A   C   O

D0485068

The Four Corners Region

Where Colorado, Utah, Arizona
& New Mexico Meet

FIRST EDITION

THE FOUR CORNERS REGION

Where Colorado, Utah, Arizona & New Mexico Meet

Sara J. Benson

The Countryman Press
Woodstock, Vermont

LEFT: *The Grand Canyon, one of the natural wonders of the Four Corners region.* Sara Benson & Mike Connolly

To my partner Mike, for sharing thousands
of miles and hundreds of photos.
This book is yours.

ISBN 978-1-58157-083-0

Cover and interior photos by the author unless otherwise specified
Book design by Bodenweber Design
Page composition by Eugenie S. Delaney
Maps by Mapping Specialists Ltd., Madison, WI © The Countryman Press

Published by The Countryman Press, P.O. Box 748, Woodstock, Vermont 05091

Distributed by W. W. Norton & Company, Inc., 500 Fifth Avenue, New York, NY 10110

Manufactured in the United States of America

10 9 8 7 6 5 4 3 2 1

GREAT DESTINATIONS TRAVEL GUIDEBOOK SERIES

Recommended by *National Geographic Traveler* and *Travel + Leisure* magazines.

[A] CRISP AND CRITICAL APPROACH, FOR TRAVELERS WHO WANT TO LIVE LIKE LOCALS.
— *USA Today*

Great Destinations™ guidebooks are known for their comprehensive, critical coverage of regions of extraordinary cultural interest and natural beauty. The authors in this series are professional travel writers who have lived for many years in the regions they describe. Each title in this series is continuously updated with each printing to ensure accurate and timely information. All the books contain more than one hundred photographs and maps.

Current titles available:

THE ADIRONDACK BOOK

ATLANTA

AUSTIN, SAN ANTONIO & THE
  TEXAS HILL COUNTRY

THE BERKSHIRE BOOK

BERMUDA

BIG SUR, MONTEREY BAY & GOLD COAST
  WINE COUNTRY

CAPE CANAVERAL, COCOA BEACH & FLORIDA'S
  SPACE COAST

THE CHARLESTON, SAVANNAH & COASTAL
  ISLANDS BOOK

THE CHESAPEAKE BAY BOOK

THE COAST OF MAINE BOOK

COLORADO'S CLASSIC MOUNTAIN TOWNS:
  GREAT DESTINATIONS

THE FINGER LAKES BOOK

THE FOUR CORNERS REGION

GALVESTON, SOUTH PADRE ISLAND &
  THE TEXAS GULF COAST

THE HAMPTONS BOOK

HONOLULU & OAHU: GREAT DESTINATIONS
  HAWAII

THE HUDSON VALLEY BOOK

THE JERSEY SHORE: ATLANTIC CITY TO CAPE
  MAY (INCLUDES THE WILDWOODS)

LOS CABOS & BAJA CALIFORNIA SUR: GREAT
  DESTINATIONS MEXICO

MICHIGAN'S UPPER PENINSULA

MONTREAL & QUEBEC CITY: GREAT
  DESTINATIONS CANADA

THE NANTUCKET BOOK

THE NAPA & SONOMA BOOK

NORTH CAROLINA'S OUTER BANKS & THE
  CRYSTAL COAST

PALM BEACH, MIAMI & THE FLORIDA KEYS

PHOENIX, SCOTTSDALE, SEDONA &
  CENTRAL ARIZONA

PLAYA DEL CARMEN, TULUM & THE RIVIERA
  MAYA: GREAT DESTINATIONS MEXICO

SALT LAKE CITY, PARK CITY, PROVO &
  UTAH'S HIGH COUNTRY RESORTS

SAN DIEGO & TIJUANA

SAN JUAN, VIEQUES & CULEBRA: GREAT
  DESTINATIONS PUERTO RICO

THE SEATTLE & VANCOUVER BOOK: INCLUDES
  THE OLYMPIC PENINSULA, VICTORIA & MORE

THE SANTA FE & TAOS BOOK

THE SARASOTA, SANIBEL ISLAND &
  NAPLES BOOK

THE SHENANDOAH VALLEY BOOK

TOURING EAST COAST WINE COUNTRY

WASHINGTON D.C., AND NORTHERN VIRGINIA

YELLOWSTONE & GRAND TETON NATIONAL PARKS
  AND JACKSON HOLE

YOSEMITE & THE SOUTHERN SIERRA NEVADA

If you are traveling to, moving to, residing in, or just interested in any (or all!) of these enchanting regions, a Great Destinations guidebook is a superior companion. Honest and painstakingly critical, full of information only a local can provide, Great Destinations guidebooks give you all the practical knowledge you need to enjoy the best of each region. Why not own them all?

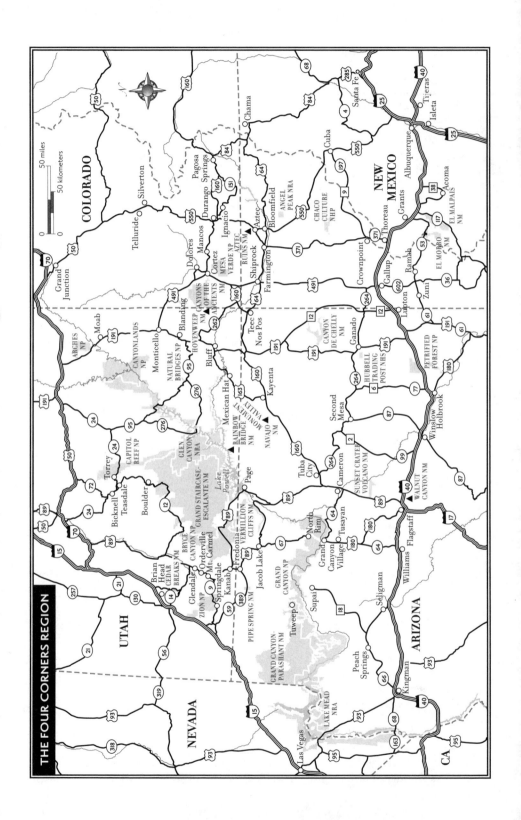

THE FOUR CORNERS REGION

Contents

ACKNOWLEDGMENTS

Writing this book would not have been possible without the wealth of regional information generously shared by those I met and talked with along the winding highways and back roads of the Four Corners region. Their local expertise, timely advice, and insights proved invaluable, especially in helping me to share with you what makes any visit to the Four Corners inspiring.

As they've done before on other successful book projects, professional photographers and writers Kim Grant and Michael Connolly Jr. contributed ideas and images that bring these pages to life. Whether they were shooting canyon landscapes or Native American dances, talking with local artisans, or recommending local chefs' eateries, their in-depth regional knowledge and artistic sensibilities give my work a more vivid sense of place. I was lucky to have them as road-trip companions and hosts, and without them I would have been lost, figuratively—and sometimes literally—speaking.

While researching and writing this guidebook, I was impressed by the strength and resilience of the Four Corners' multicultural fabric—woven of Native American, Mexican, and European threads—that wraps around this remote corner of the nation. With the weight of a troubled and yet triumphant history balanced on their shoulders, the peoples of the Four Corners carry on rituals from past centuries as they create new traditions to bind together contemporary communities. I am honored to have been a guest in their lands.

I trust that the words I have written in this guidebook will treat the people who live in this unforgettable place with dignity and respect.

—Sara Benson

INTRODUCTION

The American Southwest is a legendary landscape. For many centuries its weathered contours have been traced and retread by Native American tribes, Spanish colonial missionaries, and cowboys and pioneers. Visit once in a lifetime, or again and again, and you'll discover the wellspring of nations.

This book covers the Four Corners region, the Southwest's heartland. It circles the point where Arizona, New Mexico, Colorado, and Utah meet. This unique area encompasses some of the largest Native American–held lands in the American West, such as the Navajo Nation; awe-inspiring natural attractions like the Grand Canyon; and the ruins of ancient civilizations, including the cliff dwellings at Mesa Verde National Park. In between these places, veer off the beaten path to explore historic Route 66, America's "Mother Road." The Four Corners is enormous, justifying several return visits, not just one trip.

The natural beauty here is undeniable, with endless outdoor activities to pursue. See a full moon framed by a sandstone arch in Utah's desert. Stand atop the mesas of the Colorado Plateau, filled with Ancestral Puebloan sites. Peer into Arizona's Grand Canyon, large enough to swallow a city—and it never appears the same way twice, thanks to its serendipitous weather. Descend to the swift Colorado River as bald eagles soar above your head. Cruise along Route 66 through a petrified forest and Technicolor painted desert, then detour from Gallup to the tribal lands of Native American nations, where mountain peaks and soaring buttes each tell a story.

The Four Corners is where myths collide with dream-making realities. Monument Valley, where scores of Western movies were filmed, has a Native American history tragically different from Hollywood's tall tales. Nevertheless, wherever you wander in this vast land, you'll feel larger than life, just like vintage movie stars on the silver screen. While navigating the twists and turns of a slot canyon near Lake Powell, driving through rugged Grand Staircase–Escalante National Monument, or white-water rafting the Colorado River as it barges through the Grand Canyon, you'll feel like the first explorer to happen upon these spots. You can be transported to another time, a different way of living and thinking entirely, by attending a ceremonial dance at one of New Mexico's traditional pueblos or a grand gathering of nations at a powwow in Navajoland.

With invisible frontiers as difficult to define as to deny their existence, the Four Corners is like another country inside the borders of the United States. Scan local radio frequencies as you drive along a Bureau of Indian Affairs (BIA) Highway and catch an earful of Navajo talk and music. Time zones change, even within the same state, but the pace of life remains unhurried. There's no need to rush here. The spaghetti freeway intersections and suburban sprawl of cities is largely absent. Back roads and byways fill local maps, and there's rarely a straight line to take you from point A to point B. On many days, the journey itself is the destination.

The Four Corners is an idyllic place to lose yourself for a short vacation—or a lifetime. I always find rejuvenation here. So have painters, photographers, writers, and other artists drawn here for inspiration. Perhaps it's because the Four Corners has such a rich cultural heritage, where Native American and imported traditions still influence everyday life. In fact, the historical clashes involving Native American tribes and western settlers, Spanish missionaries, and U.S. soldiers were how our national identity was forged. To get under the skin of American history, a visit to the Four Corners will more than repay any time you've got to spend.

This guidebook aims to be in-depth and at the same time selective. It is not an encyclopedia meant to exhaustively cover every place that can possibly be visited in the Four Corners. Neither is it the kind of book that belongs sitting on a coffee table or in an armchair traveler's collection. It should be an intelligent road warrior, a constant companion on your explorations of this remote region, providing help and information when it's most needed and giving you the tools to make the most of your trip. The destination chapters reveal the best of what the region offers with insightful, informative reviews of lodgings, restaurants, cultural activities, and outdoor recreation for all travelers' budgets. All facts were carefully researched and rechecked just before this book was published—although keep in mind that things inevitably change as time goes by, even in a place as timeless as this.

Finally, it is my hope that my passion for the Four Corners region—the land, its history, and its peoples—comes alive for you on every page of this book. Open your mind, your eyes, and your heart, and let this trip be the one that changes your life forever.

—Sara Benson
Page, Arizona

THE WAY THIS BOOK WORKS

This book covers the Four Corners region where Arizona, New Mexico, Colorado, and Utah meet. For practical trip-planning advice and information, turn to the "Transportation," "Information," and "If Time Is Short" chapters. If you're looking for a destination overview to inspire a visit to the Four Corners, read the introduction to this book. If you're already intrigued by the Southwest and would like more in-depth background on the region's peoples and cultures, flip to the "History" chapter.

Each of the five main destination chapters of this complete guidebook focuses on a different part of the Four Corners region: "Flagstaff and the Grand Canyon"; "Route 66," covering parts of Arizona and western New Mexico; "Native America," including the Navajo and Hopi Nations, as well as smaller Pueblo communities; "Colorado's Plateau," focusing on the Mesa Verde country of southwestern Colorado; and "Utah's Canyon Country," ranging from the adventure town of Moab west to Zion National Park. There is limited geographical overlap between the chapters, notably Gallup, New Mexico, which is located along Route 66, but is more helpfully covered in the "Native America" chapter; and Page, Arizona, a travelers' hub for visiting the North Rim of the Grand Canyon, the canyons of southern Utah, and the Navajo Nation, but appears most usefully in the "Native America" chapter.

As you drive through the Four Corners region, turn to the regional chapter you're interested in to find recommended places to stay overnight, have a meal, or go exploring. If you already have a specific place in mind, turn to the comprehensive indexes at the back of this book, which include separate lists of lodging and dining establishments. The lodging index is organized by price, while the dining index is subdivided by price and by type of cuisine. All the entries in the regional chapters are listed alphabetically by town under the standard headings of lodging, culture, restaurants and food purveyors, recreation, and shopping.

Where relevant, each entry includes specific information (telephone number, address, Web site, opening hours, admission fees, and so on) that you should know before visiting. For full-length reviews, these details are broken out into quick-reference blocks of text at the head of each listing. The lodging and restaurant entries also provide abbreviated information about which credit cards are accepted and accessibility for travelers with disabilities. In addition, restaurant reviews indicate when reservations are recommended and any other special features. All these practical details were carefully researched, then rechecked as close as possible to the time of publication of this book. That said, this information can change from month to month, year to year. Given the great distances you'll be driving in this remote region, it always pays to call ahead to confirm that important details provided in this book are accurate at the time of your trip.

Lodging and Dining Prices

Within each regional chapter, accommodation listings are arranged alphabetically under subheadings for each city or town. Prices are based on the average double-occupancy room rate during peak summer season. Know that that off-season discounts may save you as much as 40 percent off peak-season prices. Because room rates are highly subject to change, lodging reviews in this book do not include specific prices. Lodgings are instead categorized as inexpensive, moderate, expensive, or very expensive. Likewise, restaurant reviews included in this book are arranged alphabetically under town and city subheadings. Each restaurant review also includes a separate line preceding the main review noting if the establishment is inexpensive, moderate, expensive, or very expensive. Price ranges for dining listed here represent the average cost of a dinner entree, excluding any drinks, taxes, or tip.

	Lodging	Dining
Inexpensive	Up to $70	Up to $7
Moderate	$70–$134	$7–$15
Expensive	$135–$200	$16–$25
Very Expensive	Over $200	Over $25

Credit Cards
AE—American Express
D—Discover
MC—MasterCard
V—Visa

1

HISTORY

Native American Nations and the Wild West

The many different cultures of the Four Corners region—where Arizona, New Mexico, Colorado, and Utah meet—are as varied as the natural history of the Southwest. It would take many lifetimes to learn all there is to know about this crossroads of the country, where indigenous peoples, Spanish conquistadores and colonists, and Western pioneers, miners, soldiers, and railway workers all played their parts in a sometimes tragic, but also triumphant history. The people who reside here today have just as many stories to tell. Some choose to live here because of their Native American cultural heritage, while others—scientists, artists, and outdoor enthusiasts among them—find themselves drawn to the natural world of the Four Corners, with its epic landscapes and fantastic wildlife.

NATURAL HISTORY

A riveting and complex geological history, topography ranging from desert basins and deep river canyons to towering sandstone buttes and mountain peaks, plus abundant wildlife inhabiting the Colorado Plateau and beyond, all make the Four Corners a natural wonderland. Pressing environmental concerns about climate change and drought, especially with a fast-growing population still struggling over limited water resources, make eco-consciousness important not only for residents, but also travelers in this region.

The Lay of the Land

Nowhere in the Four Corners region is the geologic past more prominently on display than at the Grand Canyon, where the Colorado River has carved away layer upon colorful layer of rock and stone, the oldest dating back 2 billion years. Nearly as impressive is the Grand Staircase, a stepped sequence of sedimentary rock layers that extends north from the Grand Canyon as it moves forward in geological time. Like a layer cake, the staircase ascends from the Chocolate and Vermillion Cliffs of northern Arizona and ends at the Pink Cliffs of Bryce Canyon. In tourist brochures, the nickname "color country" is often used to describe this area of southern Utah.

LEFT: *Evidence of a once-prosperous mining industry is found in many small towns across the Four Corners region.* Mike Connolly

During prehistoric times North America was washed over by tropical seas that advanced and retreated, leaving behind sediment, volcanic ashes, mudflats, and coastal sand dunes. In the late Cretaceous period, approximately 70 million years ago, the North American plate broke away from the European plate and slid westward over another landmass, creating a massive uplift that forcibly formed not only the Rocky Mountains, but also elevated the 130,000-square-mile Colorado Plateau, which dominates the Four Corners region today. The event also warped the earth's crust, resulting in monoclines, most famously the 100-mile-long Waterpocket Fold at Capitol Reef.

Later forces of erosion—from ice-age glaciers and the opening of the Gulf of California over 5 million years ago, to heavy rainfall and snowmelt that still fill the powerful rivers flowing out of the Rocky Mountains and toward the west today—have created many of the signature landscape features of the Four Corners region. Among the most impressive for visitors are the delicate sandstone arches and fins outside Moab, the riverine canyonlands and natural stream-cut bridges of southern Utah, the high buttes and mesas of Monument Valley, the horseshoe-shaped amphitheaters and odd-looking hoodoos of Bryce Canyon, and the sheer vertical cliffs of Zion Canyon.

Although much of the Four Corners region is desertlike, the Colorado Plateau itself is cut through by a system of rivers, notably the tributaries of the mighty Colorado River, which include the Green, San Juan, and Little Colorado Rivers. The Rio Grande is another major riverway, which runs from the San Juan Mountains of Southwestern Colorado through New Mexico on its way to the Gulf of Mexico. Despite all these rivers, there is a scarcity of water throughout the Four Corners region, which makes management of this precious natural resource a hotly debated issue. When Glen Canyon Dam opened in 1963, this controversial structure drowned some of the most beautiful, wild canyonlands in the Southwest. It also dramatically changed the flow of the Colorado River through the Grand Canyon, altering its ecology, thereby making it easier for nonnative species to aggressively invade.

Native Americans living in the Four Corners region sometimes view the natural world in a way different from that of the scientific community, and many tribes maintain a spiritual relationship with the land. The Diné (or Navajo) people, for example, believe the borders of their true homeland are defined by four sacred mountains, the modern names of which are: Mount Taylor, to the south in New Mexico; the San Francisco Peaks, to the west in Arizona; and Mount Hesperus to the north and Mount Blanca to the east, both in Colorado. Because of the sacred meanings and ceremonial importance of many natural features on tribal lands, especially rock formations, visitors should respectfully not climb them, take away any pieces as souvenirs, or leave any graffiti behind.

Biodiversity of the Colorado Plateau and Beyond

Not just the dominant feature of the landscape of the Four Corners region, the Colorado Plateau also boasts a diverse ecological system. In fact, six of the seven major life zones in North America are found here, from desert scrub and grasslands, up through the mixed conifer and deciduous forests of spots like the North Rim of the Grand Canyon, to the windswept alpine tundra of the San Francisco Peaks outside Flagstaff, Arizona, and the San Juan Mountains rising above Southwestern Colorado. Add to this the sagebrush and cacti-filled Great Basin Desert that reaches into southern Utah, and you'll find a remarkable variety of environments in which both flora and fauna can flourish.

Fierce grizzly bears and iconic herds of buffalo no longer roam the Southwest, having been killed or driven out over a century ago, although wolves and prairie dogs have been

The variety of bird life found on the Colorado Plateau is a prime attraction for visitors to the Four Corners region. Sara Benson

reintroduced in a few spots. Mammals still inhabiting the deserts and the mountains of the Four Corners region include coyotes, mountain lions, cottontail rabbits and jackrabbits, foxes, bighorn sheep, mule deer, pronghorn antelopes, and well over a dozen species of bats, which you may glimpse flying overhead at night while hunting insects.

The most common reptiles and amphibians in the Southwest are snakes and lizards, which range from harmless toads, racer snakes, noisy tree frogs, and colorful collared lizards to venomous rattlers and the bizarre-looking Gila monster, a heavy, slow-moving lizard that injects venom into its prey first by biting, then, while tenaciously hanging on, chewing its victim. Other poisonous critters to watch out for while traveling through the Four Corners region are biting black widow spiders and tarantulas, and stinging scorpions.

The Colorado Plateau attracts birders and fishers with its varied avian and aquatic wildlife. Hundreds of species of birds have been spotted in the Four Corners region alone, including an array of migratory birds that arrive in spring and fall. Showy endemic species that attract attention include bald and golden eagles, various hawks and falcons, vultures, spotted owls, and the endangered California condor, which was rein-troduced to its native habitat in northern Arizona in 1996. Common species you'll more easily see include canyon wrens, woodpeckers, woodland jays, ravens, and delicate hummingbirds. The best birding spots are found at Apache del Bosque National Wildlife Refuge south of Albuquerque, the Scott M. Matheson Wetlands Preserve near Moab, the

Mesa Verde country of Southwestern Colorado, and the Kaibab Plateau surrounding the Grand Canyon.

SOCIAL HISTORY

Native American tribes, Spanish conquistadores seeking fabled cities of gold, zealous Catholic missionaries and Mormon pioneers, scientific explorers and artists, miners seeking their fortunes in the hills, transcontinental railway workers and Harvey House girls, and U.S. soldiers and federal agencies have all shaped the remote Four Corners region of the Southwest into the multicultural meeting place that it is today.

Native Origins

During what archaeologists call the Desert Archaic period, starting around 6000 BCE (Before the Common Era), the indigenous peoples of the Southwest were primarily hunters and gatherers. Gradually, the influence of the Mesoamerican culture spread northward from what is now Mexico, bringing farming and village life to at least some of the tribes of the Four Corners region. Given the harshness of desert climates in some areas, which are ill-suited to agriculture, some indigenous peoples continued a primarily hunting-and-gathering lifestyle that was heavily influenced by the migration of game and the seasonal availability of plants. Some archaeologists argue that this lifestyle may have continued in a few areas through the time of Spanish colonization.

The Basketmaker Culture, which arose around the start of the Common Era (CE) solidified village life with domesticated animals, cultivated gardens, and seasonal hunting parties. Natural fibers were woven to make everything from footwear to watertight cooking vessels. More permanent village dwellings, including pit houses, were built. During this period, around 500 CE, indigenous peoples also began building underground ceremonial chambers, now called kivas, which often had a sacred hole (the *sipapu*), through which their ancestors were believed to have emerged into this world.

The Ancestral Puebloans, once referred to as the Anasazi, were the next culture to emerge on the Colorado Plateau. Beginning around 750 CE, Ancestral Puebloans built more extensive villages with pit house lodges surrounded by fields planted with crops such as corn, beans, and squash. As more time passed, Pueblo pottery became more varied and complex, as can be seen at many museums in the Four Corners region today, notably the Museum of Northern Arizona, the Anasazi Heritage Center in Colorado, and Edge of the Cedars State Park in Utah. Ancestral Puebloans later built their sandstone-and adobe cliff dwellings into the natural alcoves and shelves of mesas, like those at Mesa Verde National Park and Canyon de Chelly, Hovenweep, and Navajo National Monuments, as well as other key archaeological sites atop the Colorado Plateau.

At the same time, the strong influence of the Chacoan Culture flowed from the heart of Chaco Canyon in northwestern New Mexico. Chaco Canyon was once the site of Ancestral Puebloan great houses and ceremonial kivas, with an engineered network of roads and trails spreading outward through the San Juan Basin to the edges of the Colorado Plateau. A spiritual, educational, and administrative center, Chaco Canyon was an important gathering place for indigenous peoples from around 850 until 1250 CE, after which its dominance over the region waned. Today the ruins at Chaco Culture National Historic Park are still sacred to some Native Americans, particularly Pueblo peoples.

Despite popularly held misconceptions, it is a myth that the Anasazi mysteriously disappeared around 1300 CE. Both archaeologists and modern tribal descendants such as the Hopi and Zuni peoples now favor a theory of waves of migration of Ancestral Puebloan peoples, following the successive abandonment of cliff dwellings due to a combination of factors, including intense drought, scarce food resources, aggressive raiders attacking from the north (including the Athapaskan-speaking ancestors of the contemporary Navajo and Apache tribes), and a growing population that could no longer be contained or protected by the defensive advantages afforded by cliff dwellings.

Arrival of the First Foreigners: the Spaniards

During the time before European conflicts and colonization, the main routes through the Four Corners region were established by Native Americans for many different purposes, including trading, hunting, finding water sources, attending religious and ceremonial gatherings, and connecting villages. The first Europeans who cut a swath through the region were motivated by dreams of untold wealth, combined with religious fervor and scientific curiosity.

In 1540, Spanish colonial governor Francisco Vásquez de Coronado set out from New Spain (in what is now Mexico), searching for one of the fabled Seven Cities of Cibola, allegedly made of gold. Although the mythical city was never found, Coronado did leave European cultural footprints in parts of New Mexico and Arizona that had experienced little or no outside interference before. Coronado visited the Zuni people, explored sections of the Colorado River of the Grand Canyon, and passed through pueblos along the Rio Grande, including at what is now Coronado State Monument.

Things remained peaceful until 1595. Juan de Oñate Salazar, who was married to a granddaughter of Hernando Cortez, the famed Spanish conquistador who conquered the Aztec empire, was sent by King Philip II of Spain to build Catholic missions and colonize what is now New Mexico. Oñate claimed all the territory north of the Rio Grande for Spain, and ruled the province of Santa Fe with a rough hand. His outrageous demands for essential supplies from the people of Acoma Pueblo led to armed resistance in 1598. Over a dozen Spaniards died, in revenge for which Oñate killed hundreds of villagers, enslaving women and children and cutting off the left foot of some of the older men who had resisted. For this cruelty, Oñate was recalled to Mexico and eventually to Spain.

That didn't stop the expansion of colonial Spain across the Southwest, however. The seat of colonial power was the city of Santa Fe, founded in northern New Mexico in 1610. A network of Catholic mission churches, which were built partly by the forced labor of indigenous peoples, helped solidify the reach of Spanish colonial authority into traditional Pueblo communities. At that time, Pueblo peoples were under enormous pressure not only from this foreign power that built over their sacred plazas, enslaved adults and took children away, and outlawed cultural traditions as heathen sorcery and witchcraft, but also from raiding tribes from the north that made their settled agricultural way of life impossible. Starvation, frustration, and generally poor treatment by the foreign invaders led to the massive Pueblo Revolt of 1680. The revolt was led by a Tewa medicine man named Popé, who had been arrested and whipped in public by colonial authorities during a campaign targeted at suppressing native religions. The bloody revolt successfully drove the Spanish away, but only for about a decade, after which the Spaniards returned in strength to reclaim Santa Fe. The city of Albuquerque was founded in 1706.

In 1775, while Juan Bautista de Anza navigated a southern route from Mexico to the Spanish missions on the California coast, a less successful expedition left from Santa Fe in search of a northern route to California. Led by Franciscan friars Silvestre Vélez de Escalante and his superior, Francisco Antansio Dominguez, this small group of Spanish explorers ended up getting lost, but still managed to explore most of the Four Corners region, from Ancestral Puebloan sites in Southwestern Colorado, across the Green River and Great Basin Desert of Utah, south onto the Kaibab Plateau and across the Colorado River of the Grand Canyon, and finally to the Zuni Pueblo outside what is now Gallup, New Mexico, all before returning home to Santa Fe. Although the Domínguez-Escalante expedition failed to find California, the participants were the first Europeans to penetrate some of the most remote areas of the Four Corners region.

War with Mexico, Manifest Destiny, and Mormons

In the early 19th century, Spanish colonial power in the New World began to fail. Back in Europe, Napoleon Bonaparte successfully invaded the mother country, which led to dissent among the colonial ranks in New Spain. Mexico's War of Independence began in 1810 and lasted until 1821, when the Republic of Mexico was formally recognized. This newly minted republic took control of much of the Southwest, but political conflicts at home and with the United States kept its attention focused elsewhere.

The Southwest remained under Mexican authority for more than two decades, until the United States intervened in the conflict between the Republic of Mexico and Texas, which was also struggling to assert its own independence. Ten years after the Republic of Texas was declared, the U.S. simply annexed the territory in 1845. When the U.S. then offered to buy all the land between Texas and the Pacific Ocean—to accomplish the nation's "manifest destiny" to stretch from sea to shining sea (from the Atlantic to the Pacific Ocean)—Mexico refused, which sparked the Mexican-American War in 1846. Two years later, after Mexico lost the war, the Treaty of Guadalupe Hidalgo signed away much of northern Mexico to the U.S., including most of the Four Corners region covering present-day Utah, Western New Mexico, and northern Arizona.

Meanwhile, the Mormon followers of the self-declared prophet Joseph Smith had found their promised land in the forbidding, almost biblical landscapes of Utah's Great Basin Desert. After being harassed back in the East, the controversial Church of Jesus Christ of Latter-Day Saints under the leadership of Brigham Young, had struck out westward, entering the valley of the Great Salt Lake in northern Utah in 1847. The "State of Deseret" proclaimed by the Mormon church became the U.S. Territory of Utah in 1848. That didn't stop the Latter-Day Saints from establishing their own network of colonial settlements radiating into southern Utah, including at St. George and Moab. The fundamental Mormon practice of "plural marriage" (polygamy) caused conflicts with the U.S. government, which continues to some degree in isolated communities today.

"Don't Fence Me In": Pioneers, Reservations, and the Railway

Throughout the 19th century, U.S. citizens increasingly began drifting into the Four Corners region. Among the first to arrive were fur trappers and caravan traders who used the Old Spanish Trail to reach Los Angeles, California, from Santa Fe, starting in the 1830s. Other early travelers included military mapmaker John C. Frémont, who marched across the Great Basin Desert in the company of Kit Carson, a fur trapper who had guided soldiers during the Mexican-American War. As more Christian missionaries arrived in the

Southwest, too, they were often received coolly by Pueblo communities, whose populations were distrustful after having been cruelly exploited by some Spanish Catholic priests and further decimated by war, starvation, and European diseases against which indigenous peoples lacked any natural immunity.

As America's frontier expanded rapidly westward, the coercive pressure exerted by the U.S. federal government and the military on Native Americans increased. By the 1860s the repressive policies of the Office of Indian Affairs were in full swing, including the forcible removal of indigenous peoples to government-appointed reservations, where hunting was restricted and Native Americans were forced to rely on often crooked federal agents for food and basic supplies. Perhaps the most infamous example of misery induced by U.S. governmental policies was the "Long Walk" endured by Navajos in the winter of 1863–64. After making a last stand at Canyon de Chelly against U.S. forces led by Kit Carson, once a friend to many Native American tribes, the Navajo were forced to leave their traditional homeland in the Four Corners region and walk for almost three weeks to eastern New Mexico, where they had no choice but to live with their traditional enemies, the Apache, at Fort Sumner. Not until the Navajo signed a new treaty in 1868 were they allowed to return to their traditional homeland, Dinétah, in the heart of the Four Corners.

Meanwhile, the U.S. Civil War (1861–65) divided political loyalties throughout the country, including in the American West. The northern half of the Four Corners region became Union territory, while the southern area was claimed and sometimes held by the Confederacy. Once the war was over, nation building began again in earnest. The first transcontinental railroad was completed in 1869 when a gold spike was ceremonially driven into the tracks in northern Utah. Barbed wire fenced off the open ranges of the West in the 1870s, the same decade that Colorado achieved statehood and the Zuni Reservation was created by Congress. In the 1880s the Santa Fe Railway also made travel across the nation easier, passing through central New Mexico and Arizona on its way west to Los Angeles. Every 100 miles or so along the line, the Fred Harvey company built restaurants and rest stops for rail travelers, called Harvey Houses, including La Posada in Winslow, Arizona. These Harvey Houses were staffed with "proper" women from back east, known as Harvey girls, who were meant to bring a touch of civility to the male-dominated frontier. Meanwhile, the Office of Indian Affairs pushed ahead with its relentless policies of cultural assimilation. The Hopi Reservation was created in 1882 by carving out tribal lands from the Navajos, leaving a bitter aftertaste that lingers still. After running disputes over Mormon religious practices, Utah finally became a state in 1896, just in time for the dramatic turn of the 20th century.

Taming the Wilderness: From Boom Towns to Going Bust

Part and parcel of America's nation-building project was the critical issue of what to do with the vast wildernesses of the West. While some American explorers approached the question with scientific curiosity, many 19th-century pioneers saw wilderness as merely a resource to be exploited. Mining became a major industry around this time, while the forests of the Colorado Plateau afforded the growth of a timber industry, particularly in northern Arizona.

The California gold rush of 1849 brought hordes of hardscrabble miners into the West. It wasn't until the 1860s that silver was struck in the Four Corners region, starting in Mormon-controlled southern Utah, at places like Silver Reef. In 1874 silver was also found in Howardsville, now a ghost town in the San Juan Mountains sitting outside Silverton,

Colorado. In 1882 a narrow-gauge railway was constructed to connect the mines of Silverton to the frontier town of Durango, Colorado. A variety of other minerals were also mined around the Southwest and the Four Corners region, starting in the late 19th and early 20th centuries, including copper, lead, and turquoise. Gold wasn't discovered in Oatman, Arizona, near the California border, until 1915. Conveniently, that was just a few years after Arizona (and New Mexico) attained statehood in 1912.

Also in the latter half of the 19th century, scientifically minded explorers made journeys into the uncharted wilderness of the Four Corners region, one of the last areas of the U.S. to be mapped. The most famous was an expedition led in 1869 by John Wesley Powell, a Civil War veteran and professor of geology. Powell navigated the Green River from Wyoming to Moab, Utah, then persevered in following the Colorado River into the canyonlands of Utah and all the way through the Grand Canyon itself. It was the Grand Canyon that brought the most tourists into the region, especially after the turn of the 20th century. Western architect Mary Colter designed many of the historic buildings on the canyon's South Rim, which was linked by rail to Williams, Arizona, in the early 1900s.

A growing awareness of the intrinsic value of wilderness and of the need to preserve America's cultural heritage sites led to the creation of a system of national parks. President Theodore Roosevelt, a big-game hunter and outdoorsman who often visited the region, signed the Antiquities Act in 1906, which protected archaeological and geological sites around the Southwest, including Mesa Verde, Chaco Canyon, El Morro, and the Petrified Forest. He then decreed the Grand Canyon a national monument in 1908. The passage of the Organic Act in 1916 made the National Park Service (NPS) official.

During the Great Depression, President Franklin D. Roosevelt greatly expanded the NPS system. As part of his "New Deal" economic and social policy programs, he also created the Civilian Conservation Corps. During the 1930s the CCC employed almost 2 million men to build scenic byways and recreational infrastructure in parks across the nation, including the Southwest. The CCCs also accomplished large-scale public works, such as the Hoover Dam, which significantly altered the Colorado River in 1935.

Dust Bowl refugees were not the only ones being offered a "New Deal" by the Roosevelt administration, however. The Indian Citizenship Act of 1924 had granted full citizenship to all Native Americans not previously naturalized by marriage, military service, or special laws and treaties. The Indian Reorganization Act of 1934, called the "Indian New Deal," overturned previous governmental policies that encouraged private ownership of tribal lands and returned some self-government to tribal councils. It wasn't true self-determination for Native Americans yet, but it was a step in the right direction.

World War, Movie Stars, and the Mother Road

World War II brought thousands of defense workers to the shipyards and factories of the West. During the war the U.S. military secretly employed Native American Marines as "code talkers," who were able to transmit military messages that successfully evaded decryption by Nazi Germany, Japan, and other Axis powers. The code talkers used cryptographic systems built upon indigenous languages that were unknown outside North America, particularly the Navajo language. The work done by the code talkers was so top-secret that these Native American war heroes were not publicly recognized until the project was declassified in the late 1960s. The atomic bomb that finally ended World War II was developed just outside the Four Corners region in the laboratories of Los Alamos, north of Albuquerque, New Mexico, and Jemez Pueblo.

One of many historic filling stations along Route 66 in Arizona. Sara Benson & Mike Connolly

During the postwar economic boom, when the country celebrated newfound freedom and wealth, thousands of Americans took to the open road and got their kicks on Route 66. Established in 1926, this Chicago–L.A. highway had also been the main route used by Dust Bowl refugees trying to make it to California during the Depression. During the war, soldiers and factory workers had also traveled America's "Mother Road." But the heyday of Route 66 was the late 1940s and early 1950s, when motor courts, diners, and kitschy roadside attractions began popping up everywhere along the highway. Many historic Route 66 sites are still standing on stretches of the road in New Mexico and Arizona bordering the Four Corners region.

By this time, mining, oil drilling, and ranching had become key economic players in the Four Corners region. In the 1920s oil and natural gas fields were discovered in the San Juan Basin of northwestern New Mexico and Southwestern Colorado, where the resource-extraction industry boomed during the 1940s and still continues today. The small town of Grants, New Mexico, made a relative fortune in uranium mining starting in the 1950s. As it worked to fuel the nuclear arms race of the Cold War, it became the world's largest producer of mined uranium until the market collapsed in 1980. Another lucrative business has been the film industry. Hollywood westerns, especially in the 1940s and '50s, used the backdrops of the Southwest's epic landscapes to make movies about life in the Wild West. Director John Ford and actors like John Wayne made the landmarks of the Four Corners region, especially the Mitten Buttes of Monument Valley, recognizable to audiences worldwide.

Modern Faces of the Four Corners

The tumult of the 1960s and '70s not only changed the physical shape of the Four Corners region, but also changed popular attitudes toward the environment and Native Americans, gradually transforming both the natural and cultural landscapes of the Southwest into what visitors will see here today.

Because much of the Four Corners region is a desert, the allocation of natural resources such as water has long been subject to strenuous debate. In some places, artificial reservoirs have been built and rivers dammed. Perhaps the most famous of these large-scale project is Glen Canyon Dam, which flooded some of the canyonlands of southern Utah and northern Arizona in 1963. Soon afterward, a burgeoning environmental movement spearheaded by the Sierra Club, filled with activists often inspired by nature writers such as Edward Abbey, stopped the same thing from happening at the Grand Canyon in 1966. Today the issue of natural resources—who owns what, who gets to use it and for what purposes, and who profits from it—is one of the most contentious faced by the region. Property rights are taken seriously, not only on tribal lands but also by ranchers who resent the dominance of the federal government, the largest land manager in the West.

During the helter-skelter 1960s, when social protests swept a nation bogged down by a war in Vietnam, Native American activists agitated for the right to greater self-determination, accompanied by nonviolent protests and the attention-grabbing occupation of some federal lands. A series of laws enacted by Congress in the 1970s gave more power to tribal governments in the arenas of education, health care, and welfare. The Bureau of Indian Affairs began moving toward a more advisory role, and today more than 90 percent of BIA employees claim Native American heritage. The path to self-determination for indigenous peoples is far from finished, although the seeds of cultural renaissance have been sown. Economically speaking, many Native American reservations remain impoverished places, where unemployment and poor health are too common. Some tribes have invested in profitable casinos, while others have chosen tourism as a growth industry.

Whatever the future may bring, and regardless of how the most critical social and natural resource issues are dealt with, it may be sustainable tourism that offers the brightest outlook for many residents. That means it's a perfect time for curious travelers to come and contribute to the multicultural tapestry of the Four Corners region. Just remember to tread lightly and always treat the land and its many peoples with respect.

2

TRANSPORTATION

Finding Your Way Here

Despite being located at the intersection of four states—Arizona, New Mexico, Colorado, and Utah—the Four Corners region remains remote. Its rural highways and byways are rugged, especially those on Native American tribal lands. The challenges of transportation may deter many tourists, but are among the major attractions for adventurous travelers. That said, it doesn't always have to be so difficult to explore the Four Corners, which is bordered by interstate highways. Figuring out your transportation options, whether it is how to get here or how to get around this vast region, should be one of your top trip-planning priorities.

The Four Corners region is geographically spread out. In fact, many of its most popular destinations, such as the Grand Canyon and Monument Valley, are located literally in the middle of nowhere. If you're not driving your own car, you can travel here by plane, train, or bus. However, once you arrive in the Four Corners region, you'll want to arrange private transportation, such as a rental car, to get around.

GETTING TO THE FOUR CORNERS

If you're visiting the South Rim of the Grand Canyon, you'll fly into Flagstaff or Phoenix, Arizona, or Las Vegas, Nevada. If you're headed to New Mexico, Albuquerque is your point of arrival. For southwestern Colorado, the nearest major transit hub is far away in Denver. Las Vegas and Salt Lake City, Utah, are the nearest access points for southern Utah.

By Car and Motorcycle
The best way to reach the Four Corners region depends on where you want to visit first. The following directions will help get you from gateway cities (notably those with major airports) to the closest access points for exploring the Four Corners.

FROM DENVER
Denver stands at the intersection of three major interstate highways—I-25 from the north and south, I-70 heading east and west, and I-76, which branches off I-80, yet another east–west route—but you might not use any of them to access the Ancestral Puebloan sites of southwestern Colorado. From CO 470, which encircles the Mile High City, drive southwest on US 285 for almost 200 miles, passing nearby Great Sand Dunes National Park. Veer west onto CO 112 for 13 miles to join US 160 westbound. Drive for another 120 miles,

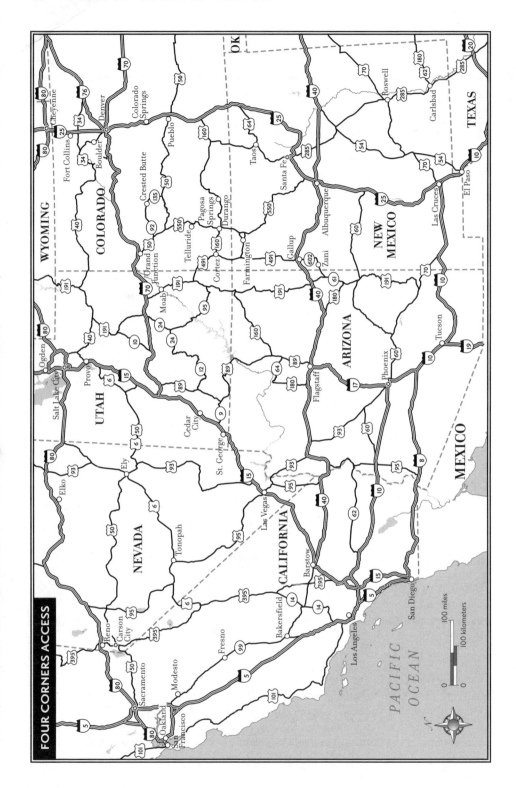

FOUR CORNERS ACCESS

passing through Pagosa Springs, to Durango, the gateway to Mesa Verde National Park. Starting from Denver, the drive to Durango should take about 6½ hours in good weather. You can reach Moab, Utah, in less time by driving west from Denver on I-70 for more than 300 miles, passing through Grand Junction, Colorado, and across the Utah state line. Look for the turnoff to Arches National Park and Moab at Crescent Junction, before reaching Green River, Utah. From Crescent Junction take US 191 south 30 miles to Moab, just beyond the national park. From Denver the drive to Moab takes about 5½ hours without stops.

FROM LAS VEGAS

Las Vegas is an excellent place to jump start your travels around the Four Corners region. Take I-15 northeast to the city of St. George, Utah, a gateway to Zion and Bryce National Parks or the North Rim of the Grand Canyon. The drive from Las Vegas takes about 2 hours to St. George (120 miles), 3 hours to Zion National Park (160 miles), 4¾ hours to Bryce Canyon National Park (250 miles), and 5½ hours to the Grand Canyon's North Rim (265 miles). From Las Vegas you can also easily reach the South Rim of the Grand Canyon, Flagstaff, and Route 66 through Arizona and New Mexico. Heading southeast of Las Vegas, take I-515 to join US 93 through Boulder City and drive over the magnificent Hoover Dam and across the Nevada–Arizona state line, after which it's a straight shot to Kingman,

Arizona. There you can get your kicks on Route 66 or take I-40 east to Flagstaff. From Las Vegas the 250-mile drive to Flagstaff takes a minimum of four hours without stops. If you're going directly to the South Rim of the Grand Canyon (275 miles, 4½ hours), take the Williams exit off I-40 west of Flagstaff, then AZ 64 north about 55 miles past the national park entrance to Grand Canyon Village. Beyond Flagstaff you can continue east on Route 66 or I-40 all the way to Gallup and Albuquerque, New Mexico. Watch for turnoffs to various points of interest along the way, including to the Hopi Nation (north of Winslow, AZ), Hubbell Trading Post National Historic Site and Canyon de Chelly National Monument (northeast of Holbrook, AZ), the Navajo Nation (north of Gallup, NM), Zuni Pueblo (southwest of Gallup, NM), Chaco Culture National Historic Park (northeast of Gallup, NM), and Acoma Pueblo, aka "Sky City" (southeast of Grants, NM).

FROM PHOENIX

Unlike other access points for the Four Corners region, Phoenix is a straight-forward place to start your trip. It's

Antique gas pumps are now showpieces at many roadside stops along old Route 66. Sara Benson

another major crossroads for out-of-state travelers: I-10 runs west to Palm Springs and Los Angeles, and east through Tucson, Arizona, to New Mexico and Texas, while I-8 connects Phoenix to San Diego. From Phoenix it's an easy 140-mile, two-hour drive north on I-17 to Flagstaff, a gateway to the Grand Canyon and Route 66. If you're headed to the Navajo Nation (to Window Rock, AZ: 330 miles, 5 hours), Mesa Verde National Park in southwestern Colorado (430 miles, 7½ hours), Albuquerque, New Mexico (470 miles, 7¾ hours), or Moab, Utah (460 miles, 7¾ hours), the quickest way to get there from Phoenix is to first drive through Flagstaff.

From Salt Lake City

There are two major options for starting out from Utah's capital city. If you want to loop through Utah's canyon country, begin by driving approximately 300 miles southwest to the city of St. George, the gateway to Zion National Park. This drive should take you just over four hours in good weather. Alternatively, it takes the same amount of time to reach the adventure town of Moab in southeastern Utah, near the Colorado border. To get to Moab from Salt Lake City, drive south on I-15 for about 50 miles to Provo, Utah, then exit onto US 6 and drive 130 miles southeast to I-70. Follow I-70 just over 20 miles east to Crescent Junction, then exit onto US 191 south another 30 miles past Arches National Park to reach Moab. From Salt Lake City the fastest way to get to Durango, Colorado (390 miles, 7 hours) or the Navajo Nation (to Window Rock, AZ: 475 miles, 8¾ hours) takes you through Moab, too.

By Plane

While some visitors drive their own cars to the Four Corners region, many arrive by plane. The following list includes major international airports around the Four Corners region, as well as the airlines that were serving those airports at press time. (Smaller regional airports with connecting express flights are listed later in this chapter, under "Getting Around the Four Corners.") For current flight schedules and airfares, contact the relevant airports or airlines directly. For driving directions from these gateway airports to the Four Corners region, see the previous section ("By Car").

Albuquerque International Sunport (ABQ), www.cabq.com/airport, 505-244-7700, 2200 Sunport Blvd. SE, Albuquerque, NM 87106. Directions: From central Albuquerque take I-25 south to exit 221, then Sunport Blvd. eastbound. Served by American Airlines, Continental Airlines, Delta Air Lines, ExpressJet Airlines, Frontier Airlines, Great Lakes Airlines, Mesa Airlines, Northwest Airlines, Southwest Airlines, United Airlines, US Airways.

Denver International Airport (DEN), www.flydenver.com, 303-342-2000, 8500 Peña Blvd., Denver, CO 80249. Directions: Northeast of downtown Denver, the airport is accessible from toll road E-470 or from I-70 eastbound (exit 284) or westbound (exit 285). Served by AirTran Airways, Alaska Airlines, American Airlines, Big Sky Airlines, Continental Airlines, Delta Air Lines, Frontier Airlines, Great Lakes Airlines, Horizon Air, JetBlue Airways, Mesa Airlines, Midwest Airlines, Northwest Airlines, Southwest Airlines, United Airlines, US Airways.

McCarran International Airport (LAS), www.mccarran.com, 702-261-5211, 5757 Wayne Newton Blvd., Las Vegas, NV 89119. Directions: From downtown Las Vegas or the Strip, take I-15 south to Tropicana Ave. (exit 37) eastbound, then Paradise Rd. south. Served by AirTran Airways, Aloha Airlines, America West Airlines, American Airlines, ATA Airlines,

Getting to the Four Corners by Car

Listed below are the estimated miles and traveling times to the major destinations in the Four Corners region. Interstate and highway speed limits vary from 55 to 75 mph.

To Albuquerque, NM, from:

City	Miles	Hours
Colorado Springs, CO	380	5:15
Denver, CO	450	6:30
El Paso, TX	265	3:45
Grand Junction, CO	380	7:45
Las Cruces, NM	225	3:15
Las Vegas, NV	575	8:15
Phoenix, AZ	470	6:30
Salt Lake City, UT	625	10:45
San Diego, CA	815	11:45
Santa Fe, NM	65	1:00
Taos, NM	135	2:30

To Durango, CO, from:

City	Miles	Hours
Colorado Springs, CO	340	6:45
Crested Butte, CO	200	4:30
Denver, CO	335	6:30
Fort Collins, CO	395	7:30
Grand Junction, CO	170	3:45
Las Vegas, NV	535	9:15
Phoenix, AZ	455	7:45
Salt Lake City, UT	395	7:00
Santa Fe, NM	240	4:15
Taos, NM	200	4:30
Telluride, CO	75	2:15

To Flagstaff, AZ, from:

City	Miles	Hours
Bakersfield, CA	480	7:00
Barstow, CA	355	5:00
Denver, CO	770	10:45
Grand Junction, CO	430	7:30
Las Vegas, NV	250	4:00
Los Angeles, CA	465	6:45
Phoenix, AZ	145	2:15
Salt Lake City, UT	520	8:45
San Diego, CA	500	7:15
Santa Fe, NM	385	5:30
Taos, NM	450	6:45
Tucson, AZ	260	4:00

To Moab, UT, from:

City	Miles	Hours
Denver, CO	355	5:30
Grand Junction, CO	115	1:45
Albuquerque, NM	390	6:30
Las Vegas, NV	460	6:30
Phoenix, AZ	460	7:45
Reno, NV	750	11:00
Salt Lake City, UT	235	4:00
Santa Fe, NM	395	7:15
Taos, NM	360	7:15
Telluride, CO	135	3:00

To St. George, UT, from:

City	Miles	Hours
Grand Junction, CO	390	5:30
Denver, CO	630	9:00
Las Vegas, NV	120	2:00
Phoenix, AZ	415	7:00
Reno, NV	535	9:15
Salt Lake City, UT	300	4:15
Santa Fe, NM	640	10:15
Taos, NM	595	11:30
Telluride, CO	470	7:45

Continental Airlines, Delta Air Lines, Frontier Airlines, Hawaiian Airlines, JetBlue Airways, Midwest Airlines, Northwest Airlines, Philippine Airlines, Southwest Airlines, Spirit Airlines, Sun Country Airlines, United Airlines, US Airways.

Phoenix Sky Harbor International Airport (PHX), www.phoenix.gov/aviation, 602-273-3300, 3400 E. Sky Harbor Blvd., Phoenix, AZ 85034. Directions: From downtown Phoenix take I-10 east to E. Sky Harbor Blvd. (exit 149). Served by AirTran Airways, Alaska Airlines, America West, American, ATA, Continental Airlines, Delta Air Lines, Frontier Airlines, Great Lakes Airlines, JetBlue Airways, Hawaiian Airlines, Midwest Airlines, Northwest Airlines, Southwest Airlines, United Airlines, US Airways.

Salt Lake City International Airport (SLC), www.slcairport.com, 801-575-2400, 1-800-595-2442, 776 N. Terminal Dr., Salt Lake City, UT 84116. Directions: From downtown Salt Lake City take I-80 west to exit 115-A, then turn right onto Bangerter Highway. Served by America West Airlines, American Airlines, Atlantic Southeast Airlines, Continental Airlines, Delta Air Lines, Frontier Airlines, JetBlue Airways, Northwest Airlines, SkyWest Airlines, Southwest Airlines, United Airlines.

By Train

The national railway service, **Amtrak**, www.amtrak.com, 1-800-872-7245, has routes that cross the Four Corners region, connecting it with the West and East Coasts, the Midwest, and the South. You'll have more seating options (for example, sleeper cars) on Amtrak trains than on Greyhound buses, but the journeys may be just as long, especially because trains do not reliably run on time. That said, there's a romantic sense of adventure in traveling through the Southwest by train, despite the inconveniences.

Long-distance Amtrak trains have dining cars, where basic meals and snacks are served. These trains may have separate lounge and observation cars, in addition to designated quiet cars, where using cell phones and audible electronic devices is prohibited and overhead lighting is dimmed. Smoking is prohibited aboard Amtrak trains, although passengers may get off briefly at scheduled stops to smoke on the platform, if state or local laws do not prohibit it.

Between the San Francisco Bay area and Chicago, the *California Zephyr* runs through Salt Lake City and Denver. The closest access points to the Four Corners region are Green River, Utah (about an hour's drive from Moab, UT) and Grand Junction, Colorado (a two-hour drive from Moab and a four-hour drive from Durango, CO). ThruWay buses connect Provo, Utah, with St. George, Utah, outside Zion National Park, taking about six hours. Amtrak's *Southwest Chief* runs between Los Angeles and Chicago, making stops in Arizona and New Mexico at Williams, Flagstaff, Winslow, Gallup, and Albuquerque. From Williams, you can board the Grand Canyon Railway (for details of this service, see "By Train" in the "Getting Around the Four Corners" section, later) for excursions to the South Rim of the Grand Canyon. Anywhere else that you decide to get off the train, you'll want to arrange in advance for a rental car, which may not be possible in smaller whistle-stop towns. Hertz car rentals are available at select Amtrak stations; book your rental car in advance through Hertz, www.hertz.com, 1-800-654-3131.

Sample fares and travel times from both the start and end points of Amtrak train routes to destinations in the Four Corners region:

Helpful road signs let you know you've found it: Route 66, America's "Mother Road." Mike Connolly

Amtrak Route	Average Trip Duration	Adult One-Way Coach Fare (Reserved Seat)
Chicago, IL–Albuquerque, NM	26 hours	$116
Chicago, IL–Denver, CO	18½ hours	$92
Chicago, IL–Flagstaff, AZ	31½ hours	$129
Chicago, IL–Salt Lake City, UT	34 hours	$126
Los Angeles, CA–Albuquerque, NM	16½ hours	$61
Los Angeles, CA–Flagstaff, AZ	10¼ hours	$58
Los Angeles, CA–Gallup, NM	13 hours	$60
San Francisco, CA–Denver, CO	36¼ hours	$93
San Francisco, CA–Salt Lake City, UT	20½ hours	$66

The best way to save money on train tickets is to purchase them online in advance. Various everyday discounts are available; for example, children ages 2 to 15 ride for half price, and seniors, students, military/veterans, and AAA members may qualify for discounts of 10 to 15 percent. Check the Amtrak Web site for more deals, including special discount fares, unlimited rail passes, and vacation packages.

Bicycles are accepted as checked baggage on Amtrak trains but may be subject to a small handling fee. All bicycles must be packaged in a sturdy container, which usually involves partially disassembling them. Most staffed Amtrak stations sell bicycle boxes.

By Bus

The nationwide bus service, **Greyhound Lines**, www.greyhound.com, 1-800-231-2222, passes through all four states in the Four Corners region. Greyhound also provides connecting services with Amtrak (see previous section), when they're called ThruWay buses. Smoking is prohibited on all Greyhound buses, although they do make frequent rest stops.

Greyhound buses may be the cheapest way to reach major cities in the Four Corners region, but they're not the most comfortable mode of travel. Greyhound stations and regularly scheduled stops include:

Arizona: Flagstaff, Holbrook, Kingman, Phoenix, Winslow

Colorado: Alamosa, Boulder, Colorado Springs, Denver, Durango, Grand Junction

New Mexico: Albuquerque, Farmington, Gallup, Grants, Las Cruces, Santa Fe, Taos

Utah: Green River, Provo, Salt Lake City, St. George

Sample fares and travel times from gateways to the Four Corners region include:

Greyhound Route	Average Trip Duration	Advance-Purchase Adult One-Way Fare
Denver, CO–Durango, CO	10 hours	$36
Las Vegas, NV–Flagstaff, AZ	5½–6 hours	$27
Las Vegas, NV–St. George, UT	2¼ hours	$27
Phoenix, AZ–Flagstaff, AZ	3 hours	$27
Salt Lake City, UT–St. George, UT	5¾ hours	$36
Santa Fe, NM–Albuquerque, NM	1 hour	$15
Taos, NM–Albuquerque, NM	2¾ hours	$27

The best way to save money on Greyhound tickets is to purchase them online at least 14 days in advance. Various other discounts are available. For example, seniors, children, students, and military/veterans may receive discounts of 5 to 40 percent off unrestricted fares. Companion fares (usually, half-off fares for the second person traveling together) may also be available. Check the Greyhound Web site for more promotional deals, special offers, and unlimited bus passes.

Bicycles are accepted as checked baggage on Greyhound buses, but they must be packaged securely in wood, canvas, or another sturdy container. A hefty surcharge may apply.

GETTING AROUND THE FOUR CORNERS

Once you've arrived at a gateway airport or city in the Four Corners region, you'll be able to get to some outlying areas by a combination of air, bus, car, train, and ferry rides. But most visitors drive themselves around according to their own schedule and a self-planned itinerary. The most popular driving route through the Southwest is nicknamed the "Grand Circle" (see www.grandcircle.org), though that's a deceptive way of describing travel through the region, because exploring the Four Corners involves more backtracking than a typical loop itinerary. If your vacation time is limited, or if you'd like to plan a quicker road trip that hits the biggest attractions in each of the four states, turn to chapter 9, "If Time Is Short," at the back of this book.

By Car and Motorcycle

Apart from the long distances involved and some bumpy backcountry roads, driving around the Four Corners region is a cinch. Rush-hour traffic and finding free parking are trouble only in cities, such as Flagstaff and Albuquerque, and at the most popular national parks—at the South Rim of the Grand Canyon, for example.

Allow more time than you think you'll need to get somewhere. You never know when you'll encounter poor road conditions, construction delays, or unexpectedly harsh, unseasonable weather. It helps to have someone who is adept at using maps to navigate for the driver, because taking the wrong road at any given unsigned rural intersection can result in an hour or more of lost travel time. Then backtracking is often the only option, because shortcuts are rare. One of the best maps available for the Four Corners region is the Indian Country Map ($4.95), published by the American Automobile Association. Club members can pick up a free copy from the nearest AAA office. Nonmembers can buy the map at AAA offices throughout the Southwest (search for locations online at www.aaa.com) and at some local bookstores and tourist offices. For fans of Tony Hillerman's mystery novels set in Navajoland, *Tony Hillerman's Indian Country Map and Guide* (Time Traveler Maps, $14.95) helps you find both real-life and fictional locations portrayed in the bestselling books. It's sold at regional bookstores and tourist shops.

If you don't drive yourself to the Four Corners region, reserve a rental car in advance for pick-up upon arrival at your gateway airport. Las Vegas is the most expensive airport for rental cars, while Albuquerque also costs more than the norm; Salt Lake City is considerably cheaper, and Denver costs even less. For a compact rental car, expect to pay at least $25 per day or $120 per week, excluding taxes and fees of up to 30 percent. It will cost significantly more for a 4WD vehicle, which often comes with restrictions on where you can drive it. Almost all rental cars have air-conditioning and an automatic transmission; some also have winter tires for inclement weather and road conditions. If you rent a car after arrival in a major town or city, keep in mind that you'll have to pay extra for transportation to/from the gateway airport, which may not be as economical.

Major car-rental agencies with airport desks and city offices around the Four Corners region:

Advantage Rent a Car, www.advantage.com, 1-866-661-2722

Alamo Rent a Car, www.alamo.com, 1-800-462-5266

Avis Car Rental, www.avis.com, 1-800-331-1212

Budget Rent a Car, www.budget.com, 1-800-527-0700

Dollar Rent a Car, www.dollar.com, 1-866-434-2226

Enterprise Rent-a-Car, www.enterprise.com, 1-800-261-7331

Hertz Rent a Car, www.hertz.com, 1-800-654-3131

National Car Rental, www.nationalcar.com, 1-800-227-7368

Payless Car Rental, www.paylesscarrental.com, 1-800-729-5377

Thrifty Car Rental, www.thrifty.com, 1-800-847-4389

Road Conditions Hotlines

For current information about road conditions in the Four Corners region, call

Arizona	1-888-411-7623
Colorado	303-639-1111
New Mexico	1-800-432-4269
Utah	801-964-6000

Getting Around the Four Corners by Car

Listed below are the estimated miles and traveling times between destinations in the Four Corners region. Interstate and highway speed limits vary from 55 to 75 mph., while traffic on local roads and in national parks usually flows no faster than 25 to 45 mph. Rough road conditions, especially on Native American tribal lands and in remote wilderness areas, may further slow down travel times, especially at night.

From Albuquerque, NM, to:

City	Miles	Hours
Aztec, NM	180	3:15
Cortez, CO	275	4:45
Durango, CO	215	4:00
Farmington, NM	185	3:15
Flagstaff, AZ	325	4:30
Gallup, NM	140	2:00
Grants, NM	80	1:15
Holbrook, AZ	235	3:15
Hopi Nation		
(Second Mesa), AZ	255	4:15
Kanab, UT	215	3:45
Moab, UT	390	6:30
Page, AZ	450	6:45
St. George, UT	585	9:30
Window Rock, AZ	165	2:30
Winslow, AZ	270	3:45
Zuni Pueblo, NM	155	2:30

From Durango, CO, to:

City	Miles	Hours
Albuquerque, NM	215	4:00
Aztec, NM	36	0:45
Cortez, CO	45	1:00
Farmington, NM	50	1:15
Flagstaff, AZ	310	5:30
Gallup, NM	175	3:30
Grants, NM	200	3:30
Holbrook, AZ	265	4:45
Kanab, UT	3:35	6:00
Mancos, CO	30	0:30
Moab, UT	160	3:00
Page, AZ	260	4:45
Pagosa Springs, CO	60	1:15
Silverton, CO	50	1:15
St. George, UT	415	7:45
Window Rock, AZ	185	3:45
Winslow, AZ	300	5:15
Zuni Pueblo, NM	210	4:15

From Flagstaff, AZ, to:

City	Miles	Hours
Albuquerque, NM	325	4:30
Durango, CO	310	5:30
Gallup, NM	185	2:45
Grants, NM	250	3:30
Holbrook, AZ	90	1:15
Hopi Nation		
(Second Mesa), AZ	120	2:00
Kayenta, AZ	150	2:45
Kingman, AZ	150	2:00
Moab, UT	320	5:45
Oatman, AZ	175	3:15
Page, AZ	135	2:30
Peach Springs, AZ	115	2:00
Seligman, AZ	75	1:15
St. George, UT	270	5:15
Tuba City, AZ	80	1:30
Tusayan		
(Grand Canyon), AZ	80	1:30
Window Rock, AZ	190	2:45
Williams, AZ	35	0:45
Winslow, AZ	60	1:00
Zuni Pueblo, NM	185	3:00

From Moab, UT, to:

City	Miles	Hours
Aztec, NM	190	3:30
Blanding, UT	75	1:15
Bryce, UT	275	4:30
Cedar City, UT	290	4:15
Cortez, CO	115	2:15
Durango, CO	160	3:00
Escalante, UT	220	4:15
Farmington, NM	185	3:30
Flagstaff, AZ	320	5:45
Gallup, NM	250	4:45
Green River, UT	55	1:00
Halls Crossing, UT	165	3:00
Hanksville, UT	110	1:45
Holbrook, AZ	315	5:30

From Moab, UT, to: (continued)			From St. George, UT, to: (continued)		
City	Miles	Hours	City	Miles	Hours
Hopi Nation			Escalante, UT	185	3:30
(Second Mesa), AZ	285	5:00	Farmington, NM	380	7:00
Kanab, UT	320	5:15	Flagstaff, AZ	270	5:15
Monticello, UT	55	1:00	Gallup, NM	445	7:30
Page, AZ	270	4:45	Green River, UT	290	4:00
Panguitch, UT	250	4:00	Halls Crossing, UT	390	6:30
Silverton, CO	175	4:00	Hanksville, UT	320	4:30
Springdale, UT	345	5:00	Holbrook, AZ	350	6:15
St. George, UT	340	4:45	Hopi Nation		
Torrey, UT	155	2:45	(Second Mesa), AZ	275	5:15
Window Rock, AZ	240	4:45	Kanab, UT	80	1:45
Zuni Pueblo, NM	285	5:30	Moab, UT	340	4:00
			Monticello, UT	395	5:45
From St. George, UT, to:			Page, AZ	155	3:00
City	Miles	Hours	Panguitch, UT	120	2:00
Albuquerque, NM	580	9:30	Silverton, CO	515	8:00
Blanding, UT	415	6:15	Springdale, UT	40	1:00
Bryce, UT	145	2:30	Torrey, UT	230	3:30
Cedar City, UT	55	1:00	Window Rock, AZ	365	7:15
Cortez, CO	370	6:45	Zuni Pueblo, NM	440	7:45
Durango, CO	415	7:30			

Check the Web sites listed above for advertisements of special discounts on multiday, weekend, and weekly car rentals. By signing up for e-mail promotions, you might earn free extra days on your car rental, discounts for on-board GPS navigational assistance, bonus frequent-flier miles, and other perks.

By Plane

Regional airports and airfields connect parts of the Four Corners region. Some are served by domestic airlines with regularly scheduled connections to major regional hubs and commuter routes, while others are reserved for charter flights and private planes. Listed below are regional airports useful for visitors. Most also offer sightseeing flights and privately chartered tours. For major international and domestic airports just outside the Four Corners region, see the "Getting to the Four Corners" section earlier in this chapter.

Canyonlands Field (CNY), www.moabairport.com, 435-259-7419, N. US 191, Moab, UT 84532. Directions: From downtown Moab take US 191 (Main St.) north. US Airways flies to Farmington, New Mexico, and Salt Lake City, Utah.

Cedar City Regional Airport (CDC), www.cedarcity.org, 435-867-9408, 2560 Aviation Way, Cedar City, UT 84720. Directions: From downtown Cedar City take UT 56 (W. 200 St.) west across I-15 (exit 59), then turn right onto N. Airport Rd. US Airways flies to Farmington, New Mexico, Las Vegas, Nevada, Phoenix, Arizona, and Salt Lake City, Utah.

Cortez Municipal Airport (CEZ), www.cityofcortez.com, 970-565-7458, 22894 County Road F, Cortez, CO 81321. Directions: From downtown Cortez take W. Main St. to US 160 /

CO 789 westbound; turn right onto County Road G, then left onto County Road F. Great Lakes Airlines flies to Denver.

Durango–La Plata County Airport (DRO), www.durangogov.org, 970-247-8143, 1000 Airport Rd., Durango, CO 81303. Directions: From downtown Durango take US 550 south to US 160 east; turn right onto CO 172 and drive south to Airport Rd. Delta Air Lines flies to Salt Lake City. United Airlines flies to Denver. US Airways flies to Phoenix.

Flagstaff (FLG), www.flagstaff.az.gov, 928-556-1234, 6200 S. Pulliam Dr., Flagstaff, AZ 86001. Directions: From downtown Flagstaff take US 89 south to I-17 (exit 337); turn left at John Wesley Powell Blvd., then right at S. Pulliam Dr. US Airways flies to Phoenix.

Four Corners Regional Airport (FMN), www.farmington.nm.us, 505-599-1395, 1300 W. Navajo St., Farmington, NM 87401. Directions: From downtown Farmington follow N. Auburn Ave. north, then turn west onto W. Navajo St. Great Lakes Airlines flies to Denver, Colorado, Gallup, New Mexico, Page, Arizona, and Phoenix, Arizona. US Airways flies to Cedar City, Utah, Moab, Utah, and Phoenix, Arizona.

Gallup Municipal Airport (GUP), www.ci.gallup.nm.us, 505-722-4896, 2111 W. Hwy. 66, Gallup, NM 87301. Directions: From downtown Gallup follow NM 118 west of NM 602. Great Lakes Airlines flies to Denver, Colorado, Farmington, New Mexico, and Phoenix, Arizona.

Grand Canyon National Park Airport (GCN), www.grandcanyonairport.net, AZ 64, Grand Canyon, AZ 86023. Directions: The airport is off AZ 64 just south of Tusayan, AZ. Charter and sightseeing flights arrive here, including from Las Vegas, Henderson, and Boulder City, Nevada, Phoenix, Arizona, and Long Beach, California.

Grand Junction Regional Airport (GJT), www.walkerfield.com, 970-244-9100, 2828 Walker Field Dr., Grand Junction, CO 81506. Directions: Take I-70 (exit 31) to Horizon Dr. northbound. Great Lakes Airlines flies to Denver, Colorado.

Kingman Airport (IGM), www.kingmanairportauthority.com, 928-757-2134, 7000 Flightline Dr., Kingman, AZ 86401. Directions: From I-40 (exit 53) drive east on Andy Devine Ave., then turn right on Mohave Airport Dr. Great Lakes Airlines flies to Phoenix and Prescott, Arizona.

Page Municipal Airport (PGA), www.cityofpage.org, 928-645-4337, 238 10th Ave., Page, AZ 86040. Directions: From downtown Page take the US 89 loop to N. Navajo Dr., then turn right on 11th Ave. and left onto Glen Canyon Dr. Great Lakes Airlines flies to Denver, Colorado, Farmington, New Mexico, and Phoenix, Arizona .

St. George Municipal Airport (SGU), www.sgcity.org/airport, 435-634-5822, 317 S. Donlee Dr., St. George, UT 84770. Directions: From downtown St. George drive west on St. George Blvd. across UT 18, then continue on S. Airport Rd. Delta Air Lines flies to Salt Lake City, Utah. United Airlines flies to Los Angeles, California.

By Train

The national railway service, **Amtrak,** www.amtrak.com, 1-800-872-7245, has cross-country train routes that connect a limited number of towns in the Four Corners region, mostly along the I-40 corridor through Arizona and New Mexico. Given the possible train delays involved, you're better off driving. For more information about Amtrak trains, including discounts and taking along bicycles as checked baggage, see the "Getting to the Four Corners" section earlier in this chapter.

Sample fares and travel times between major towns and cities in the Four Corners region:

Amtrak Route	Average Trip Duration	Adult One-Way Coach Fare (Reserved Seat)
Albuquerque, NM–Gallup, NM	2½ hours	$16
Albuquerque, NM–Flagstaff, AZ	5¼ hours	$54
Albuquerque, NM–Kingman, AZ	8 hours	$58
Albuquerque, NM–Winslow, AZ	4 hours	$41
Flagstaff, AZ–Gallup, NM	2¾ hours	$29
Flagstaff, AZ–Kingman, AZ	2¾ hours	$28
Flagstaff, AZ–Williams, AZ	½–¾ hour	$7
Flagstaff, AZ–Winslow, AZ	1 hour	$13

Two scenic railways in the Four Corners region make for unforgettable day trips or overnight excursions. Make reservations as far in advance as possible for these tourist trains; look for special discounts and package deals offered on the Web sites listed below.

The **Grand Canyon Railway**, www.thetrain.com, 928-773-1976, 1-800-843-8724, connects the Route 66 railroad town of Williams, Arizona, to Grand Canyon National Park. Vintage locomotives depart daily year-round, except December 24 and 25. The scenic trip to the South Rim of the Grand Canyon takes 2¼ hours each way. Northbound trains depart

Clamber aboard vintage locomotives at Williams, Arizona, for the trip to the South Rim of the Grand Canyon.
Mike Connolly

from the Williams depot between 9 and 10:30 AM and arrive at Grand Canyon Village between 11:15 AM and 12:45 PM. Southbound trains leave Grand Canyon Village between 3 and 4:30 PM, arriving back in Williams between 5:15 and 6:45 PM. Round-trip coach fares cost from $65 per adult ($30 to $40 per child) during peak summer season, less at other times of year. Higher classes of service such as in the club car, the observation dome car, or the luxury parlor cost much more.

Established in 1881, Colorado's **Durango & Silverton Narrow Gauge Railroad**, www.durangotrain.com, 970-247-2733, 1-877-872-4607, is one of the best train journeys in the American West. Coal-fired, steam-powered engines chug daily between downtown Durango and the historic mining town of Silverton high in the San Juan Mountains. Puffing and tooting their horns, the trains follow the historic late 19th-century rail line once used by miners, settlers, and cowboys. Today, passengers ride in enclosed vintage railcars or open-sided gondolas. It takes 3½ hours to make the 45-mile journey each way, which can be done as a scenic day trip or as an overnight excursion. During peak summer season (early May through late October), trains run one to four times daily, departing Durango in the morning and returning from Silverton in the afternoon. The standard fare in coach seats or open-air observation gondolas starts at $65 per adult ($35 per child), with quicker return options via bus from Silverton costing slightly more. Higher classes of service can cost up to twice as much. Between early March and early May, vintage locomotives also make shorter round-trip runs up Cascade Canyon along the Animas River. Round-trip excursion coach fares for this trip start at $45 per adult ($22 per child).

By Bus

The national bus service is **Greyhound**, www.greyhound.com, 1-800-231-2222. Its routes connect major cities with a few smaller towns in the Four Corners region, but they don't reach remote locations, such as national parks or Native American tribal lands. Greyhound bus services are neither fast nor frequent, so most travelers prefer to drive themselves. For more information about Greyhound buses, including discounts and taking along bicycles as checked baggage, see the "Getting to the Four Corners" section earlier in this chapter.

Sample advance-purchase fares for Greyhound buses between select towns and cities in the Four Corners region:

Greyhound Route	Average Trip Duration	Advance-Purchase Adult One-Way Fare
Albuquerque, NM–Flagstaff, AZ	6–6½ hours	$46
Albuquerque, NM–Farmington, NM	3½ hours	$34.50
Albuquerque, NM–Gallup, NM	2¼–2½ hours	$23.50
Durango, CO–Grand Junction, CO	4¼ hours	$35
Flagstaff, AZ–Kingman, AZ	2½ hours	$33.50
Flagstaff, AZ–Holbrook, AZ	1¾ hours	$23
Flagstaff, AZ–Winslow, AZ	1¼ hours	$15
Green River, UT–St. George, UT	5–7¾ hours	$37

Major cities such as Flagstaff and Albuquerque have local public buses for sightseeing around the city. Some local travel agencies offer pricey group bus tours from major cities and tourist hubs to popular regional attractions, such as the Grand Canyon. These bus tours don't usually allow visitors much time to get out and really explore. However, if you don't have a car, they may be your only option.

By Boat and Ferry

Several tour operators in the Four Corners region offer day trips, overnight excursions, and multiday aquatic adventures, from classic rafting trips down the Colorado River through the Grand Canyon to guided boat tours across Lake Powell to Rainbow Bridge inside the Navajo Nation. For detailed descriptions of these trips and recommended tour operators, see the relevant "Recreation" sections of the regional destination chapters.

In Glen Canyon National Recreation Area, the state of Utah operates a regularly scheduled car ferry service between the Halls Crossing (435-684-7000) and Bullfrog (435-684-3000) marinas. The public ferry operates year-round, with two to six departures daily in each direction. During the busy summer season, the first departure is usually at 8 or 9 AM, while the last run happens around 6 or 7 PM. The ferry crossing takes about 25 minutes each way. The one-way fare is $5 per passenger on foot or bicycle, $10 per motorcycle including all riders, and $20 for vehicles including all passengers (a surcharge applies for vehicles over 20 feet long). The ferry is occasionally out of service, so always call ahead for current hours of operation.

By Bicycle

The rough road conditions of most highways and byways in the Four Corners region, combined with busy traffic along the interstate, make road biking an unattractive option, except for endurance athletes in top condition. Many areas of the Four Corners offer superb mountain-biking opportunities, especially around Moab. Mountain-bike rentals can be expensive, however, starting from $20 a day. For more information on recreational cycling and mountain biking, see the relevant "Recreation" sections of the regional destination chapters.

By Taxi

You'll find taxi service in major towns and cities. Check under "Taxi" in the local yellow pages for more companies serving the following cities, as well as other towns and rural areas.

ALBUQUERQUE, NM

Albuquerque Cab Company, 505-883-4888

Yellow Cab, 505-247-8888

FLAGSTAFF, AZ

Allstar Taxi, 928-213-8294

Friendly Cab & Shuttle, 928-774-4444

MOAB, UT

Nomad Cab, 435-260-9986

ST. GEORGE, UT

Taxi USA, 435-656-1500

On Foot

Most of the small towns found along the back roads and byways of the Four Corners region are relatively pedestrian-friendly. The downtown core of larger cities, such as Flagstaff and Albuquerque, can be navigated on foot, although you can only get to some outlying areas via a combination of public buses and taxis or by driving.

3

FLAGSTAFF AND THE GRAND CANYON

A River Runs Through It

Experiencing the Grand Canyon for yourself—perhaps while catching sunrise breaking over the thickly forested canyon rim, or while camping underneath the stars by the Colorado River—is something not to be missed during a sojourn through the Southwest.

Carved by the mighty Colorado River over millions of years, this spectacular sight is more than a mile deep and 277 miles long. President Theodore Roosevelt once remarked, "You can not improve on it. The ages have been at work on it, and man can only mar it. What you can do is to keep it for your children, your children's children . . . as one of the great sights which every American . . . should see." Standing atop the rim today, visitors can peer down at colorful layers of ancient geology displayed in the eroded walls and spiring buttes of the canyon. There's no question why they call it grand.

The Grand Canyon was inhabited by Native Americans for many centuries before Europeans arrived, including by Ancestral Puebloan peoples, then Paiute and Navajo bands, and finally the modern Hualapai and Havasupai tribes who still live here. It was first stumbled upon by outsiders when Spanish conquistadores passed by in the mid-16th century. But it didn't become famous until John Wesley Powell led a daring expedition along the Colorado River and found passage all the way through the Grand Canyon in 1869. After the turn of the 20th century, many more tourists, photographers, scientists, and politicians showed up. Some of the buildings that sprang up on the South Rim, including in Grand Canyon Village, were designed by famed Western architect Mary Colter. The Grand Canyon Railway began transporting tourists to the canyon from Williams, Arizona, in 1909. A decade later the Grand Canyon was declared a national park, preserving it as a wildlife refuge and outdoor playground for the nation.

Even short walks along the South Rim of the Grand Canyon reward day-trippers with majestic views, while the remote North Rim—a five-hour drive away, though only 10 miles as the California condor flies—offers more of a taste of solitude. The gateway to the South Rim is Flagstaff, Arizona, a fun-lovin' university town with a touch of the Wild West and Route 66 relics still standing along Santa Fe Avenue, which runs alongside the railroad

LEFT: *Peer at colorful layers of geological history inside Grand Canyon National Park.* Sara Benson & Mike Connolly

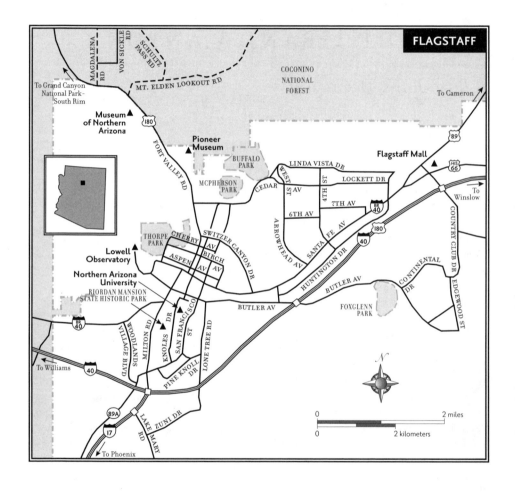

tracks downtown. Flagstaff enjoys higher mountain elevations than most of the deserts across the Southwest, making it a cool escape in summer and a winter-sports haven when the snow falls. On the drive from Flagstaff to the South Rim of the Grand Canyon, you'll pass the breathtaking Kachina Peaks Wilderness in the Coconino National Forest, a year-round destination for outdoor enthusiasts.

A short drive west of Flagstaff, the nostalgic yesteryear town of Williams (see the "Route 66" chapter) is another gateway to the South Rim of the canyon. The "Route 66" chapter appearing later in this book also covers the Hualapai and Havasupai Reservations in the western region of the Grand Canyon, offering further opportunities for backpacking, river rafting, and 4WD trips, as well as guided tours, including of the Grand Canyon West's glass-floored Skywalk. Access to these tribal lands requires a short but scenic detour along Route 66 from Seligman, about an hour's drive west of Flagstaff.

On the rustic North Rim of the Grand Canyon, you can leave the most crushing crowds behind. In fact, you might even have spectacular canyon viewpoints all to yourself. However, the North Rim is only open seasonally, usually from May through October, after which services shut down and the road eventually closes for the winter. To get to the North Rim, you'll pass through the hamlet of Jacob Lake, Arizona, due north of the national park entrance. Jacob Lake is accessible from Kanab, Utah (see the "Utah's Canyon Country" chapter), or Page, Arizona (see the "Native America" chapter).

LODGING

Flagstaff

ARIZONA MOUNTAIN INN
Innkeepers: Briany and Mary Bostwick
928-774-8959, 1-800-239-5236
www.arizonamountaininn.com
arizonamountaininn@msn.com
4200 Lake Mary Rd., Flagstaff, AZ 86001
Directions: Take I-40 exit 195 north toward Flagstaff. Turn left onto W. Forest Meadows St., then left again on Beulah Blvd., continuing underneath I-40. Turn left onto Lake Mary Rd. and drive approximately 1 mile.
Price: Moderate
Credit Cards: AE, D, MC, V
Handicapped Access: Partial

Hidden off the highway on private woodland acres, this rustic resort comprises a variety of stone and wooden cabins, each equipped with a kitchenette or full kitchen, a wood-burning stove or fireplace, ceiling fans (no air-conditioning or TVs), and barbecue grill. While the cabins are built closely together, the atmosphere is usually peaceful. Skip staying in the bed-and-breakfast suites, however. Dogs are welcome in most of the cabins. A minimum stay usually applies.

ASPEN INN BED & BREAKFAST
Innkeepers: Joe and Raquel Sanchez
928-773-0295, 1-888-999-4110
www.flagstaffbedbreakfast.com
info@flagstaffbedbreakfast.com
218 N. Elden St. (at E. Birch Ave.)
Flagstaff, AZ 86001
Price: Moderate
Credit Cards: AE, D, MC, V
Handicapped Access: No

Just a few blocks from downtown, this historic 1912 house offers European-style bed-and-breakfast rooms with private baths, cable TV, air-conditioning, telephones, mini-refrigerators stocked with snacks, and high-speed Wi-Fi Internet access. The decor tends toward minimalist art deco. Rates include an eclectic hot, cooked breakfast, but it's the warmth and helpfulness of the innkeepers that ensures repeat guests.

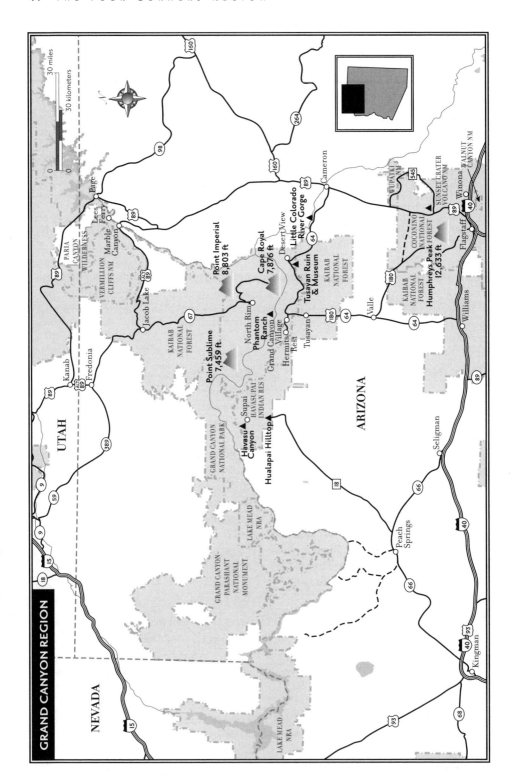

BUDGET HOST—SAGA MOTEL

928-779-3631
www.budgethost.com
820 W. Route 66 (west of S. Milton Rd.)
Flagstaff, AZ 86001
Price: Inexpensive
Credit Cards: AE, D, MC, V
Handicapped Access: Yes

Most of Flagstaff's vintage Route 66 motels are strung out by the railroad tracks on the east side of town. But the renovated Twilite Motel, which has a fetching neon sign glowing outside, is conveniently closer to downtown. Good for a quick overnight stay, it rates above the budget-motel norm, with service-oriented owners and double-paned windows to help shut out the train noise.

COMFI COTTAGES OF FLAGSTAFF

928-774-0731, 1-888-774-0731
www.comficottages.com
pat@comficottages.com
Office: 1612 N. Aztec St. (off W. Beal Rd.)
Flagstaff, AZ 86001
Directions: Follow N. Fort Valley Rd. (US 180), approximately 1.5 miles northwest of downtown Flagstaff.
Price: Very Expensive
Credit Cards: D, MC, V
Handicapped Access: Partial

These private 1920s vacation rental cottages are located in quiet residential areas within walking distance of downtown Flagstaff. Each quaint house is fully equipped with modern conveniences, including TV with VCR and DVD players, telephone, barbecue grill, and bicycles and tennis rackets to borrow. We especially liked the cottage adorned with Navajo and Hopi artwork and Southwestern-patterned quilts. Ask about the availability of Internet access when booking. A minimum stay may apply on weekends and holidays.

CONIFER HOUSE
BED & BREAKFAST INN

Innkeepers: Dave and Lauren Wright
928-774-2438, 1-888-788-3614
www.coniferhouse.com
info@coniferhouse.com
1701 W. Stevanna Way (off N. Fort Valley Rd. / US 180), Flagstaff, AZ 86001
Directions: Follow US 180 approximately 2 miles northwest of downtown.
Price: Expensive
Credit Cards: MC, V
Handicapped Access: No

In a residential neighborhood on the outskirts of Flagstaff, this modest house has five guest rooms equipped with ceiling fans, cable TV and VCR and DVD players, high-speed Internet access, romantic gas fireplaces, private baths with whirlpool tubs, and private entrances. Full hot, cooked breakfasts with dishes such as apple-cinnamon French toast are delightful. A shared kitchenette is available for guests. A two-night minimum stay applies on weekends from May through October.

ENGLAND HOUSE
BED AND BREAKFAST

Innkeepers: Laurie and Richard Dunn
928-214-7350, 1-877-214-7350
www.englandhousebandb.com
614 W. Santa Fe Ave. (at N. Bonito St.)
Flagstaff, AZ 86001
Price: Expensive
Credit Cards: D, MC, V
Handicapped Access: No

This distinguished-looking 1920s house surrounded by flowering gardens is a stone's throw west of downtown. Adorned throughout with French antiques, the inn's guest rooms are thoughtfully outfitted with extra pillows, CD player alarm clocks, and moisturizing bath-and-body products ideal for the dry Arizona climate. The spacious Song Catcher Suite has a queen-size feather

The England House Bed and Breakfast inhabits an early-20th-century stonecutter's house near downtown Flagstaff. Sara Benson & Mike Connolly

bed and a clawfoot tub in a private bathroom. As a special treat, breakfast is served on the glassed-in sunporch, warmed by a cozy hearth on chilly days.

FAIRFIELD INN FLAGSTAFF
928-773-1300, 1-888-236-2427
www.marriott.com/hotels/travel/flgfi
2005 S. Milton Rd. (at W. Saunders Dr.)
Flagstaff, AZ 86004
Directions: Take I-17 north of I-40 (exit 195).
Price: Moderate
Credit Cards: AE, D, MC, V
Handicapped Access: Yes

Charging the same rates as some roadside motels, the upscale Fairfield Inn is a bonus value. Although renovated rooms are not well-designed for business travelers (apart from offering free high-speed Internet access), they are spacious and well-equipped for leisure travelers, with superior mattresses, down pillows, and in some a microwave and mini-refrigerator. The outdoor swimming pool and hot tub are open seasonally. Rates include a free hot breakfast bar.

FALL INN TO NATURE
Innkeepers: Ron and Annette Fallaha
928-714-0237, 1-888-920-0237
www.fallinntonature.com
info@fallinntonature.com
4555 S. Lake Mary Rd., Flagstaff, AZ 86001
Directions: From I-40 (exit 195) drive north toward downtown. Turn left onto W. Forest Meadows St. Go left on Beulah Blvd., continuing underneath I-40. Turn left onto Lake Mary Rd. for approximately 2 miles.
Price: Moderate
Credit Cards: D, MC, V
Handicapped Access: No

Next to thickly wooded forests south of Flagstaff, this two-story log home is near mountains and wildflower meadows. A rural roadside bed-and-breakfast, it is equally suited for nature lovers and independent travelers. Upstairs rooms have rustic furnishings, private baths, air-conditioning and heating, TVs with VCR/DVD players, coffeemakers, and free high-speed Internet access. Children are welcome in the two-bedroom family suite, which has a full kitchen and private entrance. Rates include a full, hot cooked breakfast.

HOTEL MONTE VISTA
Manager: Jim Craven
928-779-6971, 1-800-545-3068
www.hotelmontevista.com
montev@infomagic.net
100 N. San Francisco St. (at E. Aspen St.)
Flagstaff, AZ 86001

Price: Moderate
Credit Cards: AE, D, MC, V
Handicapped Access: No

Presiding over downtown Flagstaff for more than eight decades, the venerable Monte Vista is the most elegant historic hotel in town. During its glory days, Hollywood stars such as Humphrey Bogart and Carole Lombard and western writer Zane Grey stayed here. In modern times it has been a favorite of rock stars. Each of the 50 neo-Victorian rooms and suites has cable TV, telephone, and shower and bathtub. The accommodations are all on the upper floors, with some mountain views. The hotel's cocktail lounge and downstairs coffee shop are sociable hangouts.

Sleep where movie stars have slept inside the historic Hotel Monte Vista. Sara Benson & Mike Connolly

THE INN AT NAU

General Manager: Julene Boger
928-523-1616
http://home.nau.edu/hrm/theinn/
julene.bolger@nau.edu
P.O. Box 5606, Flagstaff, AZ 86011
Directions: Take San Francisco St. south onto the Northern Arizona University (NAU) campus. At McCreary Dr. turn right at the sign past the sports field.
Price: Moderate
Credit Cards: AE, MC, V
Handicapped Access: Yes

On a university campus near downtown, this small hotel is a living laboratory managed by students. It has just 19 rooms and suites comfortably furnished with high-quality beds, cable TV, mini-refrigerators, and free high-speed Wi-Fi Internet access. For a small fee guests can use the university's state-of-the-art fitness and aquatic facilities across the street. Accommodation taxes are not charged, and rates include a breakfast buffet. Make reservations far in advance, as the inn often books up during special events.

LITTLE AMERICA HOTEL

928-779-2741, 1-800-865-1401
www.littleamerica.com/flagstaff
2515 E. Butler Ave. (at Purple Heart Trail)
Flagstaff, AZ 86004
Directions: Off I-40 exit 198
Price: Expensive
Credit Cards: AE, D, MC, V
Handicapped Access: Yes

On the east side of town, this well-appointed hotel complex is often booked out for special events. Room rates may be high, but a variety of discounts are available. The modern furnished rooms are a cut above the competition, with feather down pillows and comforters, flat-screen TVs, free high-speed Internet access, mini-refrigerators, plush carpeting, and separate dressing and sitting areas. Out back there's a wooded hiking trail, sand volleyball court, horseshoe pits, and croquet and badminton sets to borrow. There's also a fitness room and heated outdoor pool and hot tub.

RESIDENCE INN FLAGSTAFF

928-526-5555, 1-800-331-3131
www.marriott.com/
residence-inn/travel.mi
3440 N. Country Club Dr. (at E. Boulder Run Dr.), Flagstaff, AZ 86004
Directions: Off I-40 exit 201
Price: Expensive
Credit Cards: AE, D, MC, V
Handicapped Access: Yes

Meant for business travelers and extended stays, this all-suite hotel is well-suited for families or anyone traveling with pets. Nearby a golf course, this hotel looks like condo duplexes from the outside. Inside each of the studio and two-bedroom suites you'll find a fully equipped kitchen and ergonomic work desk with free high-speed Internet access. Rates include a breakfast buffet and evening social hour (Monday through Thursday). A heated outdoor pool and hot tub are open seasonally.

STARLIGHT PINES
BED AND BREAKFAST

Innkeepers: Richard Svendsen and Michael Ruiz
928-527-1912, 1-800-752-1912
www.starlightpinesbb.com
romance@starlightpinesbb.com
3380 E. Lockett Rd. (off N. Fanning Dr.)
Flagstaff, AZ 86004
Directions: Off I-40 exit 201
Price: Expensive
Credit Cards: D, MC, V
Handicapped Access: No

In an unlikely spot next to a public schoolyard, this stately Victorian house is sheltered by pine trees. Inside the oak-floored, high-ceilinged rooms you'll find fresh

Experience Flagstaff's early pioneer days for yourself at the turn-of-the-20th-century Weatherford Hotel.
Sara Benson & Mike Connolly

flowers, antiques and Tiffany lamps, fireplaces, and clawfoot tubs (no TVs). Guests are welcome to kick back on the wraparound porch with mountain views. Rates include a hot breakfast and high-speed Wi-Fi Internet access. An award-winning bed-and-breakfasts with hospitable owners, the inn is gay-friendly.

WEATHERFORD HOTEL

Manager: Matt Bial
928-779-1919
www.weatherfordhotel.com
information@weatherfordhotel.com
23 N. Leroux St. (at W. Aspen St.),
Flagstaff, AZ 86001
Price: Inexpensive
Credit Cards: AE, D, MC, V
Handicapped Access: No

For those who want a taste of history, this turn-of-the-20th-century hotel with crackling fireplaces and open-air balconies overlooking the busy streets of downtown Flagstaff offers simple accommodations, mostly without air-conditioning, TVs, or telephones. It's an authentic experience of an Old West boardinghouse, complete with thin-walled rooms that don't block out the train noise or the boisterous pub downstairs with live music playing until the wee hours. Incidentally, President Theodore Roosevelt once stayed here.

Fredonia

GRAND CANYON MOTEL

928-643-7646
175 S. Main St. (US 89-A at Pratt St. / AZ 389), Fredonia, AZ 86022
Price: Inexpensive
Credit Cards: MC, V
Handicapped Access: Yes

Much closer to southern Utah than to Flagstaff, but within easy driving distance of the North Rim of the Grand Canyon, this budget motel with amiable owners offers vintage stone-and-wood cabins equipped with cable TV and air-conditioning. Some have kitchenettes with mini-refrigerators and microwaves. Ask about discounts for multiday and weekly stays.

JUNIPER LODGE

928-643-7752
www.juniperlodge.info
465 S. Main St. (US 89-A at Lukus Lane), Fredonia, AZ 86022
Price: Inexpensive
Credit Cards: MC, V
Handicapped Access: Yes

Recently renovated and under new management, this value-priced motel offers spacious rooms with rustic log-style furniture, telephones, satellite TV, and high-speed Wi-Fi Internet access. Rely on the attached Sage House Grill for a quick, filling country-style meal.

Grand Canyon National Park— North Rim

GRAND CANYON LODGE

Regional General Manager: Jeff D'Arpa
Lodge: 928-638-2611; advance reservations: 303-297-2757, 1-888-297-2757
www.grandcanyonnorthrim.com
reserve-gcnr@xanterra.com
Grand Canyon National Park
North Rim, AZ 86052
Open: Mid-May through mid-October or early November
Price: Moderate
Credit Cards: AE, D, MC, V
Handicapped Access: Partial

A beautiful escape from the ordinary, this sprawling national park lodge sits right on the North Rim of the Grand Canyon. To enjoy sunset views from the hotel's back patio, check in before dark. Accommodations include motel rooms and a variety of cabins, from rustic duplexes to more comfortable cottages with rocking chairs on private porches with jaw-dropping canyon views. All accommodations

Rustic cabins offer a taste-of-yesteryear atmosphere on the North Rim of the Grand Canyon. Sara Benson & Mike Connolly

have phones, but no TVs. Reservations are accepted up to 13 months in advance. For same-day reservations and to check last-minute availability, call the lodge directly.

KAIBAB LODGE

928-638-2389
www.kaibablodge.com
info@kaibablodge.com
HC Box 30, Fredonia, AZ 86022
Directions: On AZ 67, 5 miles north of the national park entrance
Open: Mid-May through mid-October or early November
Price: Moderate
Credit Cards: D, MC, V
Handicapped Access: Partial

Standing by themselves in a forested meadow, these rustic country cabins are the closest lodging options outside the North Rim boundary of Grand Canyon National Park. Open only during summer, this lodge offers basic motel-style rooms in shared duplexes and larger private cabins, some of which have kitchenettes. Beware of the thin-walled older cabins, which can be frustrating if you have noisy neighbors. Check-in is available until 10 PM at the lodge. Ask about pet-friendly rooms.

Grand Canyon National Park— South Rim

Reservations for all the following lodgings in Grand Canyon Village on the South Rim of Grand Canyon National Park are accepted up to 13 months in advance. For same-day reservations and to check last-minute availability, call the local phone number listed below for each lodging. Lodgings are open year-round; rates drop during winter.

BRIGHT ANGEL LODGE & CABINS

Management: Xanterra Parks & Resorts
Lodge: 928-638-2631; advance reservations: 303-297-2757, 1-888-297-2757
www.grandcanyonlodges.com
reserve-gcsr@xanterra.com
P.O. Box 699, Grand Canyon, AZ 86023
Price: Moderate
Credit Cards: AE, D, MC, V
Handicapped Access: Partial

Built in the mid-1930s, this nationally registered historic landmark is a charming place to stay. You can't stay any closer to the South Rim, especially not when you choose one of the rustic cabins set apart from the main lodge, which is a constant hub of activity. Not all of the rooms inside the

Tourists ready for adventure outside the Bright Angel Lodge on the South Rim of the Grand Canyon.
Sara Benson & Mike Connolly

Cozy, rustic cabins surround the Bright Angel Lodge on the South Rim of the Grand Canyon.
Sara Benson & Mike Connolly

lodge have private baths, and none have TV, although all the cabins have telephones, TVs, and private baths. Some cabins are duplexes, which means sharing walls with neighbors. More deluxe cabins come with gas fireplaces.

EL TOVAR HOTEL

Management: Xanterra Parks & Resorts
Lodge: 928-638-2631; advance reservations: 303-297-2757, 1-888-297-2757
www.grandcanyonlodges.com
reserve-gcsr@xanterra.com
P.O. Box 699, Grand Canyon, AZ 86023
Price: Expensive
Credit Cards: AE, D, MC, V
Handicapped Access: Partial

This early-20th-century hotel is by far the most genteel place to sleep on the South Rim. Recently renovated rooms and suites are equipped with TVs and telephones, as well as lovely oversize bathrooms that have art-deco decor, tiled floors, and deep soaking tubs. The bedding is so comfortable that you may find it difficult to get up early enough to see the sun rise over the Grand Canyon. The hotel boasts old-fashioned wooden wraparound porches for relaxation, including the one outside the cocktail bar. Evening turn-down and room service are offered.

The El Tovar Hotel is the pinnacle of luxury on the South Rim of Grand Canyon National Park.
Sara Benson & Mike Connolly

MASWIK LODGE

Management: Xanterra Parks & Resorts
Lodge: 928-638-2631; advance reservations: 303-297-2757, 1-888-297-2757
www.grandcanyonlodges.com
reserve-gcsr@xanterra.com
P.O. Box 699, Grand Canyon, AZ 86023
Price: Moderate
Credit Cards: AE, D, MC, V
Handicapped Access: Yes

Often full with tour bus groups, the Maswik Lodge offers basic motel rooms in two-story buildings built away from the canyon rim. Each standard room has two queen-

The historic El Tovar Hotel presides majestically over the South Rim. Courtesy Xanterra Parks & Resorts

size beds, private bath, TV, and telephone. During the summer months rustic cabin rooms with TVs and phones are also available. Note the Maswik Lodge may have vacancies when other South Rim lodgings are full.

PHANTOM RANCH
Management: Xanterra Parks & Resorts
Advance reservations: 303-297-2757, 1-888-297-2757
www.grandcanyonlodges.com
reserve-gcsr@xanterra.com
P.O. Box 699, Grand Canyon, AZ 86023
Directions: Accessible only on foot or mule via the Bright Angel and South Kaibab Trails, or on river-rafting trips
Price: Inexpensive
Credit Cards: AE, D, MC, V
Handicapped Access: No

Scenically set at the bottom of the Grand Canyon beside the Colorado River, this historic ranch was built back in the 1920s. The rustic main lodge and cabins are constructed of wood and stone and blend beautifully with the natural environs. Basic accommodations are comfortably heated or cooled, depending on the weather. Both the single-sex dormitories and private cabins have bunk beds and vanity sinks. All guests share the shower house. The ranch is popular with backpackers, mule riders, and river runners, so make sure you book as far in advance as possible.

YAVAPAI LODGE
Lodge: 928-638-2631; advance reservations: 303-297-2757, 1-888-297-2757
www.grandcanyonlodges.com
reserve-gcsr@xanterra.com
P.O. Box 699, Grand Canyon, AZ 86023
Price: Moderate
Credit Cards: AE, D, MC, V
Handicapped Access: No

This lodge is located well away from the canyon rim near the South Rim's grocery store, deli, and outdoors store. It provides surprisingly pleasant motel-style rooms equipped with air-conditioning, TVs, telephones, mini-refrigerators, and coffeemakers. It's an especially good choice for active families traveling on a budget.

Jacob Lake

JACOB LAKE INN
Manager: Shayne Rich
928-643-7232
www.jacoblake.com
jacob@jacoblake.com
Junction of US 89-A at AZ 67,
Jacob Lake, AZ 86022
Price: Moderate
Credit Cards: AE, D, MC, V
Handicapped Access: Partial

Open year-round, this 1920s lodge is among the few accommodation options spread thinly between Kanab and the North Rim of the Grand Canyon. Expect plenty of hubbub and "No Vacancy" signs during summer, while winter allows more peaceful stays. Some motel rooms have cable TV, phones, and high-speed Internet access, but private cabins do not. Pets are accepted in some rooms for a nightly surcharge. The inn's bakery has yummy snacks and breakfast items to help you get started in the morning.

Tusayan

BEST WESTERN GRAND CANYON SQUIRE INN
928-638-2681, 1-800-622-6966
www.grandcanyonsquire.com
100 AZ 64, Grand Canyon, AZ 86023
Price: Moderate
Credit Cards: AE, D, MC, V
Handicapped Access: Yes

Just south of the South Rim of the Grand Canyon, this standard motel offers reasonable accommodations in the high-priced gateway town of Tusayan. All the guest rooms come with cable TV, coffeemakers, telephones, and high-speed Wi-Fi Internet access. Other amenities include an indoor hot tub and sauna, an outdoor seasonal swimming pool, and a family fun center for billiards and bowling.

THE GRAND HOTEL
General Manager: Darla Barrett
928-638-3333, 1-888-634-7263
http://the-grand-hotel-grand-canyon
.pacificahost.com
P.O. Box 3319, Grand Canyon, AZ 86023
Directions: On AZ 64 north of the airport
Price: Expensive
Credit Cards: AE, D, MC, V
Handicapped Access: Partial

This newly built motel offers some of the most spacious accommodations in Tusayan. All guest rooms have pillow-top mattresses, cable TV, coffeemakers, and brand-name bath amenities; deluxe rooms have private balconies or patios. Amenities include an indoor heated swimming pool and hot tub, small fitness room, and guest laundry facilities. Pets are accepted in some rooms.

SEVEN MILE LODGE
928-638-2291
www.angelfire.com/biz/7milelodge/
gc7mile@hotmail.com
AZ 64, Grand Canyon, AZ 86023
Price: Inexpensive
Credit Cards: MC, V
Handicapped Access: Yes

A last resort for travelers who arrive at the Grand Canyon without reservations, this family-owned motel accepts walk-in guests only. All the basic motel rooms have two queen-size beds, cable TV, coffeemakers, private baths with showers and tubs, and individual heating and air-conditioning (no phones). A solid budget choice, it will do in a pinch.

CULTURE

Archaeological Sites
For Ancestral Puebloan sites inside national parks and monuments, see the "Museums" and also "Parks and Natural Attractions" sections later in this chapter.

Architecture
GRAND CANYON VILLAGE, HERMITS REST & DESERT VIEW WATCHTOWER
928-638-7888
www.nps.gov/grca
Grand Canyon National Park—South Rim, P.O. Box 129, Grand Canyon, AZ 86023

Step inside the historic Hopi House, designed by western architect Mary Colter. Sara Benson & Mike Connolly

Open: Lodges open 24/7/365; daytime seasonal hours vary for other buildings
Admission: seven-day entry pass per vehicle $25; per individual on foot, bicycle, or motor-cycle $12

Famed early-20th-century Western architect Mary Elizabeth Jane Colter began her career building railway hotels for the Fred Harvey Co. She was a student of Southwestern art and archaeology, and her masterwork may be a collection of buildings on the South Rim of the Grand Canyon. While in Grand Canyon Village, admire sandstone-walled Hopi House,

Architect Mary Colter's whimsical Desert View Watchtower on the South Rim of the Grand Canyon. Sara Benson & Mike Connolly

an homage to tribal pueblos, now filled with Native America artisan crafts (see the "Shopping" section later). Perched on the rim itself, the stone Lookout Studio appears to have grown naturally out of the canyon's walls. By designing the rustic-style Bright Angel Lodge, Colter inspired an entire generation of national park architecture. She also crafted the detailed Southwestern interior design of the El Tovar Hotel. Standing at opposite ends of the canyon are two more whimsical structures. The primitive stonework of Hermits Rest is accented by an antique New Mexican mission bell. The Desert View Watchtower is worth climbing inside, not only for the sweeping canyon vistas but also for interior murals and the design of the building, which echoes Ancestral Puebloan dwellings.

RIORDAN MANSION STATE HISTORIC PARK

928-779-4395
www.pr.state.az.us/parks/parkhtml/riordan
409 W. Riordan Rd. (at S. Knowles Dr.), Flagstaff, AZ 86001
Directions: From downtown Flagstaff take S. Milton Rd. south, then turn left onto Riordan Rd.
Open: Daily 8:30–5, May through October; 10:30–5, November through April
Admission: Adults $6, children 7–13 $2.50, children 6 and under free

In a grove of pine trees on the Northern Arizona University campus, this historical mansion is a masterpiece of Arts-and-Crafts architecture. Built by an influential logging family, the site's two mansions are connected by a billiards room. They were designed by architect Charles Whittlesey, who also crafted the impressive El Tovar Hotel in Grand Canyon Village. The exterior of the mansions looks as rustic as a log cabin, but that belies the elegance inside, decorated with original furniture and unique photographic windows showing Southwestern scenes. Call ahead to check the schedule of guided tours, which typically depart hourly.

The timber industry built much of the Old West, including impressive Riordan Mansion.
Sara Benson & Mike Connolly

Art Galleries

Many more artists set up shop in Sedona, Arizona, but Flagstaff still has several art galleries, most of which are found downtown, especially at places like the complex at 111 E. Aspen Street Flagstaff Art Walks, with gallery openings and special events, happen downtown on the first Friday evening of every month. For open studio tours, contact the Artists' Coalition of Flagstaff (www.flagstaffarts.org, 928-779-2300). For artisan craft shops, see the "Shopping" section below.

Coconino Center for the Arts, www.culturalpartners.org, 928-779-2300, 2300 N. Fort Valley Rd. (US 180), Flagstaff. Multipurpose venue hosts rotating art exhibitions; call ahead to check schedules.

Kolb Studio, www.grandcanyon.org/kolb, 928-638-2481, Grand Canyon Village, Grand Canyon National Park—South Rim. Inside the historic studio built by the Kolb brothers, adventurous photographers who arrived at the Grand Canyon in 1901, rotating art exhibits feature paintings, photography, and prints related to nature, Native American culture, and Western history.

Cinema

Grand Canyon National Geographic IMAX Theater, www.explorethecanyon.com, 928-638-2468, National Geographic Visitor Center, AZ 64, Tusayan. Sponsored by National Geographic, this IMAX movie with an award-winning director and score has been seen by nearly 40 million people. Seasonal hours vary, but the shows usually begin hourly on the half hour. Buy discount tickets ahead of time online to skip the lines, or take a look at the interpretive displays inside the visitor center while you wait.

The historic Kolb Studio has an enviable perch on the South Rim of the Grand Canyon. Sara Benson & Mike Connolly

Harkins Flagstaff 11, www.harkinstheatre.com, 928-774-4847, 1959 S. Woodlands Village Blvd., off University Ave. west of S. Milton Rd., Flagstaff. Near downtown, Flagstaff's largest cinema has stadium seating and Dolby THX sound.

Movies on the Square, www.heritagesquaretrust.org, 928-853-4292, Heritage Square, 111 W. Birch St., Flagstaff. On Friday evenings from Memorial Day through Labor Day, this downtown park offers free screenings of family-friendly classic films and newly released movies, with live entertainment before the show.

Orpheum Theater, www.orpheumpresents.com, 928-556-1580. 15 W. Aspen St., Flagstaff, AZ. This early-20th-century theater sometimes shows classic flicks and hosts independent film festivals, such as the Flagstaff Mountain Film Festival (www.flagstaffmountainfilms.com) in March and the Southwest Native American Film Festival (www.indigenousaction.org/filmfest) in October.

Historic Places

For more historical sites around Flagstaff and the Grand Canyon, see "Architecture," above.

Museums

MUSEUM OF NORTHERN ARIZONA

928-774-5213
www.musnaz.org
3101 N. Fort Valley Rd. (US 180), Flagstaff, AZ 86001
Directions: 3 miles northwest of downtown Flagstaff
Admission: Adults $5, seniors $4, students $3, Native Americans and youth 7–17 $2, children 6 and under free
Open: Daily 9–5; closed Thanksgiving, Christmas, and New Year's Day

Finely curated exhibits bring to life the land and peoples of the Colorado Plateau. The geology and paleontology panels will engage scientific minds. The displays of Native American history, sacred rituals, and traditional and contemporary arts—ranging from Ancestral Puebloan pottery to modern murals—are a must-see attraction for Four Corners visitors. Pick up a self-guiding brochure for the nature trail and wildlife-viewing pond out back. Native American cultural festivals are held here every summer (see "Seasonal Events," below).

NORTHERN ARIZONA UNIVERSITY ART MUSEUM

928-523-3471
www.nau.edu/art_museum/
Knowles Drive at McMullen Circle, Flagstaff, AZ 86011
Admission: Donations accepted
Open: Monday through Friday 10–4:30, Saturday 10–3

A collection of three small galleries, this university-sponsored art museum puts on rotating exhibits of modern and contemporary art. The main exhibition space and Weiss Gallery are found inside the Old Main building on the Northern Arizona University campus. The former presents cutting-edge, contemporary art in all media, while the latter displays pieces from the global art and furniture collections of Marguerite Weiss, including works by Southwestern and Native American artists.

PIONEER MUSEUM

928-774-6272
www.arizonahistoricalsociety.org
2340 N. Fort Valley Rd. (US 180), Flagstaff, AZ 86001
Directions: 2 miles northwest of downtown Flagstaff
Admission: Adults $3, seniors and students 12–18 $2, children under 12 free. Free admission on the first Saturday of each month.
Open: Monday through Saturday 9–5; closed Thanksgiving, Christmas, and New Year's Day

Next to the Coconino Center for the Arts, this small historical museum is housed inside a former county hospital for the poor. On the grounds you'll find a homesteader's cabin,

Ancient pottery and other archaeological finds are on display inside the must-see Museum of Northern Arizona. Sara Benson & Mike Connolly

farm barn, root cellar, and a 1929 locomotive and Santa Fe caboose for railroad buffs. Living history demonstrations are performed by costumed volunteers during the Wool Festival in early June and over the Fourth of July holiday, when Civil War and pioneer fur-trading camps are staged here.

TUSAYAN MUSEUM

928-638-7888
www.nps.gov/grca
Grand Canyon National Park—South Rim, P.O. Box 129, Grand Canyon AZ, 86023
Directions: 3 miles west of Desert View Watchtower
Admission: Free with park entrance fee ($25 per vehicle for seven-day pass)
Open: Daily 9–5 in summer; seasonal hours vary

Most visitors start with a stroll through the 800-year-old Pueblo ruins found outside the museum. Inside you'll find a small but expertly curated room of displays about Ancestral Puebloan peoples and daily life in a Hopi pueblo, both historically and now. It's a worthwhile stop en route to the Desert View Watchtower (see "Architecture," above), especially to attend a ranger-guided walk or cultural program.

YAVAPAI OBSERVATION STATION

928-638-7888
www.nps.gov/grca
Grand Canyon National Park—South Rim, P.O. Box 129, Grand Canyon AZ, 86023
Directions: 1 mile east of Market Plaza in Grand Canyon Village

Admission: Free with park entrance fee ($25 per vehicle for seven-day pass)
Open: Daily 9–5 in summer; seasonal hours vary

This historic observation station was one of the first interpretive structures in the entire National Park Service. Its location was selected in the 1920s by scientists as the best single viewpoint on the South Rim of the Grand Canyon for examining the canyon's head-spinning geological layers. Interpretive exhibits focus on what can be seen outside the station's panoramic windows, as well as the Colorado River's role in carving out this natural wonder. Geology programs are presented daily by park rangers.

Music and Dance

For more live-music venues, see "Nightlife," below.

Flagstaff Folk Festival, www.ffotm.net/folkfest/, 928-774-9541, Coconino Center for the Arts, 2300 N. Fort Valley Rd. (US 180), Flagstaff. In mid-June this homegrown festival features three days of folk and bluegrass performances, storytelling, and musical workshops.

Flagstaff Symphony Orchestra, www.flagstaffsymphony.org, 928-774-5107, 113 E. Aspen St., Suite A, Flagstaff. For over half a century, the FSO has performed classical, pop, and chorale music concerts from September through April.

Grand Canyon Chamber Music Festival, www.grandcanyonmusicfest.org, 928-638-9215, 1-800-997-8285, Grand Canyon National Park—South Rim. Held every September at the Shrine of the Ages on the South Rim of the canyon, this chamber music concert series sells out quickly; buy tickets in advance.

Heritage Square, www.heritagesquaretrust.org, 928-853-4292, Heritage Square, 111 W. Birch St., Flagstaff. Between Memorial Day and Labor Day, all kinds of musical concerts happen at this downtown park on Thursday, Saturday, and Sunday evenings, occasionally including dance lessons with swingin' live bands. Admission is free.

Orpheum Theater, www.orpheumpresents.com, 928-556-1580. 15 W. Aspen St., Flagstaff. This historic movie house presents a lively calendar of music and performing arts events, from local bands to national touring acts and international stars.

Nightlife

Beaver Street Brewery, www.beaverstreetbrewery.com, 928-779-0079, 11 S. Beaver St., Flagstaff. Local brewpub and restaurant has big-screen sports TVs and a game room next door with billiards tables and retro video-arcade machines. The oatmeal stout and seasonal Bavarian brews are worth pouring a pint.

Bright Angel Bar, www.grandcanyonlodges.com, 928-638-2631, Bright Angel Lodge, Grand Canyon Village. Have a swig of beer in a rustic lounge painted with Grand Canyon murals, where folk and western musicians perform during busy tourist times.

Canyon Star Saloon, 928-638-3333, The Grand Hotel, AZ 64, Tusayan. Hotel bar has big-screen sports TVs and pool tables, with lively entertainment such as cowboy musicians spilling over from the restaurant. Some of the bar stools are made from cowboy saddles.

Charly's Pub, www.weatherfordhotel.com, 928-779-1919, Weatherford Hotel, 23 N. Leroux St., Flagstaff. At a historic hotel downtown, this casual corner pub is always boisterous with live music shows, including jazz, blues, and rock 'n' roll, and open-mike nights. Before sunset sidle up to a sidewalk patio table for drinks.

El Tovar Lounge, www.grandcanyonlodges.com, 928-638-2631, El Tovar Hotel, Grand Canyon Village. Grab a table on the back porch and watch the sun sink over the canyon rim. A cocktail list includes prickly-pear margaritas, along with a short menu of southwestern appetizers and desserts.

Flagstaff Brewing Company, www.flagbrew.com, 928-773-1442, 16 E. Route 66, Flagstaff. Brewing top-rated suds since 1984, this friendly brewpub usually has live local bands from Thursday through Sunday nights. The handcrafted ESB, porter, and wheat beers rate among Arizona's best.

Maswik Lounge and Sports Bar, www.grandcanyonlodges.com, 928-638-2631, Maswik Lodge, Grand Canyon Village. This casual sports bar features big-screen TVs, pool tables, and a full bar with a variety of draft beers on tap.

Monte Vista Cocktail Lounge, www.hotelmontevista.com, 928-779-6971, Hotel Monte Vista, 100 N. San Francisco St., Flagstaff. At this svelte underground bar, lipstick-red pool tables and a mix of live music and DJs that keeps hepcats and lounge lizards coming back.

Museum Club, www.museumclub.com, 928-526-9434, 3404 E. Route 66, Flagstaff. Nicknamed "The Zoo" after its days as a taxidermy shop, this 1930s roadhouse is a Route 66 landmark. True cowboy spirit reigns over a barn-size wooden dance floor that really comes alive on Friday and Saturday nights. Pony up to the 1880s mahogany bar at the back to find a roughneck pardner. Look for horseshoe tournaments, no-limit Texas hold 'em poker, off-track betting on horse racing, and karaoke nights.

Pay-N-Take Downtown Market, www.payntake.com, 928-226-8595, 12 W. Aspen St., Flagstaff. A popular meeting place for locals, this retro-looking convenience shop stocks candy, ice cream, and snacks. The bottle shop sells espresso drinks, wines by the glass or bottle, and over 100 different kinds of beer by the six-pack. Free Wi-Fi hot spot.

The Museum Club, a nightclub that was once a taxidermy shop, has a noteworthy collection of stuffed animals hanging on the walls above the dance floor. Sara Benson & Mike Connolly

Rough Rider Saloon, www.grandcanyon northrim.com, 928-638-2611, Grand Canyon National Park—North Rim.

Named in honor of Teddy Roosevelt, this casual wooden bar has some intriguing micro-brews on tap. Get yours poured into a plastic cup, then take it over to the lodge's panoramic back porch for sunset views.

San Felipe's Cantina, 928-779-6000, 103 N. Leroux St., Flagstaff. Follow the hooting and hollering of college students to this Baja-style party shack downtown. Massive margaritas and cheap beer are always on hand.

Starlite Lanes, www.starlitelanesflagstaff.com, 928-526-1138; 3406 E. Route 66, Flagstaff. Classic local bowling alley on Route 66 also serves cocktails.

Wine Loft, 928-773-9463, 17 N. San Francisco St., Flagstaff. Tucked away upstairs from the rambunctious streets, this mellow bar has comfy sofa lounges, brick walls hung with contemporary art, and an extensive selection of Belgian beers and wines by the glass.

Observatories
LOWELL OBSERVATORY
928-233-3211
www.lowell.edu
1400 W. Mars Hill Rd., Flagstaff, AZ 86001
Directions: Follow Santa Fe Ave. west of downtown. Turn right at the fork and drive up Mars Hill.
Open: March through October 9–5, November through February 12–5. Also Wednesday, Friday, and Saturday from 5:30 pm (free admission after 9:30 pm) September through May; Monday through Saturday from 5:30 pm (free admission after 10 pm) June through August; closes earlier during inclement weather. Call ahead to check schedules.
Admission: Adults $6, students and seniors $5, youths 5–17 $3, children 4 and under free

West of downtown, this working astronomical observatory is open to the public. Daytime tours, which usually begin hourly on the hour, lead visitors up into the telescope domes, then explore astronomical exhibits and watch a short multimedia show. Evening programs also take in telescope viewing of the heavens, weather permitting. Stargazing and meteor shower viewing festivals take place throughout the year.

Seasonal Events
FEBRUARY
Flagstaff Winterfest, www.flagstaffchamber.com, 928-774-4505, Flagstaff

APRIL
Northern Arizona Book Festival, www.nazbookfest.com, 928-380-8682, Flagstaff

JUNE
Hopi Festival of Arts and Culture, www.musnaz.org, 928-774-5213, Flagstaff.

Pine County Pro Rodeo, www.pinecountryprorodeo.com, 928-526-3556, 1-888-681-3556, Flagstaff

Route 66 Regional Chili Cook-off, 928-526-4314, Flagstaff

Wool Festival, www.arizonahistoricalsociety.org, 928-774-6272, Flagstaff

JULY
Independence Day Festival, www.arizonahistoricalsociety.org, 928-774-6272, Flagstaff

AUGUST
Navajo Festival of Arts and Culture, www.musnaz.org, 928-774-5213, Flagstaff

SEPTEMBER
Coconino County Fair, www.coconinoaz.gov, 928-774-5011, 1-800-559-9289, Flagstaff

Flagstaff Festival of Science, www.scifest.org, 928-527-3344, Flagstaff

Flagstaff Marathon, www.flagstaffnordiccenter.com, 928-220-0550, Flagstaff

Flagstaff Route 66 Days, www.flagstaffroute66days.com, 928-779-9541, Flagstaff

OCTOBER
Autumn in the Aspens, www.flagstaffnordiccenter.com, 928-220-0550, Flagstaff

Celebraciónes de la Gente, www.musnaz.org, 928-774-5213, Flagstaff

DECEMBER
New Year's Eve Pinecone Drop, www.flagstaff.az.gov, 928-774-5281, Flagstaff

RESTAURANTS AND FOOD PURVEYORS

Flagstaff

BLACK BEAN BURRITO BAR
928-779-9905
12 E. Route 66 (between N. Leroux St. and
N. San Francisco St.), Flagstaff, AZ 86001
Open: Daily
Price: Inexpensive
Cuisine: Californian/Mexican
Serving: B, L, D
Credit Cards: MC, V
Handicapped Access: Yes

On a pedestrian-only side street in downtown, this California-inspired Mexican
burrito joint has sidewalk tables for
munching on tortilla chips, downing a
tamarindo soda, and devouring freshly
rolled burritos full of shrimp, chicken,
beef, or grilled veggies served with a rainbow variety of salsas.

BRANDY'S RESTAURANT & BAKERY
928-779-2187
www.brandysrestaurant.com

*A healthier lifestyle enlightens Flagstaff: Look for
bicycles and vegetarian-friendly restaurants.*
Sara Benson & Mike Connolly

1500 E. Cedar Ave. (at N. West St.)
Flagstaff, AZ 86001
Directions: From downtown take E. Santa
Fe Ave. east, then turn left onto West St.
Open: Daily
Price: Moderate
Cuisine: American
Serving: B, L (daily), D (Tuesday through
Saturday)
Credit Cards: MC, V
Handicapped Access: Yes

Off the beaten path northeast of downtown,
this bustling espresso bar, bakery, and café
shows off colorful contemporary art splashed
on the walls. An in-the-know locals' spot,
here chefs use fresh ingredients in everything
from eggs Benedict done a dozen different
ways to chicken braised in honey butter with
ginger carrots and sun-dried tomato risotto.

MIZ ZIP'S
928-526-0104
2924 E. Route 66 (at E. Lakin Dr.)
Flagstaff, AZ 86001
Open: Daily
Price: Inexpensive
Cuisine: American
Serving: B, L (daily), D (Monday through
Saturday)
Credit Cards: None
Handicapped Access: Yes

At this real-deal diner, Route 66 roadsters
and cowboys in pickup trucks are often
seen in the parking lot. The old-school
menu is best for huge breakfast plates. Miz
Zip's is most famous for its homemade pies,
which have been featured in Mother Road
cookbooks.

MONSOON ON THE RIM
928-226-8844
6 E. Aspen St. (at N. Leroux St.),
Flagstaff, AZ 86001
Open: Daily
Price: Moderate
Cuisine: Pan-Asian / sushi

Serving: L, D
Credit Cards: AE, MC, V
Handicapped Access: Yes

A prime patio with tables set beside
Heritage Square park keeps this fusion
restaurant hopping. A modern menu of
pan-Asian rice bowls, noodles, curries, and
even creative sushi keeps locals and
tourists coming back for more.

MOUNTAIN OASIS
928-214-9270
11 E. Aspen St. (at N. Leroux St.)
Flagstaff, AZ 86001
Open: Daily
Price: Expensive
Cuisine: International
Serving: L, D
Credit Cards: AE, D, MC, V
Handicapped Access: Yes

Always warm and inviting, this downtown
institution serves an eclectic flavorful menu,
from falafel and grilled portobello mushroom
sandwiches with avocado aioli at lunch to
coconut curry chicken and Caribbean chicken
pasta at dinner. A homey atmosphere is the
real draw for families and even romantic
couples. Interesting microbrews are served.

SWADDEE THAI
928-773-1122
www.swaddeethai.com
115 E. Aspen St. (at San Francisco St.)
Flagstaff, AZ 86001
Open: Daily
Price: Moderate
Cuisine: Thai
Serving: L, D
Credit Cards: MC, V
Handicapped Access: Yes

An outpost of the award-winning Thai
kitchen in Scottsdale, Arizona, the Flagstaff
café has Far East flair in its design. On the
menu are savory and fruity salads, north-
eastern specialties from the Isaan region,

Thai barbecue, pineapple curries, and tofu versions of meatier mains. As a concession to tamer tongues, patrons can order on a spiciness scale of 1–5.

WHISTLE STOP CAFÉ

928-779-0079
www.beaverstreetbrewery.com
11 S. Beaver St. (at W. Phoenix Ave.)
Flagstaff, AZ 86001
Open: Daily
Price: Moderate
Cuisine: International
Serving: L, D
Credit Cards: AE, D, MC, V
Handicapped Access: Yes

South of the railroad tracks at the Beaver Street Brewery, the Whistle Stop Café has Bavarian-style microbrews on tap that are almost outshone by the handcrafted fare, including wood-fired pizzas and sandwiches, fondue platters for two, steak salads, and an apple-ginger stout cake. Beware: Portion sizes are enormous. A seasonal outdoor beer garden has partially eclipsed mountain views, while billiard tables await next door in the brewery's game room.

Fredonia

SAGE HOUSE GRILL

928-643-7712
www.juniperlodge.info
Juniper Lodge, 465 S. Main St. (US 89-A at Lukus Lane), Fredonia, AZ 86022
Open: Daily
Price: Moderate
Cuisine: American
Serving: B, L, D
Credit Cards: MC, V

Aiming for a river-running theme, this ranch-style diner sports rough-hewn tables with old-fashioned checkered cloths. The bountiful breakfast menu will fuel a full day of outdoor adventures. Hot sandwiches and gourmet burgers are cooked to order at lunch and dinner, when fresh fish, surf-and-turf platters, and pot roasts with cinnamon baked yams make an appearance. Spoon into a yummy banana split afterward.

Grand Canyon National Park— North Rim

GRAND CANYON LODGE DINING ROOM

928-638-2611 ext. 760, 1-888-297-2757
www.grandcanyonnorthrim.com
Grand Canyon National Park—
North Rim, AZ 86052
Open: Daily mid-May through mid-October
Price: Expensive
Cuisine: Southwestern
Serving: B, L, D
Credit Cards: AE, D, MC, V
Special Features: Dinner reservations required; casual attire

This remote national park lodge boasts a rustic dining room with panoramic windows. The menu of Southwestern grill items, seafood, and pasta is ho-hum, but it's the spectacular setting that makes it worthwhile. Reservations are not required for lunch, when salads, salmon and veggie burgers, and an all-you-can-eat pasta and salad bar are bargains.

Grand Canyon National Park— South Rim

ARIZONA ROOM

928-638-2631
www.grandcanyonlodges.com
Bright Angel Lodge
Grand Canyon Village, AZ 86023
Open: Daily, mid-February through December
Price: Expensive
Cuisine: Southwestern/steakhouse
Serving: L (March through October), (mid-February through December)
Credit Cards: AE, D, MC, V
Special Features: No reservations

Kick back with a cocktail and catch a sunset from the back porch of the Grand Canyon Lodge on the North Rim. Sara Benson & Mike Connolly

Don't let the rustic cowboy atmosphere fool you: The Bright Angel's tip-top dining room delivers some of the best Western cuisine in northern Arizona. Feast on hand-cut steaks, barbecue ribs, beef brisket with cider applesauce, or roasted chicken with honey-chipotle sauce. Fork into peach-blackberry streusel pie or a fresh lime tart for dessert. There's always a queue for dinner, so show up early and put yourself on the wait list, then sip a signature margarita on the open-air back porch. Holiday meals here are a special treat, especially if you're luckily seated at a table next to canyon-view picture windows.

BRIGHT ANGEL RESTAURANT
928-638-2631
www.grandcanyonlodges.com
Bright Angel Lodge,
Grand Canyon, AZ 86023
Open: Daily
Price: Moderate
Cuisine: Southwestern/American
Serving: B, L, D
Credit Cards: AE, D, MC, V

Although the Arizona Room is favored for lunch and dinner, this casual family-style restaurant is great for filling breakfasts, including Southwestern skillets, steak and eggs plates, hot biscuits with country gravy, berry-licious bowls of granola, and tall stacks of fluffy blueberry pancakes.

EL TOVAR DINING ROOM
928-638-2631 ext. 6432
www.grandcanyonlodges.com
El Tovar Hotel, Grand Canyon, AZ 86023
Open: Daily
Price: Expensive
Cuisine: International
Serving: B, L, D
Credit Cards: AE, D, MC, V
Special Features: Lunch and dinner reservations accepted up to 6 months in advance for hotel guests, 30 days for nonguests; business-casual dress

Graciously set inside the El Tovar Hotel, this dining room is adorned with one-of-a-kind woven Native American rugs and rich furnishings made of Oregon pine and native stone from the Kaibab Plateau. Unfortunately, the food varies in quality and doesn't always live up to the expectations raised by the atmosphere. Still, there's something for everyone on the menu, from mesquite-smoked pork chops with pine-nut stuffing to Mediterranean salads.

PHANTOM RANCH

Management: Xanterra Parks & Resorts
303-297-2757, 1-888-297-2757
www.grandcanyonlodges.com
P.O. Box 699, Grand Canyon, AZ 86023
Directions: Accessible only on foot or mule via the Bright Angel and South Kaibab Trails, or on river-rafting trips.
Price: Expensive
Credit Cards: AE, D, MC, V
Special Features: Advance reservations required

Simple canteen meals are dished up at this historic ranch by the Colorado River at the bottom of the Grand Canyon, including cowboy breakfasts and a hiker's stew, vegetarian chili, or steaks at dinner. There are two seatings each for breakfast and dinner;

sack lunches are available for pick-up anytime. The ranch canteen is open to backpackers and river runners who aren't overnight guests, but advance reservations are always necessary, because all the foodstuffs have to be packed in by mule train!

Jacob Lake

JACOB LAKE INN

928-643-7232
www.jacoblake.com
Junction of US 89-A at AZ 67,
Jacob Lake, AZ 86022
Open: Daily
Price: Moderate
Cuisine: American
Serving: B, L, D
Credit Cards: AE, D, MC, V
Handicapped Access: Partial

Just like at the lodge bakery (see "Food Purveyors," below), this family-owned woodsy café makes much of the food from scratch daily, from the morning flapjacks and biscuits with gravy to the famous Grand Bull sandwich (grilled ground beef, onions, mushrooms, bacon, cheese, tomatoes, and green chilies piled between thick-sliced homemade bread) at lunch or dinner. Don't skip dessert, especially not the fruity pies or lemon bars.

Bakeries, Coffeehouses, and Juice Bars

Canyon Coffee House, 928-638-2631, Bright Angel Lodge, Grand Canyon Village, Grand Canyon National Park—South Rim. Order up espresso drinks, shade-grown organic coffee, and continental breakfast items to go.

Jacob Lake Inn Bakery, www.jacoblake.com, 928-643-7232, Hwys. 67 and US 89-A, Jacob Lake. Using some of the same recipes since the 1920s, this bakery is famed for its homemade breads, deli sandwiches, muffins, pies, cakes, and cookies.

Jennifer's Bakery & Internet Cafe, 928-638-3433, AZ 64, Tusayan. Worth searching out on your way to the South Rim of the Grand Canyon, this bakery and café offers espresso drinks, fresh pastries, and free high-speed Wi-Fi Internet access.

Late for the Train, www.lateforthetrain.com, 928-779-5975, 107 N. San Francisco St., Flagstaff. In the historic Babbitt Building, this wittily named coffee shop has newspapers for perusing while you wait, plus free high-speed Wi-Fi Internet access.

Macy's European Coffee House, www.macyscoffee.net, 928-774-2243, 14 S. Beaver St., Flagstaff. On the wrong side of the railroad tracks, this punk coffeehouse is also a delish vegetarian and vegan café. Sit outside and enjoy a mixed salad, or take a slice of cheesecake or an ooey-gooey brownie to go. Free high-speed Wi-Fi Internet access.

Rendezvous Coffee House & Martini Bar, www.hotelmontevista.com, 928-779-3131, Hotel Monte Vista, 100 N. San Francisco St., Flagstaff. With a kaleidoscopic street-level view inside one of downtown's historic hotels, this classy coffeehouse also serves teas, fine chocolates, wines, hot appetizers, and cocktails.

Rough Rider Saloon, www.grandcanyonnorthrim.com, 928-638-2611, Grand Canyon National Park—North Rim. By day, this saloon transforms into an espresso bar selling bagels and baked goods in the morning.

Delis, Grocery Stores, and Ice Cream
Bright Angel Fountain, 928-638-2631, Bright Angel Lodge, Grand Canyon Village, Grand Canyon National Park—South Rim. For a scoop of ice cream, hot dogs, and other family vacation—worthy snacks, handy to the rim of the Grand Canyon.

Canyon Village Marketplace & Deli, 928-638-2262, Market Plaza, Grand Canyon Village, Grand Canyon National Park—South Rim. All-purpose grocery store on the South Rim has a convenient takeout deli.

Deli in the Pines, www.grandcanyonnorthrim.com, 928-638-2611, Grand Canyon National Park—North Rim. On the North Rim, it's a quick, easy stop for salads, sandwiches, pizza, calzones, and ice cream.

New Frontiers Natural Marketplace, 928-774-5747, 1000 S. Milton Rd., Flagstaff. Northern Arizona's best natural foods market has baskets of fresh produce and a deli with hot and cold picnic items to go.

RECREATION

Bicycling and Mountain Biking
Flagstaff has hundreds of miles of mountain-biking trails, mostly in national forest land south of town and north toward the San Francisco Peaks. For weekend warriors, the steep, technical trails in the Dry Lakes area on US 180 north of town are a challenge. For a locals' mountain-biking guide, pick up Cosmic Ray's *Fat Tire Tales and Trails: Arizona*. It's sold at **Absolute Bikes** (www.absolutebikes.net, 928-779-5969, 18 N. San Francisco St., Flagstaff), which provides sales, service, rentals, and repairs for mountain bikes and more; check the Web site for group

The San Francisco Peaks north of Flagstaff are a four-season mountain playground.

Sara Benson & Mike Connolly

rides and special events. A concrete freestyle BMX park, **The Basin** (www.flagstaff.az.gov, 928-779-7690, 1700 E. 6th Ave., Flagstaff) has three irregularly shaped bowls for polishing your trick maneuvers. For road cyclists, the paved road along the South Rim of the Grand Canyon is less busy heading westbound; rough 4WD roads to remote lookouts on the canyon's North Rim are open to mountain bikers.

Birding

The region's most important species is the rare California condor, reintroduced to its native Grand Canyon habitat in 1996. Another 250 species are found along the Colorado River corridor, mostly migratory birds and other species that use it as a winter habitat, such as bald eagles. Desert species found throughout the Sonoran and Mojave Deserts also nest in the canyon's cliffs, while goshawks, blue grouse, and spotted owls are found in the conifer forests of the Kaibab Plateau bordering both canyon rims. For casual bird-watching, visit the **Arboretum at Flagstaff** (see "Parks and Natural Attractions," below). For more information about birding hot spots, including the lakes south of Flagstaff, contact the **Audubon Society's Maricopa** chapter (www.maricopaaudubon.org, 480-829-8209).

Boating and Waterskiing

Many lakes on national forest land around Flagstaff offer limited opportunities for boating, waterskiing, and even windsurfing. **Lake Mary Narrows Recreation Area** and **Mormon Lake** are both southeast of town.

Camping

Inside Grand Canyon National Park, reservations for **North Rim Campground** (open mid-May through mid-October) and **Mather Campground** (open year-round; reservations available March through mid-November) near Grand Canyon Village on the South Rim, both of which have tent and RV sites, are necessary during peak season. Make reservations up to six months in advance (www.recreation.gov, 1-877-444-6777); for last-minute availability, ask in person at the campground. For RV sites with hookups, **Trailer Village** (www.grandcanyonlodges.com; same-day availability: 928-638-2631; reservations 303-297-2757, 1-888-297-2757) is a private campground in Grand Canyon Village. Shady tent and RV sites at semideveloped **Desert View Campground** (open mid-May to mid-October) on the east side of the South Rim are first-come, first-served.

Free dispersed camping and primitive campgrounds near the Grand Canyon are available in the **Kaibab National Forest**, including at **Ten-X Campground** (open May through October), which has first-come, first-served sites 2 miles south of Tusayan. Contact the **Tusayan Ranger Station** (928-638-2443) near the South Rim or the **North Kaibab Ranger Station** (928-643-7395) in Fredonia for regulations, restrictions, annd more information about camping near the canyon. In the **Coconino National Forest** (www.fs.fed.us/r3/coconino, 928-527-3600, 1824 S. Thompson St., Flagstaff), developed **Bonito Campground** (open early May through mid-October) near Sunset Crater and Wupatki National Monuments has first-come, first-served tent and RV sites (no hookups).

West of downtown Flagstaff, **Woody Mountain Campground & RV Park** (www.woody mountaincampground.com, 928-774-7727, 1-800-732-7986, 2727 W. Route 66, Flagstaff) is shaded by pines and has amenities such as hot showers and an outdoor heated swimming pool that's open seasonally.

Canoeing and Kayaking

For professional-level kayakers, a few river-rafting outfitters will provide customized support for technical trips through the Grand Canyon (see "River Rafting," below). Some of the lakes on national forest land south of Flagstaff (see "Fishing," below) offer canoeing and kayaking opportunities, if you bring your own equipment.

Climbing

Near downtown Flagstaff, **Vertical Relief** (www.verticalrelief.com, 928-556-9909, 205 S. San Francisco St.) climbing gym has 6,500 square feet of artificial walls mimicking all types of terrain for beginners to experts. Day passes and packages that include equipment rental and a lesson are available. Outdoor guided trips into the Coconino and Kaibab National Forests can be arranged for individuals or small groups.

Disc (Frisbee) Golf

Arizona Snowbowl, www.arizonasnowbowl.com, 928-779-1951, Snowbowl Rd., off US 180, 7 miles northwest of Flagstaff. Open during summer, this high-altitude disc golf course on national forest land starts outside Agassiz Lodge.

McPherson Park, www.flagstaff.az.gov, 928-779-7690, 1650 N. Turquoise Dr., Flagstaff. A newer disc-golf course than the old standby at **Thorpe Regional Park** (1919 N. Thorpe Rd.).

Northern Arizona University, http://home.nau.edu/outdoors/disc_golf.asp, 928-523-3229, on the south side of NAU campus, off Pine Knoll Dr., Flagstaff. Recently built 18-hole basket course is popular with students.

Fishing

While better fishing opportunities await outside Williams (see the "Route 66" chapter), the national forest land around Flagstaff protects lakes popular with anglers during the summer season (May through September). **Upper Lake Mary** has catfish, crappie, and northern pike, as well as a boat ramp, while **Lower Lake Mary, Long Lake, Ashurst Lake,** and **Marshall Lake** are stocked with trout, and **Mormon Lake** has a rustic lodge that organizes outdoor activities. **Kinnikinick Lake** is another good spot for trout fishing. All these lakes are a scenic drive southeast of Flagstaff. For fishing supplies, gear, clothing, and advice, drop by **Babbitt's Flyfishing Specialists**, 928-779-3253, 15 E. Aspen Street, Flagstaff.

Fitness Facilities

Flagstaff Athletic Club, www.flagstaffathleticclub.com, 928-779-4593, 1200 W. Route 66, Flagstaff. Full-service workout center offers trend-setting classes and massage therapy. It's equipped with cardio and cycling machines, weights, and an indoor climbing wall and swimming pool.

Northern Arizona University Recreation Center, http://home.nau.edu/recreation/, 928-523-1732, Franklin Ave. at San Francisco St., Flagstaff. Home to a high-altitude athletes' training center, this state-of-the-art university fitness center has weights, massage therapy, and a variety of fitness classes, from belly dancing and yoga to pilates and kickboxing.

Football

Northern Arizona University, http://nau.newtier.com, 928-523-5661, Lumberjack Stadium, off San Francisco St., Flagstaff. The NAU college football season typically runs from late August through mid-November.

Golf

Most golf courses in the Flagstaff area are open only to private members.

Continental Country Club, www.continentalflagstaff.com, 928-526-5125, 1-877-526-5125, 2380 N. Oakmount Dr., Flagstaff. A scenic course set at the foot of Mount Elden in the San Francisco Peaks. Semiprivate, 18 holes, 6,029 yards, par 72; cart and club rentals, driving range, lessons, pro shop, restaurant. Open May through September.

Hiking and Backpacking

Grand Canyon National Park is the best hiking destination near Flagstaff. Developed trails include easy, wheelchair-accessible rim routes to lookout points. Along both rims there are also moderate day hikes on fairly level trails, some with eye-catching views.

Warning: It's foolhardy and potentially fatal to hike down to the Colorado River in a day. Even athletes in top condition have died from dehydration while trying to do it. That's because the temperature rises rapidly the deeper into the canyon you go, especially during summer. Day hikers should respect the park-recommended turnaround points on each trail.

If you want to reach the Colorado River, plan an overnight backpacking trip. For down-and-back trips or rim-to-rim traverses, it's easier to start on the canyon's South Rim. For backpacking information and regulations, including for advance wilderness permits and waiting lists for walk-ins, contact the **Grand Canyon National Park Backcountry Information Center** (www.nps.gov/grca, 928-638-7875, P.O. Box 129, Grand Canyon, AZ 86023) in Grand Canyon Village on the South Rim and also on the North Rim. For reservations at Phantom Ranch, see the "Lodging" section, earlier in this chapter.

Many less-crowded hiking and backpacking routes can be found in the **Coconino National Forest** (928-527-3600, www.fs.fed.us/r3/coconino, 5075

Tunnels and waterfalls are part of the journey from the rim of the Grand Canyon to the Colorado River below.
Sara Benson & Mike Connolly

Take the plunge from the North Rim of the Grand Canyon to the Colorado River below.   Sara Benson & Mike Connolly

N. US 89, Flagstaff, AZ), especially in the **Kachina Peaks Wilderness,** off US 180 northwest of Flagstaff. Some trails start from the Arizona Snowbowl (www.arizona snowbowl.com, 928-779-1951). For experienced climbers the most popular trip is up **Humphrey's Peak** (12,633 ft.), Arizona's highest mountain.

Mule and Horseback Riding

By far the most popular Grand Canyon trip is on the back of trusty mules from the South Rim down to the Colorado River; make reservations as far in advance as possible. There are also beautiful trails on national forest land surrounding Flagstaff.

Canyon Trail Rides, www.canyonrides.com, 435-679-8665, P.O. Box 128, Tropic, UT 84776. For day trips atop the Grand Canyon's North Rim, mule rides depart daily from mid-May through mid-October.

Xanterra Mule Trips, www.grandcanyonlodges.com, 928-638-3283, P.O. Box 97, Grand Canyon, AZ 86023. Offers day rides on the South Rim and overnight trips to Phantom Ranch. Riders must be at least 4'7" tall, weigh less than 200 pounds fully dressed, speak English fluently, and be in good physical condition (no pregnant women allowed). Check at the Bright Angel Lodge transportation desk for waiting list and standby availability.

Parks and Natural Attractions

THE ARBORETUM AT FLAGSTAFF

928-774-1442
www.thearb.org
4001 S. Woody Mountain Rd., Flagstaff, AZ 86001
Directions: Take W. Route 66 west of downtown. Turn left onto Woody Mountain Rd. and drive 4 miles south.
Open: April through October, daily 9–5
Admission: Adults $5, youths 6–17 $2, children under 6 free

This natural woodland oasis southwest of downtown Flagstaff harbors over 100 species of birds and 2,500 high-altitude plants spread throughout gardens, ponds, wetlands, butterfly habitats, wildflower meadows, and edible gardens. One-hour guided walks are offered daily. Meet-and-greet bird of prey programs are normally conducted Friday through Monday. Look for special events and educational classes, such as nature photography and pine-needle basket weaving.

Take a mule ride or hike down into the Grand Canyon to visit historic Phantom Ranch on the Colorado River.
Courtesy Xanterra Parks & Resorts

GRAND CANYON NATIONAL PARK

928-638-7888
www.nps.gov/grca
P.O. Box 129, Grand Canyon AZ, 86023
Directions: To reach the South Rim take
US 180 northwest of Flagstaff or AZ 64
north of Williams. To visit the North Rim,
follow US 89-A southeast of Kanab, then
take AZ 67 south.
Admission: $25 per vehicle for seven-day
entry pass
Open: 24/7/365

Even short hikes reward visitors to the Grand Canyon with unforgettable views. Sara Benson & Mike Connolly

The Southwest's superstar attraction, this
enormous hole in the ground is a geological jigsaw puzzle carved out over eons by
the Colorado River. The South Rim is the
most popular destination, with lodges,
restaurants, museums, shops, and shuttle
buses for hikers, photographers, and
leisure tourists. The remote North Rim
has a more wild, rugged appeal, with 4WD
roads to solitary lookout points. For outdoor activities, such as backpacking, mule trips,
and river rafting, see the relevant headings elsewhere in the "Recreation" section of this
chapter.

PIPE SPRING NATIONAL MONUMENT

928-643-7105
www.nps.gov/pisp
406 N. Pipe Spring Rd., Fredonia, AZ 86022
Directions: On AZ 389, 15 miles west of Fredonia
Open: Daily 7–5, June through August; daily 8–5, September through May. Closed
Thanksgiving, Christmas, and New Year's Day.
Admission: Adults $5, children under 16 free

Adjoining the Kaibab Paiute Indian Reservation, this historic Mormon homestead is also a
place to learn about contemporary tribal culture and the conflicted settlement of the
American West. Guided tours of the Mormon fort (nicknamed "Windsor Castle"), where
plural wives once hid out from U.S. law enforcement, are offered daily. Wander the gardens
and orchards replanted with Native American and pioneer crops before walking along the
half-mile Ridge Trail, which has stunning views of the Arizona Strip.

SUNSET CRATER VOLCANO AND WUPATKI NATIONAL MONUMENTS

928-526-0502, 928-679-2365
www.nps.gov/sucr, www.nps.gov/wupa
Directions: From Flagstaff take US 89 north for 12 miles, then turn right at Sunset
Crater–Wupatki Loop Rd.
Open: Wupatki N.M. open daily 9–5, closed Christmas Day. Sunset Crater Volcano N.M.
open daily 9–5, November through April; 8-5, May through October. (scenic drives and
trails open sunrise to sunset)
Admission: Adults $5, children under 16 free

A half-day trip northeast of Flagstaff, these twin monuments make a fascinating detour.
Sunset Crater Volcano National Monument preserves a kaleidoscope of lava flows and cinder cones that you can drive through en route to the 800-year-old Ancestral Puebloan
ruins at Wupatki Pueblo, where paved trails let visitors respectfully view the ruins of this
ancient cultural crossroads up close.

WALNUT CANYON NATIONAL MONUMENT

928-526-3367
www.nps.gov/waca
Mailing address: 6400 N. US 89, Flagstaff, AZ 86004
Directions: 3 miles south of I-40 (exit 204)
Open: Daily 9–5, November through April; daily 8–5, May through October. Trails close
one hour earlier.
Admission: Adults $5, children under 16 free

A quiet escape from the crowds, this peaceful park just south of Flagstaff preserves Sinagua
cliff dwellings built right into the canyon walls and shaded by ponderosa pine forests. The
Island Trail leads down to the ruins; call ahead to check trail conditions during winter.

Racquet Sports

City of Flagstaff Parks and Recreation, www.flagstaff.az.gov, 928-779-7690, Flagstaff. Select
municipal and regional parks have outdoor tennis courts, including some lighted for night play.

Mormon pioneers staked a claim in the desert at Pipe Springs National Monument. Sara Benson & Mike Connolly

Flagstaff Athletic Club, www.flagstaffathleticclub.com, 928-779-4593, 1200 W. Route 66, Flagstaff. Maintains indoor racquetball and tennis courts.

Northern Arizona University Recreation Center, http://home.nau.edu/recreation/, 928-523-1732, Franklin Ave. at San Francisco St., Flagstaff. Rents equipment and has six racquetball indoor courts, as well as table tennis.

River Rafting

For Grand Canyon rafting trips on the Colorado River, the months of May through September are the busiest and the hottest. The spring and fall shoulder seasons (April, September, and October) can be beautiful times for river running. Because rafting permits for the Grand Canyon are limited, guided trips easily fill a year in advance. Experienced rafters who want to run the Colorado River themselves must enter a weighted lottery, usually held during May; for details contact the **Grand Canyon National Park River Permits Office,** www.nps.gov/grca, 928-638-7843, 1-800-959-9164, P.O. Box 129, Grand Canyon, Arizona 86023.

Arizona River Runners, www.raftarizona.com, 1-800-477-7238, P.O. Box 47788, Phoenix, AZ 85068. Organizes motorized and oar-powered trips through the Grand Canyon of varying lengths, with attractive hike-in / hike-out options.

Canyon Explorations, www.canyonx.com, 928-774-4559, 1-800-654-0723, P.O. Box 310, Flagstaff, AZ 86002. This small family-owned business offers hybrid Grand Canyon river-running trips that include oar and paddle boats and inflatable kayaks.

Canyoneers, www.canyoneers.com, 928-564-0924, 1-800-525-0924, P.O. Box 2997, Flagstaff, AZ 86003. Offers short and long guided rowing trips through the Grand Canyon in either rafts or pioneer-style cataract boats.

Diamond River Adventures, www.diamondriver.com, 928-645-8866, 916 Vista Ave., Page, AZ 86040. Long-running outfitter offers less expensive motorized and oar-powered trips through the Grand Canyon, including family-friendly trips.

OARS, www.oars.com. 209-736-4677, 1-800-346-6277, P.O. Box 67, Angels Camp, CA 95222. The Grand Canyon's original oar-powered rafting outfitter. Very experienced guides lead adventurous river trips in hard-sided dories, too, just like early western explorers. Trips also include side canyon hikes.

Outdoors Unlimited, www.outdoorsunlimited.com, 928-526-4511, 1-800-637-RAFT, 6900 Townsend Wiwona Rd., Flagstaff. For 40 years they've been guiding nonmotorized trips through the Grand Canyon powered by either oars or paddles.

Rivers & Oceans, www.rivers-oceans.com, 928-526-4575, 1-800-473-4576, 12620 N. Copeland Lane, Flagstaff. Offers guided motorized and rowing rafting trips of 1 to 16 days through the Grand Canyon for beginners to experienced rafters.

Running

Flagstaff's Northern Arizona University campus has an outdoor running track off San Francisco Street near the recreation center (see "Fitness Facilities," above). The city's burgeoning urban trail system branches out from San Francisco Street in several directions. For example, a multiuse trail leads south of campus for 5 miles to Fort Tuthill County Park. For more information on the trail system, contact the Flagstaff Department of Parks and Recreation (www.flagstaff.az.gov, 928-779-7690).

Skiing, Snowboarding, and Other Winter Sports

For cross-country skiing and snowshoeing opportunities, explore the **Coconino National Forest** (www.fs.fed.us/r3/coconino/, 928-527-3600, 1824 S. Thompson St., Flagstaff) and the **Kaibab National Forest** (www.fs.fed.us/r3/kai/, 928-638-2443, AZ 64, Tusayan) outside Flagstaff. Other winter-sports destinations include:

Arizona Snowbowl, www.arizonasnowbowl.com, 928-779-1951, Snowbowl Rd., off US 180, 7 miles northwest of Flagstaff. With a peak elevation of 11,500 feet, this ski and snowboard resort in the San Francisco Peaks has four lifts and a variety of ski runs, half of which are rated intermediate, plus a snowboarding terrain park, equipment rentals, a ski school, and basic lodgings. The season usually lasts from mid-December until mid-April.

Flagstaff Ice Arena, www.flagstaff.az.gov, 928-774-1051, Jay Lively Activity Center, 1650 N. Turquoise Dr., Flagstaff. Call ahead for open-skate hours at this family-friendly ice arena.

Flagstaff Nordic Center, www.flagstaffnordiccenter.com, 928-220-0550, US 180 mile marker 232, approximately 15 miles northwest of Flagstaff. In the lofty Coconino National Forest, this top-notch Nordic center has groomed trails, rustic lodging, cross-country ski and snowshoe rentals, races, ski lessons, and a concessions area. There's a sledding and snow play area just 1 mile farther along US 180 at Crowley Pit.

Flagstaff Winter Sports, www.flagstaffwintersports.com, 928-779-2700, 1-888-883-7669, 719 N. Humphreys St. (US 180), Flagstaff. When the Arizona Snowbowl is open, so is this store, which rents and sells ski and snowboard clothing and equipment.

Grand Canyon National Park, www.nps.gov/grca, 928-638-7875, P.O. Box 129, Grand Canyon, AZ 86023. Backcountry permits are required for overnight snowshoe and cross-country skiing trips starting from the North Rim after the road closes in late autumn. The backcountry information center on the South Rim is open daily year-round.

Swimming

Northern Arizona University Wall Aquatic Center, http://home.nau.edu/recreation/, 928-523-4509, Franklin Ave. at San Francisco St., Flagstaff. This NAU campus complex has an Olympic-size pool, diving boards, and weight room; call for recreational swim hours.

Tours

Grand Canyon National Park Shuttle Bus, www.nps.gov/grca, 928-638-7888, Grand Canyon, AZ. Free shuttle routes operate from an hour before sunrise until an hour after sunset. The green Kaibab Trail and Village routes operate year-round. The Hermits Rest route runs from March through November, taking about 80 minutes for the round-trip.

Grand Canyon Railway, www.thetrain.com, 928-773-1976, 1-800-843-8724, Grand Canyon Depot, beside Maswik Lodge, Grand Canyon Village. Scenic excursion in historic railway cars between the South Rim of the Grand Canyon and Williams, Arizona (see the "Route 66" chapter). For details about the railway, see the "Getting Around the Four Corners" section of the "Transportation" chapter, earlier in this book.

Xanterra South Rim, www.grandcanyonlodges.com, 928-638-2631, Bright Angel Lodge, Grand Canyon Village. Guided bus tours of the Grand Canyon's South Rim include sunrise and sunset trips and excursions west to Hermits Rest and east to Desert View Watchtower, all starting from Grand Canyon Village.

Park your car and take a free tour of the Grand Canyon's South Rim aboard the eco-conscious park shuttle.
Sara Benson & Mike Connolly

Navajo rugs are among the Native American artisan crafts sold inside Hopi House Sara Benson & Mike Connolly

SHOPPING

Art, Antiques, and Collectibles

Arizona Handmade Gallery, www.azhandmade.com, 928-779-3790, 13 N. San Francisco St., Flagstaff. A light-filled gallery sells functional and fine-art works in all media, including nature photography, sculpture, jewelry, paintings, handblown art glass, textile and leather art, and wood carvings by local artists.

The Artists Gallery, www.theartists gallery.net, 928-773-0958, 17 N. San Francisco St., Flagstaff. Cooperative gallery in downtown Flagstaff sells original jewelry, photography, painting, ceramics, textile art, and stone, wood, and metal works.

Books, Clothing, Gifts, Maps, and Outdoor Gear

Adventure Racing Concepts, www.adventureracingconcept.com, 928-779-5393, 719 N. Humphreys St., Flagstaff. Sells everything you'll need for trail running, camping, kayaking, rock climbing, and mountain biking, including clothing, footwear, and books.

Aspen Sports, 928-779-1935, 15 N. San Francisco St., Flagstaff. A locals' favorite, this downtown outfitter sells name-brand outdoor gear, clothing, and footwear for both sexes.

Babbitt's Backcountry Outfitters, 928-774-4775, 12 E. Aspen Ave., Flagstaff. One of Flagstaff's oldest outfitters sells and rents backpacking, camping, and hiking gear, as well as outdoor activity guidebooks and maps.

Canyon Village Marketplace General Store, 928-638-2262, Market Plaza, Grand Canyon Village. On the South Rim of the Grand Canyon, this supermarket sells and rents a limited selection of hiking, camping, and backpacking equipment for last-minute trips.

Cloud Nine Kite Shop, 928-556-9096, 612 N. Humphreys St., Flagstaff. Stop by this small shop to buy a colorful kite to fly in the San Francisco Peaks en route to the Grand Canyon.

Gene's Western Wear, www.geneswesternwear.net, 928-774-3543, 111 N. Leroux St., Flagstaff. For aspiring cowboys and rodeo hands, this appealing western-wear shop sells blue jeans, boots, belt buckles, bolos, and vests.

Grand Canyon Association Bookstore, www.grandcanyon.org, 928-638-2481, Grand Canyon National Park. The nonprofit association runs bookstores and gift shops at Kolb

Studio, Yavapai Point, and Tusayan Museum on the South Rim of the Grand Canyon and at the North Rim visitor center. At Canyon View Information Plaza near Mather Point on the South Rim, Books 'n More stocks a huge variety of books, maps, posters and prints, CDs and DVDs, kids' stuff, and more.

Peace Surplus, www.peacesurplus.com, 928-779-4521, 14 W. Route 66, Flagstaff. With the bold slogan "If It's Outdoors—It's Us!" this all-around outdoor outfitter sells backpacking, climbing, fly-fishing, skiing, and snowboarding gear at bargain prices.

Native American Trading Posts and Galleries

Hopi House, www.grandcanyonlodges.com, 928-638-2631, Grand Canyon Village. First opened to the public in 1905 by Fred Harvey, this homage to traditional Hopi dwellings was designed by Western architect Mary Colter and constructed of stone and wood by Hopi craftspeople. It exhibits Navajo rugs, Hopi kachinas, jewelry, basketry, Pueblo pottery, and more. An upstairs gallery is for serious collectors seeking museum-quality items.

Museum of Northern Arizona, www.musnaz.org, 928-774-5213, 3101 N. Fort Valley Rd. (US 180), Flagstaff. The museum's high-quality gift shop and bookstore has a gallery of handmade Native American crafts, including works by contemporary artisans. Browse the Zuni fetishes, Navajo rugs, Hopi kachinas, Pueblo pottery, silver and turquoise jewelry, sculptures, and wood carvings.

Old Adobe Traders, www.oldadobetraders.com, 928-774-2411, 204-C E. Route 66, Flagstaff. Displays woven baskets, leather wear, pottery, jewelry, storyteller dolls, sculpture, musical CDs, and textile rugs with Native American and Southwestern themes.

Pow Wow Trading Post, www.powwow.sonictech.net, 928-779-5725, 118 W. Route 66, Flagstaff. An outpost of the original trading post in Page, Arizona, this Native American—owned shop has a small selection of kachinas, Navajo rugs, Pueblo pottery and baskets, and handcrafted silver jewelry.

Winter Sun Trading Company, www.wintersun.com, 928-774-2884, 107 N. San Francisco St., Flagstaff. Family-owned shop sells Southwestern herbs, as well as Native American basketry, jewelry, baskets, kachinas, books, and music.

4

ROUTE 66

Cruising the Mother Road

The Continental Divide is literally the high point of the journey, but a drive along just about any stretch of Route 66 may become one of the highlights of your travels through the Southwest. Connecting the midwestern city of Chicago with the ocean beaches of Los Angeles in California, Route 66 shows off some of its best-preserved stretches here in the Four Corners region as it meanders through Arizona and New Mexico.

Running almost parallel to I-40 between Flagstaff, Arizona, and Albuquerque, New Mexico, Route 66 is wonderfully caught in its own time warp. Life seems to move more slowly on the rural byways and small-town main streets that interconnect to make up the route, which was officially decommissioned in 1984. Nowadays Route 66 is a veritable out-door museum of historical roadside attractions, from retro 1930s motor courts and vintage '50s-style diners to Native American trading posts and Old West mining towns. The young at heart will delight in more kitschy sightseeing spots, such as the Jackrabbit Trading Post, the Sno-Cap Drive-In, and the Wigwam Motel, while history buffs will be impressed by the restorations undertaken at landmarks such as La Posada Hotel and the Painted Desert Inn in Petrified Forest National Park.

Created by an act of Congress in 1926, Route 66 was nicknamed the "Mother Road" by novelist John Steinbeck, who wrote in the *Grapes of Wrath* about Dust Bowl refugees making the rough-and-tumble journey west along Route 66 during the Great Depression. The route was also popularly known as "The Main Street of America," as it linked an array of small towns all along its path to the Pacific Ocean. By the end of World War II, Route 66 was finally paved—just in the nick of time for the birth of the classic American road trip, which got its start in the postwar economic boom. After Nat King Cole made Bobby Troup's song "(Get Your Kicks On) Route 66" a hit in 1946, everyone seemed to be humming the tune, from Gallup, New Mexico, to Kingman, Arizona.

Ironically, World War II was also the beginning of the end for Route 66. Enamored of the German autobahn, President Dwight D. Eisenhower proposed that the United States build an ambitious interstate highway system. Bustling roadside stops along the Mother Road became ghost towns, as slowly but surely the 2,200 miles of the route were literally paved over by the interstates or bypassed. As Route 66 withered, hometown activists began

LEFT: *Another of the many historic filling stations along Route 66 in Arizona.* Sara Benson & Mike Connolly

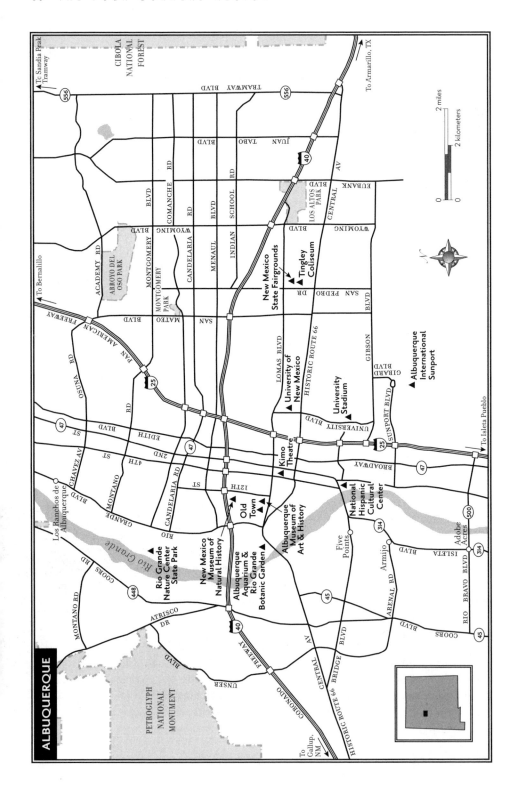

ALBUQUERQUE

making preservation efforts to keep the spirit of the Mother Road alive. While some historic places along Route 66 are gone forever, others have been rescued from the wrecking ball. Small towns such as Seligman and Kingman in western Arizona take their Route 66 heritage seriously, affording a delightful taste of yesteryear to tourists who venture off the interstate.

Often Route 66 is the most interesting way to get from point A to point B in central Arizona and New Mexico. It is also sometimes the only route available. To visit the Hualapai and Havasupai Reservations, for example, you'll need to drive at least a short distance along Route 66 to reach the western region of the Grand Canyon. Many visits to Navajo, Hopi, and Zuni tribal lands start from Gallup, New Mexico (see the "Native America" chapter), another Route 66 town. For suggested travel itineraries for day-trippers along Route 66, turn to the "Historic Places" section, later in this chapter.

LODGING

Albuquerque

ADOBE NIDO BED AND BREAKFAST
Innkeepers: Rol and Sarah Dolk
505-344-1310, 1-866-435-6436
www.adobenido.com
info@adobenido.com
1124 Major Ave. NW (off 12th St. NW)
Albuquerque, NM 87107
Directions: South of Candelaria Rd. NW, west of I-25 (exit 227)
Price: Expensive
Credit Cards: AE, D, MC, V
Handicapped Access: No

In a quiet North Valley neighborhood, this elegant adobe home has a tranquil, even romantic atmosphere and attentive hosts. All of the country-style rooms have satellite TV and high-speed Wi-Fi Internet access. Some rooms with private baths have whirlpool tubs, while all guests enjoy the outdoor Finnish sauna and billiards room. Betty's Bath & Day Spa is a recommended oasis nearby. Rates include a hot, healthy-minded breakfast. The inn is gay-friendly.

BOTTGER MANSION OF OLD TOWN
Innkeepers: Steve and Kathy Hiatt
505-243-3639, 1-800-758-3639
www.bottger.com
info@bottger.com
110 San Felipe NW, at Lomas Blvd.
Albuquerque, NM 87104
Price: Expensive
Credit Cards: AE, D, MC, V
Handicapped Access: No

For fans of classic Victorian bed-and-breakfasts, this inn in the heart of Old Town is the place. Inside a gracious 1908 mansion, whimsical, romantic rooms come with four-poster beds, lace curtains, love seats, floral wallpaper, writing desks, and ceiling fans. The manicured front lawn is ideal for taking afternoon tea. The inn is gay-friendly.

This classic Victorian bed-and-breakfast juts up against the historic adobe buildings of Old Town in Albuquerque, New Mexico. Sara Benson & Mike Connolly

CINNAMON MORNING
BED & BREAKFAST

Innkeepers: Sue and Dick Percilick
505-345-3541, 1-800-214-9481
www.cinnamonmorning.com
info@cinnamonmorning.com
2700 Rio Grande Blvd. NW (south of
Candelaria Rd. NW)
Albuquerque, NM 87104
Directions: West of I-25 exit 227
Price: Moderate
Credit Cards: AE, D, MC, V
Handicapped Access: Partial

With a gracious cat-owning host, this bed-and-breakfast makes guests feel truly welcome, placing candy bowls around the house and offering free bottled water. Fresh-faced, contemporary design cheers up rooms in the main house. The property also comprises a two-bedroom guesthouse with a full kitchen and a more private Mexican-tiled casita. Unwind on the garden patio or drive to the Rio Grande nearby for a riverside walk. High-speed Wi-Fi Internet is available. Pets welcome.

CLUBHOUSE INN & SUITES

505-345-0010, 1-866-345-0010
http://albuquerque.clubhouseinn.com
1315 Menaul Blvd. NE
Albuquerque, NM 87107
Price: Moderate
Credit Cards: AE, D, MC, V
Handicapped Access: Yes

With a convenient location near both I-25 and I-40, this residential hotel offers value-priced accommodations with complimentary high-speed Wi-Fi Internet access. A few oversize rooms and suites have balconies overlooking the courtyard, with its outdoor swimming pool. Business-class rooms and all suites have mini-refrigerators and microwaves, too. Rates include a hot breakfast buffet and complimentary gym passes.

LOS POBLANOS INN

505-344-9297
www.lospoblanos.com
info@lospoblanos.com
4803 Rio Grande Blvd. NW (north of
Montaro Rd. NW), Albuquerque, NM 87107
Price: Very Expensive
Credit Cards: AE, MC, V
Handicapped Access: Partial

A rambling, architect-designed hacienda in the countryside northwest of town, Los Poblanos is surrounded by woodlands and a lavender farm. New Mexican–style accommodations range from the McCormick Room, which faces a garden courtyard, to the two-room Field Suite inside the original 1880s adobe wing. Private guesthouses are also rented. All accommodations have high-speed Internet access and are furnished with kiva fireplaces and spa products; some also have cable TV and VCRs. Rates include a hearty breakfast made with fresh, often organic local produce and a complimentary *New York Times*.

MAUGER ESTATE
BED & BREAKFAST INN

Innkeepers: Tammy and Mike Ross
505-242-8755, 1-800-719-9189
www.maugerbb.com
maugerbb@aol.com
701 Roma Ave. NW (at 7th St. NW)
Albuquerque, NM 87102
Price: Expensive
Credit Cards: AE, D, MC, V
Handicapped Access: No

Ensconced in flowering gardens, this red-brick Queen Anne Victorian home near Old Town is a grand 19th-century mansion. Extra amenities include fresh flowers, private baths, European down comforters and pillows, mini-refrigerators, high-speed Wi-Fi Internet access, and individual heating in all rooms. Guests receive discounted day passes to a nearby fitness center with an indoor swimming pool. Rates include a buffet-style breakfast. Dogs are welcome for a surcharge. The inn is gay-friendly.

MONTEREY NON SMOKERS MOTEL
505-243-3554, 1-877-666-8379
www.nonsmokersmotel.com
2402 Central Ave. SW (west of Rio Grande Blvd. SW), Albuquerque, NM 87104
Price: Inexpensive
Credit Cards: AE, D, MC, V
Handicapped Access: Yes

Albuquerque has chain motels and business hotels lining the interstates. But this vintage Route 66 motel close to Old Town has more character, attracting both budget travelers and fresh-air lovers. The basic but tidy rooms have mini-refrigerators. Amenities include self-service laundry and an outdoor swimming pool. The no-smoking policy is strictly enforced.

OLD TOWN BED & BREAKFAST
Innkeeper: Nancy Hoffman
505-764-9144, 1-888-900-9144
www.inn-new-mexico.com
nancyhoffman@earthlink.net
707 17th St. NW (north of Lomas Blvd. NW), Albuquerque, NM 87104
Price: Moderate
Credit Cards: None
Handicapped Access: No

Although it's not actually in Old Town, it is nearby. The Pueblo revival–style architecture gives it a true southwestern feel. Choose from the sunny Garden Suite, which has a private bath, kiva fireplace, and library sitting area, or the Aerie, an upstairs room with a Mexican tiled bath and windows looking onto the treetops. Rates include a hot breakfast.

Continental Divide
STAUDER'S NAVAJO LODGE
Innkeeper: Sheree Stauder
505-862-7553
www.rainbirdtrading.com
info@rainbirdtrading.com
HC-32 Box 1, Continental Divide, NM 87312
Directions: On W. Coolidge Rd., north of I-40 exit 44
Price: Moderate
Credit Cards: None
Handicapped Access: No

Just 3 miles west of the Continental Divide off Route 66, this bed and breakfast is run by a friendly family who know the area inside out. Two private casitas, each with its own private bathroom, flank an open-air courtyard and are adorned with Native American and Mexican furnishing and antiques. Expect a welcome basket and fresh flowers. Rates include breakfast (homemade goodies, if you're lucky).

Grants
CIMARRON ROSE BED & BREAKFAST
Innkeeper: Sheri McWethy
505-783-4770, 1-800-856-5776
www.cimarronrose.com
689 Oso Ridge Rd., Grants, NM 87020
Directions: On NM 53 between mile markers 56 and 57, about 30 miles from Grants
Price: Moderate
Credit Cards: None
Handicapped Access: Yes

Standing in pine forests near the Continental Divide, this eco-conscious bed-and-breakfast run by naturalists and cultural interpreters offers varied opportunities for bird-watching, mountain biking, hiking, and cross-country skiing. The garden library has field guides, maps, and binoculars for guests to borrow. Each suite has a full kitchen, ceiling fan, and gas heater. The Cimarron Suite has mountain cabin decor, a wood-burning stove, and a clawfoot tub, while the spacious Bandera Suite has Southwestern flavor and a barbecue grill on the outdoor patio. Hot breakfasts may include homemade blue-corn pancakes, berry muffins, and free-range country eggs. Reservations are mandatory.

Holbrook

HEWARD HOUSE AT HOLBROOK BED & BREAKFAST

Innkeepers: Glenn and Linda Blansett
928-524-3411, 1-877-740-0452
www.bbonline.com/az/heward
hewardhouse@frontiernet.net
108 Crestview Dr. (off E. Navajo Blvd.)
Holbrook, AZ 86025
Directions: North of I-40 (exit 286)
Price: Moderate
Credit Cards: None
Handicapped Access: No

With modern renovations, this airy 1930s art-deco adobe house has a billiards room, cheery fireplace, and a Mexican-tiled patio with a fountain. A lot of Southwestern art is found here, including Navajo rugs, baskets, pottery, and Hopi kachinas. Although the rooms are nothing fancy—more like staying at a relative's house, in fact—the hosts are welcoming. The Cowboy Room has a claw-foot tub and a bed of rough-hewn logs.

WIGWAM MOTEL

Innkeepers: Lewis family
928-524-3048
www.galerie-kokopelli.com/wigwam
clewis97@cybertrails.com
811 W. Hopi Dr. (at N. 8th Ave.)
Holbrook, AZ 86025
Price: Inexpensive
Credit Cards: MC, V
Handicapped Access: Yes

One of the last remaining wigwam village motels, which were built across the U.S.A. from the 1930s into the '50s, Holbrook's historic landmark is the best. The motel sign's neon glow is a beacon for road-weary travelers. Furnished with folksy bedspreads and antique furniture, each of the spic-and-span guest rooms sits inside its own concrete teepee, with a classic automobile parked outside. The bathrooms are tiny and traffic noise may disturb light sleepers, but it's still a gem. Vintage curios are displayed in the lobby, where Route 66 souvenirs are sold.

Kingman

BEST WESTERN A WAYFARER'S INN & SUITES

928-753-6271, 1-800-548-5695
www.bestwestern.com
2815 E. Andy Devine Ave. (Route 66)
Kingman, AZ 86401
Price: Moderate
Credit Cards: AE, D, MC, V
Handicapped Access: Yes

The Best Western truly is the best of Kingman's roadside Route 66 motels. Many of the recently remodeled rooms come with free high-speed Wi-Fi Internet access; oversize mini-suites also have a sitting area, work desk, and king-size beds. The hot tub is open year-round, while the out-door swimming pool is open seasonally. Rates include an extended continental breakfast. Pets are allowed (subject to a deposit) for one-night stays.

HUALAPAI MOUNTAIN PARK

Manager: Mohave County Parks
928-681-5700
www.mcparks.com
6250 Hualapai Mountain Rd.
Kingman, AZ 86401
Directions: From I-40 (exit 51), take Stockton Hill Rd. south 14 miles to Hualapai Mountain Rd.
Price: Moderate
Credit Cards: MC, V
Handicapped Access: Partial

Ideal for a peaceful night's sleep under starry skies, an array of historic stone and wood cabins built by the Civilian Conservation Corps await inside this rustic mountain park. Each stand-alone cabin is unique, but all have electricity, private bath, refrigerator, stovetop, and a barbecue

Sleep peacefully inside rustic cabins built by the Civilian Conservation Corps during the Depression.
Mike Connolly

grill and picnic table outside. Some also have wood-burning fireplaces. Choose from bunk or double beds only. Guests supply their own bedding, towels, and cookware.

Peach Springs
GRAND CANYON HUALAPAI LODGE
Manager: Hualapai Tribe
928-769-2219, 1-877-716-9378
www.destinationgrandcanyon.com
info@grandcanyonresort.com
900 Route 66, Peach Springs, AZ 86434
Price: Moderate
Credit Cards: AE, D, MC, V
Handicapped Access: Yes

Travelers stay at this standard motel for the convenience of quick access to rafting and 4WD tours on the Hualapai Indian Reservation. The lobby has vaulted ceilings, a river-rock fireplace, and Native American artworks hanging on the walls. Each guest

room has either a king-size bed or two queen-size beds, plus individual heating and air-conditioning units. The front desk is open 24 hours. The lodge's family-style Diamond Creek Restaurant serves diner fare and a few Native American specialties.

HAVASUPAI LODGE
Manager: Havasupai Tribe
928-448-2111, 928-448-2201
www.havasupaitribe.com/lodge
P.O. Box 159, Supai, AZ 86435
Directions: Approximately 8.5 miles east of Peach Springs, take BIA 18 north for 65 miles to Hualapai Hilltop Highway.
Price: Moderate
Credit Cards: MC, V
Handicapped Access: No

For a rustic Grand Canyon experience, make the long drive to this Native American reservation, which is accessible only on foot or via mule train. After hiking down into Havasu Canyon (see "Hiking," below), overnight visitors can check in at the extremely basic lodge. There are only two dozen motel rooms, all with two double beds and air-conditioning, but no TVs or phones. Rates do not include the mandatory per-person fee charged for visiting the reservation. Solo travelers, especially women, may not feel safe here.

Seligman
CANYON LODGE
928-422-3255, 1-800-700-5054
www.route66canyonlodge.com
114 E. Chino Ave. (Route 66)
Seligman, AZ 86337
Price: Inexpensive
Credit Cards: AE, D, MC, V
Handicapped Access: Partial

Seligman has a slew of vintage motor courts along Route 66. This two-story motel may not have a retro neon sign like the others do, but it does offer friendly customer service, free high-speed Internet access, and discounts at local restaurants for guests. All rooms have mini-refrigerators, microwaves, and coffeemakers. Continental breakfast is complimentary.

HISTORIC ROUTE 66 MOTEL
928-422-3204
www.route66seligmanarizona.com
500 W. Chino Ave. (Route 66)
Seligman, AZ 86337
Price: Inexpensive
Credit Cards: AE, D, MC, V
Handicapped Access: Yes

Pricier than other motels in Seligman, this Route 66–themed motor court has a photoworthy neon sign out front. Each well-kept room comes with some homey touches, such as lace curtains and homespun, country-style quilts. Diverting signs inside the rooms talk about Western movie stars and other famous guests who have stayed here over the years.

Williams
THE CANYON MOTEL
Innkeepers: Shirley and Kevin
928-635-9371, 1-800-482-3955
www.thecanyonmotel.com
thecanyonmotel@aol.com
1900 E. Rodeo Rd., Williams, AZ 86046
Price: Moderate
Credit Cards: D, MC, V
Handicapped: Partial

With views of pine-covered mountains, this unique property has 18 old-fashioned flagstone cottages, accommodations inside two train cabooses, and a three-room suite in a vintage railway car, any of which make for a unique getaway. Basic motel rooms, which have cable TV, mini-refrigerators, microwaves, and coffeemakers, are not as worthwhile.

GRAND CANYON COUNTRY INN
928-635-4045
www.gccountryinn.com
info@gccountryinn.com
911 W. Route 66, Williams, AZ 86046
Price: Inexpensive
Credit Cards: AE, D, MC, V
Handicapped Access: Partial

A historic building in the heart of downtown Williams, this nonsmoking hotel has basic, motel-style rooms for travelers on a budget. If you enjoy quaint ambience and antiques, this 120-year-old hotel is a comfortable enough place to stop overnight. Rates include a continental breakfast buffet and access to an indoor heated swimming pool and hot tub.

GRAND LIVING BED & BREAKFAST
Innkeepers: Gloria and Bill Job
928-635-4171, 1-800-210-5908
www.grandlivingbnb.com
job@grandlivingbnb.com
701 Quarter Horse Rd. (off Rodeo Rd., east of N. Airport Rd.), Williams, AZ 86046

Price: Expensive
Credit Cards: AE, D, MC, V
Handicapped Access: No

On a side road north of the railroad tracks, this gracious bed-and-breakfast is all about relaxation. Every room in this two-story ranch house has its own fireplace, whirlpool tub, clawfoot soaking tub in the bathroom, and TV and VCR. Some have mountain views and are furnished with antiques. There's a library of books and videos for guests to borrow. The personable hosts craft multicourse gourmet breakfasts.

LEGACIES BED & BREAKFAST
Innkeepers: Linda and Ron Dixon
928-635-4880, 1-866-370-2288
www.legaciesbb.com
book@legaciesbb.com
450 S. 11th St. (at W. Sheridan Ave.)
Williams, AZ 86046
Price: Expensive
Credit Cards: MC, V
Handicapped Access: No

This luxurious inn surrounded by ponderosa pines has rooms outfitted with whirlpool spas, plush robes, satellite TV and DVD players, mini-refrigerators, and free high-speed Wi-Fi Internet access. Downstairs the Legacy Suite has a canopied king bed, while the adjacent Route 66 Room has retro touches. Upstairs the tropical-themed Hawaiian Room enjoys more privacy. Gourmet breakfasts feature dishes like orange-pecan French toast.

THE LODGE ON ROUTE 66
928-635-4534, 1-877-563-3266
www.thelodgeonroute66.com
lodgeon66@aol.com
200 E. Route 66, Williams, AZ 86046
Price: Moderate
Credit Cards: AE, D, MC, V
Handicapped Access: Yes

Although Route 66 through downtown Williams is lined with cheaper vintage motor courts, this recently remodeled property offers some little luxuries: superior mattresses, rich wooden furnishings, marble-topped bathrooms, flat-screen TVs, soft lighting, and Southwestern decor. Standard rooms are small, but many suites have kitchenettes, gas fireplaces, and even whirlpool tubs. Rates include an extended continental breakfast.

THE RED GARTER BED & BAKERY
Innkeeper: John Holst
928-635-1484, 1-800-328-1484
www.redgarter.com
137 Railroad Ave. (at S. 1st St.)
Williams, AZ 86046
Price: Moderate
Credit Cards: D, MC, V
Handicapped Access: Yes

A favorite stop for Grand Canyon travelers, this charming inn inhabits a late 19th-century Victorian Romanesque building that once operated as a bordello. The high-ceilinged Madam's Room has a skylight and an antique brass bed imported from N'awlins. Rumors of a resident ghost abound. The downstairs bakery serves fresh pastries and gourmet coffee. Wi-Fi Internet access is available, as are discounts for last-minute, off-season, and online bookings.

SHERIDAN HOUSE INN
Innkeepers: K. C. and Mary Seidner
928-635-9441, 1-888-635-9345
www.grandcanyonbbinn.com
sheridanhouseinn@msn.com
460 E. Sheridan Ave. (at S. Lewis St.)
Williams, AZ 86046
Price: Expensive
Credit Cards: AE, D, MC, V
Handicapped Access: No

Only a few blocks from downtown, this peaceful bed-and-breakfast has exceptionally hospitable owners, who are always happy to

Detour to La Posada Hotel, which Western architect Mary Colter considered her masterpiece, in Winslow, Arizona. Sara Benson & Mike Connolly

Winslow

LA POSADA HOTEL

Innkeeper: Allan Affeldt
928-289-4366
www.laposada.org
303 E. 2nd St. (at N. Apache Ave.)
Winslow, AZ 86047
Price: Moderate
Credit Cards: AE, D, MC, V
Handicapped Access: Limited

This rambling fantasy hacienda designed by early-20th-century Western architect Mary Colter offers superior value with a splash of colonial Mexican style. Albert Einstein, Amelia Earhart, Gene Autry, Gary Cooper, and John Wayne are among the famous folks who have slept inside this historic landmark. Every unique room exhibits a rustic Mexican or Southwestern style and is adorned with antiques, historical photos, and bold artwork. The Howard Hughes suite has a wood-burning fireplace, sitting areas, and an original mural by a Santa Fe artist. There are no phones, but rooms do have cable TV. Although restoration work is ongoing, this gorgeous historic hotel is still quite a find in dusty downtown Winslow.

give travel tips. Each room comes equipped with cable TV, a VCR or DVD player, and a stereo system. The Cedar Room has bay windows with a love seat and views of the treetops. There are also two family-size suites. When the weather is warm, full breakfasts are served on an outdoor deck among the pine trees.

CULTURE

Archaeological Sites

Stop by the Northwest New Mexico Visitor Center (505-876-2783, off I-40 exit 85, Grants, NM) for detailed information about visiting the cliff dwellings of **Casamero Pueblo**, a short drive north of Prewitt, New Mexico, on County Road 19.

CORONADO STATE MONUMENT

505-867-5351
www.nmmonuments.org
US 550 (at Kuaua Rd.), Bernalillo, NM 87004
Directions: 1.7 miles west of I-25 exit 242
Admission: Adults $3, children under 16 free; combination ticket with Jémez State Monument $5
Open: Daily 8:30–5, Wednesday through Monday

Spanish conquistador Francisco Vásquez de Coronado stumbled upon this place while looking for New Mexico's fabled Seven Cities of Gold. What he found instead was the Rio Grande Pueblo of Kuaua, which means "evergreen." Excavated during the 1930s, the ceremonial great kiva is best known for its multilayered murals. The museum inside the visitor center displays Native American and Spanish colonial artifacts.

HOMOLOVI RUINS STATE PARK
928-289-4106
www.pr.state.az.us/Parks/parkhtml/
homolovi.html
HCR 63, Box 5, Winslow, AZ 85047
Directions: From I-40 (exit 257) take
AZ 87 north.
Open: Daily dawn to dusk; closed
Christmas Day
Admission: $3 per vehicle

A sacred site to the Hopi people, this park protects Ancestral Puebloan ruins hidden in the grasslands. Some are accessible via roads and trails that pass archaeological ruins, mostly crumbling excavated walls and rocky petroglyph sites. Afterward, drive farther north on AZ 87 to Little Painted Desert County Park for colorful sunset panoramas.

At Little Painted Desert County Park, weathered geological formations appear like an artist's palette.
Sara Benson & Mike Connolly

Art Galleries
In Albuquerque the pedestrian-friendly streets of Old Town, the Nob Hill neighborhood, and downtown have plentiful art galleries displaying works by southwestern and Native American artists. For gallery hopping, the first Friday evening of each month is best.

516 Arts, www.516arts.org, 505-242-1445, 516 Central Ave. SW, Albuquerque, NM. Independent, nonprofit gallery livens up downtown with live music and spoken-word performances, too.

Double Six Gallery, www.cac66.com, 505-287-7311, 1001 W. Santa Fe Ave., Grants, NM. Run by the Cibola Arts Council, this local artists' space hosts rotating exhibitions.

La Posada Hotel, www.laposada.org, 928-289-4366, 303 E. 2nd St., Winslow, AZ. The rambling hallways and great rooms of this landmark hotel are hung with historical and contemporary artwork from the Southwest and beyond to Europe. Look for sculptures and paintings by local artists, including the tinwork *La Posada Madonna*. Taking photos is strictly prohibited, although some pieces are for sale.

Mariposa Gallery, www.mariposa-gallery.com, 505-268-6828, 3500 Central Ave. SE, Albuquerque, NM. At this fun, funky gallery, exhibitions by local artists working in all media are displayed both downstairs and upstairs, and change monthly.

Matrix Fine Art and New Grounds Print Workshop and Gallery, www.matrixfineart.com, 505-268-8952, 3812 Central Ave. SE, Albuquerque, NM. Exhibits ceramics, blown glass, sculpture, paintings, and prints by emerging New Mexico artists.

Snowdrift Art Space, www.snowdriftart.com, 928-289-8201, 120 W. 2nd St., Winslow, AZ. Regional artists display large-scale sculptures, installations, and a variety of experimental pieces.

Casinos

Route 66 Casino, www.rt66casino.com, 505-352-7866, 1-866-352-7866, 14500 Central Ave., off I-40 exit 140, Albuquerque, NM. Opposite the historic Rio Puerco Bridge, this themed casino evokes Route 66 nostalgia, from neon replicas of Twin Arrows in the parking lot to Mother Road murals inside. Slot machines, blackjack, and a nonsmoking, no-limit poker room.

Sandia Resort and Casino, www.sandiacasino.com, 505-796-7500, 1-800-526-9366, 30 Rainbow Rd. NE, off Tramway Rd. (I-25 exit 234), Albuquerque, NM. Luxe casino brings Las Vegas style to northern New Mexico. Table games, poker tournaments, video poker, a bingo hall, and a nonsmoking slot machine room.

Santa Ana Star Casino, www.santaanastar.com, 505-867-0000, 54 Jemez Canyon Dam Rd., Santa Ana Pueblo, NM. Friendly locals' casino offers craps, blackjack, roulette, video poker, slot machines, and a poker room with Texas hold 'em tournaments.

Cinema

Century 14 Downtown Albuquerque, www.centurytheatres.com, 505-243-7469, 100 Central Ave., Albuquerque, NM. Multiplex screening new releases has stadium seating, Dolby THX sound, video games, and a café.

Century Rio 24, 1-800-326-3264, 4901 Pan-American Freeway NE, Albuquerque, NM. A variety of Hollywood and independent film showings with Dolby THX and stadium-style love seats.

DynaTheater, www.nmnaturalhistory.org, 505-841-2800, New Mexico Museum of Natural History, 1801 Mountain Rd. NW, Albuquerque, NM. Natural history and adventure films are projected onto a giant Iwerks screen.

Guild Cinema, www.guildcinema.com, 505-255-1848, 3405 Central Ave. NE, Albuquerque, NM. This arthouse cinema in the Nob Hill neighborhood shows classic flicks, new independent films, and foreign movies.

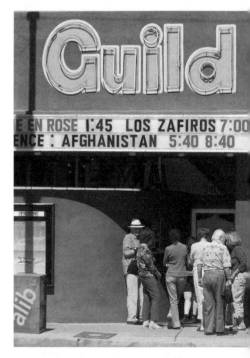

The Guild is an independent art house cinema in Albuquerque's funky Nob Hill neighborhood.
Sara Benson

Historic Places

The following day trip–size sections narrate highlights of Route 66 that you'll be able to find while driving through Arizona (www.azrte66.com) and New Mexico (www.rt66nm.org).

Still standing after 100 years, the Oatman Hotel is where movie stars Clark Gable and Carole Lombard honeymooned.
Mike Connolly

KINGMAN TO WILLIAMS, ARIZONA

Start your trip at the **Powerhouse Visitor Center** (www.kingman tourism.org, 928-753-6106, 1-866-427-7866, 120 W. Route 66, Kingman AZ), which has a diverting Route 66 museum (see "Museums," below) and gift shop. Across the street is **Locomotive Park**, with its 1928 steam engine. Pick up a walking-tour map of historic Kingman, a mining and railway town founded during Arizona's territorial days, at the visitor center. Tour the **1915 Bonelli House** (928-753-3175, 430 E. Spring St.) or detour north of town via White Cliffs Road to see a **late-19th-century wagon trail** once used to transport ore from the mines.

Follow Route 66 westbound via Beale Street across I-40 (exit 44), then turn left onto Oatman Road Grind up Gold Hill Grade over **Sitgreaves Pass** (3,523 ft.) and coast into the Old West mining town of **Oatman** (www.oatmangoldroad.com, 928-768-6222), where wild burros turned loose by miners still roam the streets. Poke around the 1902 **Oatman Hotel** and the old jail museum before backtracking to Kingman.

Follow Andy Devine Avenue, which becomes Route 66, east of Kingman to whimsical **Hackberry General Store** (928-769-2605, Hackberry, AZ), where a cherry-red 1956 Corvette convertible is parked next to vintage gas pumps. The former filling station is chockablock with Route 66 memorabilia, antiques, and frontier kitsch.

Keep heading east past Valentine and Truxton, with its landmark Frontier Motel neon sign. Drive east past **Grand Canyon Caverns** (see "Parks and Natural Attractions," below) to **Peach Springs**, where river-rafting and 4WD trips to the Grand Canyon leave from the Hualapai Lodge, including SkyWalk tours (see "Tours," below).

Route 66 continues east to the railroad town of **Seligman** (www.route66giftshop.com, 928-422-3352), where **Delgadillo's barbershop** and the **Sno-Cap Drive-In** are don't-miss historic landmarks. Leave Seligman via Crookton Road for a rolling scenic drive along a little-changed segment of Route 66, rejoining I-40 (exit 139).

Exit I-40 (exit 161) and take Bill Williams Avenue into yesteryear **Williams**, the last Route 66 town to be bypassed by the interstate system. Drive through downtown, filled with curio shops and vintage motor courts, back to I-40 (exit 165) eastbound to Flagstaff.

FLAGSTAFF, ARIZONA, TO GALLUP, NEW MEXICO

After a detour to the Grand Canyon, follow Santa Fe Avenue east of Flagstaff past US 89. Get back on I-40 (exit 204) eastbound past Winona. At exit 219 look south for a glimpse of the landmark **Twin Arrows**, all that's left of a once-busy trading post. At exit 233 detour south to out-of-this-world **Meteor Crater** (see "Parks and Natural Attractions," below).

Leave I-40 at exit 252 and follow Business 40 into downtown **Winslow** (www.winslow
arizona.org, 928-289-2434), with its **Old Trails Museum** (see "Museums," below).
Opposite is the **Standin' on the Corner Park** (www.standinonthecorner.com), with its
mural homage to the rock band The Eagles. Stop by exquisite **La Posada Hotel** (www
.laposada.org, 928-289-4366, 303 E. 2nd St., Winslow, AZ), built during the 1930s by
Western architect Mary Colter. It was one of the last of the great railway hotels built by the
Fred Harvey Company, which brought the accouterments of civilization into the Old West.
Colter oversaw every aspect of construction, from wrought-iron tulips in the foyer to
Mediterranean sunken gardens. Self-guided tour booklets are available for a small
donation.

From Winslow travel along I-40 to exit 269, where the famous "Here It Is!" sign on the
frontage road announces the famous **Jack Rabbit Trading Post** (see "Shopping," below).
Back on I-40 drive east to exit 285, then take Hopi Drive into **Holbrook**, passing the
Wigwam Motel (see "Lodging," above). At the Navajo County Courthouse, the **Old West
Museum** (928-524-6558, 100 E. Arizona St., Holbrook, AZ) is worth a quick stop to exam-
ine the antique jail.

Follow US 180 south, then east as it winds through **Petrified Forest National Park** (see
"Parks and Natural Attractions," below) and the beautiful **Painted Desert**. Near the park's
northern entrance, the **Painted Desert Inn** is a restored landmark. Built by the Civilian
Conservation Corps, it has an interior design that was influenced by the Fred Harvey
Company, architect Mary Colter, and Hopi muralists.

Exit the park and rejoin I-40 eastbound at exit 311. At exit 343 take Querino Road north,
then follow rough dirt roads east over the 1930s **Querino Canyon Bridge**. Take I-40 from
exit 346 to exit 359, then follow the north frontage road past **Chief Yellowhorse Trading
Post** (see "Shopping," below) into New Mexico. NM 118 heads east to Gallup, New Mexico.

GALLUP TO ALBUQUERQUE, NEW MEXICO
The unofficial capital of western Native America, Gallup (see the "Native America" chap-
ter) is a Route 66 gold mine. Leaving town, follow Route 66 (NM 118) eastbound past **Red
Rock State Park**. Rejoin I-40 (exit 36) eastbound. Take exit 47 at the kitschy **Continental
Divide Indian Market** (see
"Shopping," below). Follow NM 122
east all the way into **Grants**, a
uranium mining boomtown (see
"Museums," below) that went bust.
Snap a photo of the atomic neon sign
outside the defunct **Uranium Cafe**
(519 W. Santa Fe Ave.).

Leaving Grants, follow NM 122 east
onto NM 124, which winds through
quiet roadside towns: **McCarty's**,
which has a Spanish colonial mission
church; **Villa de Cubero**, where
the vintage motor courts in which
Hemingway wrote parts of *The Old
Man and the Sea* still stand; **Budville**,
a 1930s-era trading post and filling

*An abandoned filling station along historic Route 66 in
Budville, New Mexico.* Sara Benson & Mike Connolly

The kitschy folk-art exterior of the retro Aztec Motel along historic Route 66 in Albuquerque, New Mexico.

Sara Benson & Mike Connolly

station; and **Laguna,** with its early-18th-century Franciscan mission church.

At Mesita rejoin I-40 eastbound to exit 140. On the north frontage road, opposite the **Route 66 Casino** (see "Casinos," above), park and walk across the historic **Rio Puerco Bridge.** Keep driving east on the north frontage road, passing under I-40 onto Central Avenue, which passes straight through Albuquerque. In **Old Town,** walking tours depart from the **Albuquerque Museum of Art and History** (see "Museums," below), usually at 11 AM Tuesday through Sunday. Downtown, the beautifully restored **KiMo Theatre** (www.cabq.gov/kimo, 505-768-3544, 423 Central Ave. NW, Albuquerque, NM), a 1920s vaudeville house, boasts Pueblo deco architectural details and murals. Self-guided tours are usually available between 9 AM and 4 PM Monday through Friday. East of the University of New Mexico campus, the quirky **Aztec Motel** (3821 Central Ave. NE, Albuquerque, NM) is a veritable folk-art museum.

Museums

ALBUQUERQUE MUSEUM OF ART AND HISTORY

505-243-7255
www.cabq.gov/museum
2000 Mountain Rd. NW, Albuquerque, NM 87104
Open: Tuesday through Sunday 9–5
Admission: Adults $4, seniors $2, children 4–12 $1; free first Wednesday of the month and every Sunday 9–1

Next to Old Town, this thoughtful museum mixes showings by New Mexico and Native American artists with regional history exhibits and national touring shows. Docent-guided gallery walks and sculpture garden talks are free with admission. Reservations for tours of the historic Casa San Ysidro adobe in Corrales, a short drive northwest of Albuquerque, are required.

HISTORIC ROUTE 66 MUSEUM

928-753-9889
www.kingmantourism.org/route66museum
Powerhouse Visitors Center, 120 W. Andy Devine Ave., Kingman, AZ 86401
Open: Daily 9–6, March through November; daily 9–5, December through February
Admission: Adults $4, seniors $3, children under 13 free

Hands down it's the best spot in Arizona to learn about the history and pop culture of the Mother Road, from its Dust Bowl years to the hot-rodding 1950s and beyond. Highlights include life-size dioramas, colorful murals, black-and-white historical photos, and films shown in the Route 66 Theater. Tickets also include entry to the Mohave Museum of History and Arts nearby.

MOHAVE MUSEUM OF HISTORY AND ARTS

928-753-3195
www.ctaz.com/~mocohist/museum
400 W. Beale St. (at Grandview Ave.)
Kingman, AZ 86041
Open: Monday through Friday 9–5, Saturday and some Sundays 1–5
Admission: Adults $4, seniors $3, children under 13 free

In downtown Kingman, the Mohave Museum of History and Arts is a must for history buffs. Mike Connolly

A hodgepodge of historical exhibits covers Arizona Territory's early pioneer and railroad days. They also tell the story of famous local son, Western actor Andy Devine. Look for Native American cultural artifacts and artworks, as well as historical murals in the lobby. Out back you'll find an assortment of antique railway, pioneer, and mining equipment. Tickets also include entry to the Historic Route 66 Museum nearby.

NEW MEXICO MINING MUSEUM

505-287-4802, 1-800-748-2142
www.grants.org
100 N. Iron Ave. (at W. Route 66), Grants, NM 87020
Open: Monday through Friday 9–4, Saturday 9–3
Admission: Adults $3, seniors and youth $2, children under 6 free

After the discovery of a uranium mother lode in the 1950s, Grants became the world's largest uranium mining town, which was a very profitable business during the Cold War. Descend into the simulated mine shaft, then walk through first-floor history exhibits to find out why the town's once-booming industry went bust.

OLD TRAILS MUSEUM

928-289-5861
www.winslowarizona.org
212 N. Kinsley Ave. (at W. 2nd St.), Winslow, AZ 86047
Open: Tuesday through Saturday 10–4
Admission: Donations accepted

Across from the "Standin' on the Corner" park, this modest historical museum is stuffed full of treasures from yesteryear. Inside a vintage 1920s building, homegrown exhibits focus on Route 66, Native American tribes, Western ranch life, and the railroad.

WILD WEST JUNCTION AND TERRITORIAL MUSEUM
928-635-4512
www.wildwestjunction.com
321 E. Route 66, Williams, AZ 86046
Open: Hours vary seasonally
Admission: Free

Wild West Junction looks like a miniature frontier movie set with its wooden buildings and dusty wagon wheels lying about. A small museum has authentic Old West artifacts gathered from real cowboys, gambling saloons, barbershops, and boardinghouses, along with Western movie memorabilia.

Nightlife
In Albuquerque the liveliest areas for bar hopping and clubbing are found along Central Avenue downtown and in the Nob Hill district east of the University of New Mexico campus.

Black Cat, 928-422-3451, 114 W. Chino Ave., Seligman, AZ. A classic dive bar in a sleepy whistle-stop railroad town, with pool tables and a jukebox.

Burt's Tiki Lounge, www.burtstikilounge.com, 505-247-2878, 313 Gold Ave. SW, Albuquerque, NM. At this wonderfully kitschy surf-style hangout serving tropical drinks, live bands mingle with crowds of downtown locals.

Caravan East, www.caravaneast.com, 505-265-7877, 7605 Central Ave. NE, Albuquerque, NM. Get into the swing of things while two-steppin' and line dancing to live country-and-western bands; call ahead to check performance schedules.

Experience a microcosm of the Wild West at the Territorial Museum. Sara Benson & Mike Connolly

Cerbat Lanes, 928-692-1818, 3631 Stockton Hill Rd, north of I-40 exit 51, Kingman, AZ. This family-friendly PBA bowling alley has a snack bar and grill for sports fans.

Chama River Brewing Company, www.chamariverbrewery.com, 505-342-1800, 4939 Pan American Freeway, Albuquerque, NM. More of a high-end restaurant than a tap room, Chama River churns out fine brews, from honey wheat, amber, and pale ales to a seasonal barley wine.

Grand Canyon Brewery, 928-635-2445, 233 W. Route 66, Williams, AZ. Top-rated beers made by a local brewmaster are reason enough to drop by this pub with rustic, woodsy furniture, pool tables, and an outdoor patio.

Kelly's Brewpub, www.kellysbrewpub.com, 505-262-2739, 3222 Central Ave. NE, Albuquerque, NM. Inside the 1930s Jones Motor Company building on Route 66, the long bar has 20 microbrews on tap, big-screen sports TVs, and pool tables.

Launchpad, www.launchpadrocks.com, 505-764-8887, 618 Central Ave. SW, Albuquerque, NM. Long-running live-music club stages a variety of alt-rock and punk band showcases, including all-ages shows.

Lucky 66 Bowl, www.lucky66bowl.com, 505-345-2506, 6132 4th St. NW, Albuquerque, NM. Family-owned bowling alley has a pub, billiards tables, and live bands some nights.

Martini Lounge, www.theturquoiseroom.net, 928-289-2888, La Posada Hotel, 303 E. 2nd St., Winslow, AZ. By the elegant Turquoise Room restaurant, there's a stylishly retro cocktail lounge with a copper-topped bar. The Route 66 Cadillac margarita is fantastic.

Silva's Saloon, 505-867-9976, 955 Camino del Pueblo, Bernalillo, NM. Northwest of Albuquerque, this 1930s-era saloon has loads of atmosphere and sells cold beer, tortilla chips, and beef jerky. It's full of Hollywood western movie memorabilia.

Starlight Lanes, 505-771-5333, Santa Ana Star Casino, 54 Jemez Canyon Dam Rd., Santa Ana Pueblo, NM. With a UFO-themed Cosmic Bar and Grill upstairs, this bowling alley offers lanes with light and fog machines, automatic score-keeping, and a video-game arcade.

Sultana Bar, 928-635-2021, 301 W. Route 66, Williams, AZ. Inside a rehabbed 1912 movie house, this "world famous" biker bar is for serious drinking, pool playing, and darts; live bands sometimes rock the house.

Zinc Wine Bar, www.zincabq.com, 505-254-9462, 3009 Central Ave. NE, Albuquerque, NM. Posh multilevel Nob Hill restaurant offers beer and wine pours by the glass, flights of specialty liquors and wine, and occasionally live music.

Pueblos

The best place to start your journey is at the **Indian Pueblo Cultural Center** (www.indian pueblo.org, 505-843-7270, 1-866-855-7902, 2401 12th St. NW, Albuquerque, NM). The downstairs museum has informative exhibits about all of the Pueblo communities near Albuquerque, including essential etiquette for visitors. Cultural celebrations, music and dance performances, and other special events are held here.

Rising over 350 feet above the surrounding plains, **Acoma Pueblo** (www.skycity.com, 1-800-747-0181, Sky City Cultural Center, south of I-40 exit 102 or 108, Acoma, NM), also

Many pueblos in New Mexico have ceremonial plazas dominated by Spanish Catholic missionary churches.
Sara Benson

known as Sky City, dates from the 12th century. It's one of North America's oldest continuously inhabited settlements. Insightful, informative tour guides shepherd visitors around the pueblo, where families sell pottery and traditional snacks out of their adobe homes. At the mission church you'll hear the real history upon which Willa Cather's novel *Death Comes for the Archbishop* was based. Admission is by guided tour only, departing several times daily year-round. After the tour, visitors can either ride the bus back to the cultural center or clamber down a vertigo-inducing cliffside trail. Separate fees apply for visiting the cultural center's small Haak´u Museum, which hosts rotating exhibits of art, tribal history, and traditional culture.

About a 45-minute drive west of Albuquerque, **Laguna Pueblo** (www.lagunapueblo.org, 505-552-6654, off NM 124 via I-40 exit 114, Laguna, NM) centers on a town plaza dominated by the Franciscan church of San José de Laguna. Normally not open to visitors, the church has ceiling frescos that exhibit syncretism of Catholic and Native American symbolism. Ceremonial feast days with dancing happen several times per year.

A 20-minute drive south of Albuquerque, **Isleta Pueblo** (www.isletapueblo.com, 505-869-3111, off I-25 exit 215, Isleta, NM) is easily spotted by the steeple atop the 17th-century San Augustine Mission, which is now surrounded by pottery shops inside local homes. Ceremonial dances are held here on August 28 and September 4. A 40-minute drive northeast of Albuquerque toward Santa Fe, conservative **San Felipe Pueblo** (505-867-3381, off I-25 exit 252, San Felipe, NM) is open to the public on its feast day (May 1) and for an arts-and-crafts fair in October. Farther north, **Santo Domingo Pueblo** (505-465-2214, off I-25 exit 259, Santo Domingo, NM) is famous for its ceremonial corn dances held on August 4.

For information on the Zuni and Jemez Pueblos and villages on the Hopi mesas, turn to the "Culture" section of the "Native America" chapter.

Theater, Music, and Dance

Chamber Music Albuquerque, www.cma-abq.org, 505-268-1990, Symphony Center, 4407 Menaul Blvd. NE, off I-40 exit 160, Albuquerque, NM. Presents classical and American folk music and hosts an international festival of chamber music in June.

Ghost Riders, www.oatmangoldroad.com, 928-768-6222, Oatman, AZ. Hokey but nevertheless entertaining Wild West shootouts happen on the dusty streets of Oatman almost daily; call for current showtimes.

KiMo Theatre, www.cabq.gov/kimo, 505-768-3544, 423 Central Ave. NW, Albuquerque, NM. This 1920s downtown landmark stages classic and contemporary plays, musicals, opera, jazz, experimental music, ballet, and even burlesque shows.

Navajo County Courthouse, www.ci.holbrook.az.us, 1-800-524-2459, Navajo County Courthouse, 100 E. Arizona St., Holbrook, AZ. Native American dances are held in front of the courthouse on weekday evenings in summer.

New Mexico Symphony Orchestra, www.nmso.org, 505-881-8999, Symphony Center, 4407 Menaul Blvd. NE, northeast of I-40 exit 160, Albuquerque, NM. Performs classical, light operatic, and pops music at several venues around town, including concerts under the stars at Albuquerque's zoo.

Seasonal Events

JANUARY

Annual Pony Express Ride, www.ci.holbrook.az.us, 1-800-524-2459, Holbrook, AZ

Bed Races, www.oatmangoldroad.com, 928-768-3839, Oatman, AZ

FEBRUARY

Wild West Days, www.oatmangoldroad.com, 928-768-3839, Oatman, AZ

APRIL

Gathering of Nations Pow Wow, www.gatheringofnations.com, 505-836-2810, Albuquerque, NM

Railroad Days, winslowarizona.org, 928-289-2434, Winslow, AZ

MAY

Albuquerque Wine Festival, www.nmwine.com, 1-866-494-6366, Albuquerque, NM

Historic Route 66 Fun Run, www.azrt66.com, 928-753-5001, Seligman, AZ, to Golden Shores, AZ

Hualapai Downs Horse Races, www.kingmantourism.org, 928-753-2636, Kingman, AZ

Rendezvous Days, www.williamschamber.com, 928-635-4061, Williams, AZ

JUNE

National Barrel Races, www.williamschamber.com, 928-635-4061, Williams, AZ

Old West Celebration, www.ci.holbrook.az.us, 1-800-524-2459, Holbrook, AZ

JULY

4th of July Sidewalk Egg Fry Contest, www.oatmangoldroad.com, 928-768-3839, Oatman, AZ

Gathering of Eagles Art Show and Sale, www.ci.holbrook.az.us, 1-800-524-2459, Holbrook, AZ

Small Town Fourth of July Celebrations, www.williamschamber.com, 928-635-4061, Williams, AZ

AUGUST

Cool Country Cruise In and Route 66 Festival, www.williamschamber.com, 928-635-4061, Williams, AZ

Hualapai Mountain Arts and Crafts Festival, www.kingmantourism.org, 928-753-2636, Kingman, AZ

Southwest Quilt Festival, Bluegrass Contest and Train Show, www.ci.holbrook.az.us, 1-800-524-2459, Holbrook, AZ

SEPTEMBER

Andy Devine Days Parade, Community Fair and PRCA Rodeo, www.kingmantourism.org, 928-757-7919, Kingman, AZ

Feast of San Estevan, www.skycity.com, 1-888-759-2489, Pueblo of Acoma, NM

Gold Camp Days and International Burro Bisket Toss, www.oatmangoldroad.com, 928-768-3839, Oatman, AZ

Mohave County Fair, www.kingmantourism.org, 928-753-2636, Kingman, AZ

Navajo County Fair and Little Buckaroo Rodeo, www.ci.holbrook.az.us, 1-800-524-2459, Holbrook, AZ

New Mexico State Fair, www.exponm.com/fair, 505-265-3976, Albuquerque, NM

PRCA Rodeo, www.williamschamber.com, 928-635-4061, Williams, AZ

Standin' on the Corner Festival, www.standinonthecorner.com, 928-289-2434, Winslow, AZ

OCTOBER

Albuquerque International Balloon Fiesta, www.balloonfiesta.com, 505-821-1000, 1-888-422-7277, Albuquerque, NM

Ancient Way Festival, www.ancientway-route53.com/fallfestival.html, 505-287-4802, 1-800-748-2142, along NM 53 outside Grants, NM

Kingman Air and Auto Show, www.kingmantourism.org, 928-692-9599, Kingman, AZ

NOVEMBER

Weems International Artfest, www.weemsgallery.com, 505-293-6133, Albuquerque, NM

DECEMBER

Parade of Lights and Dickens Carolers, www.williamschamber.com, 928-635-4061, Williams, AZ

RESTAURANTS

Acoma Pueblo

YAAK'A CAFÉ

1-800-747-0181
www.skycity.com
Sky City Cultural Center, Acoma, NM 87034
Directions: A 20-minute drive from I-40,
either southeast of exit 102 or southwest of
exit 108.
Open: Daily
Cuisine: Southwestern
Serving: B, L
Price: Inexpensive
Credit Cards: AE, D, MC, V
Handicapped Access: Yes

Inside the pueblo's cultural center, this
casual Native American and Southwestern
café serves stomach-stuffing specialties
such as fry bread topped with red and green
chili sauces, blue-corn pancakes with a side
of peppercorn bacon, and traditional pork
and lamb stews. Fresh-baked cookies and
pastries are heavenly.

Albuquerque

66 DINER

505-247-1421
www.66diner.com
1405 Central Ave. NE
Albuquerque, NM 87106
Open: Daily
Price: Moderate
Cuisine: American
Serving: B (Saturday and Sunday), L, D
Credit Cards: AE, D, MC, V
Handicapped Access: Yes

Chicken-fried steak, meat loaf, even liver
and onions—American diner classics are
what's on the menu here, right down to the
blue plate specials and soda fountain creations. But don't come here for the food as
much as for the Route 66—era ambience,
from black-and-white tiled floors to fluo-
rescent pink and turquoise-colored
accents.

AMBROZIA CAFE AND WINE BAR

505-242-6560
www.ambroziacafe.com
108 Rio Grande Blvd. NW (at Central Ave.)
Albuquerque, NM 87104
Open: Daily
Price: Expensive
Cuisine: Eclectic
Serving: B (Sunday), D (Monday through
Saturday)
Credit Cards: AE, D, MC, V
Handicapped Access: Yes

Just outside Old Town, this historic adobe
house is adorned with red chili peppers and
Spanish colonial—style wrought-iron candelabra. The award-winning chef dreams
up Southwestern fusion dishes like lobster
hot dogs, ceviche margaritas, elk carpaccio,
and duck burgers, followed by ginger and
red-chili crème brûlée. An expert wine list
ranges from New Mexico to the West Coast
and Europe.

FLYING STAR CAFE

505-244-8099
www.flyingstarcafe.com
723 Silver Ave. SW (at 7th St. SW)
Albuquerque, NM 87103
Open: Daily
Price: Moderate
Cuisine: Bakery/American
Serving: B, L, D
Credit Cards: AE, D, MC, V
Handicapped Access: Yes

With multiple UFO-themed locations
around town, their motto is: "Life is what
you bake of it." It's part coffee shop, part
bakery, and part creative deli churning out
oversize sandwiches and salads, mostly
made with organic produce and hormone-
free animal products. Kick back with an
espresso, smoothie, or microbrewed beer,
since there are racks of magazines available
for purchase and free high-speed Wi-Fi
Internet access.

GRUET STEAKHOUSE

505-256-9463
www.gruetsteakhouse.com
3201 Central Ave. NE (west of Carlisle Blvd.
NE), Albuquerque, NM 87106
Open: Daily
Price: Expensive
Cuisine: Steakhouse
Serving: D
Credit Cards: AE, MC, V
Handicapped Access: No
Special Features: Reservations recommended

Run by local Gruet Winery, this top-cut steakhouse is atmospherically set inside the historic Monte Vista Fire Station. An all-classic steakhouse menu includes petits filets to New York strip, as well as herb-roasted chicken and grilled seafood. A star wine list favors New World vintages, including New Mexico chardonnay and Oregon pinot noir.

Feast on top-drawer steaks and New Mexican wines inside a historic firehouse at the Gruet Steakhouse in Albuquerque, New Mexico. Sara Benson & Mike Connolly

RANGE CAFE

505-867-1700
www.rangecafe.com
925 Camino del Pueblo
Bernalillo, NM 87004
Directions: From I-25 (exit 240) drive east on NM 473 for a mile, then turn right.
Open: Daily
Price: Moderate
Cuisine: New Mexican
Serving: B, L, D
Credit Cards: AE, D, MC, V
Handicapped Access: Yes

Although there are two locations in central Albuquerque, the original Range Cafe is worth the drive northwest of town, especially around sunset. A whimsical, colorful kitchen serves top-notch plates of New Mexican fare—especially blue-corn tortillas stuffed with chicken or cheese and doused in red and green chili sauces. Sip a gold-medal margarita from the bar. Choose Life by Chocolate, Death by Lemon, or one of almost a dozen other sweet endings.

SEASONS ROTISSERIE & GRILL

505-766-5100
www.seasonsonthenet.com
2031 Mountain Rd. NW (at Rio Grande Blvd. NW), Albuquerque, NM 87104
Open: Daily
Price: Expensive
Cuisine: New American
Serving: L (Monday through Friday), D
Credit Cards: AE, D, MC, V
Handicapped Access: No

In a tranquil setting near Old Town, this New American bistro is popular for its second-story outdoor patio, where you can relax with a glass or half bottle of wine from an extensive list that favors Californian and European vintages. The menu rotates with the seasons, featuring dishes like pistachio-crusted pork chops and poblano chili corn bread. There's live jazz music some nights.

SLATE STREET CAFE

505-243-2210
www.slatestreetcafe.com
515 N. Slate St. NW (at 6th St.)
Albuquerque, NM 87102
Open: Monday through Saturday
Price: Moderate
Cuisine: New American
Serving: B, L (Monday through Saturday),
D (Tuesday through Saturday).
Credit Cards: AE, D, MC, V
Handicapped Access: Yes

Downtown power brokers lunch at this creative little bistro by the courthouse. Classic egg breakfasts and house-made sandwiches, soups, and salads are done with an epicurean southwestern twist. A cheerful lime-green interior is splashed with contemporary artwork, or you can eat on the small, sunny patio. In the evening check out the soaring wine bar loft.

STANDARD DINER

505-243-1440
www.standarddiner.com
320 Central Ave. SE
Albuquerque, NM 87102
Open: Daily
Price: Expensive
Cuisine: New American
Serving: B (Sunday), L, D
Credit Cards: AE, D, MC, V
Handicapped Access: Yes

It's been said before, but this diner is anything but standard. For fans of art-deco design and fine food, stop by for mac 'n' cheese with smoked salmon, lamb loin topped with fresh basil and goat cheese, wasabi mash, or sweet potato fries. Service is attentive, and the crowd genteel.

Holbrook

BUTTERFIELD STAGE CO. STEAK HOUSE

928-524-3447
609 W. Hopi Dr., Holbrook, AZ 86025

The silhouettes of a Victorian-costumed couple light up the windows of the Butterfield Steakhouse in Holbrook, Arizona. Sara Benson & Mike Connolly

Open: Daily
Price: Expensive
Cuisine: Steakhouse
Serving: D
Credit Cards: AE, MC, V
Handicapped Access: Yes

In downtown Holbrook this country steakhouse is lit up at night with Victorian silhouettes in the windows. Friendly servers bring heaping plates of steak-and-potatoes dinners, barbecue chicken, and more. While the food isn't five-star, it's filling. Rustic tables and booths are decorated with Western movie star and railroad robber lore.

EL RANCHO RESTAURANT

928-524-3332
867 Navajo Blvd., Holbrook, AZ 86025
Open: Daily
Price: Moderate
Cuisine: Steakhouse
Serving: B, L, D
Credit Cards: MC, V
Handicapped Access: Yes

It's a little taste of New Mexico, but on the other side of the Arizona border. An unlikely-looking diner attached to a motel, it attracts local cowboys and families with its spicy salsas and red-hot chili sauces. The 1960s color palette and furnishings are outrageously retro.

MESA ITALIANA RESTAURANT
928-524-6696
2318 Navajo Blvd., Holbrook, AZ 86025
Open: Monday through Saturday
Price: Moderate
Cuisine: Steakhouse
Serving: D
Credit Cards: AE, D, MC, V
Handicapped Access: Yes

North of I-40, this Italian restaurant dishes up old-school favorites like baked eggplant, scampi, linguini, cannelloni, chicken cacciatore, and house-made tiramisu and tartufo for dessert. Its popular sports bar has a crowd-pleasing menu of comfort food like onion rings, popcorn shrimp, and grilled pork chops.

Kingman
DAMBAR STEAKHOUSE
928-753-3523
www.cyberfork.com/dambar/
1960 E. Andy Devine Ave. (at Stockton Hill Rd.), Kingman, AZ 86401
Open: Daily
Price: Expensive
Cuisine: Western
Serving: L, D
Credit Cards: MC, V
Handicapped Access: Yes

East of downtown, this casual cowboy joint pulls in local crowds. If you're not ravenous, stick with the simple chicken salad, burgers (including veggie versions), and steak or chicken fajitas. Hungrier patrons can fork into baby back ribs, chicken-fried steak, grilled catfish, and a variety of mesquite-broiled steak cuts.

HUBB'S BRUNSWICK BISTRO
928-718-1800
www.hotel-brunswick.com

315 E. Andy Devine Ave. (at N. 3rd St.)
Kingman, AZ 86401
Open: Monday through Saturday
Price: Expensive
Cuisine: Western/Southwestern
Serving: L (Monday through Friday),
D (Monday through Saturday)
Credit Cards: AE, D, MC, V
Handicapped Access: Yes

Be seated inside an elegant historic hotel that dates to Arizona's territorial days. The sophisticated menu changes with the seasons but always features classics like Caesar salads with blackened shrimp or grilled burgers topped with blue cheese, as well as more innovative Southwestern fare. The wine list is above par.

Oatman
OATMAN HOTEL
928-768-4408
181 Main St., Oatman, AZ 86433
Open: Daily
Price: Inexpensive
Cuisine: American
Serving: L
Credit Cards: MC, V
Handicapped Access: No

Attached to a historic hotel, this roughshod saloon is where dollar bills are tacked to the walls and cold beers are slung across the bar to thirsty patrons, most of whom are bikers or ghost hunters. The back-to-basics grill menu includes tasty buffalo burgers with "burro ears" (fried potatoes) on the side.

Seligman
ROAD KILL CAFE & OK SALOON
928-422-3554
502 W. Chino Ave. (Route 66)
Seligman, AZ 86337
Open: Daily
Price: Moderate
Cuisine: American
Serving: B, L, D

Credit Cards: AE, D, MC, V
Handicapped Access: Yes

Surprisingly, this tongue-in-check carnivorous roadhouse, where their motto is, "They always surrender when they're stuck on the fender," has a bountiful salad bar, plus other simple selections for vegetarians. The Western grill menu includes more exotic meat dishes, too, such as elk, duck, and buffalo burgers.

WESTSIDE LILO'S CAFE
928-422-5456
415 W. Chino Ave (Route 66),
Seligman, AZ 86337
Open: Daily
Price: Moderate
Cuisine: American/German
Serving: B, L, D
Credit Cards: AE, D, MC, V
Handicapped Access: Yes

This cozy parlor eatery with a shaded outdoor patio serves honest-to-goodness, country-style cooking. The home-baked foodstuffs, from morning biscuits and gravy, to bowls of soup served with fresh bread, to filling plates of chicken-fried steak with carrot cake for dessert, are standouts. Service is fast and friendly.

Williams
OLD SMOKEY'S RESTAURANT
928-635-1915
624 W. Route 66, Williams, AZ 86046
Open: Daily
Price: Inexpensive
Cuisine: Diner
Serving: B, L
Credit Cards: AE, D, MC, V
Handicapped Access: Yes

It feels as if you're dining inside an Old West pioneer cabin at this charming, yesteryear 1946 pancake house, itself an authentic piece of Route 66 memorabilia. Chubby Checker and Elvis Presley are among the famous faces who have eaten here. Huge breakfasts are served all day, with hot lunch dishes on the menu, too.

PANCHO MCGILLICUDDY'S
928-635-4150
141 W. Railroad Ave. (at N. 1st St.)
Williams, AZ 86046
Open: Daily
Price: Moderate
Cuisine: Mexican/American
Serving: L, D
Credit Cards: AE, D, MC, V
Handicapped Access: Yes

An unlikely but nevertheless entertaining combination of an Irish-themed bar with a Mexican-American kitchen, this airy restaurant opposite the railroad depot is a sociable spot, especially with a frozen margarita at tables on the flower-bedecked patio. The New Mexican, Southwestern, and Mexican fare is above average.

PINE COUNTRY RESTAURANT
928-635-9718
107 N. Grand Canyon Blvd. (at W. Railroad Ave.), Williams, AZ 86046
Open: Daily
Price: Moderate
Cuisine: American
Serving: B, L, D
Credit Cards: AE, D, MC, V
Handicapped Access: Yes

A family-style restaurant handy to the railroad depot, it's always packed with tourists and locals alike who come for the country-style home cooking. Don't miss the tempting glass display case of unbelievably rich fruit pies, cream pies, and cakes that really corral the crowds.

RED RAVEN RESTAURANT
928-635-4980
www.redravenrestaurant.com
135 W. Route 66 (at S. 1st St.),
Williams, AZ 86046

Open: Tuesday through Sunday
Price: Expensive
Cuisine: New American
Serving: L, D
Credit Cards: AE, D, MC, V
Handicapped Access: No

Williams's most upscale dining room, the
Red Raven is a creative New American
bistro that offers deluxe options for vegetarians. Meanwhile, omnivores can fork
into charbroiled mahi mahi with avocado
and Havarti cheese or Asian-inspired ginger beef laid on salad greens.

TYPHOON SALOON & RESTAURANT
928-635-4308
321 E. Route 66, Williams, AZ 86046
www.wildwestjunction.com
Open: Tuesday through Sunday
Price: Moderate
Cuisine: Western/steakhouse
Serving: L, D
Credit Cards: MC, V
Handicapped Access: Yes

At the dry (i.e., no alcohol) Typhoon
Saloon, the barbecue ribs, steaks, and
chicken wings are a delish mouthful. Soups,
salads, and burgers also appear on the family-friendly menu. Take a seat on the back
veranda overlooking Route 66, or sit inside
when live bands play. Cowboy skits are
sometimes staged here, because it's all
about Old West–style fun.

Winslow

THE TURQUOISE ROOM
928-289-2888
www.theturquoiseroom.net
La Posada Hotel, 303 E. 2nd St.,
Winslow, AZ 86047
Open: Daily
Price: Expensive
Cuisine: Southwestern
Serving: B, L, D
Credit Cards: AE, D, MC, V
Handicapped Access: Yes
Special Features: Reservations recom-
mended; full bar

This elegant dining room pays homage to
the Santa Fe Railway's legendary *Southwest
Chief*. High-caliber Southwest cuisine by
chef John Sharpe is served on reproduc-
tions of early-20th-century dishware
designed by Western architect Mary Colter.
The contemporary Southwestern menu
changes seasonally but always features
locally grown produce from Flagstaff farmers' markets and fresh seafood shipped
from Boston, New Orleans, and Alaska. At
breakfast, experiment with the corn-bread
pudding with prickly-pear cactus syrup or
blue-corn enchiladas. Innovative lunch and
dinner menus include a few old-fashioned
dishes that imitate the whistle-stop fare
once served by the Fred Harvey Co.
Suggested wine pairings feature vintages
grown in California vineyards.

Food Purveyors
Fort Beale Temperance Saloon, www.fortbeale.com, 928-753-1235, 318 E. Beale St.,
Kingman, AZ. Next to an old-fashioned mercantile shop, this place retains the atmosphere
of Arizona during its wild territorial days, with a player piano and gunfight reenactments
on weekends. Drop by for burgers, fruit pies, and root beer floats.

Java Cycle Coffee House, 928-635-1117, 326 W. Route 66, Williams, AZ. When you need a
java jump start, stop by this former bicycle shop, which has a small local art gallery, board
games, and espresso bar serving snacks. Free high-speed Wi-Fi Internet access.

Mr. D'z Route 66 Diner, 928-718-0066, 105 E. Andy Devine Ave., Kingman, AZ. Near the
Powerhouse Visitor Center, this retro-themed diner with classic cars parked out front sells
homemade root beer that tastes delectably of caramel.

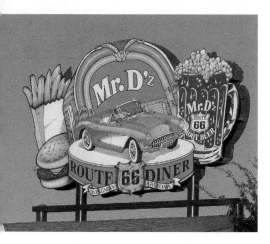

Mr. D'z makes its own caramel-tasting root beer. In fact, it's so good that they're often sold out of bottled six-packs. Sara Benson & Mike Connolly

Route 66 Malt Shop & Grill, www.route66maltshop.com, 505-242-7866, 1720 W. Central Ave., Albuquerque, NM. Inside a former filling station with antique gas pumps out front, this retro soda fountain makes homemade root beer and whips up flavored sodas and ice-cream shakes and floats.

Satellite Coffee, 505-256-0345 www.satcoffee.com, 3513 Central Ave. NE, Albuquerque, NM. A funky offshoot of the Flying Star Cafe (see "Restaurants," above) has four locations around town, all making fine espressos and teas and ice-blended drinks.

The Seattle Grind, 928-289-2859, 106 E. 2nd St., Winslow, AZ. An arty oasis by the railroad tracks, this independent café brews up icy and hot espresso drinks and teas, with a menu of pastries, bagels, and other noshes.

Seligman Sundries, www.seligmansundries.com, 928-422-4795, 109 W. Route 66, Seligman, AZ. With signs advertising "Coffee!" in several languages, this historic Route 66 place sells ice-cream fountain treats, espresso drinks, and unique coffee blends. Free Wi-Fi Internet access available.

Sno-Cap Drive-In, 928-422-3291, 301 E. Chino Ave., Seligman, AZ. Along an authentic stretch of the Mother Road, this wonderfully eccentric landmark vends ice cream, milk-shakes, and hot grilled snacks. Take photos of the prankster signs and Route 66 memora-bilia.

Twisters '50s Soda Fountain, 928-635-0266, 417 E. Route 66, Williams, AZ. This nostal-gic diner that captures the spirit of Route 66 makes ice-cream sundaes, sodas, and other old-time treats.

RECREATION

Baseball

Albuquerque Isotopes, www.albuquerquebaseball.com, information 505-924-2255, tick-ets 505-883-7800, Isotopes Park, 1601 Avenida Cesar Chavez SE, off I-25 exit 223, Albuquerque, NM. An affiliate of the MLB Florida Marlins, this AAA minor-league base-ball team plays home games near the university campus from April to September.

Bicycling and Mountain Biking

Albuquerque provides some excellent single-track opportunities for mountain bikers, most famously the seasonal trails accessed via **Sandia Peak Tramway** (www.sandiapeak

.com, 505-856-7325, 10 Tramway Loop NE, Albuquerque, NM), where mountain-bike rentals are available. Experienced riders head for **Cedro Peak in the Cibola National Forest** (www.fs.fed.us/r3/cibola, 505-281-3304, 11776 NM 337, Tijeras, NM) east of Albuquerque. Beginners take to the sandy single-track alongside the **Rio Grande in Albuquerque**, where an urban network of paved bicycle paths also exists (www.cabq.gov/recreation/bicycle, 505-768-2680). With access to the paved **Paseo del Bosque** bike trail, **Tingley Beach** (www.cabq.gov, 505-768-2000, Albuquerque BioPark, 1800 Tingley Dr. SW, Albuquerque, NM) rents mountain bikes during summer. The **Albuquerque Century & Downtown Criterium** (www.albuquerquecentury.com, 505-837-9400) road races happen in early June.

The **Ancient Way Cycling Tour** (www.grants.org, 505-287-4802, 1-800-748-2412) is a scenic road cycling race held outside Grants in mid-October. It follows NM 53 up to El Malpais National Monument and the Continental Divide. Stop by the **Northwest New Mexico Visitor Center** (505-876-2783, off I-40 exit 85, Grants, NM) for more information on mountain-biking trails in the **Zuni Mountains**, most famously the **Quartz Hill route** through Zuni and Bonita Canyons, and around **Mount Taylor.**

Northwest of downtown Kingman, the **Cerbat Foothills** have short, hilly multiuse trails that are open to mountain bikers. For road cycling, less-trafficked stretches of Route 66 are ideal for scenic long-distance rides. **Tour de Acoma** (www.skycity.com, 1-888-759-2489) is held on the Acoma and Laguna Pueblo reservations in late September.

Soak up the southwestern sun at Satellite Coffee in the funky Nob Hill neighborhood of Albuquerque, New Mexico. Sara Benson & Mike Connolly

Birding

Albuquerque is one of the most diverse birding spots in the country, from wetlands along the Rio Grande to the higher elevations of the Sandia Mountains, where owls may be seen after dark during summer and rosy finches nest in winter. Start at the **Rio Grande Nature Center State Park** (www.rgnc.org, 505-344-7240, 2901 Candelaria Rd. NW, Albuquerque, NM), where over 200 species have been spotted along walking trails that wind through sand flats, wetlands, and the *bosque*, a cottonwood-covered river bottom. The river provides habitat for sandhill cranes, kingfishers, bald eagles, roadrunners, hummingbirds, and many migratory winter species along the flyway.

Although it's a 90-minute drive south of Albuquerque, serious birders won't want to miss **Apache del Bosque National Wildlife Refuge** (www.fws.gov, www.friendsofthebosque.org, 505-835-1828, NM 1 south of US 380, off I-25 exit 139, Socorro, NM), with Rio Grande wetlands and riparian forests at the edge of the Chihuahuan Desert. The **Festival of the Cranes** happens during mid-November.

In western Arizona, **Havasu National Wildlife Refuge** (www.fws.gov, 760-326-3853, Topock, AZ) preserves prime habitat for shorebirds, falcons, hawks, owls, and other avian species alongside the Colorado River, including in Topock Gorge and marshy wetlands nearby; for a birding checklist, download the online brochure.

Boating, Canoeing, Fishing, and Kayaking

Experienced paddlers can launch canoes and kayaks from underneath bridges over the **Rio Grande** in central Albuquerque, but ask for local advice first. At the Albuquerque BioPark, **Tingley Beach** (www.cabq.gov, 505-768-2000, 1800 Tingley Dr. SW, Albuquerque, NM) rents family-friendly pedal boats during summer.

Swimming, fishing, and canoe trips to secluded, deep-water **Clear Creek Canyon** outside Winslow, Arizona, start from **McHood Park** (www.ci.winslow.az.us, 928-289-5714). To get there take AZ 87 south of Winslow, then turn left on AZ 99. For fishing trips into **Topock Gorge**, in western Arizona near the state line, contact **Captain Doyle's River Excursions** (www.funfishing.net, 928-768-2667, 1-866-284-3262, Topock, AZ).

Camping

Albuquerque has a few privately owned RV parks. Northwest of the city adjacent to Coronado State Monument (see "Archaeological Sites," above), the **Coronado Campground** (505-980-8256, 106 Kuaua Rd., Bernalillo, NM) has developed and undeveloped tent and RV sites (hookups available).

South of Kingman, **Hualapai Mountain Park** (www.mcparks.com, 928-681-5700, RV park reservations 1-877-757-0915, 6250 Hualapai Mountain Rd., Kingman, AZ) has shady first-come, first-served tent sites and RV sites with hookups; it's open May through October. Near **Meteor Crater** there's a full-service private RV park (928-289-4002, 1-800-478-4002, off I-40 exit 233, Winslow, AZ). **Homolovi Ruins State Park** (see "Archaeological Sites," above) has tent and RV sites with electrical hookups; the campground is open April through mid-November.

Remotely located on the Hualapai Indian Reservation next to the Colorado River, primitive **Diamond Creek Campground** (www.destinationgrandcanyon.com, 928-769-2219, 1-877-716-9378) is accessible only via a high-clearance 4WD road from Peach Springs. The campground is usually open from mid-March through October. You must purchase a camping permit first at the Hualapai Lodge (see "Lodging," above); inquire about road conditions and the weather forecast before making the trip.

Free dispersed tent camping is usually allowed in national forests and on other federal recreational lands. For more information contact the **Northwest New Mexico Visitor Center** (505-876-2783, off I-40 exit 85, Grants, NM) or the **Bureau of Land Management's Rio Puerco Field Office** (www.nm.blm.gov, 505-761-8700, 435 Montano Rd. NE, Albuquerque, NM).

Disc (Frisbee) Golf

Albuquerque's oldest course at **Roosevelt Park** (www.cabq.gov/parks, 505-867-8650, Coal Ave. SE at Spruce St., off I-25 exit 223) is not the only game in town. Also try the tees **opposite Ladera Golf Course** (Ouray Rd. NW off Unser Blvd. north of I-40 exit 154) or the more technical desert course at **Brent Baca Memorial** (Los Picaros Rd. SE, off I-25 exit 220) near the airport.

Fitness Facilities

There are few indoor gyms along Route 66. Book hotels with workout facilities instead.

Bikram's Yoga, www.bikramyogaburque.com, 505-243-4688, 724 Central Ave. SE, Albuquerque, NM. Drop-in classes teach hatha yoga poses and breathing exercises in a heated room.

High Desert Yoga, www.highdesertyoga.com, 505-232-9642, 4600 Copper St. NE, north of Central Ave., Albuquerque, NM. Multi-style yoga studio in the Nob Hill neighborhood; call ahead to check schedules.

Liberty Gym, www.libertygym.com, 505-884-8012, 2401 Jefferson St. NE, Albuquerque, NM. Basic, no-frills fitness center has weights and cardio machines.

Premiere Fitness, www.winslowfit.com, 928-289-2188, 200 W. 2nd St., Winslow, AZ. This gym has over 10,000 square feet of workout space, including express circuits, cardio and strength-training machines, spin bikes, free weights, and group classes.

YogaNow, www.yoganow.org, 505-232-4717, 215 Gold St. SW, Albuquerque, NM. Offers a variety of drop-in yoga classes downtown for all levels of experience.

Football

The **University of New Mexico Lobos** men's football team (http://golobos.cstv .com, tickets 505-925-5627, UNM Stadium, Avenida Cesar Chavez at University Blvd., Albuquerque, NM) plays from September through November. Also at the UNM stadium, the **New Mexico Bowl** (www.newmexicobowl.com, 505-925-5999) matches up the MWC and WAC college football conferences in late December.

Golf

For information about municipal Arroyo del Oso, Ladera, and Puerto del Sol golf courses or the driving range at Balloon Park, contact the **Albuquerque Department of Parks and Recreation** (www.cabq.gov/golf, 505-1-888-8115).

Cerbat Cliffs Golf Course,

http://parks.cityofkingman.gov/golf.asp, 928-753-6593, 1001 Gates Ave., off Stockton Hill Rd., I-40 exit 51, Kingman, AZ. Low-key municipal course for begin-

Prankster jokes and Route 66 relics abound at the Sno-Cap Drive-in in Seligman, Arizona. Sara Benson & Mike Connolly

ner and intermediate skill levels. Public, 18 holes, 6,502 yards, par 71; club and cart rentals, driving range, pro shop, snack bar.

Championship Golf Course at UNM, www.unmgolf.com, 505-277-4546, 3601 University Blvd. SE, Albuquerque, NM. The most bang for your buck is found at this nationally renowned course, locally nicknamed "The Monster." Public, 18 holes, 7,248 yards, par 72; cart and club rentals, lessons, pro shop, putting and chipping greens, restaurant.

Coyote del Malpais Golf Course, www.coyotedelmalpaisgolfcourse.com, 505-285-5544, 2001 George Hanosh Blvd., Grants, NM. A scenic lake-strewn course beneath majestic Mount Taylor. Public, 18 holes, 7,087 yards, par 71; club and cart rentals, driving range, lessons, pro shop, snack bar.

Elephant Rocks Golf Course, www.elephant-rocks.com, 928-635-4935, 2200 Golf Course Dr., Williams, AZ. PGA-designed highlands course is an escape from the desert heat. Public, 18 holes, 6,695 yards, par 72; club and cart rentals, driving range, pro shop, 1930s-era clubhouse. Open March through November.

Paa-Ko Ridge Golf Club, www.paakoridge.com, 505-281-6000, 8666-898-5987, Clubhouse Dr., north of I-40 exit 175, Sandia Park, NM. Award-winning course with native vegetation and Sandia Mountains views. Public, 27 holes, 9,466 yards, par 108; club and cart rentals, driving range, lessons, pro shop, putting and chipping greens, restaurant.

Sandia Golf Course, www.sandiagolf.com, 505-798-3990, Sandia Resort & Casino, 30 Rainbow Rd. NE, off Tramway Blvd., east of I-25 exit 234, Albuquerque, NM. Newly opened course is scenically perched above the city in the Sandia Mountains. Public, 18 holes, 7,722 yards, par 72; club and cart rentals, driving range, pro shop, putting and chipping greens, restaurant, snack bar.

Santa Ana Golf Club, www.santaanagolf.com, 505-867-9464, 288 Prairie Star Rd., Santa Ana Pueblo, NM. Near Twin Warriors Golf Club, this top-ranked national course dotted with lakes offers unlimited daily play. Public, 18 holes, 7,145 yards, par 72; cart and club rentals, lessons, pro shop, putting and chipping greens, restaurant.

Twin Warriors Golf Club, www.santaanagolf.com, 505-771-6155, 1301 Tuyuna Trail, Santa Ana Pueblo, NM. A grassy links-style course surrounded by piñon trees and high desert offers Sandia Mountains vistas. Public, 18 holes, 7,736 yards, par 72; cart and club rentals, driving range, lessons, pro shop, putting green.

Valle Vista Country Club, www.vallevistagolf.com, 928-757-8744, 9868 Concho Dr., Kingman AZ. A relatively challenging course by the Hualapai Mountains. Semiprivate, 18 holes, 6,266 yards, par 72; club and cart rentals, driving range, lessons, pro shop.

Hiking and Backpacking

Around Albuquerque, the **Sandia Mountains** are crisscrossed by seasonal hiking trails, including those easily accessed via the **Sandia Peak Tramway** (www.sandiapeak.com, 505-856-7325, 10 Tramway Loop NE, Albuquerque, NM). Farther west outside Grants, stop by the **Northwest New Mexico Visitor Center** (505-876-2783, off I-40 exit 85, Grants, NM) for advice about summiting **Mount Taylor** (10,301 ft.).

Detour northeast of Peach Springs for a more adventurous backpacking trip on the **Havasupai Reservation** (www.havasupaitribe.com, 928-448-2111, 928-448-2201). Hike the challenging 10-mile trail down into **Havasu Canyon,** where you can overnight at the tribe's basic lodge (see "Lodging," above) or primitive campground (site reservations 928-448-2141/2121/2174/2180), then day hike to **Beaver Falls** and the **Colorado River.** Register and pay the tribal entry fee at the tourist office upon arrival. Beware that theft and violent crimes against backpackers have occurred recently on tribal lands, especially at the campground and while hiking on trails. Solo travelers should avoid this trip.

Northwest of downtown Kingman, the **Cerbat Foothills** have a multiuse trail system (http://parks.cityofkingman.gov, 928-757-7919), where you may spot raptors and desert tortoises along the historic **Camp Beale Loop.** A 30-minute drive south, **Hualapai Mountain Park** (www.mcparks.com/hmp/hiking.html, 1-877-757-0915) has developed and more rugged hiking trails at higher elevations.

For many more hiking opportunities, see "Parks and Natural Attractions," below.

Horseback Riding

Cedar Crest Stables, www.cedarcreststables.com, 505-281-5197, 47 Snowline Rd., Cedar Crest, NM. East of Albuquerque, guided trail rides explore the Sandia Mountains.

Mountain Ranch Stables, www.mountainranchresort.com, 928-635-2693, off I-40 exit 171, Williams, AZ. Short trail rides in the Kaibab National Forest from April through October.

Oatman Stables, www.oatmanstables.com, 928-768-3257, P.O. Box 301, Oatman, AZ 86433. From October through May, offers trail rides, overnight pack trips, and working cattle drives.

Parks and Natural Attractions

For information about Grand Canyon West and the Skywalk on the Hualapai Indian Reservation, see the "Tours and Guided Adventures" section, below.

ALBUQUERQUE AQUARIUM AND RIO GRANDE BOTANIC GARDEN
505-768-2000
www.cabq.gov/biopark
2601 Central Ave. SW, Albuquerque, NM 87104
Open: Daily 9–5 (till 6 pm Saturday and Sunday, June through August); last ticket sold 30 minutes before closing. Closed Thanksgiving, Christmas, and New Year's Day.
Admission: Adults $7, seniors and children 3–12 $3, children under 3 free

The Albuquerque BioPark, which encompasses Tingley Beach (see "Boating," above) and the city's zoo, has an outstanding aquarium stocked with species from the Rio Grande south to the Gulf of Mexico. An oasis in the desert, the Rio Grande Botanic Garden grows desert and wetlands species and harbors a butterfly pavilion, Japanese garden, and a 1930s-era heritage farm featuring living-history demonstrations.

EL MALPAIS NATIONAL MONUMENT AND CONSERVATION AREA
505-783-4774
www.nps.gov/elma
Directions: Visitor center on NM 53, 23 miles southwest of I-40 (exit 81)

Open: Daily dawn to dusk
Admission: Free

A volcanic badlands desert of lava flows, cinder cones, and caves, El Malpais is a jagged wilderness. Two highways run alongside the monument, while the Chain of Craters Backcountry Byway (County Road 42) is a 32-mile 4WD dirt adventure for high-clearance vehicles. Popular with tourists is the privately owned Bandera Volcano ice cave (www.ice caves.com, 1-888-423-2283), accessed via a graded dirt road off NM 53 about 5 miles south of the visitor center. Self-guided tours of the ice cave (adults $9, seniors $7, children 5–12 $4) are usually available from 8 AM until an hour before sunset.

EL MORRO NATIONAL MONUMENT
505-783-4226
www.nps.gov/elmo
HC 61 Box 43, Ramah, NM 87321
Directions: From I-40 (exit 81) take NM 53 south for 42 miles.
Open: Visitor center open daily 9–5 in winter, 9–6 during spring and fall, 9–7 Memorial Day through Labor Day. Trails close one hour later.
Admission: Adults $3, children under 16 free

At El Morro ("the bluff"), Ancestral Puebloans once lived on the beautiful mesa top, which offers panoramas of the Zuni Mountains and the nearby volcanic wilderness of El Malpais National Monument. Access is via a hiking trail that passes Newspaper Rock, which is inscribed with ancient petroglyphs and more modern scribbling by Spanish colonial explorers and early western pioneers.

El Morro's Newspaper Rock has been spreading the word among travelers for hundreds of years.
Sara Benson

GRAND CANYON CAVERNS
928-422-3223, 928-422-4565
www.gccaverns.com
900 Route 66, Peach Springs, AZ 86434
Directions: 22 miles west of Seligman, AZ
Open: Daily 10–4. Call ahead for winter hours (November through February); closed Christmas Day.
Admission: Regular tour: adults $12.95, children 4–12 $9.95. Explorers tour: $44.95 per person.

The 80th anniversary of the discovery of these caves was recently celebrated. The 45-minute tours, which depart every half hour, start and end with an ear-popping elevator ride and require less than a mile of walking. There's also a curio shop, diner, motel, RV park, and 24-hour gas station here.

METEOR CRATER

928-289-2362, 1-800-289-5898
www.meteorcrater.com
P.O. Box 30940, Flagstaff, AZ 86003
Directions: Off I-40 exit 233, west of Winslow, AZ
Open: Daily 8–5. Extended hours daily 7–7 late May to September 15. Open 8–1 on
Thanksgiving; closed Christmas Day.
Admission: Adults $15, seniors $13, children 6–17 $6, children under 6 free

Created in less than 10 seconds, this 50,000-year-old astrogeological landmark is deeper
than the Statue of Liberty is high. At this ultra-kitschy roadside attraction, the museum is
a hodgepodge of space paraphernalia, including artifacts from early Apollo missions and a
meteorite fragment that weighs a whopping 1,406 pounds. Catch the 10-minute video
about meteorite impacts and collisions, then spy on the vast impact crater (where NASA
astronauts once trained) by using telescopes from the indoor observation areas. Sturdy
shoes are a must for guided crater rim hikes, which are offered several times daily.

PETRIFIED FOREST NATIONAL PARK

928-524-6228
www.nps.gov/pefo
1 Park Rd., Petrified Forest, AZ 86028
Directions: The north entrance is off I-40
(exit 311). Eastbound travelers should take
I-40 exit 285 into Holbrook, then drive 19
miles southeast on US 180 to the south
entrance.
Open: Daily 8–5 October through
February; 7–6 March to mid-May and
September; 7–7 mid-May through August
Admission: seven-day entry pass $10 per
vehicle

This widely scattered "forest" is made up of
broken fossilized logs, which crystallized
into quartz over 225 million years ago during the Triassic period. Bask in the ben-
tonite badlands of the Painted Desert, where
the land changes colors with the angle of the
sun and minerals in the earth, and check
out the petroglyphs at Newspaper Rock. The
paved 28-mile scenic drive passes hiking
trailheads, panoramic viewpoints, and
archaeological and geological features of
interest, including Blue Mesa and Puerco
Pueblo. Ranger-led walks often start near
the park's southern entrance at the
Rainbow Museum, which contains the cast
of dinosaur fossils found nearby in 1984.

*Ancient logs are scattered naturally along the hills
and hiking trails of Petrified Forest National Park.*
Sara Benson & Mike Connolly

PETROGLYPH NATIONAL MONUMENT
505-899-0205
www.nps.gov/petr/
6001 Unser Blvd. NW, Albuquerque, NM 87120
Directions: 3.5 miles north of I-40 exit 154
Open: Daily 8–5; closed New Year's Day, Thanksgiving, and Christmas
Admission: Parking on weekdays/weekends $1/$2

In the sprawling suburbs of Albuquerque, this petite park protects a wealth of petroglyph sites reached via walking trails in windswept Rinconanda, Boca Negra, and Piedra Marcadas Canyons. The Volcanoes day-use area has more strenuous hiking trails leading to overlooks. Drop by the visitor center for an orientation, trail guides, and natural science exhibits.

SANDIA PEAK TRAMWAY
505-856-7325
www.sandiapeak.com
10 Tramway Loop NE, Albuquerque, NM 87122
Directions: 9 miles north of I-40 (exit 167) via Tramway Blvd., or 6 miles east of I-25 (exit 234) via Tramway Rd.
Admission: Round-trip tickets: adults $17.50, seniors and teens 13–20 $15, children 5–12 $10, children under 5 free
Open: Wednesday through Monday 9–8 and Tuesday 5–8; extended summer hours daily 9–9

This is one of the world's longest tramways. Rides begin among cacti in the desert and rise over 3,800 feet to an observation deck with views of pine-forested Sandia Peak (10,378 ft.). During summer the skiers' chairlift transports hikers and mountain bikers farther uphill (for details about these activities see the relevant subheadings elsewhere in the "Recreation" section of this chapter).

Racquet Sports
Centennial Park, http://parks.cityofkingman.gov, 928-757-7919, 3333 Harrison St., off E. Beverly Ave., northeast of I-40 exit 51, Kingman, AZ. Community center maintains four tennis courts and two indoor racquetball courts.

City Park, http://ci.winslow.az.us/parks_facilities.htm, 928-289-5714, between Cherry, Colorado, Pope, and Maple Sts., Winslow, AZ. Has racquetball and outdoor tennis courts.

Jerry Cline Tennis Complex, www.cabq.gov/recreation, 505-256-2080, 7205 Constitution Ave. NE, off I-40 exit 162, Albuquerque, NM. The largest municipal tennis complex has 18 reservable courts, including some lighted for night play; drop-in doubles, backboards, and ball-machine rentals available.

River Rafting
Hualapai River Runners, www.destinationgrandcanyon.com, 928-769-2219, 1-877-716-9378, Hualapai Lodge, Peach Springs, AZ. Organized by the Hualapai Tribe, one-day motorized rafting trips include a 4WD road trip to the Colorado River at the bottom of the Grand Canyon, a hike to Travertine Falls, a white-water run, and snacks, drinks, and lunch.

Rock Climbing

Stone Age Climbing Gym, www.stoneageclimbinggym.com, 505-341-2016, 4201 Yale Ave. NW, off I-25 exit 277, Albuquerque, NM. New Mexico's largest indoor climbing gym provides opportunities for bouldering, top roping, and lead climbing. Day passes, equipment rental, classes, and custom guided trips available.

Suntoucher Mountain Guides, www.suntoucher.com, 505-400-5590, 505-400-2529, 2900 Vista del Rey NE, Albuquerque, NM. Offers rock-climbing classes, women's clinics, and guided trips in the Sandia Mountains wilderness accessed via the tramway.

Running

In Albuquerque the University of New Mexico campus has an outdoor running track located off Central Avenue SE. Elsewhere, quieter stretches of Route 66 are ideal for long-distance training on blacktop and gravel. Trail runners also have some beautifully forested and rugged desert options (see "Hiking," earlier).

Skiing, Snowboarding, and Other Winter Sports

Sandia Peak Tramway, www.sandiapeak.com, 505-242-9052, snow report 505-857-8977, 10 Tramway Loop NE, Albuquerque, NM. It can't compare with Taos, but Albuquerque's scenic tramway accesses a winter ski area with four chairlifts and 30 trails, a ski school, rentals, pro shop, café, and snowboarders' terrain park.

You can also go snowshoeing on hiking trails in the **Sandia Mountains** around Albuquerque. There are rugged, steep cross-country skiing trails in the **Cibola National Forest** (www.fs.fed.us/r3/cibola, 505-876-2783, off I-40 exit 85, Grants, NM) around **Mount Taylor**. In mid-February, the **Mount Taylor Winter Quadrathlon** (www.mttaylorquad.org, 505-287-4802) is a brutal 42-mile race to the summit and back by road biking, running, cross-country skiing, and snowshoeing.

West of Flagstaff, **Williams** (www.williamschamber.com, 928-635-4061) has an outdoor ice-skating rink open from Thanksgiving through New Year's.

Swimming

Centennial Pool, http://parks.cityofkingman.gov, 928-757-7910, 3333 Harrison St., off E. Beverly Ave., northeast of I-40 exit 51, Kingman, AZ. Outdoor municipal pool has a waterslide; open during summer only.

City Park, http://ci.winslow.az.us, 928-289-5714, between Cherry, Colorado, Pope, and Maple Sts., Winslow, AZ. Has a year-round indoor swimming pool and summer-only outdoor pool.

McHood Park, http://ci.winslow.az.us, 928-289-5714, off AZ 99, Winslow, AZ. A 10-minute drive from downtown Winslow, this municipal park has outdoor swimming holes. To get here take AZ 87 south to AZ 99, then turn left.

West Mesa Aquatic Center, 505-836-8718, 6705 Fortuna Rd. NW, at Coors Blvd. NW, off I-40 exit 155, Albuquerque, NM. Olympic-size indoor pool has a diving board, while the family-friendly indoor and outdoor recreation pools have waterslides. To find more municipal pools, contact the Albuquerque Parks and Recreation Department (www.cabq.gov/recreation, 505-857-8650).

Williams Aquatic Center, www.williamsarizona.gov, 928-635-3005, 315 W. Railroad Ave., Williams, AZ. Call ahead for public swim hours in the indoor lap pool.

Tours and Guided Adventures

For details of the Grand Canyon Railway between Williams and the South Rim of the Grand Canyon, see the "Getting Around the Four Corners" section of the "Transportation" chapter, earlier in this book.

Albuquerque Convention & Visitors Bureau, www.itsatrip.org, 505-842-2282, 1-800-284-2282, Plaza Don Luis, off Romero Ave. NW, Albuquerque, NM. The city tourism office offers free self-guided walking tour pamphlets, all downloadable online.

Albuquerque Hang Gliding, www.albuquerquehanggliding.com, 1-800-615-9086, Albuquerque, NM. Offers tandem hang-gliding rides and lessons for beginners.

Beautiful Balloons Co., www.beautifulballoonsco.com, 1-800-367-6625, Albuquerque, NM. Long-established outfitters offer hot-air balloon rides at sunrise and sunset (two-person minimum).

Grand Canyon West, www.destinationgrandcanyon.com, 928-769-2219, 1-877-716-9378, Hualapai Lodge, P.O. Box 246, Peach Springs, AZ. The Hualapai Tribe offers a variety of guided tours, including out to the Skywalk, a glass cantilever bridge suspended 4,400 feet above the Colorado River of the Grand Canyon.

Taste New Mexico vintages at the Casa Rondena Winery on the rural outskirts of Albuquerque. Sara Benson & Mike Connolly

Saloon Row Ghost Tours, www.saloonrowghosttour.com, 928-600-3024, 117 W. Railroad Ave., Williams, AZ. Offers paranormal and ghost-hunting tours of downtown Williams almost nightly, year-round.

Skyspan Adventures, www.skyspanadventures.com, 505-250-2300, 1-877-759-7726, 5600 McLeod Rd. NE, Albuquerque, NM. Experienced pilot who has flown in a hot-air balloon from North America to Africa offers early morning flights.

The Vineyard Express, www.thevineyardexpress.net, 505-292-3657, 1-888-501-2665, Albuquerque, NM. Organizes guided winery tours by limo coach that allow guests to meet the winemakers and vineyard growers.

SHOPPING

Art, Antiques, and Collectibles
Most Route 66 towns have quaint shops
selling antiques and collectibles.

Bubbee's Goodz, 928-718-1188, 402 E.
Beale St., Kingman, AZ. Downtown
Kingman is chockablock with antiques
shops. Standing on a corner, Bubbee's has
a small but select collection of artifacts
from Arizona's pioneer, Native American,
and Western days, plus railroad memorabilia, antique kitchen goods, and vinyl
records.

*Nostalgic yesteryear souvenir shops are found all
along Route 66.* Sara Benson & Mike Connolly

Fort Beale Mercantile,
www.fortbeale.com, 928-753-1235, 314
and 318 E. Beale St., Kingman, AZ. This old-fashioned downtown landmark sells the real
McCoy: genuine Western antiques and collectibles from chaps to cowboy hats, pioneer
housewares, and reproduction vintage clothing for guys and gals.

La Posada Hotel, www.laposada.org, 928-289-4366, 303 E. 2nd St., Winslow, AZ. Browse
Southwestern, Mexican, and Native American–made goods in the art gallery, then peek
inside the lobby gift shop, which sells collectible reproduction Mary Colter–designed
dishware, antique rings, petrified wood, and local-interest books.

Books, Maps, Outdoor Gear, and Souvenirs
Angel & Vilma Delgadillo's Route 66 Gift Shop, www.route66giftshop.com, 928-422-
3352, 217 E. Route 66, Seligman, AZ. It has spawned imitators, but Seligman's original

Route 66 gift shop wins points for nostalgia. It's attached to the famous barbershop owned by Angel Delgadillo, the
"Guardian Angel" of Route 66 preservation in Arizona.

Continental Divide Indian Market, off
I-40 exit 47, Continental Divide, NM.
Although the kitschy souvenirs are unre-
markable, this is literally the high point
of the Mother Road—so why not pick up a
rubber tomahawk or discount moccasins
here?

**Historic Route 66 Association of
Arizona,** www.azrt66.com, 928-753-
5001, Powerhouse Visitor Center, 120 W.
Route 66, Kingman, AZ. Nonprofit gift
shop by the railroad tracks stocks road-

*Old Town Albuquerque is a happy hunting ground of
artists' shops and garden courtyards.*
Sara Benson & Mike Connolly

trip maps, Route 66 coffee-table books, and all sorts of souvenirs, including luggage emblazoned with Route 66 logos.

Jack Rabbit Trading Post, www.jackrabbit-tradingpost.com, 928-288-3230, off I-40 exit 269, Joseph City, AZ. Opened in 1949, this souvenir shop is famous for its "Here It Is!" billboard campaign along Route 66. Take a photo of yourself saddling the giant jackrabbit outside as trains roar past, then wander inside for Route 66 memorabilia and Western curios.

Jim Gray's Petrified Wood Co., www.petrifiedwoodco.com, 928-524-1842, 147 US 180 at AZ 77, Holbrook, AZ. Outside the national park's south entrance, this warehouse of petrified wood, rough mineral rocks, fossils, and polished logs has a lapidary workshop churning out high-priced bookends, carvings, and jewelry.

Rainbow Rock Shop, 928-524-2384, 101 Navajo Blvd., Holbrook, AZ. Watched over by prehistoric dinosaurs handmade from colorful cement, this local shop displays geodes, petrified wood, and other souvenirs.

REI, www.rei.com, 505-247-1191, 1550 Mercantile Ave. NE, off I-25 exit 228, Albuquerque, NM. Expert outdoor retailer sells hiking, biking, camping, snow sports, and paddling gear, including clothing, shoes, and outdoor activity guidebooks and maps.

Route 66 Casino, www.rt66casino.com, 505-352-7866, 1-866-352-7866, 14500 Central Ave., off I-40 exit 140, Albuquerque, NM. Giant casino has a larger-than-life gift shop full of Route 66–themed souvenirs representing every state along the Mother Road.

The town of Seligman, Arizona, doesn't miss a chance to have fun with its Route 66 heritage.
Sara Benson & Mike Connolly

Seligman Sundries, www.seligmansundries.com, 928-422-4795, 109 W. Route 66, Seligman, AZ. This revitalized general store has historical displays of antique soda fountain and pharmacy goods. Buy Route 66 souvenirs and coffee beans roasted on site.

Sportz Outdoor, www .sportzoutdoor.com, 505-387- 9400, 6915 Montgomery Blvd. NE, east of I-25 exit 229, Albuquerque, NM. Cycling, running, hiking, swimming, skiing, snowboarding, and yoga clothing and equipment are sold here. Knowledgeable staff offer advice and events information.

You know you've finally arrived at the Jack Rabbit Trading Post in Joseph City, Arizona. Sara Benson & Mike Connolly

Native American Trading Posts and Galleries

Albuquerque's Old Town has dozens of art galleries for works by Native American artists, some of whom sell directly to tourists on the sidewalks around the plaza.

Chief Yellowhorse Trading Post, off I-40 exit 359, Lupton, AZ. Backed by canyons west of the state line, this famous roadside souvenir shop was run by Chief Yellowhorse, a Navajo trader and World War II airman, until his death in 1999. Buffalo were once corralled here.

McGee's Hopi Traders, www.mcgeeshopitraders.com, 928-524-1977, 2114 E. Navajo Blvd., Holbrook, AZ. This family-owned business has been in operation since the 1930s. The whimsical two-story adobe building houses a Native American art gallery specializing in Hopi and Navajo pottery, rugs, jewelry, and art.

Mohave Museum of History and Arts, 928-753-3195, 400 W. Beale St., Kingman, AZ. Tiny historical museum has a fine artisan gift shop filled with Navajo pottery, Hopi kachinas, Pueblo storyteller dolls, handmade jewelry and dream catchers, and books.

Sky City Cultural Center, www.skycity.com, 1-888-759-2489, south of I-40 exit 102 or 108, Acoma, NM. Spacious gift shop displays jewelry and artisan crafts made by the tribe, as well as Southwestern books and fine-art prints.

Thunder Eagle Native Art, 928-635-9260, 221 W. Route 66, Williams, AZ. This serene downtown gallery shop sells Native American artwork and traditional artisan crafts at fair prices, with guarantees of authenticity.

Turquoise Teepee, 928-635-4709, 114 W. Route 66, Williams, AZ. It may look more like a garage sale than a typical trading post, but this historic curio shop with an unmistakable neon sign is worth browsing for its antique Native American jewelry.

5

NATIVE AMERICA

Tribal Lands and Peoples

Once you drive over the border onto one of the Southwest's tribal reservations, it feels like you've stepped into another world. While the physicality of the place may look the same as the U.S. state you've just left behind, the spiritual impact of every mountain and rock formation jutting above the endless horizon feels vastly different. It is easy to imagine this is where the ancestors of modern Native Americans once walked. For the people who live here today, these reservations are hard-won homelands where ceremonial traditions such as powwows and corn dances are still conducted, just as in centuries past. Visitors who show respect for the land and its people are welcome here.

Whether your trip takes you deep inside the Navajo Nation, atop the high mesas of the Hopi people, or into more compact Native American communities such as the Zuni Pueblo, you'll likely start your journey from the cultural crossroads of Gallup, New Mexico. The unofficial capital of Indian country, the city of Gallup is also a major stopover on Route 66, which is covered in an earlier chapter of this book. From Gallup travelers can drive south to visit the Zuni Pueblo or northwest to Window Rock, the capital of the Navajo Nation, then make their way west to the historic Hubbell Trading Post and north to Chinle, the gateway to Canyon de Chelly National Monument.

Another entrance to the region is the city of Page, set beside Lake Powell in northern Arizona. Backed by a dam, the massive Glen Canyon National Recreation Area dominates the region. From Page a few travelers head west to the Grand Canyon's North Rim (see the "Flagstaff and Grand Canyon" chapter), but most travel east into Navajoland to visit Monument Valley, with its landmark Mitten Buttes made famous by old-fashioned Hollywood westerns, or directly to the Hopi mesas, which are also accessible from Winslow (see the "Route 66" chapter). Travelers starting from Albuquerque (see the "Route 66" chapter) have the best advantage for visiting the Ancestral Puebloan ruins of Chaco Culture National Historic Park near Farmington and Aztec, before heading north over the New Mexico–Colorado border to the cliff dwellings of Mesa Verde National Park (see the "Colorado's Plateau" chapter).

No matter where you choose to roam in this essential part of the Four Corners region, there are a few basic rules of cultural etiquette to observe while you are a guest on Native

LEFT: *Ladders are part of hiking into the canyons of Natural Bridges National Monument.* Sara Benson

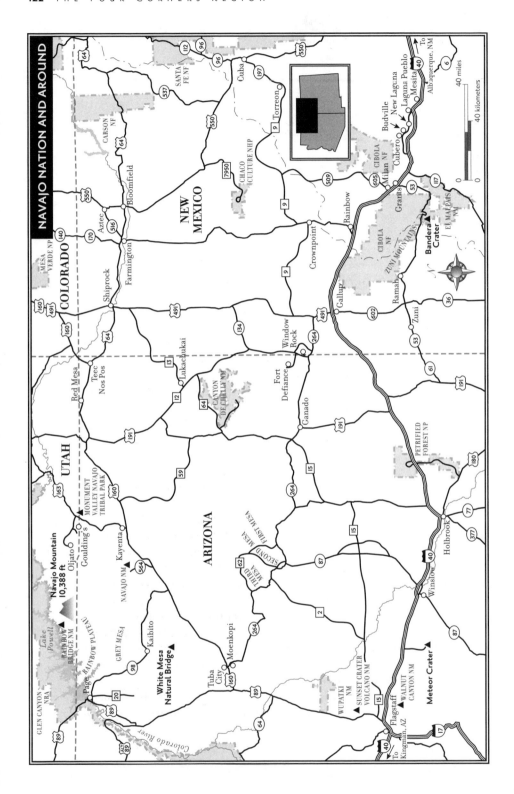

NAVAJO NATION AND AROUND

American tribal lands. Photography or recording devices of any kind might not be allowed, or their use may be subject to restrictions and require purchasing a special permit. Always ask permission before taking any photographs or video recordings, especially of local residents and at any cultural ceremonies or festivals. Respect all private property signs, and do not venture off-road either on foot or in your vehicle. Taking any souvenir artifacts is strictly prohibited, as is climbing on ruins and rock formations. Modest dress is appreciated (long pants or a skirt, and a shirt with sleeves), especially if you are invited to attend a ceremonial event that is open to the public, during which you should listen and watch with respect, which means no talking, applauding, or approaching the participants. Ask at tribal tourism offices for more specific advice about the places you are visiting. Last, alcohol is often banned on Indian reservations, which means you should not bring any alcohol with you onto tribal lands, even if you don't intend to consume it there.

Don't forget that the Navajo Nation and the state of New Mexico observe Daylight Saving Time, when clocks are set ahead one hour from the second Sunday in March until the first Sunday in November. Arizona stays on Mountain Standard Time (MST) year-round.

To visit other Native American tribal lands closer to Albuquerque, where the Indian Pueblo Cultural Center is located, turn to the "Route 66" chapter.

LODGING

Many of the places to stay on or near tribal lands are chain hotels and motels, because independent inns are few and far between. Camping is sometimes a good option (see "Recreation," below). Note that nightly accommodation taxes of 18 percent or more typically apply at hotels and motels located on the Navajo Nation.

Cameron

CAMERON TRADING POST LODGE
928-679-2231, 1-800-338-7385
www.camerontradingpost.com
P.O. Box 339, Cameron, AZ 86020
Directions: On US 89, 2 miles north of AZ 64
Price: Moderate
Credit Cards: AE, D, MC, V
Handicapped Access: Yes

A 30-minute drive from the South Rim of Grand Canyon, this historic roadside trading post has a well-kept, multilevel motel. It's also slightly misleadingly called the Grand Canyon Hotel, but don't let the remote location by itself deter you. Some of the standard rooms have handcrafted fur-niture and balconies with canyon views. All are equipped with cable TV, telephones, coffeemakers, and air-conditioning. The family-style restaurant serves American diner fare and gargantuan Navajo tacos.

CHINLE
Best Western Canyon de Chelly Inn
928-674-5874, 1-800-327-0354
www.bestwesternarizona.com
100 Main St. (BIA 102), Chinle, AZ 86503
Price: Moderate
Credit Cards: AE, D, MC, V
Handicapped Access: Yes

Although it doesn't have as many amenities as Chinle's other hotel, the Best Western charges less for its rooms, which vary in quality from darkish to recently updated. All come with satellite TVs and coffeemakers; some have balconies, too. Inquire if the indoor heated pool, hot tub, and steam room have reopened. The basic Junction Restaurant next door serves three square meals a day, including Navajo tacos.

HOLIDAY INN CANYON DE CHELLY
928-674-5000, 1-800-315-2621
www.holidayinn.com

Off BIA 27, Chinle, AZ 86503
Price: Moderate
CreditCards: AE, D, MC, V
Handicapped Access: Yes

Built on the site of old Garcia's Trading Post, this is the best hotel near Canyon de Chelly National Park. It's clean, modern, and convenient for an overnight stop. Standard rooms have cable TV, work desks, bathtubs, mini-refrigerators, microwaves, and coffeemakers. Welcome amenities include free high-speed Wi-Fi Internet access and an outdoor swimming pool.

THUNDERBIRD LODGE

928-674-5841, 1-800-679-2473
www.tbirdlodge.com
tbirdlodge@frontiernet.net
P.O. Box 548, Chinle, AZ 86503
Price: Moderate
Credit Cards: AE, D, MC, V
Handicapped Access: Yes

Offering the only lodgings inside Canyon de Chelly, the vintage T-Bird Lodge consists of low-lying pink adobe buildings shaded by cottonwood trees planted in the 1930s by the Civilian Conservation Corps. Basic rooms are equipped with ceiling fans, air-conditioning, heating, cable TV, and telephones. The furnishings feel rustic, with Navajo paintings hung on the walls. Tour guides for 4WD and horseback trips into the canyon can be hired here.

Farmington

CASA BLANCA INN

Innkeepers: David and Shirley Alford
505-327-6503, 1-800-550-6503
www.casablancanm.com
info@casablanca.com
505 E. La Plata St. (east of Court Ave.)
Farmington, NM 87401
Price: Moderate
Credit Cards: AE, MC, V
Handicapped Access: Yes

In a split-level hacienda atop a bluff, this residential neighborhood bed-and-breakfast offers travelers simple luxuries. From the handcrafted furniture to the Navajo woven rugs and Latin American textiles, nearly everything here has artful flair. Rooms are outfitted with down pillows and comforters, telephones, cable TV, high-speed Internet access, mini-refrigerators, microwaves, and coffeemakers with bean grinders. The Hideaway Room accesses a seasonal outdoor hot tub, while the upper-floor Vista Grande Suite has an enclosed sunporch. Rates include a breakfast buffet.

HOLIDAY INN EXPRESS

505-325-2545, 1-888-465-4329
www.hiexpress.com
2110 Bloomfield Blvd. (AZ 64)
Farmington, NM 87401
Price: Moderate
Credit Cards: AE, D, MC, V
Handicapped Access: Yes

The best pick of Farmington's upscale chains, this hotel has an indoor pool and hot tub, outdoor barbecue grills, and self-service guest laundry. All rooms come with satellite TVs, work desks, mini-refrigerators, microwaves, and coffeemakers, while suites have VCRs, too. Rates include high-speed Wi-Fi Internet access, a breakfast buffet, and free passes to a nearby fitness gym.

KOKOPELLI'S CAVE BED & BREAKFAST

Innkeeper: Lindy Poole
505-325-2461, 505-325-7855
www.bbonline.com/nm/kokopelli/
kokoscave@hotmail.com
3204 Crestridge Dr. (north of E. 30th St.)
Farmington, NM 87401
Price: Very Expensive
Credit Cards: AE, MC, V
Handicapped Access: No

For fans of quirky one-of-a-kind spots, an overnight stay in this cave dug 70 feet underground is an absolute treasure. Carved by a geologist out of sandstone, this one-bedroom home has a full kitchen, electricity, running hot and cold water, a waterfall shower, and flagstone hot tub. Guests must be in good physical shape because entering the cave requires hiking on a rugged trail down a steep ladder. Check-in is at the owner's house.

SILVER RIVER ADOBE INN

Innkeepers: David Beers and Diana Ohlson
505-325-8219, 1-800-382-9251
www.silveradobe.com
reservations@silveradobe.com
3151 W. Main St. (east of US 170)
Farmington, NM 87401
Price: Moderate
Credit Cards: AE, MC, V
Handicapped Access: No

Get off the beaten path at this rustic country lodge at the confluence of the San Juan and La Plata Rivers, on the west side of town. Standing atop a sandstone cliff, the house has a trio of eco-conscious guest accommodations, each with a private entrance, full bath, and a kitchenette in the guest suite. French doors open off living areas onto a peaceful riverside patio. Rates include a full healthy breakfast.

THE REGION INN

505-325-1191, 1-888-325-1191
www.theregioninn.com
reservations@theregioninn.com
601 E. Broadway (AZ 64, at Scott Ave.)
Farmington, NM 87401
Price: Moderate
Credit Cards: AE, D, MC, V
Handicapped Access: Yes

Farmington has no shortage of cheap motels, but it's worth paying a bit more to stay at this well-kept property. Standard rooms are spacious, equipped with mini-refrigerators, ceiling fans, individual climate controls, cable TV, and high-speed Internet access. Guests enjoy the outdoor swimming pool and complimentary breakfast buffet. Reservations are essential.

Fort Defiance
HOZHO RETREAT CENTER

Manager: Good Shepherd Mission
928-729-2322
www.goodshepherdmission.org
goodshepherdmission618@yahoo.com
P.O. Box 618, Fort Defiance, AZ 86504
Directions: From I-40 exit 357 take BIA 12 north for 29 miles to AZ 264, then BIA 112 northwest 7 miles. At the first stop sign, turn right, then take the next left at the post office.
Price: Inexpensive
Credit Cards: None
Handicapped Access: Yes

At this Episcopal retreat center west of Window Rock, guest rooms inside the stone cottage are open to indepedent travelers when no groups are scheduled. Most of the spartan rooms are equipped with bunk beds, although a few have full-size beds. The hostel-like common areas include a living area with cable TV and a full kitchen.

The El Rancho Hotel is where Hollywood movie stars once stayed in Gallup, New Mexico. Sara Benson & Mike Connolly

Gallup

EL RANCHO HOTEL

505-863-9311, 1-800-543-6351
www.elranchohotel.com
elrancho@cnetco.com
1000 E. Route 66, Gallup, NM 87301
Price: Moderate
Credit Cards: AE, D, MC, V
Handicapped Access: Partial

A historic Route 66 landmark, this 1937
hotel has a vintage neon sign promising
"The Charm of Yesterday, the Convenience
of Tomorrow." Built for Hollywood stars
that once made Western movies nearby,
this rambling hotel has a Southern planta-
tion portico leading inside a soaring lobby
adorned with Native American artwork.
While not luxurious, all of the antique
rooms and suites have cable TV; some have
balconies above the outdoor swimming
pool. Basic motel rooms are in a less attractive annex.

HAMPTON INN GALLUP–WEST

505-722-7224, 1-800-426-7866
www.hamptoninn.com
111 Twin Buttes Rd. (off I-40 exit 16)
Gallup, NM 87301
Price: Moderate
Credit Cards: AE, D, MC, V
Handicapped Access: Yes

At the quiet western edge of town near the
interstate, this newly built business hotel
has Route 66–themed interior design and
loads of extra amenities, including high-
speed Wi-Fi Internet access, an indoor
swimming pool and hot tub, a tiny workout
room, and a hot breakfast buffet all included
in the rates. The staff are refreshingly
professional.

Kayenta

ANASAZI INN—TSEGI CANYON

928-697-3793
www.anasaziinn.com

Soaring interior of the El Rancho Hotel. Sara Benson &
Mike Connolly

info@anasaziinn.com
P.O. Box 1543, Kayenta, AZ 86033
Directions: On US 160, 10 miles west of
Kayenta
Price: Moderate
Credit Cards: MC, V
Handicapped Access: Yes

In a remote location at the mouth of Tsegi
Canyon, this single-story motel has basic,
wood-paneled rooms with cable TVs, telephones, and sometimes kitchenettes. Rooms
are darkish but are clean and feel almost like
a cabin in the woods. Beware that those fac-
ing the highway are noisier. The café serves
diner meals, including Navajo tacos.

BEST WESTERN WETHERILL INN

928-697-3231, 1-800-780-7234
www.bestwestern.com/wetherillinn

P.O. Box 175, US 163, Kayenta, AZ 86033
Price: Moderate
Credit Cards: AE, D, MC, V
Handicapped Access: Yes

A typical chain motel beside the highway, this two-story Best Western is cheered up with Southwestern accents. Standard guest rooms have satellite TVs and air-conditioning, while some rooms enjoy free high-speed Internet access. The indoor pool is open year-round. Rates include a continental breakfast, while the family-style Golden Sands Restaurant stands next door.

HAMPTON INN KAYENTA
928-697-3170, 1-800-426-7866
www.hamptoninn.com
P.O. Box 1217, US 160, Kayenta, AZ 86033
Price: Moderate
Credit Cards: AE, D, MC, V
Handicapped Access: Yes

Offering the most peaceful atmosphere of any of Kayenta's hotels, this well-run chain offers spacious rooms with comfy beds and free high-speed Internet access. An outdoor swimming pool is open seasonally. Rates include a continental breakfast buffet served in the rustic ranch-style dining room. Conveniently for road trippers, the lobby is open 24 hours.

Kykotsmovi
HOPI CULTURAL CENTER INN
928-734-2401
www.hopiculturalcenter.com
info@hopiculturalcenter.com
P.O. Box 123, Kykotsmovi, AZ 886039
Directions: Off AZ 264, on the Second Mesa
Price: Moderate
Credit Cards: AE, D, MC, V
Handicapped Access: Yes

The only tourist hotel on Hopi tribal lands, this simple inn offers basic motel-style accommodations beside the museum.

Although well-worn rooms don't come with many amenities, it's your only option in the entire area. The inn's family-style restaurant serves reliable Southwestern fare and a few Native American specialties.

Marble Canyon
CLIFF DWELLERS LODGE
928-355-2261, 1-800-962-9755
www.cliffdwellerslodge.com
HC67, Box 30, Marble Canyon, AZ 86036
Directions: On US 89-A, 9 miles west of Navajo Bridge
Price: Moderate
Credit Cards: AE, D, MC, V
Handicapped Access: Yes

This single-story motor court near Lees Ferry is the place to come for a sociable atmosphere. The cozy guest units found inside adobe-style buildings have satellite TVs and coffeemakers. The lodge's lively restaurant and bar serve heaping plates of ranch-style cooking and beers from around the world.

LEES FERRY LODGE
AT VERMILION CLIFFS
928-355-2231, 1-800-451-2231
www.leesferrylodge.com
info@leesferrylodge.com
HC67, Box 1, Marble Canyon, AZ 86036
Directions: On US 89-A, 3.5 miles west of Navajo Bridge
Price: Moderate
Credit Cards: AE, D, MC, V
Handicapped Access: Yes

With rustic two-story buildings backed against gorgeous sandstone cliffs, this motel is ideal for active travelers who'd rather stay outside town closer to the wilderness. Wood-paneled rooms have kitschy pine furnishings, plaid and Southwest-patterned bedspreads, and gas fireplaces, but no TVs. There are only a dozen rooms, so reservations are advised.

Monument Valley

The Monument Valley Resort, www.navajo nationparks.org, an upscale 90-unit hotel being built inside the tribal park, is scheduled to open in mid-2008.

GOULDING'S LODGE

435-727-3231
www.gouldings.com
gouldings@gouldings.com
P.O. Box 360001
Monument Valley, UT 84536
Directions: On Monument Valley Rd., off US 163
Price: Moderate
Credit Cards: AE, D, MC, V
Handicapped Access: Yes

This is the traditional place to stay while visiting Monument Valley. This historic trading post lodge has an authentic Wild West atmosphere. All rooms have cable TV and VCRs or DVD players. A library of free movies to borrow includes classic Hollywood Westerns filmed nearby. Standard rooms come with mini-refrigerators, coffeemakers, and individual heating and air-conditioning units. Some rooms also have balconies. Guest amenities include a heated indoor swimming pool, small fitness room, free high-speed Wi-Fi Internet access, restaurant, trading post gallery, and complimentary museum and nightly slide-show admission for guests.

Navajo Dam

D'S BED AND BREAKFAST

Innkeeper: Chuck Pearson
505-632-0044
www.dsbandb.com
host@dsbandb.com
P.O. Box 6517, Navajo Dam, NM 87419
Directions: From NM 173 west of Navajo Dam, take Country Road 4265 south
Price: Moderate
Credit Cards: None
Handicapped Access: No

A contemporary house near Navajo Dam, this inn offers four simple bedrooms with adjacent shared bathrooms on the upper floor. Rooms have country-style furnishings, and guests enjoy free high-speed Wi-Fi Internet access. Don't miss the horizon views from wraparound porches. Secure boat storage is available for guests.

Page

CANYON COLORS BED & BREAKFAST

Innkeepers: Rich and Bev Jones
928-645-5979, 1-800-536-2530
www.canyoncolors.com
canyoncolors@webtv.net
225 S. Navajo Dr. (at 3rd Ave.)
Page, AZ 86040
Price: Moderate
Credit Cards: AE, MC
Handicapped Access: Partial

In a residential neighborhood near downtown, this back-to-basics bed-and-breakfast is run by hospitable Belgian hosts. Contemporary guest rooms all have private baths, air-conditioning, cable TV/VCRs, mini-fridges, and perhaps a wood-burning stove or whirlpool tub. Outside are a seasonal swimming pool and a patio with barbecue grills. Rates include a full breakfast. French and German are spoken.

COURTYARD PAGE

928-645-5000, 1-800-321-2211
www.marriott.com
600 Clubhouse Dr. (off US 89)
Page, AZ 86040
Price: Expensive
Credit Cards: AE, D, MC, V
Handicapped Access: Yes

On the outskirts of town near the Lake Powell National Golf Course, Page's most popular business hotel is an older property, but the atmosphere is sociable. Over 150 guest rooms are equipped with cable TVs, microwaves, mini-refrigerators, and free high-speed Wi-Fi Internet access. An outdoor heated swimming pool is open seasonally. There's also a fitness room for guests.

DAYS INN & SUITES

Manager: Traci Varner
928-645-2800, 1-877-525-3769
www.daysinn.net
961 N. US 89 (at Haul Rd.), Page, AZ 86040
Price: Moderate
Credit Cards: AE, D, MC, V
Handicapped Access: Yes

The helpful, professional staff make a real difference at this roadside chain motel, which has an outdoor swimming pool and hot tub. Standard rooms have cable TV, mini-refrigerators, and telephones, while oversize suites with separate sitting areas may have whirlpool tubs. Rates include an extended continental breakfast and free high-speed Internet access. Pets allowed.

HOLIDAY INN EXPRESS

928-645-9000, 1-800-315-2621
www.hiexpress.com
751 N. Navajo Dr., Page, AZ 86040
Price: Moderate
Credit Cards: AE, D, MC, V
Handicapped Access: Yes

Near downtown Page, this multistory business-class hotel has standard rooms with motel-style furnishings, satellite TVs, coffeemakers, mini-refrigerators, and microwaves. Some rooms and suites are equipped with kitchenettes or full kitchens. Guests enjoy free high-speed Wi-Fi Internet access and a seasonal outdoor swimming pool. Rates include a continental breakfast bar.

MOTEL 6 PAGE

Manager: Alice Yellowman
928-645-5888, 1-800-466-8356
www.motel6-page.com

637 S. Lake Powell Blvd. (US 89)
Page, AZ 86040
Price: Inexpensive
Credit Cards: AE, D, MC, V
Handicapped Access: Yes

Rising above the typical standards of a chain motel, this pet-friendly property has efficient, courteous staff and oversize rooms with all the usual amenities, including cable TV, telephones, and individual heating and air-conditioning units. Some rooms on upper floors have mountain views. High-speed Wi-Fi Internet access is complimentary.

Tuba City

QUALITY INN NAVAJO NATION

928-283-4545, 1-800-644-8383
www.choicehotels.com
P.O. Box 247, Tuba City, AZ 86045
Directions: Main St. (BIA 101) at
Moenave Rd.
Price: Moderate
Credit Cards: AE, D, MC, V
Handicapped Access: Yes

Next to a trading post and museum, this reliable chain has low-lying motel buildings and a laid-back atmosphere. All the guest rooms, some of which are pet-friendly, have high-speed Internet access and satellite TV. Guest amenities include a coin-op laundry. Out front there's a coffee shop offering high-speed Wi-Fi Internet access. The family-style Hogan Restaurant is next door.

Window Rock

QUALITY INN NAVAJO NATION CAPITAL

928-871-4108, 1-877-424-6423
www.choicehotels.com
48 W. AZ 264, Window Rock, AZ 86515
Price: Moderate
Credit Cards: AE, D, MC, V
Handicapped Access: Yes

Although most tourists stay in nearby Gallup, Window Rock does have this standard pet-friendly motel within walking distance of the tribal museum. Basic rooms with exterior access also have cable TV, coffeemakers, work desks, individual heating, and air-conditioning, and some have mini-fridges. Rates include breakfast, although the attached Dine Restaurant also serves three filling meals a day.

Zuni Pueblo

THE INN AT HALONA

Innkeepers: Roger and Elaine Dodson Thomas
505-782-4118, 505-782-4547, 1-800-752-3278
www.halona.com
halona@nm.net
23-B Pia Mesa Rd., Zuni, NM 87327

Price: Moderate
Credit Cards: MC, V
Handicapped Access: Yes

A lovely retreat in the heart of the Zuni Pueblo, this welcoming bed-and-breakfast inn inhabits two 1940s missionary adobe houses around a fountain courtyard. The interiors are adorned with Southwestern arts and crafts. Private rooms may or may not have attached baths, however. Ask for one upstairs for a more peaceful night's sleep. Rates include a hot, cooked breakfast. The common lounge has satellite TV and a VCR, while each room has its own telephone. The general store next door sells basic groceries and takeout dinners. The Pueblo museum, historical sites, and co-op art galleries are all within walking distance. Check in between 4 and 7 PM (MST).

CULTURE

Archaeological Sites

AZTEC RUINS NATIONAL MONUMENT

505-334-6174
www.nps.gov/azru
84 County Road 2900 (Ruins Rd.)
Aztec, NM 87410
Open: Daily 8–5, extended summer hours 8–6. Closed Thanksgiving, Christmas, and New Year's Day.
Admission: seven-day entry pass per adult $5, children under 16 free

On the Animas River, this low-key monument protects an Ancestral Puebloan ceremonial center. The excavated ruins are bigger than a football field. The highlight is a reconstructed Great Kiva, which gives visitors a better idea of what the ancient ruins of sacred sites found at Chaco

Walk among ancient houses at Aztec Ruins National Monument in New Mexico. Sara Benson & Mike Connolly

Culture National Historic Park and pueblos around southwestern Colorado might have looked like originally. The on-site museum screens interesting videos and lends self-guided walking tour brochure pamphlets.

CHACO CULTURE NATIONAL HISTORIC PARK

www.nps.gov/chcu
505-786-7014
P.O. Box 280, Nageezi, NM 87037
Directions: From US 550, about 3 miles southeast of Nageezi, it's a 21-mile trip on rutted dirt roads via County Roads 7900 and 7950.
Open: Daily sunrise to sunset. Visitor center open daily 8–5; closed Thanksgiving, Christmas, and New Year's Day.
Admission: seven-day entry pass per vehicle $8

Although it's out of the way nowadays, Chaco Canyon was a thriving center of Ancestral Puebloan culture between 850 and 1250 CE. From the visitor center, a paved scenic loop road passes five major Chacoan sites, all accessible via walking paths. The popular Petroglyph Trail links the ceremonial great houses of Pueblo Bonito and Chetro Ketl. Interpretive guides and back-country permits are available at the visitor center. The small observatory out back offers night-sky and daytime solar viewing.

Explore the ancient ruins of Chaco Culture National Historic Park. Sara Benson & Mike Connolly

NAVAJO NATIONAL MONUMENT

928-672-2700
www.nps.gov/nava
HC71 Box 3, Tonalea, AZ 86044
Directions: On NM 564, north of US 160 west of Kayenta
Open: Daily 9–5; extended summer hours Monday through Friday 8–5, Saturday through Sunday 8–7
Admission: Free

This peaceful park protects a trio of Ancestral Puebloan cliff dwellings, some of which can be glimpsed from viewpoints positioned along delightful nature trails with interpretive signs about culture and natural history. See the ancient ruins up close on independent hikes (free permits required) or guided tours (call ahead to check schedules).

SALMON RUINS MUSEUM AND RESEARCH LIBRARY

505-632-2013
www.salmonruins.com
P.O. Box 125, Bloomfield, NM 87413
Directions: 10 miles east of Farmington on AZ 64

Pioneer structures stand behind the Salmon Ruins Museum in New Mexico. Sara Benson & Mike Connolly

Open: Monday through Friday 8–5, Saturday 9–5, Sunday 12–5, November through April;
Monday through Friday. 8–5, Saturday 9–5, Sunday 9–5, May–October. Closed
Thanksgiving, Christmas, and New Year's Day.
Admission: Adults $3, seniors $2, children 6–16 $1, children under 6 free

Offering a variety of cultural experiences, this historical complex at the side of the highway
preserves an 11th-century Ancestral Puebloan great house and a 19th-century pioneer
homestead. A walking trail takes visitors by replicas of indigenous pit houses, Navajo
hogans, tipis, and a sweat house. At the ruins entrance, an archaeological and cultural
museum has rotating exhibitions and
hosts guest lecturers.

Art Galleries

The city of Gallup usually hosts an **Arts
Crawl** (www.gallupnm.org, 505-722-
2228) on the second Friday evening of
each month, when artists' studios are
open to the public and galleries have
openings. But you can walk around downtown anytime to see brightly painted
Native American–themed murals on several of Gallup's historic buildings.
Informative brochures about the murals
are available from the Gallup Chamber of

*Peek inside a Native American–style pithouse at the
Salmon Ruins Museum in New Mexico.* Sara Benson &
Mike Connolly

Commerce (www.gallupnm.org, 505-722-2228, 103 W. Route 66, Gallup, NM).

Artifacts Gallery, www.artifacts-gallery.com, 505-327-2907, 302 E. Main St., Farmington, NM. Downtown gallery shows off works by local artists, including watercolors, pastels, oil paintings, handcrafted jewelry, pottery, prints, and photography.

Emerson Gallery, www.emersongallery.com, 505-599-8597, 121 W. Main St., Farmington, NM. An expert dealer in Native American fine art, this warmly lit space displays original paintings, fabric art, etchings, prints, jewelry, and Navajo folk art.

Feat of Clay, 505-334-3663, 108 S. Main Ave., Aztec, NM. Cooperative art gallery sells ceramics, pottery, and works in a variety of other media by regional artists.

For more art and crafts by indige-nous artists, from Navajo rugs to carved Zuni fetishes, turn to "Native American Trading Posts and Galleries" under "Shopping," below.

Cinema

Animas 10, www.allentheatresinc.com, 505-327-7915, 4601 E. Main St., Farmington, NM. In the Animas Valley Mall, multiplex shows newly released Hollywood flicks.

El Morro Theater, www.ci.gallup.nm.us, 505-726-0050, 207 W. Coal Ave., Gallup, NM. Sometimes screens independent movies and classic movies, including an annual UFO film festival in October and intercultural film fest in November.

The historic El Morro Theater in Gallup, New Mexico, has a quirky, independent lineup. Sara Benson

Farmington Cinematheque, www.sjc.cc.nm.us, 505-566-3430, San Juan College Little Theatre, 4601 College Blvd., Farmington, NM. Screens independent, documentary, and foreign films twice a month during autumn.

Red Rock 6, www.allentheatresinc.com, 505-726-0800, 3711 Church Rock St., Gallup, NM. On the outskirts of town, multiplex screens newly released Hollywood movies.

Westates Theatres Page Mesa Theater, 928-645-9565, 42 S. Lake Powell Blvd., Page, AZ. Single-screen cinema shows new Hollywood blockbusters.

Historic Places

AZTEC MUSEUM AND PIONEER VILLAGE
505-334-9829
www.aztecnm.com

125 N. Main Ave. (US 550, at W. Chaco St.), Aztec, NM 87410
Open: Monday through Saturday 10–4; extended summer hours Monday through Saturday 9–5
Admission: Adults $3, children 12–17 $1, children under 12 free

This hodgepodge local museum is easily spotted by the antique farm equipment, pioneer cabin, blacksmith's shop, bank, and other historical buildings out back. Inside you'll find a variety of Southwestern and Old West artifacts, from Spanish colonial armor to 19th-century cowboy doodads, antique photographs, and minerals and fossils.

JÉMEZ STATE MONUMENT
505-829-3530
www.nmmonuments.org
P.O. Box 143, Jemez Springs, NM 87025
Directions: On NM 4, 1 mile north of Jemez Springs
Open: Wednesday through Monday 8:30–5
Admission: Adults $3, children under 16 free; combination ticket with Coronado State Monument $5

On a self-guided tour, learn about the history of Towa Pueblo and the 17th-century Spanish colonial missionaries who built the enormous Catholic church that now lies in ruins. Inside the visitor center a small museum presents the cultural and historical viewpoints of the indigenous peoples whose descendants still live in Jemez Pueblo. No photography allowed.

HUBBELL TRADING POST NATIONAL HISTORIC SITE
928-755-3475
www.nps.gov/hutr
P.O. Box 150, Ganado, AZ 86505
Directions: On AZ 264, .5 mile west of US 191
Open: Daily 8–5 mid-September to mid-May, 8–6 late May to early September. Closed Thanksgiving, Christmas, and New Year's Day.
Admission: Free; historic home tours $2 per person

This authentic 19th-century store on the Navajo Nation—in fact, it's the oldest trading post in the Southwest—also operates as a living museum. It looks much as it did during the Old West days, with adobe rooms layered with gorgeous Navajo rugs and dis-

A trip to Hubbell Trading Post National Historic Site is like taking a step back in time. Sara Benson & Mike Connolly

playing artisan crafts, handworked jewelry, and everyday items like cookware and basic general-store supplies. Guided tours visit the original Hubbell homestead next door.

Native American baskets are displayed and sold at Hubbell Trading Post National Historic Site. Sara Benson & Mike Connolly

Museums

For museums in the Zuni and Jemez Pueblos and on the Hopi mesas, see "Pueblos," below.

EXPLORE NAVAJO INTERACTIVE MUSEUM

928-283-5441
www.explorenavajo.com
Moenave Rd. at Main St.
Tuba City, AZ 86045
Open: Monday through Saturday 8–6, Sunday 12–6
Admission: Adults $9, seniors $7, youths 7–12 $6, children 6 and under free

Based on exhibits from the 2002 Winter Olympic Games in Salt Lake City, this custom-built museum mimics the shape of a traditional Navajo hogan. Inside visitors will find tribal arts, cultural, and historical displays, from narratives of the "Long Walk" that the Navajos took during the mid-19th-century to short films about the spiritual significance of constellations in the night sky over Navajoland. Museum tickets are also valid for viewing the Navajo code talker exhibits at the Tuba City Trading Post next door (see "Shopping," below).

FARMINGTON MUSEUM AT GATEWAY PARK

505-599-1174
www.farmingtonmuseum.org
3041 E. Main, Farmington, NM 87402
Open: Monday through Saturday 8–5
Admission: Donations accepted

On the east side of town beside the Animas River, this gigantic complex has surprisingly modern exhibits. Take a ride inside a simulated oil rig and find out about lucrative resource extraction in the San Juan Basin, then step inside the full-scale replica of the historic Three Waters Trading Post. Exhibits cover the city's history, and works by local plein-air painters are displayed during summer. The museum also runs the E^3 Children's Museum & Science Center near downtown and the Riverside Nature Center at Animas Park (see "Parks and Natural Attractions," below).

GOULDING'S MUSEUM

435-727-3231
www.gouldings.com
Goulding's Lodge, P.O. Box 360001, Monument Valley, UT 84536
Directions: On Monument Valley Rd., off US 163
Open: Daily 8–8 (limited hours November through March)
Admission: Individuals $2

Atmospherically set inside an original 1920s trading post nearby Monument Valley, this tiny two-story museum tells the history of the adventuresome Goulding family and also the Hollywood stars they invited to Monument Valley, like actor John Wayne and director John Ford, who made the valley world-famous by filming Western movies here. The antique photographs and movie memorabilia collections are diverting.

NAVAJO CODE TALKERS EXHIBIT
928-697-3534
Burger King, US 160, Kayenta, AZ 86033
Open: Daily 7–10
Admission: Free

Perhaps a more unlikely location for a mini-museum there never was. These home-grown historical displays, hidden away inside a local fast-food restaurant, tell about the valuable work that Navajo code talkers did to help the Allies win World War II. Much of the memorabilia and many photographs were in fact donated by friends and families of the code talkers themselves.

NAVAJO NATION MUSEUM
928-871-7941
www.discovernavajo.com
P.O. Box 1840, Window Rock, AZ 86515
Directions: Off AZ 264, east of BIA 12
Open: Tuesday through Friday 8–8, Monday and Saturday 8–5
Admission: Donations accepted

At the Navajo Nation Library, this small museum has rotating exhibits about the history and culture of the Diné people, from 19th-century trading posts to tribal debates with the U.S. government over land rights. Outside by the parking lot is a replica of a traditional Navajo hogan. Ask at the information desk about visiting the tribal council chambers, adorned with colorful murals. Reservations are required for tours, which may be available when the council is not in session; call ahead for more information.

ST. MICHAEL'S MISSION MUSEUM
928-871-4171
P.O. Box 680, St. Michaels, AZ 86511
Directions: South of AZ 264, approximately 4 miles west of BIA 12
Open: Usually Monday through Friday 9–5; call ahead to check hours
Admission: Donations accepted

There are many historical mission churches around the Navajo Nation, some of which are still active Episcopal and Catholic parishes, including St. Michael's. Behind the lovely tree-shaded stone church is a small historical museum. Exhibits display valuable Navajo arts, crafts, and artifacts from the 17th century when Franciscan friars first arrived here. Most interesting are early 20th-century photos of everyday life on the Navajo Nation.

STORYTELLER MUSEUM
505-722-3730
www.southwestindian.com

Gallup Cultural Center, 201 E. Route 66, Gallup, NM
Open: Monday through Friday 10–4
Admission: Donations accepted

Hidden upstairs from a coffee bar near the railroad tracks, this museum has a captivating collection of authentic Native American belongings, with many pieces donated by local families and artists. Exceptionally well-curated exhibits delve into the cultural rituals and artisan crafts of a variety of indigenous peoples around the Four Corners region. The first-floor gallery shop vends exquisite jewelry, pottery, and other works by tribal artists. For historical exhibits about World War II Navajo code talkers, visit the Gallup Chamber of Commerce (www.gallupnm.org, 505-722-2228), a few doors west.

Music, Dance, and Theater

Civic Center Foundation for the Performing Arts, www.fmtn.org, 505-599-1148, 1-877-599-3331, Miriam M. Taylor Theater, 200 W. Arrington St., Farmington, NM. Community theater presents Broadway-style and contemporary stage shows.

Gallup Courthouse, www.gallupnm.org, 505-722-2228, 201 W. Hill St., Gallup, NM. From Memorial Day through Labor Day, Native American dances takes place nightly (weather permitting) at the plaza by the courthouse, attracting huge crowds.

Gallup Cultural Center, www.southwestindian.com, 505-863-4131, 201 E. Route 66, Gallup, NM. Festivals, musical concerts, and Native American cultural performances happen here.

Gallup Performing Arts Center, www.gpac.info, 505-722-2258, 1500 S. 2nd St., Gallup, NM. Nonprofit group schedules musical and performing arts events around town, including a jazz-and-blues festival in October.

San Juan Symphony, www.sanjuansymphony.org, 505-566-3430, San Juan College, Henderson Performance Hall, 4601 College Blvd., Farmington, NM. Performs classical, pops, light opera, and folk music, and works by 20th-century composers from September through April.

Sandstone Productions, www.fmtn.org/sandstone, 505-599-1407, Lions Wilderness Park Amphitheater, 5800 College Blvd., Farmington, NM. Outdoor summer theater features modern plays.

Silhouette Performing Arts Series, www.sanjuancollege.edu, 505-566-3430, San Juan College Performance Hall and Little Theatre, 4601 College Blvd., Farmington, NM. Orchestral concerts, touring musicians, choirs, and jazz bands perform between September and May.

Summer Terrace Series, 505-599-1174, Gateway Park, 3041 E. Main St., Farmington, NM. On Saturday evenings from June through September, free, family-friendly programs are held outdoors by the river, including storytelling under the stars.

Theatre Ensemble Arts, www.tearts.org, 505-327-0076, P.O. Box 5425, Farmington, NM 87499. Award-winning community group stages independent productions of contemporary plays.

Nightlife

49er Lounge, www.elranchohotel.com, 505-863-9311, El Rancho Hotel, 1000 E. Route 66, Gallup, NM. Have a stiff drink or a cocktail where John Wayne once imbibed. This dark hideaway inside the historic El Rancho Hotel has vintage Western movie-star memorabilia.

The Bowl, 928-645-2682, 24 N. Lake Powell Blvd., Page, AZ. Downtown dive bar has foosball and billiards tables, video games, live music, and a small bowling alley.

Bowlero Lanes, 505-325-1857, 3704 E. Main St., Farmington, NM. Retro bowling alley has a shiny new sports bar with big-screen TVs and billiards tables.

Dam Bar, www.damplaza.com, 928-645-2161, 644 N. Navajo Dr., Page, AZ. Next to the Gunsmoke Saloon, this circular bar is well-positioned for watching sports on big-screen TVs, with interesting, hard-to-find microbrews on tap.

Driftwood Lounge, www.lakepowell.com, 928-645-2433, Lake Powell Resort, Wahweap Marina, Page, AZ. Skip the Rainbow Room restaurant. Instead watch the sun set over Lake Powell from the waterfront picture windows of this casual bar, which shows sports on satellite TVs.

Gunsmoke Saloon, www.damplaza.com, 928-645-2161, 644 N. Navajo Dr., Page, AZ. The most popular nightspot in Page, this energetic bar and club has a dance floor, billiards and foosball tables, video games, and live music and DJs some nights. No cover.

Ken's Old West Restaurant & Lounge, 928-645-5160, 718 Vista Ave., Page, AZ. Barn-size cowboy steakhouse has live bands and country-and-western dancing, mostly on weekends.

SunRay Park and Casino, www.sunraygaming.com, 505-566-1200, 39 County Road 5568, Farmington, NM. Open until at least 2 AM nightly, this casino has plenty of booze, slot machines, and live music in the evenings. Live horse racing is held here from early May through mid-July.

Three Rivers Tap and Game Room, www.threeriversbrewery.com, 505-324-2187, 101 E. Main St., Farmington, NM. The only brewpub around has a delicious honey wheat and several other signature brews on tap, with billiards tables in the game room a few doors east.

Pueblos

All visitors to the Jemez and Zuni Pueblos and the Hopi mesas should start their journey at the official visitor center. Tribal staff provide maps and essential information about cultural etiquette (including restrictions on photography), tourist attractions, shopping, and special events.

The Three Rivers Eatery and Brewery is a lively gathering place in downtown Farmington, New Mexico. Sara Benson & Mike Connolly

A:SHIWI A:WAN MUSEUM & HERITAGE CENTER

505-782-4403
www.ashiwi.org
Ojo Caliente Rd., Zuni, NM 87327
Directions: From Gallup take NM 602 south for 25 miles. Veer right onto BIA 4 for 5 miles, then turn right onto NM 53 for 6 more miles.
Admission: Donations accepted
Open: Usually Monday through Friday 9–5; call ahead to verify hours

After signing in and picking up a map at the Pueblo of Zuni visitor center (505-782-7238), drive into the village straight to this modest-looking museum. Fascinating exhibits teach visitors about the history of the Zuni people, from early Spanish explorers who arrived in 1540 looking for gold to the tribe's modern struggles with the U.S. government over land rights. Cultural displays explain about traditional spirituality, including the hand-carved fetishes that Zuni artists are best known for. The museum gift shop has a limited selection of books, pottery, carvings, and handworked silver jewelry. Within walking distance are two cooperatively owned artisan craft shops and the Catholic mission church on the main plaza of the pueblo, where sacred traditional dances take place.

HOPI CULTURAL CENTER AND MUSEUM

928-734-2401
www.hopiculturalcenter.com
P.O. Box 67, Second Mesa, AZ 86043
Directions: Off AZ 264 on the Second Mesa
Open: Monday through Saturday 9–5; seasonal hours may vary
Admission: Adults $3, children $1

Before visiting any of the Hopi pueblos on the First, Second, or Third Mesas nearby, drop by this small museum. Because each of the Pueblo villages has its own etiquette for visitors, ask here for advice about responsible tourism. The museum's exhibits range from the prehistory of the tribe uncovered by later archaeological excavations to ceremonial practices and the history of the cultural clashes after Europeans arrived. An art gallery displays finely worked jewelry, kachinas, basketry, and other tribal crafts next door. On weekends, events often take place in the plaza outside, including arts-and-craft fairs and traditional drumming, dancing, and chanting. Dress respectfully during your visit, preferably wearing long pants or a skirt. Remember that visitor recordings of any kind (including photography, videos, and sketching) are strictly prohibited on Hopi tribal lands.

WALATOWA VISITOR CENTER

505-834-7235
www.jemezpueblo.com
7413 NM 4, Jemez Pueblo, NM 87024
Directions: From Albuquerque take I-25 north to exit 242, then NM 44 west to US 550 north. Turn right onto NM 4 near San Isidro.
Open: Daily 8–5
Admission: Donations accepted

At the side of the highway that winds into the mountains past pottery shops and later Jémez State Monument (see "Historic Places," above), this Pueblo visitor center has a small museum. Find out about the history and culture of this unusual pueblo, which was settled after the Pueblo Revolt of 1680, and about the unique Towa dialect of the Jemez people, who are known for being storytellers. Browse the tribal basketry and pottery on display before heading off to the hot springs (see "Spas and Hot Springs," below).

Seasonal Events

JANUARY

Casper Baca Rodeo Series, www.casperbacarodeo.com, 505-287-9534, Farmington, NM

FEBRUARY

Literary Festival, www.gallupnm.org, 505-722-2040, Gallup, NM

MARCH

Annual UFO Symposium, www.aztecufo.com, 505-330-4616, Aztec, NM

APRIL

Annual After Tax Spring Fling, www.winesofthesanjuan.com, 505-632-0879, Farmington, NM

Annual Apple Blossom Contest Pow-Wow, www.sjc.cc.nm.us, 505-566-3321/3357, AZ 64 between Farmington and Bloomfield, NM

Four Corners Classic USTRC Team Roping Competition, www.gofarmington.com, 505-325-0279, 1-888-325-0279, Farmington, NM

MAY

Eastern Navajo Arts and Crafts Festival, www.discovernavajo.com, 928-810-8501, Torreon / Star Lake Chapter House, AZ

Farmington Invitational Balloon Festival, www.gofarmington.com, 505-325-0279, 1-888-325-0279, Farmington, NM

Native American Arts and Crafts Auction, www.nps.gov/hutr, 928-755-3475, Hubbell Trading Post, Ganado, AZ

Ralph Johnson Memorial Rodeo, www.discovernavajo.com, 928-810-8501, Ganado, AZ

RiverFest, www.gofarmington.com, 505-325-0279, 1-888-325-0279, Farmington, NM

Shiprock Marathon, www.shiprockmarathon.com, 928-810-8501, Shiprock, NM

JUNE

Drums of Summer, www.navajonationparks.org, 435-727-5870, Monument Valley, UT

Fiesta Days, www.aztecchamber.com, 505-334-9551, Aztec, NM

Lions Club Rodeo, www.gallupnm.org, 505-722-2040, Gallup, NM

Natoni Horse Race, www.discovernavajo.com, 928-810-8501, Rocky Ridge, AZ

Navajo Nation Museum Music Festival, www.discovernavajo.com, 928-871-7941, Window Rock, AZ

JULY

4th of July Celebrations, www.discovernavajo.com, 928-810-8501, Window Rock, AZ

4th of July Rodeo, www.casperbacarodeo.com, 505-287-9534, Kayenta, NM

Animas River Blues Festival, www.animasriverblues.com, 505-334-9551, Aztec, NM

Balloon Rally, www.aztecchamber.com, 505-334-9551, Aztec, NM

Land of Enchantment Rod Run, www.gofarmington.com, 505-325-0279, 1-888-325-0279, Farmington, NM

Monument Valley Independence Day Celebration, www.navajonationparks.org, 435-727-5870, Monument Valley, AZ

Narbona Pass Classic, www.discovernavajo.com, 928-810-8501, Crystal / Sheep Springs, NM

AUGUST

Gallup Inter-Tribal Indian Ceremonial, www.gallupintertribal.com, 505-863-3896, Gallup, NM

Connie Mack Amateur Baseball World Series, www.cmws.org, 505-327-9673, Farmington, NM

San Juan County Fair, www.gofarmington.com, 505-325-5415, 1-800-448-1240, Farmington, NM

Zuni Tribal Fair, www.zunitourism.com, 505-782-4371, Zuni, NM

SEPTEMBER

Aztec Founder's Day, www.aztecchamber.com, 505-334-9551, Aztec, NM

Antique Truck Show, www.aztecchamber.com, 505-333-2599, Aztec, NM

Navajo Nation Fair, www.navajonationfair.com, 928-871-6478, Window Rock, AZ

Totah Festival Indian Market & Pow Wow, www.gofarmington.com, 505-325-0279, 1-888-325-0279, Farmington, NM

Wines of the San Juan Harvest Festival, www.winesofthesanjuan.com, 505-632-0879, Farmington, NM

Zuni Fair, www.ashiwi.org, 505-782-7238, Zuni, NM

OCTOBER

Festival of Cultures, www.gallupnm.org, 505-722-2228, Gallup, NM

Four Corners Storytelling Festival, www.gofarmington.com, 505-325-0279, 1-888-325-0279, Farmington, NM

NMRA Rodeo Finals, www.casperbacarodeo.com, 505-287-9534, Farmington, NM

Oktoberfest, www.aztecchamber.com, 1-888-838-9551, Aztec, NM

Pumpkin Festival, www.pagelakepowelltourism.com, 928-645-2741, 1-888-261-7243, Page, AZ

Shiprock Navajo Fair, www.discovernavajo.com, 928-810-8501, Shiprock, NM

NOVEMBER
Page–Lake Powell Hot Air Balloon Regatta, www.pagelakepowelltourism.com, 928-645-4216, 1-888-261-7243, Page, AZ

DECEMBER
Festival of Lights, www.pagelakepowelltourism.com, 928-645-2741, 1-888-261-7243, Page, AZ

Imagine the Enchantment Christmas Festival, www.aztecchamber.com, 505-333-2599, Aztec, NM

Luminaria Lights, www.nps.gov/hutr, 928-755-3475, Hubbell Trading Post, Ganado, AZ

Navajo Nativity, www.gofarmington.com, 505-325-0279, 1-888-325-0279, Farmington, NM

Red Rock Balloon Rally, www.redrockballoonrally.com, 505-722-2228, Gallup, NM

Riverglo, www.gofarmington.com, 505-325-0279, 1-888-325-0279, Farmington, NM

Salmon Ruins Holiday Arts and Crafts Fair, www.salmonruins.com, 505-632-2013, Aztec, NM

RESTAURANTS

For more basic places to stop and eat as you're passing through remote places, especially on Navajo and Hopi tribal lands, see also the "Lodging" section above.

Aztec

MAIN STREET BISTRO
505-334-0109
www.aztecmainstreetbistro.com
122 N. Main Ave. (US 550)
Aztec, NM 87410
Open: Monday through Saturday
Price: Inexpensive
Cuisine: Deli
Serving: B, L
Credit Cards: MC, V
Handicapped Access: Yes

A friendly little oasis in downtown Aztec, opposite the local history museum, this petite deli and kitchen makes toasty sandwiches, garden salads, house-made soups, and fresh-baked quiches and pastries.

Order a picnic lunch to go, then enjoy it at the parasol-shaded patio tables outside. Free Wi-Fi Internet access available.

RUBIO'S
505-334-0599
116 S. Main St. (US 550), Aztec, NM 87410
Open: Daily
Price: Moderate
Cuisine: Mexican
Serving: L, D
Credit Cards: AE, D, MC, V
Handicapped Access: Yes

Inside a historic building decorated with colorful murals right in downtown Aztec, this family-style Mexican restaurant is a pretty spot to stop and catch your breath while you fork into New Mexican favorites like enchiladas, tacos, and plates of fresh tortillas topped with cheese and red- and green-chili sauces. Ingredients are fresh and often raised locally, which makes it delicious.

Farmington

ANDREA KRISTINA'S KAFE

505-327-3133
www.andreakristinas.com
218 W. Main St. (at N. Allen Ave.)
Farmington, NM 87401
Open: Monday through Saturday
Price: Moderate
Cuisine: New American
Serving: B, L, D
Credit Cards: MC, V
Handicapped Access: Yes

Hidden at the back of an independent bookstore, this bustling kitchen makes small batches of deli sandwiches, garden-fresh salads, and homemade soups. Many of the café's signature items exhibit a Southwestern twist, like the Hemingway Sandwich (sliced roast beef, avocado, and green-chili cream cheese). Gourmet pastries and espresso drinks are available to go, or enjoy them at wooden tables set cozily beside the bookshelves.

BOON'S FAMILY THAI BBQ

505-325-5556
321 W. Main St. (at S. Behrend Ave.)
Farmington, NM 87401
Open: Monday through Saturday
Price: Moderate
Cuisine: Thai
Serving: L, D
Credit Cards: AE, D, MC, V
Handicapped Access: Yes

A diminutive downtown eatery, reliable Boon's serves a menu of Thai standards that are several notches above par, from a rainbow of curry flavors to the classic barbecue dishes. Service is friendly and quick. Boon's also has a second branch in the nearby town of Aztec at 104 S. Main Avenue (505-334-1234).

LOS HERMANITOS

505-326-5664
www.loshermanitos.com
3501 E. Main St. (east of S. Browning Pkwy.), Farmington, NM 87402
Open: Monday through Saturday
Price: Moderate
Cuisine: New Mexican
Serving: B, L, D
Credit Cards: AE, D, MC, V
Handicapped Access: Yes

Splashed with colorful murals and south-of-the-border artwork, this festive eatery serves authentic New Mexican cuisine and more innovative recipes created by the same family who also run the second Los Hermanitos restaurant west of downtown. Wake up to chorizo egg dishes, or show up later in the day for stuffed sopapillas, stacked enchiladas, and sizzling fajitas.

THREE RIVERS EATERY & BREWERY

505-324-2187
www.threeriversbrewery.com
101 E. Main St. (at S. Orchard Ave.)
Farmington, NM 87401
Open: Daily
Price: Expensive
Cuisine: American
Serving: L, D
Credit Cards: AE, D, MC, V
Handicapped Access: Yes

In a 1912 redbrick building, this comfy downtown brewpub is always hopping, especially after dark. Crowds gather not only for the delicious microbrews on tap, but also for hearty fare like hickory-smoked ribs, biscuit-battered catfish, "drunken" marinated rib eye steak, and green-chili chicken soup. Daily specials include all-you-can-eat pasta nights and half-price gourmet Angus burgers. A few doors down you'll find the tap and game room (see "Nightlife," above).

Gallup

EARL'S

505-863-4201
1400 E. Route 66 (off I-40 exit 22)
Gallup, NM 87310
Open: Daily
Price: Moderate
Cuisine: American
Serving: B, L, D
Credit Cards: AE, MC, V
Handicapped Access: Yes

In business for more than 60 years, this old-fashioned diner is best known for the invited Native American artisans who circulate among the tables, chatting with customers and selling their wares. (If you'd prefer not to be approached, there's a convenient sign you can put on your table.) The home-cooked food here ranges from New Mexican enchiladas to country-style chicken-fried steaks, with sweet fruit and cream pies for dessert.

OLYMPIC KITCHEN

505-863-2584
3200 W. Route 66 (off I-40 exit 16)
Gallup, NM 87301
Open: Daily
Price: Moderate
Cuisine: Mexican
Serving: B, L, D
Credit Cards: AE, D, MC, V
Handicapped Access: Yes

Route 66 running through Gallup has more than its fair share of diners, but this Greek-run joint offers fantastic value. There's an extensive wine list and a giant menu with several pages devoted just to Greek, Italian, and Mexican cuisine. It's the authentic-tasting falafel, shawarma, and gyro plates that are sure to please.

RANCH KITCHEN

505-722-5696
3001 W. Route 66, Gallup, NM 87301
Open: Daily
Price: Moderate
Cuisine: Steaks/Southwestern
Serving: B, L, D
Credit Cards: AE, D, MC, V
Handicapped Access: Yes

A landmark on Route 66, the restaurant is remarkable just for the kitschy-cool sign out front. Dating back to the 1950s, this rustic Western steakhouse and ranch dining room boasts a hearty menu of Southwestern favorites, from mesquite-grilled chicken, ribs, and beef to eggs topped with green-chili sauce at breakfast. The waitstaff are friendly, too.

Marble Canyon

CLIFF DWELLERS LODGE

928-355-2261
www.cliffdwellerslodge.com
HC67, Box 30, Marble Canyon, AZ 86036

The Ranch Kitchen is just one of Gallup's many Route 66 landmarks. Sara Benson & Mike Connolly

Directions: On US 89-A, 9 miles west of Navajo Bridge
Open: Daily
Price: Expensive
Cuisine: Western/steakhouse
Serving: B, L (during winter, Saturday through Sunday only), D
Credit Cards: AE, D, MC, V
Handicapped Access: Yes

A rustic restaurant where the staff seem to know almost everyone's name, this spot dishes up the best Western grill and cookhouse fare for miles around. Chatty waitresses bring out huge breakfast plates of pancakes and egg scrambles at breakfast, steak-and-cheese and California club sandwiches at lunch, and barbecue and surf-and-turf feasts for dinner. The bar stays lively late into the evening.

Monument Valley
STAGECOACH DINING ROOM
435-727-3231
www.gouldings.com
P.O. Box 360001
Monument Valley, UT 84536
Directions: On Monument Valley Rd., off US 163
Open: Daily
Price: Expensive
Cuisine: American
Serving: B, L, D
Credit Cards: AE, D, MC, V
Handicapped Access: Yes

Upstairs at historic Goulding's Lodge, this casual family-style restaurant has picture windows looking out onto the beautiful sandstone buttes and mesas of nearby Monument Valley. The overstuffed country-style menu of American, Mexican, and Western fare includes homemade stews and local specialties like Navajo fry bread served with drizzled honey. Service is laid back.

Page
BLUE CORN RESTAURANT
928-645-8851
Quality Inn Lake Powell, 287 N. Lake Powell Blvd. (US 89), Page, AZ 86040
Open: Daily
Price: Moderate
Cuisine: Mexican/Southwestern
Serving: B, D
Credit Cards: AE, D, MC, V
Handicapped Access: Yes

Tribally owned and operated by the Navajo Nation, this casual restaurant inside a chain hotel may look suspiciously empty. Yet there's no better place in town to try a Navajo taco: fry bread piled high with pinto beans, seasoned beef, shredded lettuce and cheese, diced tomatoes and onions, and sliced jalapeño chilies. During the day, the family-friendly dining room has a few distant views of Glen Canyon.

DAM BAR & GRILLE
928-645-2161
www.damplaza.com
644 N. Navajo Dr. (at US 89)
Page, AZ 86040
Open: Daily
Price: Expensive
Cuisine: Southwestern
Serving: L, D
Credit Cards: MC, V
Handicapped Access: Yes

Although this polished-looking pub appears to promise more than it can always deliver, the fun, funky Southwestern menu of salads, sandwiches, and more will more than fill you up. "Dam Big Burgers" and huge plates of nachos topped with green chilies could easily feed two hungry hikers or river rafters. Wash it all down with tasty microbrews from the bar (see "Nightlife," above).

FIESTA MEXICANA
928-645-4082
125 S. Lake Powell Blvd. (US 89), Page, AZ
Open: Daily
Price: Moderate
Cuisine: Mexican/American
Serving: L, D
Credit Cards: AE, D, MC, V
Handicapped Access: Yes

Colorfully brightening up Page's main drag, this rambunctious Mexican eatery is always jumping. Though busy, it's still the place to come after sunset for a fruity margarita. Service is iffy, but the welcome menu of Mexican-American favorites will sate any appetite, ranging from Baja-style fish tacos to the spicy *camarones diablo* (devil shrimp).

STROMBOLLI'S
928-645-2605
711 N. Navajo Dr. (at US 89)
Page, AZ 86040
Open: Daily
Price: Inexpensive
Cuisine: Italian
Serving: L, D
Credit Cards: MC, V
Handicapped Access: No

For famished road trippers, there's no better place in Page to stuff yourself silly with fresh-baked calzones that are as big as your head, wagon-wheel-size pizzas, and thickly sliced garlic bread. Because service can be slow, takeout is recommended. Then you can chow down at outdoor tables underneath an awning striped by the colors of the Italian flag or out by Lake Powell.

Food Purveyors

Andrea Kristina's Kafe, 505-327-3133, 218 W. Main St., Farmington, NM. Bookstore's espresso bar serves fresh-brewed or blended coffee drinks and chai teas (see also "Restaurants," above).

Beans Gourmet Coffee House, www.damplaza.com, 928-645-6858, 644 N. Navajo Dr., Page, AZ. In-the-know locals' place for a caffeinated pick-me-up and pastries. Free Wi-Fi Internet access available.

Chile Shop, www.artifacts-gallery.com, 505-327-2907, 302 E. Main St., Farmington, NM. Inside Artifacts Gallery (see "Art Galleries," above), this culinary specialty shop sells hot-and-spicy southwestern foodstuffs made with chilies.

The Coffee House, 505-726-0291, 203 W. Coal Ave., Gallup, NM. Downtown coffee shop has an art gallery and coffee, teas, espresso, and fresh-made noshes to jump-start your morning.

Main Street Bistro, 505-334-0109, 122 N. Main Ave. (US 550), Aztec, NM. At this colorful café (see also "Restaurants," earlier), baristas brew up hot lattes and frothy cappuccinos.

Something Special Bakery and Tea Room, 505-325-8183, 116 N. Auburn Ave., north of Main St., Farmington, NM. Whimsical cottage offers freshly baked pastries and sugary desserts, elegant pots of tea, and light, vegetarian-friendly meals.

The Vanilla Moose, 505-334-6712, 1721 W. Aztec Blvd. (NM 516), Aztec, NM. Cute as a button, this butter-yellow roadside cottage serves ice-cream shakes, floats, and sweet nostalgia treats.

RECREATION

Boating and Water Sports

Many marinas and shops around Lake Powell and in Page rent water-sports equipment and watercraft.

Lake Powell Resorts & Marinas, www.lakepowell.com, 1-888-896-3829, 100 Lakeshore Dr., Page, AZ. Rents houseboats at Wahweap, Bullfrog, and Halls Crossing marinas. Also offers wakeboard and waterskiing instruction, guided fishing trips, and scenic cruises.

Navajo Lake State Park, www.nmparks.com, 505-632-2278, 1448 NM 511, Navajo Dam, NM. New Mexico's largest lake offers all kinds of water sports, including waterskiing, jet skiing, houseboating, cruising, sailing, and scuba diving. Several marinas nearby rent fishing boats and water-sports equipment.

Rivers & Oceans, www.rivers-oceans.com, 928-526-4575, 1-800-473-4576, 12620 N. Copeland Lane, Flagstaff. Arranges multiday sea-kayaking tours of Lake Powell.

Twin Finn Diving, www.twinfinn.com, 928-645-3114, 811 Vista Ave., Page, AZ. Full-service PADI shop rents sit-upon and sea kayaks for Lake Powell trips.

Camping

National parks and other federal recreation lands offer developed campgrounds with tent and RV sites and basic facilities (such as flush toilets, water). Most campgrounds have limited first-come, first-served campsites, including at Chaco Culture National Historical Park (see "Archaeological Sites," earlier), Natural Bridges National Monument, Canyon de Chelly National Monument, and inside Glen Canyon National Recreation Area (see "Parks and Natural Attractions," below). Other recommended campgrounds:

Angel Peak Campground, www.blm.gov/nm, 505-599-8900, County Road 7175, off US 550 approximately 15 miles southeast of Bloomfield, NM. Has tent sites with vault toilets (no water), atop a remote canyon in Angel Peak Recreation Area.

Lake Powell Resorts & Marinas, www.lakepowell.com, 1-888-896-3829, Glen Canyon National Recreation Area, AZ and UT. Private campgrounds provide tent and RV sites with full hookups at Wahweap Marina outside Page, Arizona, and Bullfrog and Halls Crossing in southern Utah.

Monument Valley Tribal Park, www.navajonationparks.org, 435-727-5874/5870, off US 163, Monument Valley, UT. Campsites with views of red-rock cliffs have picnic tables and flush toilets available.

Navajo Lake State Park, www.newmexico.reserveworld.com, 505-632-2278, 1-877-644-7787, 1448 NM 511, Navajo Dam, NM. Offers tent and RV sites with electrical hookups, some reservable six months in advance.

Spider Rock Campground, www.spiderrockcampground.com, 928-674-8261, off BIA 7, Chinle, AZ. About 10 miles east of the Canyon de Chelly visitor center, a hospitable local host offers shady tent and RV sites on the forested canyon rim and overnight stays in a forked Navajo timber-and-adobe hogan.

Cycling and Mountain Biking

In Farmington, New Mexico, mountain bikers hit the **Road Apple Trail**, which starts behind San Juan College and heads to Farmington Lake. The **Road Apple Rally** (www.roadapplerally.com) happens in early October. Shorter, easier trails around Farmington include **Kinsey's Ridge** at the end of Foothills Boulevard and Piñon Mesa, on NM 170 about 3 miles north of Main Street. Outside the nearby town of Aztec, the **Alien Run** (www.aztecufo.com) mountain-bike race in late April passes an alleged UFO crash site.

Around Gallup, popular mountain-biking routes include the **Pyramid and Church Rock Trails** inside **Red Rock Park** (505-722-3839, NM 566, Churchrock, NM), about 5 miles east of town, and the **High Desert Trail system,** matching a variety of skill levels with eagle-eye views from the mesas, off Chino Road, 3 miles north of Gallup via US 491.

Many of the rugged 4WD roads within **Glen Canyon National Recreation Area** (www.nps.gov/glca, 928-608-6200, P.O. Box 1507, Page, AZ 86040) are open to mountain bikers. **Lakeside Bikes** (www.lakesidebikes.net, 928-645-2266, 118 6th Ave., off US 89, Page, AZ) offers rentals, repairs, and guided rides near Lake Powell.

Fishing

For fishing regulations and to buy licenses online, contact the **New Mexico Game and Fish Department** (www.wildlife.state.nm.us, 505-476-8000). Contact **Navajo Fish and Wildlife** (www.navajofishandwildlife.org, 928-871-6451/6452, P.O. Box 1480, Window Rock, AZ 86515) for fishing permits, regulations, and a list of lakes on the Navajo Nation that are stocked with rainbow trout, bluegill, and catfish.

East of Aztec, New Mexico, at **Navajo Lake State Park** (www.nmparks.com, 505-632-2278, 1448 NM 511, Navajo Dam, NM), fishers catch trout, salmon, bass, northern pike, catfish, and crappie. Marina shops selling fishing tackle and renting watercraft surround the lake (see "Boating and Water Sports," above). The **San Juan River,** including near Navajo Dam, is the place for fly-fishing. Local outfitters offer guide services and fly-fishing lessons, including **Aztec Anglers** (www.aztecanglers.com, 1-800-811-8211), **Resolution Guide Service** (www.sanjuanfishing.com, 1-888-328-1858, Rainbow Lodge, County Road 4277 off NM 173, Navajo Dam, NM), and **Sandstone Anglers** (www.sandstoneanglers.com, 1-888-339-9789, 83 County Road 2929, Aztec, NM).

Fly fishers can also cast on the **Colorado River** at Lees Ferry, west of Page, Arizona. Hire guides through **Marble Canyon Outfitters** (www.leesferryflyfishing.com, 928-645-9235, 1-800-533-7339, P.O. Box 6032, Marble Canyon, AZ 86036).

Fitness Facilities

Blue Mesa Studio, 505-793-5760, 505-402-8582, 1717 E. 20th St., Farmington, NM; 109 W. Chaco St., Aztec, NM. Pilates and a variety of drop-in yoga classes; call ahead for schedules.

Health and Human Performance Center, www.sanjuancollege.edu, 505-566-3410, San Juan College, 4601 College Blvd., Farmington, NM. Cardio and weight machines, a small indoor track, climbing wall, and outdoor equipment rentals.

Royal Spa Fitness Center, 505-326-2211, 2101 Bloomfield Highway, Farmington, NM. Cardio and weight machines, tennis and racquetball courts, a heated indoor swimming pool, sauna, steam room, and aerobics classes.

Golf

Hidden Valley Country Club 505-334-3248, 29 County Road 3025, Aztec, NM. Rolling grasslands with desert scenery of unique rock formations. Public, 18 holes, 6,100 yards, par 70; cart rentals, clubhouse, restaurant.

Lake Powell National Golf Course, www.golflakepowell.com, 928-645-2023, 400 Clubhouse Dr., Page, AZ. Four-star municipal greens with distant views of Lake Powell. Public, 18 holes, 7,064 yards, par 72; club rentals, driving range, lessons, pro shop.

Piñon Hills Golf Course, www.farmington.nm.us, 505-326-6066, 2101 Sunrise Pkwy., Farmington, NM. Top-rated municipal golf course has sandstone canyons and long arroyos (dry washes). Public, 18 holes, 7, 249 yards, par 72; driving range, lessons, pro shop, restaurant.

Riverview Golf Course, 505-598-0140, 64 County Road 6520, Kirtland, NM. Championship layout has a classic front nine followed by a high-desert back nine, with views of Shiprock and the La Plata Mountains. Public, 18 holes, 6,853 yards, par 72; club and cart rentals, driving range, pro shop, putting and pitching greens, snack bar.

Hiking and Backpacking

There are many hiking trails made for all skill levels in **Chaco Culture National Historic Park** (see "Archaeological Sites," above), at **Navajo National Monument,** and around **Glen Canyon National Recreation Area** (see "Parks and Natural Attractions," below). In Navajoland the rugged backpacking routes to **Rainbow Bridge** around either the south or north side of Navajo Mountain take total self-sufficiency, a good topographic map, and excellent route-finding skills. Watch out for flash floods and check the weather forecast first. Mandatory camping and hiking permits are issued in advance by the **Navajo Parks and Recreation Department** (www.navajonationparks.org, 928-871-6647) and in person at the **Antelope Canyon Tribal Park Office** (928-698-2808, Coppermine Rd., Page, AZ).

Horseback Riding

For guided trips in Monument Valley and Canyon de Chelly, see "Tours and Guided Adventures," below.

In the canyons of Navajo National Monument, hiking trails lead to ancient cliff dwellings.

Sara Benson & Mike Connolly

Parks and Natural Attractions

ANTELOPE VALLEY–LAKE POWELL NAVAJO TRIBAL PARK

928-698-2808
www.navajonationparks.org
P.O. Box 4803, Page, AZ 86040
Park Office: Off Coppermine Rd. (AZ 98/BIA 20), 3 miles south of Page
Open: Entrance station daily 8–5, March through October; Lower and Upper Antelope Canyon open year-round for guided tours only
Admission: Individuals $6, children 7 and under free (excluding guided tour fees)

Among the most popular slot canyons in the Southwest, the carved sandstone passages of hidden Upper and Lower Antelope Canyons stun the daily crowds of visitors. Tour guides are required for entrance to both Upper and Lower Antelope Canyon (for recommended tour operators, see "Tours and Guided Adventures," below). If you wish to independently explore Water Holes Canyon, the required hiking permits are sold at the tribal park's main office. Watch out for flash floods, and always check the weather forecast first.

BISTI/DE-NA-ZIN WILDERNESS

505-599-8900
www.nm.blm.gov
Field Office: 1235 La Plata Highway
Farmington, NM 87401
Directions: From Farmington take NM 371 south for 36.5 miles, then turn left onto gravel NCM Road 7297 for 2 miles.
Open: 24/7/365
Admission: Free

In a remote area not often visited by tourists, the Bureau of Land Management (BLM) protects an outdoor geological wonderland of eroded shale hills presenting some of the Southwest's most playful and otherworldly landscapes. Photographers should arrive before sunset to catch the most atmospheric lighting. Full moon hikes are an ethereal experience.

Artificial Glen Canyon Dam dominates the natural landscape outside Page, Arizona. Mike Connolly

CANYON DE CHELLY NATIONAL MONUMENT

928-674-5500
www.nps.gov/cach
P.O. Box 588, Chinle, AZ 86503
Directions: On BIA 7, 3 miles east of US 191 in Chinle
Open: Visitor center open daily 8–5; closed Christmas Day. Scenic drives open 24/7/365.
Admission: Free

In the heart of the Navajo Nation, this canyon monument protects ancient archaeological sites, including rock-art petroglyphs. Visitors are free to independently take scenic drives past viewpoints along the south and north rim and to walk the steep, rocky White House Ruins Trail down for about a mile into the canyon. For more in-depth journeys into the canyon via 4WD vehicles or on horseback, a Navajo tour guide is required (see "Tours and Guided Adventures," below).

Sandstone formations glow at sunset around Glen Canyon National Recreation Area. Sara Benson

FOUR CORNERS MONUMENT

928-871-6647
www.navajonationparks.org
P.O. Box 2520, Window Rock, AZ 86515
Directions: Off US 160, northeast of Teec Nos Pos
Open: Daily 8–5, October–May; 7–8, May–September
Admission: Individuals $3

Although it doesn't offer much more than souvenir shops, this tribal park proves irresistible to anyone who wants to snap a photo of themselves standing on the concrete memorial that marks the point where all four states—Arizona, Utah, Colorado, and New Mexico—meet.

GLEN CANYON NATIONAL RECREATION AREA

www.nps.gov/glca, www.glencanyonnha.org
928-608-6200
P.O. Box 1507, Page, AZ 86040
Directions: Carl Hayden Visitor Center is off US 89, west of Glen Canyon Dam.
Open: Carl Hayden Visitor Center open daily 8–6 during summer, 8–5 spring and fall, 8–4 December through February. Seasonal tour hours vary.
Admission: seven-day entry pass per vehicle $15

An epic landscape of drowned canyons, artificial lakes, and desert washes, this million-acre-plus recreational area offers a wealth of opportunities for outdoor activities, from mountain biking and hiking to all kinds of water sports, including boating, kayaking, waterskiing, and swimming (see "Boating and Water Sports," above). For helpful information, stop by the Carl Hayden Visitor Center, from where guided tours of Glen Canyon Dam depart. The main marinas are at Wahweap, Bullfrog, and Halls Crossing. Detours to historic Lees Ferry on the Colorado River near Navajo Bridge will reward history buffs and nature lovers; it's a 40-mile drive west of Page, Arizona.

MONUMENT VALLEY NAVAJO TRIBAL PARK

435-727-5874/5870
www.navajonationparks.org
P.O. Box 360289, Monument Valley, UT 84536
Directions: Off US 163, north of Kayenta
Open: Visitor center daily 6–8, May through September; 7–7, October through April.
Scenic drive open daily 6–8:30, May through September; 8–4:30, October through March.
Park closed Thanksgiving and Christmas Day.
Admission: Individuals $5, children under 10 free

Sacred to the Diné people, Monument Valley became famous when Western director John Ford and other Hollywood stars like John Wayne arrived here to make movie magic. Climb the deck outside the visitor center for panoramic views of the Mitten Buttes. The views are even more impressive if you drive on the rough dirt road down into the valley. Guided 4WD tours that venture off the tourist loop, as well as horseback rides and overnight trips, can be arranged at the entrance (see "Tours and Guided Adventures," below).

NATURAL BRIDGES NATIONAL MONUMENT

435-962-1234
www.nps.gov/nabr
HC-60 Box 1, Lake Powell, UT 84533
Directions: On UT 475, north of UT 95, about 35 miles west of Blanding, UT
Open: 24/7/365. Visitor center daily 8–5; closed Thanksgiving, Christmas, and New Year's Day.
Admission: seven-day entry pass per individual $3, per vehicle $6

Look up after hiking down to the river inside Natural Bridges National Monument. Sara Benson

Indigenous peoples once made their home inside this windswept canyon. Today a scenic driving loop passes by viewpoints and hiking trailheads that lead via ladders down into the canyon right underneath the sacred sandstone arches. Evening ranger programs often include stargazing, because the night skies here are remarkably clear.

RIVERSIDE NATURE CENTER

505-599-1422
www.farmingtonmuseum.org/naturecenter.html
Animas Park, off Browning Pkwy., Farmington, NM 87401
Open: Tuesday through Saturday 1–6, Sunday 1–5
Admission: Free

Run by the educational Farmington Museum (see "Museums," above), this peaceful city park protects a swath of wetlands next to an oxbow bend in the Animas River. Come for wildlife watching and to wander through xeriscape demonstration gardens. Docents lead birding walks, stargazing events, and storytelling programs for families.

Racquet Sports

Farmington, New Mexico, has an indoor recreational center (505-599-1184, www.farm ington.nm.us, 1101 Fairgrounds Rd., Farmington, NM) with five racquetball courts. Contact the Farmington Department of Parks and Recreation (505-599-1184) for the locations of outdoor tennis courts in city parks, including those lighted for night play.

Rock Climbing

Rock climbing on the Navajo Nation is forbidden, which includes Monument Valley, because many rock formations are sacred sites to the Diné people.

Outside Gallup, **Mentmore Rock Climbing Area** offers dozens of bolted top-rope and sport climbs. To get there from NM 118, take County Road north for 1 mile, then drive west on Mentmore Road.

For indoor climbing gyms, see "Fitness Facilities," above.

Spas and Hot Springs

Northwest of Jemez Pueblo (see "Pueblos," earlier), downtown **Jemez Springs** has indoor bathhouses for soaking in mineral waters; make advance appointments for spa treatments. The historic **Jemez Springs Bathhouse** (www.jemezspringsbathhouse.com, 505-829-3303, 1-866-204-8303, #062 Jemez Springs Plaza, Jemez Springs, NM) offers private concrete tubs, while **Giggling Springs** (www.gigglingsprings.com, 575-829-9175, 040 Abousleman Loop, Jemez Springs, NM) has a rock-rimmed soaking pool by the natural cold-plunge Jemez River. For directions to rustic hot-springs pools that are free for public entry and open for day use only, contact the **Santa Fe National Forest** (www.fs.fed.us/r3/sfe, 505-829-3535, P.O. Box 150, Jemez Springs, NM 87025).

Swimming

See also "Fitness Facilities," above.

Brookside Park Pool, www.fmtn.org, 505-599-1188, 1901 N. Dustin Ave., Farmington, NM. Call ahead for lap and public swim hours at this outdoor summer pool.

Farmington Aquatic Center, www.fmtn.org, 505-599-1167, 1151 N. Sullivan Ave., Farmington, NM. Indoor year-round facility offers an Olympic-size pool, diving boards, and a waterslide.

Gallup Aquatic Center, 505-726-5460, 620 S. Boardman Ave. (NM 564), Gallup, NM. Recently built complex has indoor competition-size lap pools, a waterslide, and lazy river ride.

Navajo Lake State Park, www.nmparks.com, 505-632-2278, 1448 NM 511, Navajo Dam, NM. New Mexico's largest lake offers swimming (see "Boating and Water Sports," above).

Page Swimming Pool, 928-645-4380, 454 S. Lake Powell Blvd. (US 89), Page, AZ. Call ahead for public lap swim and aquatic exercise hours.

Tours and Guided Adventures

For boating tours on Lake Powell and to Rainbow Bridge, see "Boating and Water Sports," above. Even for popular trips listed below, same-day reservations may be available.

Antelope Canyon Navajo Tours, www.navajotours.com, 928-698-3384, P.O. Box 4586, Page, AZ. Standard tours of Upper Antelope Canyon (see "Parks and Natural Attractions," above) and extended photography trips led by Navajo guides.

Antelope Canyon Tours, www.antelopecanyon.com, 928-645-9102, 1-866-645-9102, 22 S. Lake Powell Blvd. (US 89), Page, AZ. Navajo-owned and operated company offers stan-

River runners launch from historic Lees Ferry for rafting trips through the Grand Canyon of the Colorado River. Sara Benson & Mike Connolly

dard and extended photography tours of Upper Antelope Canyon (see "Parks and Natural Attractions," above).

Colorado River Discovery, www.raftthecanyon.com, 1-888-522-6644, 130 6th Ave., Page, AZ. Arranges smooth-water float trips from Glen Canyon Dam to Lees Ferry, passing by petroglyphs and a famous horseshoe bend in the Colorado River.

Ken's Tours, www.lowerantelope.com, 928-606-2168, P.O. Box 117, Page, AZ 86040. Offers guided tours of Lower Antelope Canyon.

Lake Powell Resorts & Marinas, www.lakepowell.com, 1-888-896-3829, 100 Lakeshore Dr., Page, AZ. Offers scenic Lake Powell cruises and guided boat tours from Wahweap Marina to Rainbow Bridge.

Monument Valley Hot Air Balloon Co., www.monumentvalleyballooncompany.com, 602-480-6030, 1-800-843-5987, Monument Valley, UT. Unforgettable rides give you sky-high views of the mesas.

Overland Canyon Tours, www.overlandcanyon.com, 928-608-4072, 697 N. Navajo Blvd. (US 89), Page, AZ 86040. For standard tours of Upper Antelope Canyon and adventurous trips to remote Canyon X with an experienced photographer guide.

Roy Black's Tours, www.blacksmonumentvalleytours.com, 928-309-8834, Monument Valley, UT. Navajo guides for 4WD jeep, hiking, and horseback tours of Monument Valley can be hired upon arrival or reserved in advance. Ask about overnight stays in a Navajo hogan.

Thunderbird Lodge, www.tbirdlodge.com, 1-800-679-2473, P.O. Box 548, Chinle, AZ 86503. Reliable 4WD jeep, hiking, horseback, and guided driving tours of Canyon de Chelly National Monument are fairly priced.

SHOPPING

Books, Maps, and Outdoor Gear
For outdoor-equipment rentals, see "Fitness Facilities," above.

Andrea Kristina's Bookstore & Kafe, www.andreakristinas.com, 505-327-3133, 218 W. Main St., Farmington, NM. Independent bookstore carries a fine selection of new titles, with an espresso bar at the back.

Carl Hayden Visitor Center, www.nps.gov/glca, 928-608-6404, US 89 west of Glen Canyon Dam, Page, AZ. Carries a wealth of natural history and outdoor activity books, plus topographic quadrangle maps for hiking and backpacking adventures.

Native American Trading Posts and Galleries
The Navajo Nation is dappled with authentic trading posts, the biggest and best-known of which are listed below. The famous **Crownpoint Navajo Rug Auction** (www.crownpoint rugauction.com, 505-786-7386) is usually held on the third Friday of each month at Crownpoint, New Mexico, about 25 miles north of Thoreau (I-40 exit 53) via NM 371. For the Hubbell Trading Post in Ganado, see "Historical Sites," above. The **Hopi mesas** (see

"Pueblos," above) also have many **roadside shops and galleries** owned by tribal artisans that sell silver jewelry, pottery, kachinas, and other handmade crafts. At the Zuni Pueblo (see "Pueblos," above), stop by the visitor center for a map and directions to tribal-owned cooperative gallery shops selling carved fetishes, silver jewelry, and other traditional and contemporary artworks.

Fifth Generation Trading Company, 505-326-3211, 232 W. Broadway, Farmington, NM. Since the late 19th century, this trading post has stocked Southwestern sandpaintings, Navajo rugs and pottery, alabaster sculptures, and other tribal crafts.

Foutz Trading Company, 505-368-5790, 1-800-383-0615, www.foutztrade.com, AZ 64, Shiprock, NM. Old-fashioned shop carries Navajo folk art, beadwork, drums, sandpaintings, alabaster sculptures, woven baskets, kachinas, and hand-painted pottery.

Goulding's Trading Post, www.gouldings.com, 435-727-3231, Goulding's Lodge, off US 163, Monument Valley, UT. After browsing the artisan gift shop at Monument Valley Tribal Park, drive to this historic trading post nearby, which also specializes in Navajo arts and crafts and gives rug-weaving demonstrations daily.

Navajo Arts & Crafts Enterprise, www.gonavajo.com, 1-866-871-4095, off AZ 64 east of BIA 12, Window Rock, AZ. Tribal-owned artisan crafts cooperatives sell Navajo rugs, pottery, jewelry, and musical CDs. The biggest store is in Window Rock, with satellite branches in Cameron, Chinle, Kayenta, and Shiprock.

Richardson's Trading Company, www.richardsontrading.com, 505-722-4762, 222 W. Route 66, Gallup, NM. In downtown Gallup's long lineup of Indian trading posts and pawn shops, this family-owned outpost has been open since 1913. Richardson's guarantees authentic goods directly purchased from Native American artisans. Whether you're looking for Navajo rugs, Zuni silverwork, or Hopi kachinas—or just browsing.

Shiprock Trading Company, www.shiprocktrading.com, 505-324-0881, 1-800-210-7847, 301 W. Main St., Farmington, NM. Innovative gallery shows off a variety of contemporary fine arts, tradi-

Authentic Navajo rugs are found inside many trading posts across the Four Corners region. Sara Benson & Mike Connolly

tional crafts, and unique collectibles made by tribal artisans
from as far away as Santa Fe.

Two Grey Hills Trading Post,
www.twogreyhills.com, 505-789-
3270, HCR 330, Box 70, Tohatchi,
NM 87325. Far from the tourist
hordes, this Navajo-owned-and-
operated general store is accessed
via a rough dirt road off NM 491,
about 25 miles north of Gallup. The
back room is piled high with
authentic local Navajo weavings,
from small floor rugs and saddle
blankets to museum-quality wall-
sized tapestries.

Tuba City Trading Post, 928-283-
5441, Main St. at Moenave Rd.,
north of US 160, Tuba City, AZ.
Historic brick-built trading post
building has the octagonal shape of
a traditional Navajo hogan and a
small selection of artisan crafts,
books, and CDs.

*Trading posts and pawn shops are chockablock in
downtown Gallup, New Mexico.* Sara Benson & Mike Connolly

6

COLORADO'S PLATEAU

Mesas, Mines, and Rocky Mountains

Famous for its ski resorts and mountain highs, Colorado also protects some of the most impressive archaeological sites in the Four Corners region, if not the entire Southwest. Forget about the knife-edged geographical boundaries ratified by the U.S. government when Colorado became a state in 1876. Think back to earlier times before barbed wire fenced off the open range, and even before ranchers, miners, cowboys, rowdy outlaws, and bawdy bordello girls arrived in the Wild West. Imagine instead how things looked when tribes of indigenous peoples roamed the Colorado Plateau, building intricate, defensive cliff dwellings into the sides of mesas thickly covered in native forests.

What is now southwestern Colorado was once a thriving center of Ancestral Puebloan culture, whose remnants can still be seen today dotted all over the countryside. The premier attraction is Mesa Verde National Park, where guided tours and trails let visitors get up close to some of the most well-known ancient cliff dwellings. To leave more of the crowds behind, venture to Canyon of the Ancients National Monument north of Cortez or out to Hovenweep National Monument near the Utah border, both places where atmospheric ancient Native American ruins await personal rediscovery at the end of dusty county roads. Amateur archaeologists can get hands-on experience at a real-life working dig at Crow Canyon Archaeological Center, while bookworms are fascinated by the Anasazi Heritage Center museum exhibits outside Dolores.

When you've had your fill of ancient archaeological sites, southwestern Colorado has a lot more to offer independent travelers. The tourist hub of Durango is a university town that sports some authentic Old West appeal, from leather goods shops and custom cowboy-hat makers to Victorian saloons with player pianos and vaudeville acts, all found downtown by the historic railway depot. With residents that love the outdoor lifestyle, Durango is also full of cycling and mountain-biking shops, river-rafting and fly-fishing outfitters, and ski and snowboard rental outlets to equip everyone for any sport in all four seasons.

For a tamer excursion, hop on board the Durango & Silverton Narrow Gauge Railroad, which winds its way alongside the Animas River into the San Juan Mountains to the 19th-century mining boomtown of Silverton. For more high-altitude thrills, drive from Durango to Silverton and back on the San Juan Skyway, a scenic byway that clambers over

LEFT: *Lose the crowds on trails around the ruins of Hovenweep National Monument, near the Colorado-Utah border.* Sara Benson & Mike Connolly

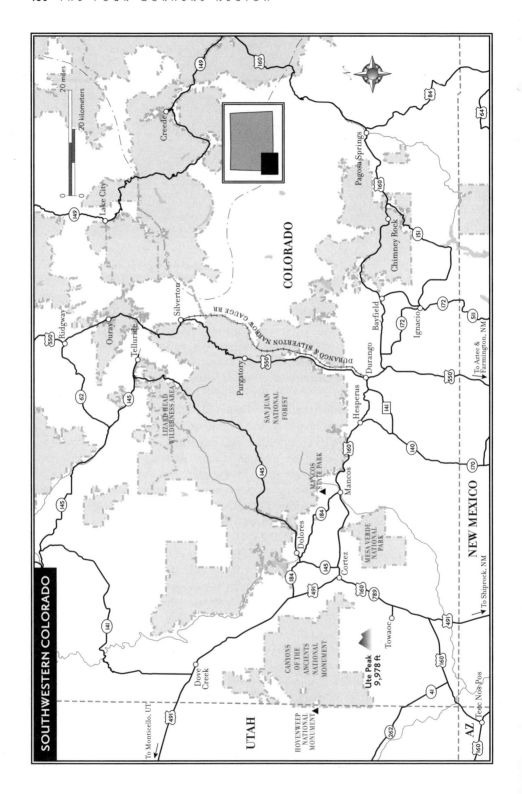

SOUTHWESTERN COLORADO

breathtaking mountain passes. Explore east of Durango, where you can soak away in hot pools by the river in Pagosa Springs, or head west into Mesa Verde country, where horseback riding stables offer trail rides to alpine lakes and meadows. West of Mesa Verde National Park, the small town of Cortez is at a crossroads, from where you can continue north to Dolores and eventually Moab (see "Utah's Canyon Country" chapter) or drive south past landmark Sleeping Ute Mountain into the Navajo Nation (see the "Native America" chapter).

Navigating around southwestern Colorado is much more straightforward than elsewhere in the Four Corners region, but weather is a bigger factor here. It can snow at higher elevations even during summer, which is nevertheless the best all-around time to visit. In winter be prepared for icy road conditions that may require putting chains on snow tires. In remote mountain towns such as Silverton, many businesses shut down completely during the off-season, roughly from late October until early May, while even popular attractions such as the Durango & Silverton Narrow Gauge Railroad and Mesa Verde National Park severely curtail their services. Bigger places like Durango are year-round destinations, but they're dominated by skiers and snowboarders once the snow falls.

LODGING

Cortez

BEST WESTERN TURQUOISE INN & SUITES
970-565-3778, 1-800-547-3376
www.cortezbestwestern.com
info@mesaverdehotel.net
535 E. Main St. (US 160), Cortez, CO 81321
Price: Moderate
Credit Cards: AE, D, MC, V
Handicapped Access: Yes

This upmarket chain has spacious rooms with a host of amenities, including free high-speed Internet access, coffeemakers, microwaves, mini-refrigerators, and cable TV. Some suites have hot tubs or fireplaces, while others are big enough to fit families, who also enjoy the outdoor swimming pool and indoor waterfall jetted pool. Rates include an expanded continental breakfast and free samples of homemade fudge from the gift shop. Pets are allowed for a surcharge.

BUDGET HOST INN BEL RAU LODGE
970-565-3738, 1-888-677-3738
www.budgethostmesaverde.com

2040 E. Main St. (US 160)
Cortez, CO 81321
Price: Moderate
Credit Cards: AE, D, MC, V
Handicapped Access: Yes

This independently owned budget motel on the outskirts of Cortez may be showing its age, but it's an excellent value in the off-season. The older rooms are quite roomy and are equipped with heating and air-conditioning, cable TV, and free Wi-Fi Internet access. Kitchenettes are available. There's an outdoor picnic area and seasonal swimming pool and hot tub. Rates include continental breakfast. Pets are welcome.

CANYON OF THE ANCIENTS GUEST RANCH
970-565-4288
www.canyonoftheancients.com
canyon_of_the_ancients@yahoo.com
7986 County Road G, Cortez, CO 81321
Directions: From US 160/191 southwest of Cortez, take County Road G 15 miles west.
Price: Very Expensive
Credit Cards: MC, V
Handicapped Access: Yes

On pastoral ranchlands near the Utah border, this retreat rents private cottages tucked away inside McElmo Canyon, where Butch Cassidy once stashed loot. The minimalist adobe cottage has a kitchen, mosaic-tiled tub, and flat-screen TV. The historic stone house built by a cowboy has a full kitchen and kiva fireplace. Deluxe tipis have platform beds and shared shower and bath facilities. There are hilly footpaths, cottonwood groves, petroglyphs, and ancient ruins to explore. A two-night minimum stay usually applies.

HOLIDAY INN EXPRESS MESA VERDE–CORTEZ

970-565-6000, 1-888-465-4329
www.hiexpress.com
2121 E. Main St. (US 160), Cortez, CO 81321
Price: Moderate
Credit Cards: AE, D, MC, V
Handicapped Access: Yes

This welcoming, recently renovated chain hotel at the edge of town has loads of extras, including in-room satellite TV, high-speed Wi-Fi Internet access, a fully equipped fitness room, sauna, whirlpool, and complimentary breakfast buffet. Suites have microwaves and in-room refrigerators; special family-friendly suites come with bunk beds and video-game consoles for kids. Pets are accepted.

THE INN AT MCELMO CANYON

Innkeepers: Eric and Una Johnson
970-564-0240, 1-866-833-0240
www.theinnatmcelmocanyon.com
inquiries@theinnatmcelmocanyon.com
19601 County Road G, Cortez, CO 81321
Directions: From US 160/491 southwest of Cortez, take County Road G more than 25 miles west.
Price: Expensive
Credit Cards: AE, MC, V
Handicapped Access: Yes

This rustic bed-and-breakfast resides on beautiful ranchlands near the Utah border. The decor is simple yet elegant, with en-suite baths, feather beds, down comforters, high-class sheets, all-natural soaps and lotions, and maybe fresh flowers on the nightstand. The Lizard Head Suite has a whirlpool tub and private deck, while the Powder Horn Suite has a full kitchen. Ask about off-season rates and golfing and skiing discounts.

THE KELLY PLACE

Innkeepers: Jerene Waite and Marc Yaxley
970-565-3125, 1-800-745-4885
www.kellyplace.com
kelly@kellyplace.com
14663 County Road G, Cortez, CO 81321
Directions: From US 160/491 southwest of Cortez, drive 10.2 miles west on County Road G. Turn right at the Kelly Place sign, then bear left onto a mile-long dirt road.
Price: Moderate
Credit Cards: D, MC, V
Handicapped Access: No

Right inside McElmo Canyon, this adobe bed-and-breakfast is also an archaeological excavation site. Choose from rustic guest rooms with private baths in the main lodge, duplex cottages with kitchenettes, or the private cabin with a fireplace and whirlpool tub. Books, magazines, movies, and high-speed Wi-Fi Internet access are available in the lodge. When the sun shines, unwind on the flagstone patio or wander the grounds to pick fresh fruit from the orchards and explore Ancestral Puebloan ruins. Rates include a breakfast buffet.

SUPER 8 MOTEL—CORTEZ / MESA VERDE AREA

970-565-8888, 1-800-800-8000
www.super8.com
505 E. Main St. (US 160), Cortez, CO 81321
Price: Inexpensive
Credit Cards: AE, D, MC, V
Handicapped Access: Yes

Although Cortez has a long line of retro independent motels along Main Street, not all are as reliable as this budget-conscious chain, where the fair rates include high-speed Wi-Fi Internet access and continental breakfast. Rooms may be nothing fancy, but they're spotlessly clean and equipped with individual air-conditioning and heating units.

UTE MOUNTAIN LODGE AND CASINO
Manager: Ute Mountain Ute Tribe
970-565-8837, 1-888-565-8837
www.utemountaincasinocom
hotel@utemountaincasinocom
Mailing Address: 3 Weeminuche Dr. (at Yellowjacket), Towaoc, CO 81334
Directions: 11 miles south of Cortez on US 160/491
Price: Inexpensive
Credit Cards: AE, D, MC, V
Handicapped Access: Yes

While the service is not as professionally polished as tired travelers might hope for, this Native American—owned casino hotel offers oversize guest rooms with Southwestern accents. Well-kept suites have separate sitting and sleeping areas, king-size sleigh beds, microwaves, mini-refrigerators, and cable TV.

Dolores

CIRCLE K RANCH
970-562-3826, 1-800-477-6381
www.ckranch.com
vacation@ckranch.com
27758 CO 145, Dolores, CO 81323
Directions: 26 miles northeast of Dolores on CO 145
Price: Moderate
Credit Cards: D, V
Handicapped Access: Yes

In the San Juan Mountains, this rustic dude ranch is a base camp for fishing, hunting, and horseback riding during summer. While the nonsmoking motel and lodge rooms are very basic, the "full plan" available for groups of two or more people includes three hearty meals and discounts on trail rides. Even more attractive are the private cabins in a pine forest that have airy decks, full kitchens, and bathrooms. The main lodge has a roaring fireplace for gathering on cooler evenings. Pets may be accepted.

DOLORES MOUNTAIN INN
970-882-7203, 1-800-842-8113
www.dminn.com
701 Railroad Ave. (at 7th St.)
Dolores, CO 81323
Price: Moderate
Credit Cards: AE, D, MC, V
Handicapped Access: Yes

In the tiny town of Dolores, this nonsmoking motel offers spacious rooms and family-size suites with one or two bedrooms and a kitchen. All have cable TV, private showers with bathtubs, and individual heating and air-conditioning. Guest amenities include VCR rentals and free high-speed Wi-Fi Internet access. The inn is within walking distance of downtown restaurants and the brewpub, but expect noise from the highway just outside. Pets are accepted for a small surcharge.

DUNTON HOT SPRINGS
Manager: Clare Evans
970-882-4800
www.duntonhotsprings.com
info@duntonhotsprings.com
52086 West Fork Rd., Dolores, CO 81323
Directions: Take CO 145 approximately 13 miles north of Dolores, then turn left onto County Road 38 (W. Dolores Rd., aka W. Fork Rd.) before Stoner. From there, it's a 22-mile drive, including 9 miles of unpaved roads.
Price: Very Expensive
Credit Cards: MC, V
Handicapped Access: No

Only a few lodgings in the Four Corners region rate as highly as this luxury hot-springs hideaway in the San Juan Mountains. All of the historic hand-hewn log houses have been painstakingly restored and outfitted with Western furnishings plus all the amenities, including high-speed Wi-Fi Internet access. Nonsmoking accommodations range from a quirky tipi with a California king-size bed and shared bath to the honeymoon house with a Rajasthani wedding bed and gas fireplace. Rates cover three meals a day and unlimited soaks in the hot springs. À la carte activities include yoga in the historic Pony Express building, guided fly-fishing trips, horseback rides, and heli-skiing. A two-night minimum stay is usually required. Pets may be accepted for a daily surcharge.

LEBANON SCHOOLHOUSE BED & BREAKFAST

Innkeepers: Ken and Laura Hahn
970-882-4461, 1-877-882-4461
www.lebanonschoolhouse.com
info@lebanonschoolhouse.com
24925 County Road T, Dolores, CO 81323
Directions: Drive north on CO 491 past Empire Electric, turn right onto Lebanon Rd. (County Road 25) and drive 6.9 miles to the stop sign.
Price: Moderate
Credit Cards: D, MC, V
Handicapped Access: Partial

This early 20th-century schoolhouse has just five rooms and is furnished throughout with lovely antiques. Some guest rooms have private baths. Each has something special to distinguish it from the rest, for example, the Art Room, which is stocked with arts and crafts supplies and has a separate loft bed for kids. Even more private is the 1920s cottage, the tree-shaded Teachery. Rates include a full breakfast (pumpkin waffles with maple syrup, if

you're lucky). Guests have access to a shared kitchen and Internet access in the common area. The inn is gay-friendly. Well-behaved dogs may be allowed. Ask about discounts for teachers.

OUTPOST MOTEL, CABINS AND RV PARK

Managers: The Wagner family
970-882-7271, 1-800-382-4892
www.doloreslodging.com
outpostmotel@centurytel.net
1800 Central Ave. (at CO 145)
Dolores, CO 81323
Price: Moderate
Credit Cards: AE, D, MC, V
Handicapped Access: Yes

This mom-and-pop motel sits on the San Juan River at the outskirts of Dolores. While the motel rooms are nothing fancy, they do have kitchenettes (bring cookware and utensils). Much better are the quaint housekeeping cabins, all of which have full kitchens, log-style furnishings, country quilts on the beds, and front porches with flower pots. Each cabin can accommodate four to eight guests.

RIO GRANDE SOUTHERN HOTEL AND B&B

Innkeeper: Susi Sieber
970-882-7527, 1-866-882-3026
www.riograndesouthernhotel.com
101 S. 5th St. (at Railroad Ave.)
Dolores, CO 81323
Price: Moderate
Credit Cards: D, MC, V
Handicapped Access: No

Recently renovated and lovingly restored, this historic property faces the town square. Step into the turn-of-the-20th-century lobby with its comfy leather club chairs and imagine how it looked when Teddy Roosevelt and Western novelist Zane Grey slept here. True to the inn's historical theme, guest rooms are outfitted in Victorian style with sconces, flowered carpeting, and lacy curtains. Rates include a hot breakfast served in the charming café.

Durango

4920 FOR RAILROAD FANATICS

Innkeepers: Jim and Pat Conway
www.all-railroads.com/4920.html
jconway@con-cor.com
970-247-0916, 1-888-255-7826
4920 N. County Road 203
Durango, CO 81301
Open: May through September
Price: Moderate
Credit Cards: AE, D, MC, V
Handicapped Access: No

Run by self-confessed railroad fanatics and model train manufacturers, this summer vacation home in the heart of the Animas Valley rents two suites for travelers who share their hobby. You can watch trains make their way along the historic Durango & Silverton Railroad line, then spend an evening perusing the large collection of train videos in the library. Rates include a help-yourself breakfast that's available anytime in the kitchenette area. A three-night minimum stay is required. The property is nonsmoking. Children are welcome.

APPLE ORCHARD INN

Innkeepers: Celeste and John Gardiner
970-247-0751, 1-800-426-0751
www.appleorchardinn.com
info@appleorchardinn.com
7758 County Road 203, Durango, CO 81301
Directions: Take US 550 approximately 6 miles north of Durango. Turn left on Thimble Lane, then right on County Road 203.
Price: Expensive
Credit Cards: AE, D, MC, V
Handicapped Access: Partial

On a rural property surrounded by fruit trees in the Animas Valley, this award-winning inn offers four guest rooms in the farmhouse and six country cottages. The main house is gorgeously appointed with cherry wood floors, a river-rock fireplace, and original artwork. All rooms and cottages have private baths, while some cottages also have whirlpool tubs, king-size sleigh beds, and French doors that open onto private patios with views of the San Juan Mountains. Rates include a full hot gourmet breakfast and afternoon snacks and cookies, plus access to the garden hot tub. This inn is gay-friendly.

BEST WESTERN MOUNTAIN SHADOWS

970-247-5200, 1-800-521-5218
www.bestwestern.com
3255 Main Ave. (US 550)
Durango, CO 81301
Price: Moderate
Credit Cards: AE, D, MC, V
Handicapped Access: Yes

Unmistakable for its glass-domed swimming pool and hot tub next to the highway, this chain motel is an economical choice. The solid furnishings are reminiscent of a mountain cabin or ski lodge. Guest rooms are also equipped with work desks, microwaves, mini-refrigerators, coffeemakers, heating and air-conditioning, and cable TV. Rates include high-speed Wi-Fi Internet access and an expanded continental breakfast.

BLUE LAKE RANCH

Innkeepers: Shirley and David Alford
970-385-4537, 1-888-258-3525
www.bluelakeranch.com
bluelake@frontier.net
16000 CO 140, Hesperus, CO 81326
Directions: Take US 160 west from Durango to Hesperus, then CO 140 south of mile marker 17.
Price: Expensive
Credit Cards: None
Handicapped Access: Yes

On the way to Mesa Verde National Park, this luxurious bed-and-breakfast sits on

200 private acres of piñon and juniper pines and heirloom gardens beside pacific Blue Lake with a dramatic backdrop of mountain peaks. Accommodations are rustic yet elegant, ranging from private cabins to shared casitas and historic homes. Each has a unique assortment of amenities, from kiva fireplaces and deep soaking tubs to full kitchens. All accommodations have telephones, TVs with VCRs, refrigerators, microwaves, coffeemakers with grinders, and free high-speed Wi-Fi Internet access. Rates include a Southwestern breakfast buffet with fresh fruit and hot tamales. The inn is gay-friendly.

BLUE SPRUCE CABINS

Manager: Kent Wilson
970-884-2641, 1-888-884-2641
www.bluesprucervpark.com
info@bluesprucervpark.com
1875 County Road 500, Bayfield, CO 81122
Directions: From the junction of US 550 and E. 15th St., drive east 2 blocks to Florida Rd. (County Road 240). Continue to County Road 501, then turn left onto County Road 500.
Price: Moderate
Credit Cards: MC, V
Handicapped Access: No

On Vallecito Lake, a humble RV park has well-equipped housekeeping cabins with simple, rustic log-style furniture, kitchenettes, private bathrooms with showers, DirecTV, and front porches for breathing in the fresh country air. Amenities include high-speed Wi-Fi Internet access, laundry facilities, an exercise room, and a games recreation room. Some cabins are pet-friendly.

COUNTRY SUNSHINE
BED AND BREAKFAST

Innkeepers: Walter and Jodi Hammerle
970-247-2853, 1-800-383-2853
www.countrysunshine.com
inn@countrysunshine.com
35130 US 550 N., between mile markers 34 and 35, Durango, CO 81301
Directions: Drive approximately 12 miles north of downtown Durango.
Price: Moderate
Credit Cards: AE, D, MC, V
Handicapped Access: No

It's the hospitality of hosts who always go the extra mile that makes any stay here memorable. Inside their relaxing home, the oversize rooms have knotty pine–paneled walls, king-size beds, private bathrooms, TVs and VCRs, and sometimes an antique writing desk or gas fireplace. Hot breakfasts feature oatmeal-blueberry pancakes and other specialties. Snacks and drinks are available all day, with delectable desserts served every evening. There's a library, outdoor hot tub, and high-speed Wi-Fi Internet access for guests. German is spoken.

DOUBLETREE HOTEL DURANGO

970-259-6580, 1-800-222-8733
www.durango.doubletree.com
501 Camino Del Rio (at E. 6th St.)
Durango, CO 81301
Price: Expensive
Credit Cards: AE, D, MC, V
Handicapped Access: Yes

For upscale accommodations within walking distance of downtown Durango's restaurants and shops, this waterfront hotel fits the bill. Spacious rooms and suites with sitting areas enjoy complimentary high-speed Internet access and are equipped with ergonomic work desks, down pillows, and luxury mattresses; some have private balconies overlooking the Animas River. A state-of-the-art fitness center and free airport shuttle are perks.

THE GABLE HOUSE BED & BREAKFAST

Innkeeper: Heather Bryson
970-247-4982

www.durangobedandbreakfast.com
805 E. 5th Ave. (at E. 8th St.)
Durango, CO 81301
Price: Expensive
Credit Cards: MC, V
Handicapped Access: No

This lovely Queen Anne Victorian with a signature wraparound wooden porch is a nationally registered historic site, which makes staying here even more atmospheric. On a residential side street near downtown, this quiet and elegant inn is run by a hospitable hostess. Charming rooms are decorated with antique furnishings, lace curtains, white coverlets, and patterned wallpapers; some have private baths, but there are no TVs or air-conditioning. Smoking is only allowed outside.

GENERAL PALMER HOTEL
970-247-4747, 1-800-523-3358
www.generalpalmer.com
gphdurango@yahoo.com
567 Main Ave. (at W. College Dr.)
Durango, CO 81301
Price: Moderate
Credit Cards: AE, D, MC, V
Handicapped Access: Yes

This modest Victorian hotel in downtown Durango is a turn-of-the-20th-century landmark within spitting distance of the train station. The gorgeous lobby and library are adorned with antiques, overstuffed couches and chairs, and elegant wall sconces. In old-fashioned guest rooms with frilly decor, you'll find a few modern conveniences such as air-conditioning, telephones, and cable TV. Rates include a continental breakfast.

JARVIS SUITE HOTEL
970-259-6190, 1-800-824-1024
www.jarvishoteldurango.com
jarvis@frontier.net
125 W. 10th St. (at Main Ave.)
Durango, CO 81301

One of downtown Durango's many historic places to comfortably bed down overnight. Sara Benson

Price: Moderate
Credit Cards: AE, D, MC, V
Handicapped Access: Yes

This apartment-style hotel offers down-to-earth value for roomy lodgings downtown, if you're not very fussy about amenities or interior design. Its suites all have full kitchens, plus telephones and cable TV. The staff are professional, and free cookies are served every afternoon. Rates include breakfast, guest laundry facilities, and parking.

THE LELAND HOUSE
BED & BREAKFAST
Innkeeper: Kirk Komick
970-385-1920, 1-800-664-1920
www.leland-house.com
stay@rochesterhotel.com
721 E. 2nd Ave. (at E. 7th St.)
Durango, CO 81301
Price: Very Expensive
Credit Cards: AE, D, MC, V
Handicapped Access: Yes

Managed by the Rochester Hotel, these roomy bed-and-breakfast lodgings are found inside a quaintly restored 1920s house located across the street from the hotel. All of the 10 suites have private baths. Studios also have kitchenettes, while larger suites have full kitchens, gas fireplaces, and private bedrooms with separate sitting areas. The two-bedroom Pittman Suite boasts a private balcony. Rates include a full breakfast. The inn is gay-friendly.

LIGHTNER CREEK INN

Innkeepers: Scott and Ellen Martin
970-259-1226, 1-800-268-9804
www.lightnercreekinn.com
info@lightnercreekinn.com
999 County Road 207, Durango, CO 81301
Directions: From Durango, take US 550 south, then US 160 west for 3 miles, and turn right onto County Road 207.
Price: Moderate
Credit Cards: AE, D, MC, V
Handicapped Access: No

A favorite of wedding parties and honeymooners, this secluded bed-and-breakfast is so restful that it feels more remote than it actually is, being just a quick drive from downtown. Spacious guest rooms inside the century-old farmhouse are outfitted with antiques and satellite TV, CD players, and telephones. Larger suites in the carriage house have more amenities like private entrances, fireplaces, mini-refrigerators, and free Wi-Fi Internet access. Neither rooms nor suites have air-conditioning, however. There's an outdoor hot tub overlooking the creek. Rates include a full hot breakfast.

NOBODY'S INN

www.nobodysinn.com
nobodysinn@frontier.net
920 Main Ave. (at E. 9th St.)
Durango, CO 81301
Price: Expensive
Credit Cards: AE, D, MC, V
Handicapped Access: No

Perched inside a 19th-century building downtown, this four-room inn has a unique concept: a hotel with no reception desk or concierge. After checking yourself in, head upstairs to where contemporary apartment-style rooms each have a kitchenette or fully equipped kitchen, telephone, cable TV, central air-conditioning, high-speed Wi-Fi Internet access, and a private (sometimes detached) bathroom. The bedding defines luxurious, with high thread-count sheets, down pillows, and lofty duvets. Avoid the noisier rooms overlooking Main Avenue. Amenities include a washer/dryer for guests.

RED CLIFF HOUSE

Innkeepers: Connie Morse and Dave Sime
970-247-3065, 1-877-972-5433
www.redcliffhouse.com
redcliff@redcliffhouse.com
3935 County Road 250, Durango, CO 81301
Directions: Drive north of Durango on US 550 for approximately 5 miles, turn right at County Road 252, then right again onto County Road 250.
Price: Moderate
Credit Cards: AE, D, MC, V
Handicapped Access: No

Just one vacation rental is offered here, the Aspen Grove Retreat. Nestled under red cliffs by the Animas River, this contemporary suite comes with its own hot tub, sunroom, private bath, telephone, satellite TV, and a fully equipped kitchen stocked with everything you'll need to make your own breakfast, including fresh produce from the innkeepers' organic orchards, gardens, and berry patches. Children are welcome and the accommodations are gay-friendly. A two- or three-night minimum stay is required.

ROCHESTER HOTEL

970-385-1920, 1-800-664-1920
www.rochesterhotel.com

stay@rochesterhotel.com
721 E. 2nd Ave. (at E. 7th St.)
Durango, CO 81301
Price: Expensive
Credit Cards: AE, D, MC, V
Handicapped Access: No

For Western movie buffs and those who love cowboy lore, this offbeat Victorian hotel has just 15 historic rooms arranged around a garden courtyard. While the rooms are small and antiques themselves, complete with creaky floorboards, ceiling fans, and thin walls, they're nevertheless charming. The top-notch management gives guests little luxuries, such as upscale bath amenities and complimentary iced tea and cookies in the afternoon. Rates include a hot breakfast.

SIESTA MOTEL
970-247-0741, 1-877-314-0741
www.durangosiestamotel.com

info@durangosiestamotel.com
3475 N. Main Ave. (US 550)
Durango, CO 81301
Price: Moderate
Credit Cards: AE, D, MC, V
Handicapped Access: Yes

North of downtown, this gem has a retro motel sign with a giant cactus and a vaquero taking a snooze out front. The family-run motor court surrounds a small courtyard. The pet-friendly, wood-paneled rooms are comfortable for penny pinchers, although the furnishings are 1970s-era. Kitchenettes and full kitchen units are available. There's free high-speed Wi-Fi Internet access and an outdoor hot tub in the gazebo.

STRATER HOTEL
970-385-8864, 1-800-247-4431
www.strater.com
699 Main Ave. (at W. 7th St.)
Durango, CO 81301

The Strater Hotel is one of downtown Durango's many historic Western lodgings. Sara Benson

Price: Expensive
Credit Cards: AE, D, MC, V
Handicapped Access: Yes

This Victorian-era hotel filled with memorabilia has stood proudly on the same corner of downtown Durango for more than 120 years. Notice the hand-carved sandstone details outside the redbrick building. Oversize guest rooms are turned out with walnut antiques and flowered wallpapers, while being equipped with modern amenities such as cable TV and free high-speed Wi-Fi Internet access. Rates include free soaks in the indoor hot tub and an expanded continental breakfast. Room service is available at dinner time, when libations are poured in the sociable spiritorium with its cozy fireplace.

Mancos

ENCHANTED MESA MOTEL
970-533-7729, 1-866-533-6372
www.enchantedmesamotel.com
vacastorena6@aol.com
862 W. Grand Ave. (Business Loop 160)
Mancos, CO 81328
Price: Inexpensive
Credit Cards: AE, D, MC, V
Handicapped Access: Yes

Although the motel-style accommodations with standard furnishings are nothing special, the bargain rates, guest laundry facilities, free high-speed Wi-Fi Internet access, a barbecue grill, pool tables, and complimentary snacks and goodies in the lobby make it a decent budget option. Kitchenette units are available. Pets accepted for a small surcharge.

FLAGSTONE MEADOWS RANCH B&B
Innkeeper: Harris Court
970-533-9838, 1-800-793-1137
www.flagstonemeadows.com
moreinfo@flagstonemeadows.com
38080 County Road K4, Mancos, CO 81328

Directions: From US 160 turn right on County Road 39, then left on County Road K4.
Price: Moderate
Credit Cards: MC, V
Handicapped Access: No

Open year-round, this beautiful lodge set beside a mountain meadow is secreted away in the countryside. Each of eight serene suites has a private bath and charming touches like hand-pieced quilts, Western memorabilia, or romantic fireplaces. Rates include breakfast, evening dessert, and complimentary soft drinks, coffee, and tea. A two-night minimum stay applies in summer.

JERSEY JIM FIRE LOOKOUT TOWER
Innkeepers: Jersey Jim Foundation
970-533-7060
www.firelookout.net/Individ_Lookouts/US057_Jersey_Jim.htm
P.O. Box 1032, Mancos, CO 81328
Directions: Drive approximately 14 miles north of Mancos on unpaved Forest Road 561.
Open: Late May to mid-October
Price: Inexpensive
Credit Cards: None
Handicapped Access: No

If you have no fear of heights, try this historic fire lookout perched in the San Juan National Forest at an elevation of nearly 10,000 feet. There's just one double bed inside the lookout, which was rebuilt in the 1960s, but the sweeping views from high above a meadow encircled by aspen trees make it worthwhile. There is no electricity or running water either, but there is a propane-fueled kitchen and wall lamps. Bring bedding, water, an ice chest for food, and binoculars. Reservations for the summer season are accepted beginning on March 1 and often fill within days; call between 1 and 5 PM (MST).

LOST CANYON LAKE LODGE

Innkeepers: Tom and Sally Garrison
970-882-7871
www.lostcanyonlakelodge.com
tomandsally@lostcanyonlakelodge.com
15472 County Road 35.3, Mancos, CO 81328
Price: Moderate
Credit Cards: MC, V
Handicapped Access: No

Hosts who genuinely care about you having a good time during your sojourn in Colorado put this bed-and-breakfast over the top. On the upper floor of the main house, two of the relaxing guest rooms have king-size beds and lake views, while smaller ones have queen-size beds and a loft. A private log cabin with a full kitchen stands by the lake. In the morning, the hostess may share her recipes for home-cooked breakfasts, which are included in the rates. At night go stargazing on the outdoor hot-tub deck.

RIVER BEND
BED & BREAKFAST

Innkeeper: Mary Hooper
1-866-403-7063
www.riverbendbandb.com
info@riverbendbandb.com
42505 US 160, Mancos, CO 81328
Price: Expensive
Credit Cards: AE, D, MC, V
Handicapped Access: No

This low-slung ranch house on the highway east of downtown Mancos has just five fan-cooled guest rooms and suites with pine-paneled walls and a Southwestern theme. The Four Corners Suite also has a whirlpool tub, rain shower, satellite TV, and private courtyard. For families with pets, the two-bedroom cabin has a full kitchen, air-conditioning, and mountain-view decks. Amenities include laundry facilities, a shared kitchen, and outdoor hot tub.

SUNDANCE BEAR LODGE

Innkeepers: Susan and Bob
970-533-1504, 1-866-529-2480
www.sundancebear.com
sue@sundancebear.com
38890 CO 184, Mancos, CO 81328
Price: Moderate
Credit Cards: D, MC, V
Handicapped Access: No

Among the most popular places to stay in Mesa Verde country, this rustic country lodge stays open year-round. Choose from two guest rooms in the main house, a romantic log cabin with a full kitchen and river-rock lined bathroom, or the three-bedroom house. Both of the bed-and-breakfast guest rooms come furnished with Navajo rugs and private baths, while the larger room also has a gas fireplace and TV. Breakfast is not included in the rates for cabin or house rentals; however, pets are accepted in either for a surcharge.

WILLOWTAIL SPRINGS

Innkeepers: Peggy and Lee Cloy
970-533-7592, 1-800-698-0603
www.willowtailsprings.com
bookings@willowtailsprings.com
P.O. Box 89, Mancos, CO 81328
Price: Expensive
Credit Cards: MC, V
Handicapped Access: No

With three romantic hideaways set beside a private lake in the La Plata Mountains, Willowtail Springs is a tranquil retreat. Borrow a rowboat or the canoe for an afternoon, or take bird-watching walks in the early morning. The sunny bungalows and the three-bedroom log home all have a full kitchen, gas fireplace, entertainment center, quaint country furnishings, pine floors, and original artwork. Rates include a continental breakfast, fresh flowers, bath amenities, and Wi-Fi Internet access in the main office. There's a three-night minimum stay during summer.

Mesa Verde National Park

FAR VIEW LODGE
General Manager: Lynn Mitchell
Lodge: 970-529-4422; advance reservations: 602-331-5210, 1-800-449-2288
www.visitmesaverde.com
info@visitmesaverde.com
Mesa Verde National Park, P.O. Box 277
Mancos, CO 81328
Directions: 15 miles from the national park entrance along the main road
Open: May through October
Price: Moderate
Credit Cards: AE, D, MC, V
Handicapped Access: Yes

This is the only lodging inside Mesa Verde National Park. It's worth paying the premium prices charged for retro motel rooms because the high-plateau location has breathtaking vistas. Although the low-lying buildings' walls are thin, the atmosphere remains restful. Standard rooms have

The rooms at Mesa Verde National Park's Far View Lodge are elevated above the mesa, with panoramic windows and patios for guests. Sara Benson & Mike Connolly

phones, mini-refrigerators, coffeemakers, and private balconies, but not much else. More spacious Kiva Rooms have hand-crafted furnishings and beds with pillow-top mattresses. The lodge's handy location opposite a park visitor center gives you an edge on securing same-day tickets for tours of Ancestral Puebloan cliffs dwellings.

Pagosa Springs
To book vacation rental homes, condos, and ranches around Pagosa Springs, contact Pagosa Central Reservations, www.pagosa accommodations.com, 1-800-945-0182.

AMERICA'S BEST VALUE INN & SUITES HIGH COUNTRY LODGE
Managers: Alberta and Steve Nickerson
970-264-4181, 1-800-862-3707
www.highcountrylodge.com
rooms@highcountrylodge.com
3821 E. US 160, Pagosa Springs, CO 81147
Price: Moderate
Credit Cards: AE, D, MC, V
Handicapped Access: Yes

East of downtown on a woodland hilltop above the highway, this comfy motel is family-owned. Choose standard or larger motel rooms with microwaves or refrigera-

Rustic furnishings match the relaxed ambience at the Far View Lodge inside Mesa Verde National Park.
Courtesy ARAMARK

tors, or wander through the groves of trees behind the main building to newly built cabins that have individual heating, private bathrooms, satellite TV, and telephones (the biggest also have full kitchens). Rates include a continental breakfast buffet. Pets are welcome for a per-stay surcharge.

KEYAH GRANDE
Innkeepers: Barbara and Alan Sackman
970-731-1160, 1-800-577-9769
www.keyahgrande.com
guestservices@keyahgrande.com
13211 W. US 160, Pagosa Springs, CO 81147
Directions: Drive 10 miles west of Pagosa Springs.
Price: Very Expensive
Credit Cards: AE, D, MC, V
Handicapped Access: No

Straight out of *Lifestyles of the Rich and Famous*, this guest ranch is located on an elk reserve favored by hunters. The Spanish-style hacienda house has eight luxurious rooms and suites adorned with museum-quality art and furniture from around the world. Expect exceptional linens, whirlpool tubs, satellite TV, and high-speed Wi-Fi Internet access among the amenities. Indulge in personalized spa services or go horseback riding in summer and snowshoeing or cross-country skiing in winter. At any time of year, sit upon the balcony for stargazing by the African fire pit. Sky-high rates include an artisanal breakfast, dinner, and lunch upon request, all prepared by a Cordon Bleu–trained chef.

THE SPRINGS RESORT
Manager: Stan Zuege
970-264-4168, 1-800-225-0934
www.pagosahotsprings.com
165 Hot Springs Blvd. (off US 160, at San Juan St.), Pagosa Springs, CO 81147
Price: Expensive
Credit Cards: AE, D, MC, V
Handicapped Access: Yes

The Springs Resort is adjacent to the famous bathhouse, which is the real reason you've come to this rural Colorado town. This is not really a high-end spa resort, however. Essentially it's a clean, comfortable multistory motel within walking distance of downtown. All the standard rooms are air-conditioned and have telephones and TVs; Grande Rooms also come with kitchenettes. Rates include 24-hour access to the hot springs, including when the pools are not open to the public and until 6 PM after checkout. There's a juice bar and café by the lobby. Pets are accepted for a surcharge.

Silverton
THE BENT ELBOW HOTEL
970-387-5775, 1-877-387-5775
www.thebent.com
lglenn@thebent.com
1114 Blair St. (at W. 11th St.)
Silverton, CO 81433
Price: Moderate
Credit Cards: AE, D, MC, V
Handicapped Access: No

Formerly a bordello and saloon, this historic hotel on Silverton's main street offers just six nonsmoking rooms and suites with double or queen-size beds, private baths, cable TV, telephones, and wired/wireless high-speed Internet access. The cozy Cottage Room suite also has a full kitchen. Room rates include a full breakfast, and room service is available whenever the restaurant is open downstairs. The hotel's balcony is ideal for watching all the activity in the town's streets.

CANYON VIEW MOTEL
970-387-5400
www.canyonviewmotel.com
info@canyonviewmotel.com
661 Greene St. (at E. 7th St.)
Silverton, CO 81433
Price: Inexpensive

Credit Cards: MC, V
Handicapped Access: Yes

Owned by a friendly family, this small motel in Silverton's downtown historic district is a well-kept budget option for a quick overnight stay. With rustic wood-paneled exteriors, newly built rooms have standard motel furnishings, including microwaves, coffeemakers, cable TV, and heating and air-conditioning. Pets are welcomed with biscuits.

ELEVATED SLEEP AND SUPPER

970-903-4132
www.sleepandsupper.com
1337 Empire St.
Silverton, CO 81433
Price: Expensive
Credit Cards: None
Handicapped Access: No

Why choose an old-fashioned hotel room when you can have an artistically designed house all to yourself? This restored turn-of-the-20th-century house in downtown Silverton boasts many of the modern amenities missing from other hostelries, including satellite TV, a stereo with an iPod dock, an indoor fireplace, a professional kitchen, and an outdoor courtyard with a barbecue pit. Gourmet four-course suppers are available for a surcharge.

GRAND IMPERIAL HOTEL

970-387-5527, 1-800-341-3340
www.grandimperialhotel.com
info@grandimperialhotel.com
1219 Greene St. (at E. 12th St.)
Silverton, CO 81433
Price: Moderate
Credit Cards: MC, V
Handicapped Access: No

Dating from the late 19th century, the Grand Imperial is among Silverton's atmospheric period lodgings, with creaky wooden floorboards and staircases to boot. The high-ceilinged rooms and suites with sitting areas

are outfitted with neo-Victorian furnishings, floral wallpaper, and dainty white bedspreads, as well as private baths, telephones, and ceiling fans. Ask for top-floor accommodations for the best mountain views.

THE HISTORIC VILLA DALLAVALLE INN

Innkeeper: Gerald and Nancy Swanson
970-387-5555, 1-866-387-5965
www.villadallavalle.com
info@villadallavalle.com
1257 Blair St. (at E. 13th St.)
Silverton, CO 81433
Price: Moderate
Credit Cards: MC, V
Handicapped Access: No

This downtown property is among Silverton's earliest 20th-century boardinghouses, and you can rest assured that the tradition of hospitality runs in the family. Each guest room is decorated with antique furnishings from a different period of this mining boomtown's history. All have private baths, TVs, telephones, and views of the San Juan Mountains. There's an indoor hot tub for guests. Rates include a breakfast buffet and evening libations.

INN OF THE ROCKIES
AT THE HISTORIC ALMA HOUSE

Innkeeper: Pam Welty
970-387-5336, 1-800-267-5336
www.innoftherockies.com
innoftherockies@hotmail.com
220 E. 10th St. (at Blair St.)
Silverton, CO 81433
Price: Moderate
Credit Cards: AE, D, MC, V
Handicapped Access: No

In Silverton's downtown historic district, this Victorian bed-and-breakfast has a gracious hostess. Inside a charming century-old house, each guest room is individually designed; some have shared baths, while others have private baths with antique clawfoot tubs, or gas fireplaces and mountain views. Rates include a full breakfast and sometimes chocolate cake and sherry in the afternoon. An outdoor hot tub awaits in the backyard gazebo.

THE TELLER HOUSE HOTEL
970-387-5423, 1-800-342-4338
www.tellerhousehotel.com
reservations@tellerhousehotel.com
1250 Greene St. (at W. 12th St.)
Silverton, CO 81433
Price: Moderate
Credit Cards: D, MC, V
Handicapped Access: No

Built in the late 19th century by a local brewer, this family-friendly historic hotel in Silverton's downtown historic district has affable staff. Simple but spacious rooms have Victorian decor, shared or private baths, and free high-speed Wi-Fi Internet access. Some have mountain views. Peak-season rates may include a delightful breakfast served at the hotel's French-American patisserie.

THE WYMAN HOTEL & INN
Innkeepers: Rodger and Tana Wrublik
970-387-5372, 1-800-609-7845
www.thewyman.com
thewyman@frontier.net
1371 Greene St. (at E. 13th St.)
Silverton, CO 81433
Price: Expensive
Credit Cards: AE, D, MC, V
Handicapped Access: No

With the proudest ambience of any hotel in Silverton, the Wyman is a historic landmark. All rooms have feather beds with down pillows and duvets, private baths, telephones, ceiling fans, TVs with VCRs and DVD players, and complimentary high-speed Wi-Fi Internet access. Deluxe rooms also have whirlpool tubs. Unique accommodations are found in the courtyard caboose, which boasts a fireplace. Although the rates are among the most expensive in town, they do include a full breakfast, afternoon tea, and evening wine and cheese hour.

CULTURE

Archaeological Sites
CANYONS OF THE ANCIENTS NATIONAL MONUMENT
970-882-5600
www.co.blm.gov/canm/
Information: Anasazi Heritage Center
27501 CO 184, Dolores, CO 81323
Open: Visitor center open daily 10–4,
November through February; 9–5,
March through October
Admission: Free

The Anasazi Heritage Center (see "Museums," below) should be your first stop for its excellent exhibits and the excavated Domínguez and Escalante Pueblos out back. The museum's visitor information desk has pamphlets with maps for exploring the monument on your own, from the popular Lowry Pueblo National

Solitary ruins are hidden down rough dirt roads inside Canyons of the Ancients National Monument.
Sara Benson & Mike Connolly

Historic Landmark to more solitary ruins, such as Painted Hand Pueblo, with its signature rock paintings and petroglyphs, and Sand Canyon Pueblo, with its far-reaching views. Many outlying sites are accessible only via rough dirt roads, which may be impassable after storms.

CHIMNEY ROCK ARCHAEOLOGICAL AREA

970-883-5359
www.chimneyrockco.org
P.O. Box 1662, Pagosa Springs, CO 81147
Directions: 3 miles south of US 160 on CO 151
Open: Daily 9–4:30, mid-May through September; guided tours usually at 9:30, 10:30, 1, and 2
Admission: Tours per adult $8, children 5–11 $2, children under 5 free

About an hour's drive east of Durango, this Ancestral Puebloan site inside a national forest surrounded by Southern Ute tribal lands has been a focus of excavations since the 1960s. It now operates as an educational and protected archaeological site that is open to the public for guided walking tours atop the high mesa of Chimney Rock. Bring sturdy shoes, a hat, and drinking water for the 1-mile walking tour on a partially paved trail that circles the Great Kiva and the pueblo. Reservations are required for workshops in traditional Native American arts and crafts, including pottery and basketry.

CROW CANYON ARCHAEOLOGICAL CENTER

970-565-8975, 1-800-422-8975
www.crowcanyon.org
23390 County Road K, Cortez, CO 81321
Directions: From Cortez take CO 491 north for 1.5 miles. Turn left at County Road L and drive 1 mile west. Turn left onto County Road 23, which curves to the left after 1 mile and becomes County Road K.
Open: Tours usually available Wednesday and Thursday June through August; call ahead to check availability.
Admission: Tours including lunch per adult $50, child 10–17 $25

West of Mesa Verde National Park outside Cortez, this working archaeological center and educational campus conducts field research in collaboration with Native American tribal members. It offers visitors a unique opportunity to take day tours that include digging alongside real-life archaeologists in the Goodman Point Pueblo excavation site and analyzing artifacts in a scientific laboratory.

HAWKINS PRESERVE

970-565-1151
www.cortezculturalcenter.org
Directions: From S. Broadway (CO 491) south of Main St. in downtown Cortez take W. 7th St. east to S. Cedar St., then turn right and drive south to Verde Vu Dr.
Open: Daily sunrise to sunset
Admission: Free

This small conservation area within Cortez's city limits protects the Hawkins Pueblo, an Ancestral Puebloan site. The preserve sidles along McElmo Creek in a woodland of piñon and juniper trees that also make it a good spot for birding. The preserve has hiking and biking trails, a picnic area, and public restrooms.

HOVENWEEP NATIONAL MONUMENT

970-562-4282
www.nps.gov/hove
McElmo Route, Cortez, CO 81321
Directions: Paved roads lead to the visitor center from Cortez (take County Road G / McElmo Canyon Rd.), and from Highway 191 south of Blanding, Utah.
Open: Daily 8–5; extended hours in summer. Closed Thanksgiving, Christmas, and New Year's Day.
Admission: seven-day entry pass per individual $3, per vehicle $6

Leave the tourist crowds of Mesa Verde behind at this wonderfully remote site near the Utah–Colorado border. It comprises six Ancestral Puebloan villages, with brick towers built atop mesas and along the vertiginous sides of canyons. Start your visit outside the visitor center at the Square Tower Group, which holds a collection of over 30 kiva ruins connected by a peaceful hiking trail. High-clearance vehicles are recommended for visiting the outlying archaeological sites located along unmaintained dirt roads.

MESA VERDE NATIONAL PARK

970-529-4465
www.nps.gov/meve
P.O. Box 8, Mesa Verde, CO 81330
Directions: Entrance off US 160 between Cortez and Durango. A paved road continues approximately 20 miles to Chapin Mesa Visitor Center and beyond.
Open: 24/7/365
Admission: seven-day entry pass per vehicle $10 ($15 Memorial Day through Labor Day)

The region's most visited archaeological sites are the stunning cliff dwellings found within this national park. Delve into Ancestral Puebloan cultures here, starting with the Chapin Mesa Archaeological Museum, which includes historical dioramas and Native American art and cultural artifacts. Rangers lead seasonal guided tours of the famous Cliff Palace and Balcony House, as well as other archaeological sites, some of which are also open for self-guided tours. The main Cliff Palace loop road is open year-round

Dizzying ladders are a part of some ranger-guided tours at Mesa Verde National Park. Sara Benson

but only during daylight hours (varies seasonally). The paved loop road around Wetherill Mesa, which has several hiking trailheads and more cliff dwellings, is open only during summer. Same-day tickets for ranger-guided tours of the cliff dwellings are first-come, first-served, so it's best to arrive at the Chapin Mesa or Far View Visitor Centers as soon as they open in the morning to secure a spot.

View Ancestral Puebloan cliff dwellings at Mesa Verde National Park. Sara Benson & Mike Connolly

UTE MOUNTAIN TRIBAL PARK

970-749-1452, 1-800-847-5485
www.utemountainute.com/tribalpark.htm
P.O. Box 109, Towaoc, CO 81334
Directions: Drive 20 miles south of Cortez to the US 160/491 split.
Open: Tours usually offered April through October; reservations required
Admission: Half-/full-day tours per person $22/$42

Unique tours led by tribal members visit cliff dwellings; inspect artifacts, pictographs, and petroglyph panels; and provide Native American interpretations of geological formations. All tours require travel on gravel roads (take your own vehicle or hire transportation provided by the tribe). The full-day tour that visits cliff dwellings requires climbing ladders and taking a 3-mile hike. Private trips to more remote areas of the park can be arranged. Near the tribal park entrance is a visitor center with a small cultural museum.

Art Galleries

Durango has the most art galleries in southwestern Colorado. For more works by indigenous artists, turn to "Native American Trading Posts and Galleries" under "Shopping," below.

Blue Raven Gallery, www.blueravengalleryco.com, 1-866-545-9189, 1250 Greene St., Silverton. This gallery owned by a sculptor showcases oil and watercolor paintings, mixed-media works, handmade jewelry, and wood carvings by local artists.

Cortez Cultural Center, www.cortezculturalcenter.org, 970-565-1151, 25 N. Market St., Cortez. Multipurpose venue hosts small rotating art shows, with interesting exhibitions including works by Native American artists during summer and fall.

Durango Arts Center, www.durangoarts.org, 970-259-2606, 802 E. 2nd Ave., Durango. Shows works in all media by local artists and national traveling exhibitions.

Ellis West Gallery, www.elliswestgallery.com, 970-382-9855, 822 Main Ave., Durango. This tasteful contemporary gallery exhibits prints, art glass, and jewelry by regional Colorado artists.

Image Counts, www.imagecounts.com, 970-382-0055, Main Mall, 835 Main Ave., Durango. This framing shop sells limited editions of nature photography, including from around the Southwest.

Karyn Galbadon Fine Arts, www.karyngabaldon.com, 970-247-9018, 680 Main Ave., Durango. Although the focus is on landscape and abstract painting, this gallery also carries works by local artists in wood, clay, bronze, and metal, including jewelry.

Kendall Mountain Gallery, www.nrphotography.com/kendallmountaingallery.asp, 913-522-1320, 1240 Blair St., Silverton. Open daily May through October, this small space displays outdoor photography and ceramic and stoneware pottery by San Juan Mountains residents.

Open Shutter Gallery, www.openshuttergallery.com, 970-382-8355, 755 E. 2nd Ave., Durango. This fine-art gallery hosts top-notch photographic exhibitions by local and international artists, with an unexpected variety of subject matter.

Rain Dance Gallery, www.raindance gallery.com, 970-375-2708, 945 Main Ave., Durango. A homey space exhibits contemporary Western and Native American works, including pottery, jewelry, weavings, art glass, sculpture, and photography.

Sorrel Sky Gallery, www.sorrelsky.com, 970-247-3555, 1-866-878-355, 870 Main Ave., Durango. The daughter of a well-known jewelry artist, this impressive gallery's director is an expert in Southwestern and Native American artworks. Inside the gallery you'll find ceramics, oil paintings, watercolors, and pastel drawings, woven baskets, sculptures, and mixed-media creations.

Wild Spirit Gallery, www.wildspirit gallery.com, 970-264-9453, 480 San Juan St. (US 160), Pagosa Springs. This rustic Western gallery carries oil paintings, limited-edition etchings, wood carvings, and bronze sculptures, often depicting cowboy landscapes and Native American ways of life.

Downtown Durango abounds with Native American and contemporary art galleries. Sara Benson

Casinos

Sky Ute Casino, www.skyutecasino.com, 970-563-3000, 1-888-842-4180, 14826 CO 172 N (about 16 miles south of Durango via US 160), Ignacio. With the only nonsmoking gaming rooms in the Four Corners, this casino runs blackjack and poker tables, video poker and slot machines, and bingo. Professional boxing events are held here.

Ute Mountain Casino, www.utemountaincasino.com, 970-565-8800, 1-800-258-8007, 11 miles south of Cortez on US 160/491, Towaoc. Offers blackjack and poker table games, video poker, a bingo hall, and the largest number of nickel slots in the Four Corners region. Rock concerts are staged here.

Cinema

The small-scale **Durango International Film Festival,** www.durangofilm.org, 970-375-7779, is a juried competition with screenings in late February and early March.

Abbey Theatre, www.abbeytheatre.com, 970-385-1711, 128 E. College Ave., Durango. Small arthouse cinema shows independent, foreign, and documentary films.

Fiesta Theatre, www.allentheaters.com, 970-523-6900, 23 W. Main St., Cortez. Marked by a vintage sign, this tiny cinema screens Hollywood movies downtown.

Gaslight Twin Cinema, www.translux movies.com, 970-247-8133, 102 E. 5th St., Durango. Twin movie theater shows first-run, foreign, and independent films.

High Five Cinema, www.transluxmovies.com, 970-247-9799, 900 Trans-Lux Dr., off Camino del Rio (US 550), Durango. At the Durango Mall, this multiplex cinema with Dolby digital sound and stadium seating shows newly released Hollywood flicks.

A touch of Hollywood in the real Old West: the Fiesta Theatre in downtown Cortez. Sara Benson

Starz Film Series, www.atheatregroup.org, 970-387-5337, Miners Union Theatre, 1069 Greene St., Silverton. Shows classic movies, short films, and documentaries six times per year.

Dance

3rd Ave. Dance Company, www.dancedurango.com, 970-259-4122, 1309 E. 3rd Ave., Durango. Amateur local troupe has a diverse repertoire, including works by nationally known guest choreographers.

Cortez Cultural Center, www.cortezculturalcenter.org, 970-565-1151, 25 N. Market St., Cortez. In summer, traditional Native American dances are usually performed several nights per week, followed by a cultural program (see "Theater," below).

Historic Places

HISTORIC DOWNTOWN DURANGO
1-800-525-8855
www.durango.org
Durango Area Tourism Office, 111 S. Camino del Rio (at Gateway Dr.), Durango, CO 81302
Open: Visitor center open daily 8–5

On the National Register of Historic Districts, downtown Durango retains the flavor of the Wild West, with its landmark late-19th-century buildings still standing. Where miners' hardware and pioneer mercantile shops once stood, now you'll find Western outfitters selling custom-fitted hats, handcrafted silver belt buckles, and the like. Don't miss the Victorian-era General Palmer Hotel (see "Lodging," above), which looks much as it did during the town's early days. Drop by the Durango & Silverton Railroad depot, too (see "Museums," below). Once you've finished strolling atmospheric Main Street, have a drink at the old-fashioned Diamond Belle Saloon (see "Nightlife," below).

HISTORIC SILVERTON
970-387-5654, 1-800-752-4494
www.silvertoncolorado.com
Silverton Chamber of Commerce & Visitors Center, US 550 and CO 110
Silverton, CO 81433
Open: Visitor center open daily 10–4, November through April; 9–5, May–June and October; and 9–6, July through September

On the National Register of Historic Districts, historic downtown Silverton has the rough-and-tumble feel of a *Deadwood* episode. If you close your eyes you can almost imagine the brothel girls, roughshod miners, and well-to-do local elite parading along the streets. Today the dusty main thoroughfare of Greene Street and notorious Blair Street are both lined with art galleries and trading posts, small-town restaurants, and Victorian-style hotels and bed-and-breakfast inns. At the visitor center pick up a self-guided walking tour brochure, which includes a stop at the 1902 county jail, now open during summer as a historical museum.

HOWARDSVILLE GHOST TOWN
www.ghosttowns.com/states/co/howardsville
Directions: Take US 550 past the courthouse and museum. Turn right onto County Road 2 and drive approximately 2 miles to the signposted turnoff.
Open: 24/7/365
Admission: Free

As a precursor to Silverton's mining boom, this silver-mining town high in the San Juan Mountains arose in 1874. By the early 1930s it had faded away, but a few wooden buildings are still standing. After you're done snapping periodlike photos, take the interesting tours available nearby at Old Hundred Gold Mine and Mayflower Mill (see separate reviews, below).

MAYFLOWER MILL TOUR

970-387-0294

Directions: Take US 550 past the courthouse and museum. Turn right onto County Road 2 and continue for approximately 4 miles.

Open: Tours available 10–5 daily, late May to September

Admission: Adults $6.50, seniors $5.50, children under 13 free

Optimistically constructed during the Depression, this modern mill was made for refining all of the precious metals formerly mined in Howardsville, including gold, silver, copper, lead, and zinc. Today it's one of the best-preserved metal mills in the West. Proceeds from interesting self-guided tours benefit the Silverton Historical Society.

OLD HUNDRED GOLD MINE TOUR

970-387-5444, 1-800-872-3009

www.minetour.com

P.O. Box 430, Silverton, CO 81433

Directions: Take US 550 past the courthouse and museum. Turn right onto County Road 2. Go 2 miles past the Mayflower Mill, then 2 miles farther to Howardsville ghost town. Cross the creek and immediately turn right onto County Road 4. After .25 mile, fork left onto County Road 4-A and drive another .75 mile.

Open: Tours depart hourly 10–4, mid-May to mid-October.

Admission: Adults $16.95, seniors $14.95, children 5–12 $7.95, children under 5 free

This fascinating tour of an authentic gold mine dating from 1872 takes visitors on a miners' tram straight into the heart of Galena Mountain, then teaches them how to pan for gold. Tours start at the miner's original 1904 bunkhouse, clearly visible on the hillside. Bring a sweater or jacket because the tunnels average 48 degrees Fahrenheit. A family-friendly attraction, the mine is also wheelchair-accessible.

Museums

ANASAZI HERITAGE CENTER

970-882-5600

www.co.blm.gov/ahc/

27501 CO 184 (north of CO 145), Dolores, CO 81323

Open: Daily 10–4, November through February; 9–5, March through October

Admission: Adults $3, children under 18 free

The jumping-off point for backroad explorations of Canyons of the Ancients National Monument (see "Archaeological Sites," above), this museum's multisensory cultural exhibits focus on art, archaeology, and the history of Ancestral Puebloan peoples.

CENTER OF SOUTHWEST STUDIES

970-247-7456

www.swcenter.fortlewis.edu

Fort Lewis College, 1000 Rim Dr. (off E. 8th Ave.), Durango, CO 81301

Directions: Take E. 8th St. east of downtown, then turn left on E. 8th Ave. After 1.1 miles, turn left onto Fort Lewis Dr., then left again onto Rim Dr.

Open: Sunday through Wednesday and Friday 1–4, Thursday 1–7
Admission: Free

This small museum stages exhibitions of Native American art, archaeology, cultural traditions, and history themed around the Four Corners region. The museum's cornerstone is a
permanent collection of Southwestern textiles by Navajo, Pueblo, and Hispanic artisans of
both sexes representing eight centuries of tradition.

DURANGO & SILVERTON NARROW GAUGE RAILROAD MUSEUM

970-247-2733, 1-877-872-4607
www.durangotrain.com
479 Main Ave. (at W. 5th St.)
Durango, CO 81301
Open: Daily 7–6 during summer; other
seasonal hours vary, so call ahead
Admission: Free

For railroad fans, history buffs, and
curious tourists, this museum on the
opposite side of the railroad tracks from
the main depot is maintained by enthusiastic volunteers. Clamber around vintage railroad cars, peruse the historical
photos and railway maps, and talk with
the old-timers about local history
while vintage trains from the Durango
& Silverton Railroad (see the
"Transportation" chapter) are puffing
away outside in the engine yard.

*The historic Durango & Silverton Narrow Gauge
Railroad departs year-round. The railroad museum is
across the tracks from the main depot in Durango.*
Sara Benson

MANCOS PIONEER MUSEUM

970-553-7434
www.mancosvalley.com
Mancos Visitor Center, Main St. at Railroad Ave., Mancos, CO 81328
Open: Monday 10–5, Tuesday through Saturday 9–4
Admission: Free

Inside the visitor center, this tiny museum touches on the history of the Mancos Valley,
including the founding Wetherill family and interesting characters like Western fiction
writer Louis L'Amour, who once resided nearby in the La Plata Mountains. Pick up a self-
guided walking tour brochure for the historic downtown district here.

SOUTHERN UTE MUSEUM

970-563-9583
www.southern-ute.nsn.us
14826 CO 172, Ignacio, CO 81137
Open: Monday through Friday 8–5
Admission: By donation

Located next to the casino, this walk-through museum has just a few rooms of modest exhibits put together by the Southern Ute tribe. Highlights include video interviews with contemporary leaders and elders; and meticulous displays of traditional art and crafts.

THE ANIMAS MUSEUM

970-259-2402
www.animasmuseum.org
3065 W. 2nd Ave. (at W. 31st St.), Durango, CO 81302
Open: Tuesday through Saturday 10–4, November through April; Monday through Saturday 10–6, May through October
Admission: Adults $2.50, children 12 and under free

Inside an early 20th-century schoolhouse, this community museum displays local history, including relics of cowboys and rural life, Ute tribal arts and cultural artifacts, and exhibits about the natural history of the San Juan Mountains and Animas River areas.

Music
See also "Nightlife," below.

Abbey Theatre, www.abbeytheatre.com, 970-385-1711, 128 E. College Ave., Durango. Occasionally schedules independent live-music shows and events.

Cortez Cultural Center, www.cortezculturalcenter.org, 970-565-1151, 25 N. Market St., Cortez. During the summer, cultural programs are held here almost nightly, including performances by Native American tribal musicians and dancers.

Community Concert Hall, at Fort Lewis College, www.durangoconcerts.com, 970-247-7657, 1000 Rim Dr., Durango. Local music groups and national touring artists, from rock and blues to classical music and chorales, take the stage.

Music in the Mountains, www.musicinthemountains.com, 970-385-6820, Durango and Pagosa Springs. Classical music festival happens from mid-July through mid-August, with dozens of orchestral, chamber, conservatory, and pops music concerts around town.

Scoot'n Blues, www.scootnblues.com, 970-259-1400, 900 Main Ave., Durango. Inside a brick building, this cross between an Irish pub and a motorcycle bar is big enough to handle crowds of locals and tourists and serves tons of good grub. Live bands perform frequently.

Silverton Brass Band, www.silverton colorado.com, 970-387-5654, Silverton. Just follow your ears to find this irascible brass band of pranksters marching through the streets of Silverton every Sunday afternoon during the summer tourist season.

Durango has the liveliest nightlife in southwestern Colorado, from plentiful brewpubs to rockin' live-music venues. Sara Benson

Storyville, www.durangobeat.org, 970-259-1475, 1150-B Main Ave., Durango. This downtown bar and grill hosts a variety of live musical acts, including the sounds of local country-and-western, blues, and rock bands, as well as national touring acts.

The Summit, www.durangosummit.com, 970-247-2324, 600 Main Ave., Durango. Hidden up a narrow flight of stairs, this tiny live-music venue puts together a calendar of punk, rock, hip hop, and other sounds with a bar serving microbrews, plus pool tables, foosball, video golf, a jukebox, and DJs some nights.

Nightlife

Bear Creek Saloon, www.bearcreeksaloon.net, 970-264-5611, 475 Lewis St., Pagosa Springs. A locals' hangout with bottles of Colorado microbrews, rustic wooden furnishings, billiards tables, retro and sports video-game machines, and karaoke nights.

Carver Brewing Co., www.carverbrewing.com, 970-259-2545, 1022 Main Ave., Durango. This polished downtown brewpub is a popular place to grab a pint of Colorado Trail Nut Brown Ale. There's a beer garden and sometimes live music, too.

Columbine Bar, 970-533-9906, 123 W. Grand Ave., Mancos. This redbrick building hides one of Colorado's oldest continuously operating bars, open since 1903. They're still serving ice-cold beer and burgers to crowds who come to play pool and darts and listen to live bands.

Diamond Belle Saloon, www.strater.com, 970-247-4431, 1-800-247-4431, 699 Main Ave., Durango. Inside the historic Strater Hotel, this atmospheric old-fashioned saloon is where Louis L'Amour was inspired to write some of his Western novels. A variety of live music happens almost nightly, from acoustic singer-songwriters to ragtime pianists.

Dolores River Brewery, www.doloresriverbrewery.com, 970-882-4677, 100 S. 4th St., Dolores. Drawing locals and tourists alike, this small-town brewery may be just getting on its feet but is already serving up superior suds. Occasionally there's live music.

Far View Lodge, www.visitmesaverde.com, 970-529-4422, Mesa Verde National Park. This upstairs patio at the Far View Lodge has panoramic views of the ancient mesa and an exceptional list of wine and cocktails.

JJ's Riverwalk Restaurant & Pub, 970-264-9100, 326 & 356 E. US 160, Pagosa Springs. Long-standing pub puts on a congenial happy hour with sunset views of the San Juan River.

Lady Falconburgh's Barley Exchange, 970-382-9664, 640 Main Ave., Durango. Head downstairs to where bohemian college students crowd around a bar with over three dozen brews on tap and dozens of more hard-to-find beer brands in bottles.

Main Street Brewery, 970-564-9112, 21 E. Main St., Cortez. This spacious downtown restaurant crafts a variety of Bavarian-style brews, with guest beers on tap and bottled imports, too. The menu of pub grub is hit-or-miss.

Miners Tavern, 970-387-9885, 1069 Greene St., Silverton. This locals' watering hole is inside a building that has been standing for over 100 years, during which time it has variously been a labor union meeting place, dance hall, and mortician's business.

Moe's Starlight Lounge, 970-259-9018, 937 Main Ave., Durango. This hip martini bar is a fabulous homage to mid-century modern design, with live jazz and DJ nights. The cool cocktails are rated, from beginner through advanced.

Pagosa Brewing Company, www.pagosabrewing.com, 970-731-2739, 100 N. Pagosa Blvd., off Bastille Dr. behind the Wild Hare, Pagosa Springs. Although it's difficult to find, this award-winning brewmasters' tasting room and beer garden are exactly what every ski town needs. Make sure you sip the Powder Day IPA.

Pride of the West, 970-387-5150, 1323 Greene St., Silverton. A high-altitude biker bar, this restaurant saloon has pool, darts, dancing, live music, and plenty of beer and spirits. Live-music shows happen nightly during summer, with reggae to roots-rock sounds.

Silverton Brewery, www.silvertonbrewing.com, 970-387-5033, 1333 Greene St., Silverton. Handcrafted brews are made in small batches

A microbrewery in downtown Cortez with an ancient deity, the kokopelli, as its mascot. Sara Benson

inside this wooden clapboard building, the first brewery to open in Silverton since Prohibition. Try the Doppelbock Diamond or unusual barley wine.

Ska Brewing, www.skabrewing.com, 970-247-5792, 545 Turner Dr., Durango. While this isn't a bar and it's open only during the day, don't miss a visit to the most punk brewmasters in southwestern Colorado. Down a pint of the Steeltoe Stout or the True Blonde Ale once, and you're hooked. Call ahead for directions.

Steamworks Brewing Co., www.steamworksbrewing.com, 970-259-9200, 801 E. 2nd Ave., Durango. Off Main Avenue, this cavernous brewpub has a long list of rotating brews, from the classic Steam Engine Lager and spicy Ale Diablo to guest taps, too.

Theater

A Theatre Group, www.atheatregroup.org, 970-387-5337, Miners Union Theatre, 1069 Greene St., Silverton. Award-winning small theater company produces popular plays during summer and winter seasons.

Bar D Chuckwagon, www.bardchuckwagon.com, 970-247-5753, 1-888-800-5753. Famous Old West dinner shows with loads of barbecue and cowboy music held on a ranch near Durango from Memorial Day through Labor Day, rain or shine.

Cortez Cultural Center, www.cortezculturalcenter.org, 970-565-1151, 25 N. Market St., Cortez. Cultural programs take place almost every night during summer, including lectures by a Navajo code talker and Native American flute concerts.

Diamond Circle Theatre, www.diamondcirclemelodrama.com, 970-247-3400, Strater Hotel, 699 Main Ave., Durango. Old West melodramas and vaudeville shows entertain inside the historic Strater Hotel in downtown Durango.

Seasonal Events

JANUARY
Snowdown Winter Festival, www.snowdown.org, 1-800-525-8555, Durango

FEBRUARY
Winterfest, www.pagosachamber.com, 970-264-2360, 1-800-252-2204, Pagosa Springs

Winter Folk Music Festival, www.pagosachamber.com, 970-731-5582, Pagosa Springs

MARCH
Durango Independent Film Festival, www.durangofilmfestival.com, 970-375-7779, Durango

Four States Agricultural Exposition, www.fourstatesagexpo.com, 970-565-3414, Cortez

Hozhoni Days, www.fortlewis.edu/student_life/native_american_center/hozhoni_days.asp, 1-877-352-2656, Durango

APRIL
Durango Bluegrass Meltdown, www.durangomeltdown.com, 970-259-7200, Durango

MAY
Mesa Verde Country Indian Arts & Culture Festival,
www.mesaverdecountry.com/tourism, 970-561-115, Cortez, Dolores, Mancos, and Towaoc

JUNE
Animas River Days, www.durango.org, 1-800-525-8555, Durango

Dolores River Festival, www.doloresriverfestival.com, 970-882-4018, Dolores

Four Corners Arts & Crafts Fiesta, www.cortezculturalcenter.org, 970-565-1151, Cortez

Indiefest Music Festival, www.folkwest.com, 1-877-472-4672, Pagosa Springs

Mancos Days, www.mancosvalley.com, 970-533-7434, Mancos

Ute Mountain Bear Dance, www.utemountaincasino.com, 970-565-8800, Towaoc

Ute Mountain Roundup, www.utemountainroundup.com, 970-565-1151, Cortez

JULY

Durango Cowgirl Classic, www.durango.org, 1-800-525-8855, Durango

Montezuma County Fair, www.co.montezuma.co.us, 970-565-3414, Cortez

Red Ryder Roundup Rodeo, www.harmanartmuseum.com, 970-264-2332, Pagosa
Springs

AUGUST

Archuleta County Fair, www.archuletacountyfair.com, 970-264-2388, Pagosa Springs

Dawg Days Chili Cook-off, www.cortezculturalcenter.org, 970-565-1151, Cortez

Durango & Silverton Narrow Gauge Railfest, www.durangotrain.com, 970-247-2733,
1-877-872-4607, Durango and Silverton

La Plata County Fair, http://co.laplata.co.us/fairgrounds/LaPlataCountyFair, 970-382-
6471, Durango

Main Avenue Juried Arts Festival, www.durango.org, 970-259-2606, Durango

Escalante Days, www.doloreschamber.com, 970-882-4018, Dolores

Four Corners Folk Festival, www.folkwest.com, 1-877-472-4672, Pagosa Springs

Mesa Verde Country Wine & Art Festival, www.mesaverdecountry.com, 970-565-8227,
1-800-530-2998, Mesa Verde National Park

Montezuma Float Balloon Rally, www.mesaverdecountry.com, 970-565-3414, Cortez

Ute Mountain Pow Wow, www.utemountaincasino.com, 970-565-8800, Towaoc

SEPTEMBER

Arts & Crafts Fall Colorfest, www.cortezculturalcenter.org, 970-565-1151, Cortez

Colorfest Balloon Rally and Wine & Cheese Tasting, www.pagosachamber.com, 970-
264-2360, 1-800-252-2204, Pagosa Springs

Mancos Valley Balloon Festival and Juried Art Fair, www.mancosvalley.com, 970-533-
7434, Mancos

Mountain Chile Cha Cha, www.folkwest.com/chile, 1-877-472-4672, Pagosa Springs

Western Heritage and Plein Air Art Exhibit, www.cortezculturalcenter.org, 970-565-
1151, Cortez

OCTOBER

Bordello Ball, www.silvertoncolorado.com, 970-387-5527, Silverton

Durango Cowboy Gathering, www.durangocowboygathering.org, 970-382-7494, Durango

Mancos Medicine Horse Music Festival, www.medicinehorsecenter.org/events, 970-533-
7403, Mancos

Octoberfest, www.pagosachamber.com, 970-264-2360, Pagosa Springs

DECEMBER

Mancos Old-Fashioned Christmas, www.mancosvalley.com, 970-533-7434, Mancos

RESTAURANTS

Cortez

DRY DOCK RESTAURANT & PUB

970-564-9404
www.thedrydock.com
200 W. Main St. (US 160), Cortez, CO 81321
Open: Daily
Price: Expensive
Cuisine: Seafood/Southwestern
Serving: D
Credit Cards: AE, D, MC, V
Handicapped Access: Yes

At the edge of downtown, this laid-back family restaurant serves up seafood and steaks, as well as Italian pastas, Mexican classics like fajitas and enchiladas, and pub-style fare, from green-chili cactus burgers to salsa-topped chicken sandwiches. Peruse a long list of signature martinis and specialty cocktails like the Dreamsicle or the Drunken Monkey.

FRANCISCA'S RESTAURANT

970-565-4093
125 E. Main St. (US 160), Cortez, CO 81321
Open: Tuesday through Saturday
Price: Moderate
Cuisine: Mexican
Serving: L (Wednesday through Friday),
D (Tuesday through Saturday)
Credit Cards: MC, V
Handicapped Access: Yes

Downtown homey Francisca's dishes up Mexican-American favorites, including cheesy enchiladas and slow-roasted pork with green chili sauce. All of the tortillas, tamales, and pillowy sopapillas are homemade, and fruity margaritas are mixed by the pitcherful.

HOMESTEADERS

970-565-6253
www.thehomesteaders.com
45 E. Main St. (US 160), Cortez, CO 81321
Open: Monday through Saturday; daily during summer
Price: Moderate
Cuisine: American/Mexican
Serving: L, D
Credit Cards: MC, V
Handicapped Access: Yes

A traveler's best bet for breakfast, this homespun café throws red-and-white checkered cloths on wooden tables with high-backed country chairs. Barbecue, sirloin steaks, and sandwiches made with fresh-baked bread are on the lunch and dinner menu, but the old-fashioned buttermilk pancakes and fluffy omelettes are the real eye-openers.

ON THE BAYOU

970-565-4079
801 E. Main St. (US 160), Cortez, CO 81321
Open: Tuesday through Saturday
Price: Moderate
Cuisine: Cajun/Creole
Serving: L, D
Credit Cards: MC, V
Handicapped Access: Yes

Obscured by a row of chain motels and strip malls, this gem run by folks from Louisiana is worth digging up. Their menu of Southern classics is the real deal, from golden hush puppies and po' boy sandwiches to jumbo bowls of jambalaya and shrimp étouffée. The family-style restaurant has Gulf Coast touches, complete with fishing nets and a Cajun country jukebox.

Dolores

DOLORES RIVER BREWERY

970-882-4677
www.doloresriverbrewery.com
100 S. 4th St. (at Central Ave.)
Dolores, CO 81323
Open: Tuesday through Saturday
Price: Moderate
Cuisine: American
Serving: D
Credit Cards: MC, V
Handicapped Access: Yes

Down by the railway tracks, this youthful brewpub pulls in crowds of convivial locals and passersby not only for original microbrews on tap, but also for a top-notch menu of pub grub, including exotic pizzas (Thai curry or chicken cordon bleu, anyone?) and calzones. Take your pint out onto the patio or stay cozy indoors when it's chilly outside.

OLD GERMANY RESTAURANT, LOUNGE & BEER GARDEN

970-882-7549
200 S. 8th St. (at Railroad Ave.)
Dolores, CO 81323
Open: Tuesday through Saturday
Price: Moderate
Cuisine: European
Serving: D
Credit Cards: MC, V
Handicapped Access: Yes

Locals know where to find a big breakfast: at Durango's Brickhouse Café. Sara Benson

An unexpected find by the river, this German beer garden has a reasonable restaurant where families fill up on schnitzel and pork roast hearty enough to see them through a whole day of exploring remote ruins in Canyons of the Ancients National Monument. However, the best menu offerings are homemade soups and the salad bar.

Durango

937 MAIN; KEN & SUE'S PLACE

970-259-2616
937 Main Ave. (at W. 9th St.)
Durango, CO 81301
Open: Daily
Price: Expensive
Cuisine: New American
Serving: L (Monday through Friday), D
Credit Cards: AE, D, MC, V
Handicapped Access: Yes

A perennial favorite, this distinguished downtown bistro serves up a New American menu with flair. Relax among the well-heeled crowds and sip a top-notch cocktail before forking into lobster ravioli or chipotle pork chops followed up by signature cranberry crème brûlée for dessert. Service is faultless.

BRICKHOUSE CAFE & COFFEE BAR

970-247-3760
www.brickhousecafe.com
1849 Main Ave. (at W. 19th St.)
Durango, CO 81301
Open: Daily; shorter winter hours
Price: Inexpensive
Cuisine: American
Serving: B, L
Credit Cards: MC, V
Handicapped Access: No

This is the kind of spot where everyone greets each other by name. But don't be shy about stepping off the front porch and into the country Victorian–style dining room for a homemade malted waffle, plate of biscuits and gravy, or deli-style sandwich with a salad of organic greens. Breakfast is served all day, and the atmosphere is family-friendly.

CARVER BREWING CO.

970-259-2545
www.carverbrewing.com
1022 Main Ave. (at E. 10th St.)
Durango, CO 81301
Open: Daily
Price: Moderate
Cuisine: American
Serving: B, L, D
Credit Cards: AE, D, MC, V
Handicapped Access: Yes

This polished downtown brewpub serves a solid three meals a day, from vegetarian breakfasts like portabello-mushroom eggs Benedict to hearty pub sandwiches and soup-filled bread bowls at lunch, and sirloin tips braised with their Colorado Trail Nut Brown Ale at dinner. When the sun shines, grab a table on the back patio.

CYPRUS CAFE

970-385-6884
www.cypruscafe.com
725 E. 2nd Ave. (at E. 7th St.)
Durango, CO 81301
Open: Monday through Saturday
Price: Expensive
Cuisine: Mediterranean
Serving: L, D
Credit Cards: AE, D, MC, V
Handicapped Access: No

Follow the garden path and step inside this gorgeous cream-colored house hidden off Durango's main street. With an elegant atmosphere and breezy patio, this Mediterranean restaurant features a tempting Greek and Italian menu, with more adventurous entrees at dinner, such as rigatoni with shrimp and spinach and salt-roasted duck with cranberry-cardamom chutney. The seafood is sustainably harvested and the meats locally raised.

DURANGO DINER

970-247-9889
www.durangodiner.com
957 Main Ave. (at W. 10th St.)
Durango, CO 81301
Open: Daily
Price: Inexpensive
Cuisine: American
Serving: B, L
Credit Cards: None
Handicapped Access: Yes

If you're craving no-nonsense diner fare, this Old West institution downtown has wooden booths that are always packed. The menu packs a punch, with breakfast served all day, including specialties like blueberry pancakes, biscuits and gravy with a dollop of green chili sauce, and the kitchen-sink omelette, if you dare. Portion sizes are gigantic.

EAST BY SOUTHWEST

970-247-5533
www.eastbysouthwest.com
160 E. College Dr. (at E. 2nd Ave.)
Durango, CO 81301
Open: Daily
Price: Expensive
Cuisine: Fusion
Serving: L (Monday through Saturday), D
Credit Cards: AE, D, MC, V
Handicapped Access: Yes

Ranging far across the Pacific Rim to Japan and back via South America, the menu at this fun-loving fusion restaurant is nothing if not adventurous. Start off with Hawaiian *poke* (marinated and spiced raw fish), then move on to Kumamoto oysters on the half shell or pork pot stickers with jalapeño sauce. Wash it all down with a mojito or a smooth sake cocktail.

MAMA'S BOY

970-247-0060
www.mamasboydurango.com
2659 Main Ave. (at W. 27th St.)

Durango, CO 81303
Open: Daily
Price: Moderate
Cuisine: Italian
Serving: D
Credit Cards: AE, D, MC, V
Handicapped Access: No

In a white house at the outskirts of downtown, fine tweaks to classic Italian dishes make the hearty fare beloved by firefighters and tourists alike. Try the rock shrimp and bay scallops drizzled with dill cream sauce or the ravioli Florentine with herbed spinach. New York–style pizza, calzones, and huge hero sandwiches are popular at lunch or for a quick takeout meal.

THE PALACE RESTAURANT & QUIET LADY TAVERN

970-247-2018
www.palacedurango.com
505 Main Ave. (at W. 5th St.)
Durango, CO 81301
Open: Daily
Price: Moderate
Cuisine: American
Serving: L, D
Credit Cards: AE, D, MC, V
Handicapped Access: Yes

Next to the historic railway depot, this old-fashioned neo-Victorian tavern and restaurant has quaint decor, from floral wallpaper to the curled sconces on the walls. No other place in town can beat these lunch specials: tasty, filling plates of curried chicken salad, homemade soups and salads, and the reliable Reuben sandwich for $10 or less. Service is attentive.

SEASONS ROTISSERIE & GRILL

970-382-9790
www.seasonsofdurango.com
764 Main Ave. (at E. 8th St.)
Durango, CO 81301
Open: Daily
Price: Expensive

Cuisine: New American
Serving: L (Monday through Friday), D
Credit Cards: AE, D, MC, V
Handicapped Access: Yes

With an award-winning wine list, this warm and inviting downtown restaurant with honey-colored walls proffers a swank menu of worldly tastes, from hoisin-glazed baby back ribs with spicy Asian slaw to Kobe beef carpaccio, along with local favorites like grilled Colorado lamb sirloin. True to the establishment's name, the innovative menu changes with the seasons.

SERIOUS TEXAS BAR-B-Q

970-247-2240
www.serioustexasbbq.com
3535 N. Main Ave. (US 550)
Durango, CO 81301
Open: Daily
Cuisine: Barbecue
Serving: L, D
Credit Cards: MC, V
Handicapped Access: Yes

If you've been to the Lone Star State, you'll approve of the tender beef brisket, succulent pork spare ribs, and pulled pork with cherry-chipotle salsa served here. Grab a drink out of the silver washtub filled with ice-cold sodas and Texas label beers, then order side dishes of cheesy potatoes, pinto beans, and homemade pie. Savor it all out on the patio, or get takeout to go.

STEAMWORKS BREWING CO.

970-259-9200
www.steamworksbrewing.com
801 E. 2nd Ave. (at E. 8th St.)
Durango, CO 81301
Open: Daily
Price: Moderate
Cuisine: Southwestern/Mexican
Serving: L, D
Credit Cards: AE, D, MC, V
Handicapped Access: Yes

Come here for mighty microbrews like Third Eye IPA, but think about staying for the food. Carnivores fork into the Southwest steak salad and pork chops with an orange-poblano BBQ sauce; vegetarians have options, too. The Southwestern menu, which shows Tex-Mex and Cajun influences, has red chili icons next to the hottest, spiciest dishes.

Hesperus

THE KENNEBEC CAFE AND BAKERY

970-247-5674
www.kennebeccafe.com
4 County Road 124 (off US 160), Hesperus
Directions: At the La Plata Canyon turnoff, about 10 miles west of Durango
Open: Tuesday through Sunday
Price: Expensive
Cuisine: New American
Serving: L, D
Credit Cards: MC, V
Handicapped Access: Yes
Special Features: Reservations accepted

Worth the drive out of town, this charming house surrounded by gardens in the La Plata Mountain range is run by chef-owners who take pride in a contemporary American bistro menu that exhibits European influences and features fresh produce and organic meats. Don't miss the signature dessert creations. Sunday brunch features apple-walnut pancakes and brioche French toast.

Mancos

ABSOLUTE BAKERY & CAFE

970-533-1200
110 N. Main St. (at Grand Ave.)
Mancos, CO 81328
Open: Daily
Price: Inexpensive
Cuisine: Eclectic
Serving: B, L
Credit Cards: MC, V
Handicapped Access: Yes

This high-ceilinged, antique-looking bakery and café is always busy with foot traffic. Follow the smell of freshly baked loaves, pastries, and desserts up to the espresso bar. Or sit down at a table by the bookcases and enjoy a garden-fresh salad or sandwich served with a tall, cool glass of lavender lemonade or iced tea.

PANGAEA

970-533-9809
145 W. Grand Ave. (at Main St.)
Mancos, CO 81328
Open: Daily
Price: Moderate
Cuisine: Eclectic
Serving: L, D
Credit Cards: MC, V
Handicapped Access: No

Easily spotted by the rainbow-striped umbrellas and picket fence out front, this converted house boasts a modern café of American comfort food with a twist, including whopping chipotle barbecue chicken sandwiches and other feasts at lunch. Everything is freshly made, and Sunday brunches are worth detouring for.

MILLWOOD JUNCTION

970-533-7338
101 Railroad Ave. (at US 160)
Mancos, CO 81328
Open: Daily
Price: Expensive
Cuisine: Steak/seafood
Serving: L (Monday through Friday), D
Credit Cards: MC, V
Handicapped Access: Yes

This behemoth, family-friendly restaurant just off the highway is always full of tourists and locals. When the sun shines, grab a table on the patio and dig into a free-ranging menu of steaks, ribs, pasta, and blackened catfish, along with a 25-item salad bar. Friday nights feature an all-you-can-eat seafood buffet.

Mesa Verde National Park

THE METATE ROOM RESTAURANT

970-529-4422
www.visitmesaverde.com
Far View Lodge, P.O. Box 277
Mancos, CO 81328
Open: Daily early May to early November
Price: Expensive
Cuisine: Southwestern
Serving: D
Credit Cards: AE, D, MC, V
Handicapped Access: Yes
Special Features: No reservations

The airy, elegant Metate Room is a breed apart from many other national park lodge restaurants. Consistently from year to year, chef Todd Halnier devises a Southwestern fusion menu, including dishes made with produce like that once eaten by Ancestral Puebloans, such as locally raised corn, beans, squash, and cactus. The Rocky Mountain elk tenderloin and hickory-smoked buffalo strip steak are standouts, as is the sommelier-chosen wine list. The Cliff Palace is an unbelievable whopper of a decadent dessert.

Pagosa Springs

ALLEY HOUSE GRILLE

970-264-0999
214 Pagosa St. (US 160)
Pagosa Springs, CO 81147
Open: Tuesday through Saturday
Price: Expensive
Cuisine: International
Serving: D
Credit Cards: AE, MC, V
Handicapped Access: No
Special Features: Reservations recommended

With a well-polished atmosphere, this downtown gem is a local favorite. Not only is the wine list notable, but the menu of globally influenced fusion fare is delec-

Chef Todd Halnier's creative cuisine makes the Metate Room at Far View Lodge inside Mesa Verde National Park a don't-miss dining experience. Courtesy ARAMARK

table. The talented kitchen turns out everything from curried chicken, mesquite-grilled pork chops, and pesto grilled shrimp with Israeli-style paella to gourmet pizzas that please adults and kids alike.

DOGWOOD CAFE

970-731-2324
www.cafedogwood.com
10 Solomon Dr., Pagosa Springs, CO 81147
Directions: Off US 160 at Piedra Rd., behind the Super 8 motel
Open: Wednesday through Sunday
Price: Moderate
Cuisine: Southern
Serving: B (Saturday through Sunday), L, D (Wednesday through Sunday)
Credit Cards: MC, V
Handicapped Access: Yes

Run by expatriates from Georgia, the Dogwood Cafe is the place for real, down-home-style Southern cooking. Sit down at a cozy table inlaid with bright mosaic tiles with a passion fruit margarita or hurricane cocktail in hand. Order fried catfish with okra and sweet potato casserole at lunch, or classic shrimp and grits with a side of fried pickles at dinner. Brunch featuring N'awlins-style beignets is served on weekends.

FARRAGO MARKET CAFE

970-264-4600
175 Pagosa St. (US 160)
Pagosa Springs, CO 81157
Open: Daily
Price: Inexpensive
Cuisine: New American
Serving: B, L
Credit Cards: MC, V
Handicapped Access: Yes

An inspirational find on the east side of downtown, this bakery and market marries fresh local produce with a globally minded menu. The result? Healthy, delicious salads, stuffed sandwiches, homemade soups, baked goodies, specialty coffees, and homemade desserts. Service may be slow, but it's usually worth the wait. Free high-speed Wi-Fi Internet access available.

KIP'S GRILL AND CANTINA

970-264-3663
121 N. Pagosa Blvd. (off US 160)
Pagosa Springs, CO 81147
Open: Daily
Price: Inexpensive
Cuisine: Mexican-American
Serving: L, D
Credit Cards: MC, V
Handicapped Access: Yes

This locals' haunt is earmarked by a red-hot chili sign. Inside the South of the Border—themed watering hole, good ol' Pabst Blue Ribbon beer is on tap and the tiny kitchen dishes up spicy fare like buffalo burgers stuffed with mozzarella cheese and green chilies, and Baja-style fish tacos. The patio out front is open during balmy weather.

Silverton

THE BENT ELBOW

970-387-5775
www.thebent.com
1114 Blair St. (at E. 11th St.)
Silverton, CO 81433
Open: Daily May through October
Price: Moderate
Cuisine: American
Serving: L (daily), D (Sunday through Friday, June through August)
Credit Cards: AE, D, MC, V
Handicapped Access: Yes

On the ground floor of a historic hotel, this convivial restaurant often has live music in the evenings. The cozy, turn-of-the-20th-century atmosphere comes complete with Victorian costumed servers and antique bottles lining the saloon walls. The home-style Western menu includes favorites like hot roast beef sandwiches and full-on steak-and-potatoes dinners.

HANDLEBARS

970-387-5395
www.handlebarsco.com
117 W. 13th St. (at Greene St.)
Silverton, CO 81433
Open: Daily May through October
Price: Moderate
Cuisine: Western/Southwestern
Serving: L, D
Credit Cards: MC, V
Handicapped Access: Yes

The busiest restaurant in Silverton, this 19th-century saloon has a casual, family-friendly atmosphere. Hot, heaping plates of all things Western and Southwestern are served, from buffalo chili and cream of green chili soup to slabs of barbecue baby back ribs and chicken-fried steak. If you come in sporting a mustache (handlebars, get it?), the jolly staff may take your photo and hang it by the bar.

Even day-trippers in a hurry to catch the next train back to Durango have time for an old-fashioned lunch in downtown Silverton. Sara Benson

NATALIA'S 1912 FAMILY RESTAURANT

970-387-5300
www.natalias1912.com
1159 Blair St. (at 12th St.)
Silverton, CO 81433
Open: Daily May through October
Price: Moderate
Cuisine: American
Serving: L, D
Credit Cards: AE, D, MC, V
Handicapped Access: Yes

Silverton is full of turn-of-the-20th-century buildings that have been rehabbed into restaurants. This former bordello decorated with historical photos, antique furnishings, and curios is justifiably popular for its hot-and-cold lunch buffet and salad bar. It's a convenient value for day-trippers catching the next train back to Durango. During summer there's often live music and a small patio with mountain views.

THE PICKLE BARREL

970-387-5713
www.thepicklebarrel.com
1304 Greene St. (at E. 13th St.)
Silverton, CO 81433
Open: Daily (Tuesday through Saturday during winter)
Price: Moderate
Cuisine: American
Serving: L, D
Credit Cards: MC, V
Handicapped Access: Yes

Inside a late 19th-century mercantile shop building from the town's early mining days, this family-friendly restaurant boasts quick service and a full bar with a selection of wines. Expect sweet-potato fries, gourmet burgers, and classic sandwiches with a twist at lunch, and pastas, prime rib, and steaks with fully loaded baked potatoes at dinner.

Bakeries, Coffeehouses, and Juice Bars

Avalanche Coffee House, 970-387-5282, 1067 Blair St., Silverton. A charming alpine hut brews French-pressed coffee and espresso drinks, perfect with a bagel, pastry, sandwich, salad, or homemade soup.

Durango Bagel, 970-385-7297, 106 E. 5th St., Durango. At this perfect college-town bagel shop, the schmears are generous and there's a fridge full of all-natural bottled juices.

Down to Earth Cafe and Juice Bar, 970-882-2660, 1319 Railroad Ave. (CO 145), Dolores. At the Dolores Wellness Center, this brand-new smoothie bar and health-conscious deli makes a mean latte.

Harmony Works and Juice Bar, 970-264-6633, 145 Hot Springs Blvd., Pagosa Springs. Inside the hot springs resort, come here for healthy smoothies, soups, salads, sandwiches, and light dinners of spa cuisine.

Jean-Pierre Bakery, www.jeanpierrebakery.com, 970-385-0122, 601 Main Ave., Durango. This French-owned bakery and café has artful display cases filled with scrumptious pastries and oven-fresh breads to grab and go.

Mad Mama's Pies, 970-387-5877, 1157 Greene St., Silverton. Serving home-baked fruit and cream pies to die for, Mad Mama's also makes takeout picnic lunches.

Magpie's Newsstand Café, 970-259-1159, 707 Main Ave., Durango. Catch up on dozens of magazines and newspapers while you down a daily dose of caffeine.

Main Book Company, 970-565-8158, 34 W. Main St., Cortez. Next to a tranquil art gallery, this independent bookstore has a civilized espresso bar at the back stocked with biscotti and sugary treats.

Mesa Mocha Espresso Bar, 602-331-5210, Far View Terrace, Mesa Verde National Park. Opposite the Far View Visitor Center, this espresso bar also serves up banana shakes, baked goodies, and healthy wrap sandwiches.

Pagosa Baking Co., 970-264-9348, 238 Pagosa St., Pagosa Springs. With old-fashioned cinnamon rolls, lemon cookies, and brownies galore, this hometown bakery satisfies any sweet tooth.

Silver Bean, 970-946-4404, 410 W. Main St., Cortez. Set inside a shiny Airstream trailer south of downtown, this quirky place brews strong espresso and hands out free Oreo cookies (while supplies last) with any purchase.

Steaming Bean Coffee Co., www.the bean.com, 970-385-7901, 915 Main Ave., Durango. For a hot cup o' joe made from freshly roasted, shade-grown, and often fairly traded organic beans, head for this sociable coffeehouse.

Hot coffee and espresso drinks are brewed inside an Airstream trailer parked outside downtown Cortez.
Sara Benson & Mike Connolly

Victoria's Parlor, 970-264-0204, 274 Pagosa St., Pagosa Springs. Step inside a Victorian house for European-style tea, coffee, pastries, desserts, and hot lunches.

Delis, Desserts, and Ice Cream

The Choke Cherry Tree, www.thechokecherrytree.com, 970-731-4951, 1-800-809-0769, 4760 W. US 160, Pagosa Springs. This alpine house sells homemade caramels, fudge, toffee, chocolate truffles, and signature chocolate-and-caramel confections.

Once Upon a Sandwich, 970-565-8292, 7 W. Main St., Cortez. Busy deli sells custom-made sandwiches with all the fixin's and beer-battered sweet-potato fries. There are ooey-gooey ice cream concoctions for dessert.

Smedley's Ice Cream Parlour, 970-387-5713, 1314 Greene St., Silverton. On Silverton's historic main street, this old-fashioned creamery makes its own flavors on site.

Grocery Stores and Markets

Cortez Farmers' Market, www.cortezfarmmarket.com, 970-565-3123, off Main St. between S. Elm St. and S. Chestnut St., Cortez. Buy farm-fresh produce and more between 7:30 AM and noon on Saturday during the growing season (usually April through October).

Nature's Oasis, www.shopnaturesoasis.com, 970-247-1988, 1123 Camino Del Rio, Durango. A large health-oriented grocery store on the outskirts of downtown Durango stocks organic produce, bulk foods, and freshly made deli sandwiches, soups, and salads.

Zuma Natural Foods, 970-533-7300, 121 Railroad Ave., Mancos. On the south frontage road of US 160, this small natural foods market is a community gathering place.

Recreation

Bicycling and Mountain Biking

Durango is southwestern Colorado's hub for road cycling and mountain biking. Paved recreational paths, long-distance highway routes, and hundreds of miles of single-track trails in the mountains and river valleys, even along old stagecoach roads, await. For trail tips, ask around at local bike shops or contact any tourist information office (see the "Information" chapter). Cycling races and events are held year-round, notably the **Iron Horse Bicycle Classic** (www.ironhorsebicycleclassic.com), which races the train from Durango to Silverton on Memorial Day weekend, and the **Escalante Days Mountain Bike Race** (www.doloreschamber.com, 970-882-4018) in mid-August at Dolores.

Durango Cyclery, www.durangocyclery.com, 970-247-0747, 143 E. 13th St., Durango. Sells cycling equipment, repairs bikes, and organizes free-for-all rides weekly.

Durango Mountain Resort, www.durangomountainresort.com, 970-247-9000, 1-800-982-6103, 1 Skier Place, Durango. In summer, this ski resort rents mountain bikes for adults and kids and operates chairlifts that access over 50 miles of trails at varying difficulty levels.

Hassle Free Sports, www.hasslefreesports.com, 970-259-3874, 2615 Main Ave., Durango. Sells, rents, and repairs road and mountain bikes; reservations available online.

Kokopelli Bike & Board, www.kokopellibike.com, 970-565-4408, 1-800-565-6736, 30 W. Main Ave., Cortez. A shop for sales, service, and rentals. Ask about local trails and their nonprofit club, which organizes group rides.

Mobius Cycles & Café, www.mobiuscycles.com, 970-387-0777, 1309 Greene St., Silverton. Repairs and sells bicycles, makes espresso drinks, and offers trail tips and free Wi-Fi Internet access.

Monty's Town Bike Rental, 970-426-2807, 143 E. 13th St., Durango. Rents in-town cruiser bikes for adults and kids.

Mountain Bike Specialists, www.mountainbikespecialists.com, 970-247-4066, 949 Main Ave., Durango. Sells and repairs bicycles. Provides information about group rides, events, and clinics.

Pedal & Powder, www.pagosapedalandpowder.com, 970-731-0338, 1-800-368-1430, 100 Country Center Dr., Pagosa Springs. Offers road and mountain bike rentals for adults and children, including kids' trailers.

Pedal the Peaks, www.pedalthepeaks.biz, 970-259-6880, 598B Main Ave., Durango. Sells, rents, and repairs bicycles; call ahead to check availability for tandem bicycle and kids' mountain bike rentals.

SouthWest Adventure Guides, www.mtnguide.net, 970-259-0370, 1-800-642-5389, 1205 Camino del Rio, Durango. Offers mountain-biking shuttle services and half- or full-day guided tours.

Birding

With its diversity of environments, southwestern Colorado offers a chance to see more than 100 different species of birds that inhabit the Colorado Plateau. Inside **Mesa Verde National Park** (www.nps.gov/meve, 970-529-4465), visitor centers sell birding checklists and offer advice for birders. To visit riparian areas, follow the Mancos River outside the town of Mancos, especially at **Mancos State Park** (http://parks.state.co.us/Parks/Mancos/, 970-533-7065, 42545 County Road N, Mancos). For more information on birding hot spots, check out the **Colorado Birding Society** Web site (http://home.att.net/~birdertoo/).

The **Ute Mountain–Mesa Verde Birding Festival** (www.utemountainmesaverde birdingfestival.com, 970-561-1151) takes place in May. Many events start at the Cortez Cultural Center (25 N. Market St.), with birding tours offered of the nearby Hawkins Preserve, Mesa Verde National Park, and Ute Mountain Tribal Park (see "Archaeological Sites," earlier).

Camping

Camping is technically a year-round activity in Colorado, but most visitors avoid snow camping during winter. To rent backpacking and camping equipment, drop by **Pine Needle Mountaineering** (www.pineneedle.com, 970-247-8728, 1-800-607-0364, 835 Main Ave., Durango).

At Mesa Verde National Park, **Morefield Campground** (www.visitmesaverde.com, 602-331-5210, 1-800-449-2288) has 435 tent and RV sites, as well as canvas tent rentals with cots inside; it's usually open from early May through mid-October. Contact **ReserveAmerica** (www.reserveamerica.com) for camping reservations at other federal recreation lands (1-877-444-6777, 518-885-3639). First-come, first-served campgrounds (a few of which have reservable sites) and free dispersed camping is available in the **San Juan National Forest** (www.fs.fed.us/r2/sanjuan/, 970-247-4874, 15 Burnett Court, Durango), which has field offices in Dolores, Pagosa Springs, and Silverton. For state park campsites and cabins, contact the **Colorado Department of Natural Resources** (http://parks.state.co.us/Reservations/, 303-470-1144, 1-800-678-2267). **Mancos State Park** has two camping yurts with ceiling fans, electricity, propane heaters, and kitchenettes. Private campgrounds catering mostly to RVs are plentiful in southwestern Colorado, too, especially around Durango and Cortez. Basic cabins and tent and RV sites are found at a primitive campground inside **Ute Mountain Tribal Park** (www.utemountainute.com/tribalpark, 970-565-3751, 1-800-847-5485).

Canoeing and Kayaking

Several outfitters offer guided trips on the Animas River outside Durango.

Durango Rivertrippers Rafting, www.durangorivertrippers.com, 970-259-0289, 1-800-292-2885, 720 Main Ave., Durango. Rents inflatable kayaks and provides lessons for Animas River trips.

Flexible Flyers Rafting, www.flexibleflyersrafting.com, 970-247-4628, 1-800-346-4628, 2344 County Road 225, Durango. Rents inflatable kayaks for Animas River trips.

Four Corners Riversports, www.riversports.com, 970-259-3893, 360 S. Camino del Rio, Durango. Offers canoe and kayaking instruction at beginning to advanced levels.

Mountain Waters Rafting, www.durangorafting.com, 970-259-4191, 1-800-585-8243, 643 Camino del Rio, Durango. Rents inflatable kayaks and guides to accompany Animas River trips.

Outlaw Rivers & Jeep Tours, www.outlawtours.com, 970-259-1800, 1-877-259-1800, 555 Main Ave., Durango. Rents inflatable kayaks and inner tubes for floating down the Animas River.

Peregrine River Outfitters, www.peregrineriver.com, 970-385-7600, 1-800-598-7600, 64 Ptarmigan Lane, Durango. Arranges guided inflatable kayak trips on the Dolores and San Juan Rivers and into the Gunnison Gorge Wilderness.

Disc Golf

Cortez Centennial Park, www.cityofcortez.com/parks.shtml, 970-564-4080, 600 N. Park St., Cortez. This 18-hole basket disc golf course scenically surrounds a duck pond.

Fishing

The trout fishing is fantastic in southwestern Colorado's mountain streams and rivers, particularly the **Animas River** outside Durango, the **Dolores River**, and the **San Juan River** through Pagosa Springs. Specially stocked reservoirs include **Vallecito Reservoir**, northeast of Durango in the San Juan National Forest, as well as around Pagosa Springs at **Williams Creek Reservoir** to the north and **Echo Canyon Reservoir** to the south. For fishing regulations and reports and to buy licenses online, contact the **Colorado Division of Wildlife** (http://wildlife.state.co.us/fishing/, 303-291-7539, 1-800-244-5613). For guided fishing trips, rental equipment, and supplies:

Animas Valley Anglers, www.gottrout.com, 970-259-0484, 264 W. 22nd St., Durango. Arranges guided wading and float trips along the Animas River, plus a small selection of new and used gear.

Circle K Guest Ranch, www.ckranch.com/fly_fishing.htm, 970-562-3826, 1-800-477-6381, 27758 CO 145, Dolores. On a remote ranch northeast of Dolores, fly-fishing guides are available for daylong wading and overnight horseback trips to secluded mountain streams. The ranch sells fishing licenses, rents equipment, and gives lessons.

Duranglers Flies and Supplies, www.duranglers.com, 970-385-4081, 1-888-347-4346, 923 Main Ave., Durango. Top-notch outfitter offers fly-fishing workshops, private lessons, and custom guided trips; it also rents and sells all the equipment you could possibly need.

Let It Fly, www.flyfishpagosa.com, 970-264-3189, 1501 W. US 160, Pagosa Springs. Small family-owned shop sells equipment and supplies, offers information about local fishing spots, and can put visitors in touch with knowledgeable guides.

Fitness Facilities

Cortez Recreation Center, www.cityofcortez.com/reccenter.shtml, 970-564-4080, 425 Roger Smith Ave., Cortez. A small indoor track surrounds the workout area. There's also a climbing wall, racquetball courts, fitness classes, and a swimming pool complex.

Durango Community Recreation Center, www.durangogov.org, 970-375-7300, 2700 Main Ave., Durango. Day passes cover use of the mountain-view fitness room, indoor track, climbing wall, racquetball courts, and aquatics area.

Durango Sports Club, www.durangosportsclub.com, 970-259-2579, 1600 Florida Rd., Durango. Full-service gym has state-of-the-art cardio workout machines, weight training, a rock-climbing wall, racquetball courts, and aerobics, yoga, and martial arts classes.

Pagosa Health & Fitness Club, 970-264-2880, 450 Lewis St., Pagosa Springs. High-tech gym equipped with cardio and weight training machines offers aerobics, spinning, yoga, and pilates classes.

Silverton Movement Center, www.silvertonmovementcenter.com, 970-387-5187, 124 E. 13th St., Silverton. This community workout center has indoor cardio and weight machines and a variety of classes, from belly dancing to yoga and pilates.

Golf

Conquistador Golf Course, http://cityofcortez.com/golfcourse.shtml, 970-565-9208, 2018 N. Dolores Rd., Cortez. Swing down this rolling course with views of the La Plata Mountains, Mesa Verde, and Sleeping Ute Mountain. Public, 18 holes, 6,963 yards, par 72; club and cart rentals, driving range, pro shop, snack bar. Open March to mid-November.

Dalton Ranch Golf Club, www.daltonranch.com, 970-247-8774, 589 County Road 252, Durango. One of the top courses in southwestern Colorado is scenically set in the Animas River Valley. Semiprivate, 18 holes, 6,934 yards, par 72; club rentals, driving range, putting greens. Open April through October.

Hillcrest Golf Club, www.golfhillcrest.com, 970-247-1499, 2300 Rim Dr., Durango. With smooth fairways, these hillside links overlooking town are for fast play. Public, par 71, 18

The Animas River runs through Durango, offering scenic cycling, hiking, and walking trails. Sara Benson

holes, 6,838 yards; driving range, lessons, pro shop, snack bar. Open February through November.

Pagosa Springs Golf Club, www.golf pagosa.com, 970-731-4755, 1 Pines Club Place, Pagosa Springs. Come for the fresh air and mountain scenery, with greens lined by piñon trees and ponderosa pines. Public, par 107, 27 holes, 10,409 yards; club and cart rentals, lessons, pro shop, restaurant. Open April through November.

Hiking and Backpacking

A variety of developed trails and ranger-led hikes await inside **Mesa Verde National Park** (see "Parks and Natural Attractions," later). Less-trammeled trails lead around **Canyons of the Ancients National Monument** (see "Archaeological Sites," earlier).

The **Animas River valley** and spectacular **mountains around Durango** offer easy nature trails, moderate half-day hikes, and challenging climbs that top out at an elevation of 13,000 feet. The **Durango Area Tourism Office** (www.durango.org, 1-800-525-8855, 111 S. Camino del Rio, Durango) and **San Juan Public Lands Center** (www.fs.fed.us/r2/sanjuan/, 970-247-4874, 15 Burnett Court, off US 160, Durango) have detailed information about hiking trails, some of which are just a short drive from downtown. Experienced backpackers can plot out trips into **Chicago Basin** in the **Weminuche Wilderness**, accessed via the Durango & Silverton Narrow Gauge Railroad (see "Getting Around the Four Corners" in the "Transportation" chapter). The **San Juan Mountains Association** (www.sjma.org, 970-385-1210) offers advice for hikers and backpackers, including online trip-planning guides.

The **La Plata Mountains** and **Dolores River valley** outside Mancos offer opportunities for more solitary hikes on easy to difficult trails. For information about the most popular trails, drop by the **Visitor Center** in Mancos (www.mancosvalley.com, 970-533-7434, Main St. at Railroad Ave., Mancos). To access more remote wilderness trails outside Pagosa Springs, stop by the **San Juan National Forest's Pagosa Field Office** (www.fs.fed.us/r2/sanjuan/, 970-264-2268, 180 2nd St., Pagosa Springs) first.

Horseback Riding

Colorado is classic cowboy ranch country, where rolling mountain meadows beckon newbie riders and experienced equestrians alike. Book a day ride, overnight pack trip, all-inclusive dude ranch vacation, or even an old-fashioned stagecoach journey or romantic winter sleigh ride.

Bartels' Mancos Valley Stage Line, www.thestagecoach.com, 970-533-9857, 1-800-365-3530, 4550 County Road 41, Mancos. Between May and September, authentic Western stagecoach trips head into Weber Canyon for lunch or sunset steak dinners.

Big Corral Riding Stables, www.vallecitolakeoutfitter.com, 970-884-9235, 17716 County Road 501, Bayfield. Experienced family-owned outfitter east of Durango arranges day rides, overnight and drop trips, and hunting excursions.

Buck's Livery, www.buckslivery.com, 970-385-2110, Durango Mountain Resort, 61 County Road 248, Durango. Explore the San Juan National Forest and Cascade Canyon with horses and mules, perhaps taking a sunset dinner ride or overnight pack trip into the backcountry. Sleigh rides depart during winter.

Circle K Ranch, www.ckranch.com, 970-562-3826, 1-800-477-6381, 27758 CO 145, Dolores. This down-home country dude ranch offers horseback rides and overnight pack and hunting trips during summer.

Echo Basin Ranch, www.echobasin.com, 970-533-7000, 43747 County Road M, Mancos. This guest ranch offers a variety of family-friendly horseback rides.

Over the Hill Outfitter, www.overthehilloutfitters.com, 970-385-7656, 4140 County Road 234, Durango. Expert outfitters leads pack trips along the spine of the Continental Divide and from Durango to Silverton, returning via the historic narrow-gauge railway.

Rapp Corral, www.rappguides.net, 970-247-8454, 51 Haviland Lake Rd., Durango. In the San Juan National Forest, about 20 miles north of Durango, this scenic ranch offers horseback trail rides and horse-drawn carriage, sleigh, and wagon rides.

Rimrock Outfitters, www.rimrockoutfitters.com, 970-533-7588, 12175 County Road 44, Mancos. In the La Plata Mountains, this traditional cowboy ranch offers river and forest trail rides (including breakfast trips), pack trips, and carriage and sleigh rides.

Rustler's Roost Ranch, www.rustlersroostranch.com, 970-533-1570, 1-800-758-1667, 5964 County Road 41, Mancos. Horse stables and outfitters offer extreme high-altitude backcountry trips for experienced riders, tamer trail rides, and overnight pack trips.

San Juan Outfitting, www.sanjuanoutfitting.com, 970-259-6259, 186 County Road 228, Durango. Experienced family-owned outfitter leads rides along the Continental Divide and in Canyons of the Ancients National Monument between spring and fall.

The Medicine Horse Center, www.medicinehorsecenter.org, 970-533-7403, P.O. Box 1074, Mancos, CO 81328. Adaptive rides provide therapeutic recreation for children and adults with disabilities.

Racquet Sports

Cortez Recreation Center, www.cityofcortez.com/reccenter.shtml, 970-564-4080, 425 Roger Smith Ave., Cortez, CO. The city maintains two indoor racquetball courts. For outdoor tennis courts, head to Parque de Vida, off N. Mildred Road north of US 160.

Durango Community Recreation Center, www.durangogov.org, 970-375-7300, 2700 Main Ave., Durango. The city has two indoor racquetball courts open to the public. For outdoor tennis courts, head to the municipal Mason Center at 301 East 12th Street.

River Rafting

Almost all the white-water rafting action in southwestern Colorado happens on the **Animas River,** usually from the peak snow-melt run-off in June through the season's end in September. Durango has the most river-running outfitters, including:

Durango Rivertrippers Rafting, www.durangorivertrippers.com, 970-259-0289, 1-800-292-2885, 720 Main Ave., Durango. Family-owned outfitter caters to adults and children, with short Animas River trips and multiday journeys on the Dolores River.

Flexible Flyers Rafting, www.flexibleflyersrafting.com, 970-247-4628, 1-800-346-4628, 2344 County Road 225, Durango. For family-friendly Animas River float trips.

Four Corners Whitewater, www.raft-kayak.com, 970-259-4608, 1-888-723-8925, 360 S. Camino Del Rio, Durango. Offers Animas River trips and a rafting guide school.

Mild to Wild Rafting, www.mild2wildrafting.com, 970-247-4789, 1-800-567-6745, 50 Animas View Dr., Durango. Runs guided trips on the Animas and Dolores Rivers, on the San Miguel River outside Telluride, and through the box canyons of the Piedra River.

Mountain Waters Rafting, www.durangorafting.com, 970-259-4191, 1-800-585-8243, 643 Camino del Rio, Durango. With 25 years of experience, this outfitter offers Animas River trips for families, raft-and-rail excursions to Silverton, and full-day class IV trips on the Piedra River.

Outlaw Rivers & Jeep Tours, www.outlawtours.com, 970-259-1800, 1-877-259-1800, 555 Main Ave., Durango. Offers easy and challenging guided rafting trips on the Animas and Piedra Rivers, including multiday adventures and raft-and-rail combo packages.

Peregrine River Outfitters, www.peregrineriver.com, 970-385-7600, 1-800-598-7600, 64 Ptarmigan Lane, Durango. Offers short Animas River trips for novices and full-day and multiday trips on the Dolores and Animas Rivers, as well destinations farther afield. Ask about fishing trips and educational tours with on-board naturalists and artists.

Rock, Ice, and Mountain Climbing

Cortez Recreation Center, www.cityofcortez.com/reccenter.shtml, 970-564-4080, 425 Roger Smith Ave., Cortez, CO. Equipped with a 35-foot-tall naturalistic rock climbing wall and two belaying systems and three ropes for partners to practice with.

Durango Community Recreation Center, www.durangogov.org, 970-375-7300, 2700 Main Ave., Durango. Fitness center has a 30-foot-tall naturalistic rock climbing wall.

San Juan Mountain Guides, www.ourayclimbing.com, 970-325-4925, P.O. Box 1214, Ouray. At a far-flung base camp north of Durango, experts teach beginner to advanced courses and lead guided rock and ice climbing trips in the San Juan Mountains.

Southwest Adventure Guides, www.mtnguide.net, 970-259-0370, 1-800-642-5389, 1205 Camino del Rio, Durango. From introductory courses to guided classic climbs and advanced skills clinics, this outfitter tackles it all: rock, ice, and alpine mountain climbing.

Running

For trails in and around Durango and special events, contact **Durango Motorless Transit** (www.go-dmt.org). In May, Durango's **Narrow Gauge 5K and 10-mile runs** are among

Colorado's oldest foot races. In April, Cortez's **Pueblo-to-Pueblo Run** (www.cortezcultural center.org, 970-565-1151) features an 11-mile, 10K and 2K fun run and walk. But nothing compares to the **Hard Rock Hundred Mile Endurance Run** (www.run100s.com/HR/), which follows backcountry routes in the San Juan Mountains outside Silverton every July.

Skiing, Snowboarding, and Other Winter Sports

Major ski resorts like Telluride north of Silverton and Wolf Creek east of Pagosa Springs are outside the Four Corners area. But around Durango and throughout Mesa Verde Country there are opportunities for downhill and cross-country skiing, snowboarding, snowshoeing, snowmobiling, ice-skating, and sledding. Some of the best Nordic skiing and snowshoeing trails are found inside **Mesa Verde National Park** (see "Archaeological Sites," above). There are also plenty of cross-country trails in the mountains around Cortez, Dolores, and Mancos; contact local tourist information offices (see the "Information" chapter) for more details.

Purgatory at Durango Mountain Resort, (www.durangomountainresort.com, 970-247-9000, 1-800-982-6103, 1 Skier Place, Durango) has almost a dozen lifts and 85 downhill skiing trails, half of which are graded intermediate. There are also two terrain parks for snowboarding and tubing and a Nordic center for cross-country skiing. Ski lessons and rentals, guided snowmobile tours, and ski biking are also available.

North of Durango, **Silverton Mountain,** (www.silvertonmountain.com, 970-387-5706, Silverton) is a minimalist high-altitude resort for extreme downhill skiing on fresh powder, with new terrain opening daily. During peak winter season it is open for guided skiing only; there are per-day skier limits, so advance reservations are highly recommended.

West of Durango, **Ski Hesperus,** (www.skihesperus.com, 970-259-3711, 9848 US 160) is a family-friendly snow-sports facility with two lifts leading to trails rated beginner through advanced, as well as inner tubing and terrain areas, an ice-skating pond, and cross-country skiing trails. Rental equipment and lessons are available.

Outdoor outfitters that rent winter sports equipment include:

Alpenhaus Ski Center, 970-731-4755, Fairfield Pagosa Resort, 262 Simmons Place, Pagosa Springs. Rents skis, snowboards, snowblades, and sleds, and sells ski equipment and clothing; online bookings available.

Chapman Hill Rink and Ski Area, www.durangogov.org, 970-375-7395, 500 Florida Rd., Durango. Has an indoor ice-skating rink with a fireplace viewing room and an outdoor rope-tow ski hill primarily for lessons.

Durango Dog Ranch, www.durangodogranch.com, 970-259-0694, County Road 124, Hesperus. Ride-along or drive-yourself dogsledding tours explore national forest lands west of Durango.

Hassle Free Sports, www.hasslefreesports.com, 970-259-3874, 2615 Main Ave., Durango. Rents, sells, and repairs skis, snowshoes, and boots; online reservations available.

Outlaw Tours, www.outlawtours.com, 970-259-3500, 1-877-259-1800, 555 Main Ave., Durango. Arranges guided snowmobile rides during winter.

Pagosa Ski Rentals, www.skipagosa.com, 970-264-2866, 350 Pagosa St., Pagosa Springs. A full-service ski shop offers equipment rental packages and weekly discounts.

Pedal & Powder, www.pagosapedalandpowder.com, 970-731-0338, 1-800-368-1430, 100 Country Center Dr., Pagosa Springs. Offers ski and snowboard rentals, sales, and service; online bookings available.

Pine Needle Mountaineering, www.pineneedle.com, 970-247-8728, 1-800-607-0364, 835 Main Ave., Durango. Rents snowshoes, skis, and boots, and sells ski equipment.

San Juan Ski Company, www.sanjuanski.com, 970-259-9671, 1-800-208-1780, Durango Mountain Resort, 1831 Lake Purgatory Dr., Durango. Private company offers rugged snow-cat trips for backcountry powder skiing on remote national forest lands. Winter reservations are accepted starting in mid-September.

Ski Barn & Dr. Feelgood's, www.discovercolorado.com/skibarn/, 970-247-1923, 1-800-796-7472, 3533 Main Ave., Durango. Rents ski and snowboard equipment and sells winter-sports gear and accessories.

SouthWest Adventure Guides, www.mtnguide.net, 970-259-0370, 1-800-642-5389, 1205 Camino del Rio, Durango. For backcountry ski trips and avalanche courses.

The Boarding Haus, 970-259-8182, 2607 Main Ave., Durango. This skateboard and BMX shop rents snowboards and sells boarding gear and clothing.

Spas and Hot Springs

Advance bookings are recommended at day spas. Hot springs don't usually require reservations, but always call ahead to confirm public-access hours.

Amaya Natural Therapeutics, 970-247-3939, 230 E. College Dr., Durango. Set aside time for a hot-tub soak or a sweat bath in the cedar sauna before picking from a full menu of therapeutic services.

Chipeta Sun Lodge and Spa, www.chipetaspa.com, 970-626-5007, 1-800-633-5868, 304 S. Lena, Ridgway. For a high-altitude yoga class or a spa indulgence on the way back from skiing at Telluride, drop by this deluxe lodge.

Orvis Hot Springs, www.orvishotsprings.com, 970-626-5324, 1585 County Road 3, off US 550, Ridgway. Humble hippie heaven has hot-springs pools by the roadside and some indoors, too. Massage treatments happen inside tranquil yurts.

Queen Bee Skin Care, www.queenbeepagosa.com, 970-731-3690, P.O. Box 4512, Pagosa Springs, CO 81147. Revered skin-care specialist has just one intimate treatment room on the shores of Lake Pagosa.

Signature Salon & Health Spa, www.signaturehealthsystems.com, 970-247-7769, 1521 Main Ave., Durango. Full-service salon and spa offers Finnish saunas, mud treatments, body scrubs, massage, and skin care and salon services, in addition to homeopathic remedies and alternative health therapies.

Spaaah Shop & Day Spa, www.spaaahshop.com, 970-375-1866, 934 Main Ave., Durango. This pure makeup and skin care vendor has a small, attentively staffed day spa downtown.

The Springs Resort, www.pagosahotsprings.com, 970-264-4168, 1-800-225-0934, P.O. Box 1799, Pagosa Hot Springs, CO 81147. Like a Disneyland for hot-springs lovers, this gargantuan complex set beside the San Juan River has 16 different pools, whose temperature is measured and posted frequently by the staff. If you're a hot-springs hedonist, try the "Lobster Pot." Don't forget to climb the cliffs to the upper pool for sunset views. There's also a heated lap pool, a freshwater whirlpool tub, and a spa for massage, body care, and salon services. Swimwear is required in the pools.

Trimble Spa & Natural Hot Springs, www.trimblehotsprings.com, 970-247-0111, 970-247-0212, on Trimble Rd. (County Road 203) off US 550, Durango, CO 81302. Just north of Durango, this simple hot-springs retreat has two mineral pools and an Olympic-size swimming pool, all family-friendly.

Swimming

Some hot-springs resorts listed in the previous section have heated swimming pools, too.

Cortez Recreation Center, www.cityofcortez.com/reccenter.shtml, 970-564-4080, 425 Roger Smith Ave., Cortez. Family-oriented community center has an indoor competition lap pool, recreation pool, lazy river pool, and enclosed inner-tube slide.

Durango Community Recreation Center, www.durangogov.org, 970-375-7300, 2700 Main Ave., Durango. Aquatic center comes equipped with a leisure pool, waterslide, diving board pool, and hot tub; call for open-swim hours.

Tours and Guided Adventures

In addition to guided trips offered by outdoor outfitters, here are some more recommended agencies offering unique tours of southwestern Colorado. For details about the historic Durango & Silverton Narrow Gauge Railroad, see the "Getting Around the Four Corners" section of the "Transportation" chapter, earlier in this book.

Durango Soaring Club, www.soardurango.com, 970-247-9037, 27290 US 550 N, Durango. Between mid-May and mid-October this club north of Durango offers sailplane rides with San Juan Mountains and Animas River views, weather permitting; advance reservations recommended.

Get Out Adventures, www.getoutadventures.com, 970-759-8212, 520 Main Ave., Durango. Guides 4WD tours through the San Juan Mountains or a slickrock canyon on the New Mexico side of the border.

New Air Helicopters, www.new-air.com, 970-259-6247, 1-800-417-0105, Animas Airpark, Flight Line Rd., Durango. Short scenic helicopter tours fly over La Plata Canyon and into the San Juan Mountains.

Outlaw Rivers & Jeep Tours, www.outlawtours.com, 970-259-1800, 1-877-259-1800, 555 Main Ave., Durango. Guided off-road tours travel via 4WD vehicles, ATVs, and snowmobiles during winter. Daylong excursions via jeep and train visit Silverton.

Redwood Llamas, www.redwoodllamas.com, 970-560-2926, 1708 Greene St., Silverton. Offers guided pack trips and one-day clinics that qualify visitors to take leased llamas packing into the wilderness independently.

Rocky Mountain Balloon Adventures, www.pagosaviews.com, 970-731-8060, Fairfield Pagosa Activities Center, 42 Piñon Causeway, Pagosa Springs. Offers participatory hot-air balloon rides above pine forests and lakes.

San Juan Backcountry, www.sanjuanbackcountry.com, 1-800-494-8687, 1123 Greene St., Silverton. Family-owned business arranges customized 4WD tours, guided fishing trips, and trailhead transport for backpackers and mountain climbers.

Silver Summit Jeep Rental, www.silversummitrvpark.com, 970-387-0240, 1-800-352-1637, 640 Mineral St., Silverton. For do-it-yourself types, this company rents 4WD jeeps with unlimited mileage for trips around the San Juan Mountains.

Soaring Colorado, www.soaringcolorado.com, 970-769-2357, Tall Timber Resort, 1 Silverton Star, Durango, CO. At the exclusive Tall Timber Resort, go ziplining in the mountains, over rivers, and through a treetop canopy between May and September.

SouthWest Adventure Guides, www.mtnguide.net, 970-259-0370, 1-800-642-5389, 1205 Camino del Rio, Durango. Offers mountain-biking and backpacking tours, rock climbing and mountaineering courses, and summer-only shuttles into the San Juan Mountains around Durango, as well as farther afield.

Thin Air Mountain Tours, www.thinairmountaintours.com, 970-749-9191, 46825 US 550, Durango. Takes guided 4WD tours along unpaved back roads at breathtaking altitudes, including hair-raising rides over Black Bear Pass and down into Telluride.

Triangle Jeep Rental, www.trianglejeeprental.com, 970-387-9990, 1-877-522-2354, 864 Greene St., Silverton. Rents convertible 4WD Jeep Wranglers for full-day mountain excursions around Silverton. Ask about discounts for multiday rentals and motel stays.

Shopping

Art, Antiques, and Collectibles
See also "Art Galleries" listed in the "Culture" section, earlier in this chapter.

Artisans of Mancos, www.artisansofmancos.com, 970-533-7040, 101 Grand Ave., Mancos. Diamonds in the rough are sometimes found inside this local artists' cooperative gallery, which displays works in all media, including jewelry, paintings, prints, sculptures, and metalwork.

Clay Mesa Gallery, www.claymesa.com, 970-565-1902, 29 E. Main St., Cortez. A husband-and-wife team display their uniquely glazed plates decorated with Southwestern, Native American, and Mexican themes.

Durango Arts Center, www.durangoarts.org, 970-259-2606, 802 E. 2nd Ave., Durango. The innovative gallery shop stocks high-quality works by Colorado artists, including ceramics, blown glass, wood carvings, photographs, jewelry, and metal sculptures.

Earthen Vessel, www.earthenvessel.com, 970-247-1281, 1-800-881-1281, 115 W. 9th St., Durango. Browse functional, down-to-earth pottery covered in colorful glazes.

Lime Berry, www.shop.limeberryonline.com, 970-375-9199, 925 Main Ave., Durango. A whirlwind of art and gifts from around the world, this shop also carries contemporary Southwestern and Native American paintings, weavings, and sculptures.

Books, Clothing, Maps, Gifts, and Outdoor Gear

Appaloosa Trading Company, www.appaloosadurango.com, 970-259-1994, 501 Main Ave., Durango. At this family-owned store by the train depot, shop for silver and leather goods, such as cowboy boots, belts, and buckles, all handmade in Colorado.

Backcountry Experience, www.bcexp.com, 970-247-5830, 1-800-648-8519, 1205 Camino del Rio, Durango. All-around outdoor outfitter carries full lines of camping, backpacking, climbing, and winter sports gear, including footwear and active clothing.

Buffalo Hand Made, 970-533-7236, 245 N. Main St., Mancos. Small specialty shop displays handcrafted leather gloves and accessories made from buffalo, elk, and white-tailed deer. Carved wooden bowls and paintings by local artists are also on display.

Durango Traditions, www.durangotrdns.com, 970-259-7509, 1-888-544-5800, 658 Main Avenue, Durango. Marketing upscale Western styles for town and country, this women's apparel store offers personalized wardrobe service.

Gardenswartz Outdoors, 970-259-6696, 780 Main Ave., Durango. While the main store at 863 Main Avenue caters to hunters and fishers, this smaller branch focuses on outdoor sports, including camping, backpacking, skiing, and snowboarding gear.

Goodman's Department Store, www.goodmanspagosa.com, 970-264-5460, 401 Pagosa St., Pagosa Springs. In business for over a century, Goodman's is a one-stop shop for outdoor and Western apparel. Admire the antique metal-embossed ceiling while you shop.

Hell Bent Leather and Silver, www.hellbentleather.com, 970-247-9088, 741 Main Ave., Durango. This contemporary shop with a sassy attitude sells handcrafted jewelry and artistic leather bags and belts with original beaded Southwestern and Western designs.

Lantern Dancer Gallery, www.lanterndancer.com, 970-264-6446, 136 E. Pagosa St., Pagosa Springs. Sells contemporary Southwestern jewelry, from turquoise bracelets and necklaces to silver earrings and pendants, as well as pottery and fine art.

Main Book Company, www.mainbookco.com, 970-565-8158, 34 W. Main St., Cortez. Stocks a wide selection of new books, including regional interest titles and outdoor activity guidebooks and maps, plus an espresso bar.

Maria's Bookshop, www.mariasbookshop.com, 970-247-1438, 960 Main Ave., Durango. Owned by a family of unicyclists, this independent bookstore has vast handmade shelves full of all kinds of good books and occasionally hosts author events.

Mesa Verde Bookstore, www.mesaverde.org, 970-529-4445, 1-800-305-6053, Mesa Verde National Park. Nonprofit association operates bookshops stocked with natural history and cultural guides, maps, prints, and other souvenirs at Mesa Verde National Park visitor centers and the Colorado Welcome Center in Cortez (see the "Information" chapter).

Moonlight Books and Gallery, 970-264-5666, 434 Pagosa St., Pagosa Springs. Pagosa's independent bookstore houses a small local art gallery and sells tickets for musical concerts and other community events.

It's no surprise to see fine leather goods for sale in downtown Durango, since Colorado is ranching country.
Sara Benson

Nathaniel's of Colorado, www.nathanielsofcolorado.com, 970-533-9740, 121 Grand Ave., Mancos. There's no better place to get personalized service from a hat maker who has catered to Hollywood celebrities. Made-to-measure felt hats are handcrafted from beaver and rabbit fur by Native American master hatter Nate Funmaker.

Overland Fine Sheepskin & Leather, www.overland.com/stores/durango.asp, 970-259-2005, 1-800-754-8345, 546 Main Ave., Durango. With 30 years of experience, they sell fur and leather apparel and accessories, from coats and hats to gloves and belts, including products crafted from beaver, mink, and sheepskin.

Pine Needle Mountaineering, www.pineneedle.com, 970-247-8728, 1-800-607-0364, 835 Main Ave., Durango. All-around outdoor outfitter has a huge selection of Osprey packs, in addition to loads of other backpacking, camping, climbing, hiking, and skiing gear, including footwear, accessories, guidebooks, maps, and rental stock.

Quality Bookstore, 970-565-9125, 34 W. Main St., Cortez. This polished downtown bookstore is a local gathering spot, especially around the espresso bar. It has an encyclopedia's worth of regional and local titles, as well as a Southwestern art gallery.

Switchback Mountain Gear, www.switchbackpagosa.com, 970-264-2225, 1-866-829-0339, 465 Pagosa St., Pagosa Springs. This outdoor outfitter carries brand-name camping, hiking, backpacking, skiing, and snowshoeing gear, as well as footwear, maps, and outdoor activity guidebooks.

Through the Lens, www.durangophotography.com, 970-247-8626, 634 Main Ave., Durango. If you can't resist getting an Old West costumed photo, come here with your loved ones to get gussied up as a bordello girl, cowboy, or outlaw gunslinger.

Weathertop Wovens, 970-387-5257, 1335 Greene St., Silverton. Linger by the demonstration loom inside this cozy workshop, which sells unique woven apparel, particularly shawls, pullovers, and jackets, along with artistic Celtic silver pins.

Native American Trading Posts and Galleries

A Shared Blanket, www.asharedblanket.com, 970-247-9210, 736 Main Ave., Durango. Low-key Native American gallery emphasizes Zuni fetishes, Navajo weavings, contemporary Pueblo pottery, Alaskan musical instruments, wood sculptures, and jewelry.

Mesa Verde Pottery, 970-565-4492, 1-800-441-9908, 27601 US 160 E., Cortez. Primarily a factory showroom for handmade Native American pottery, this warehouse also stocks works by Navajo, Hopi, and Zuni artists, from Southwestern rugs and drums to jewelry, kachinas, and fine-art prints.

Notah Dineh Trading Company & Museum, www.subee.com/nd, 970-565-9607, 1-800-444-2024, 345 W. Main Ave., Cortez. Open since the 1960s, this established trading post has a museum-worthy collection of classical and traditional Navajo rugs, including the largest-known rug sporting the Two Grey Hills pattern. There are stunning displays of kachinas, sandpaintings, beadwork, basketry, and jewelry.

Ortega's Indian Trading Post, 970-387-5744, 1228 Greene St., Silverton. Run by sixth-generation traders, this delightfully jumbled shop carries works by Navajo, Hopi, and Zuni artisans, including jewelry, sandpaintings, rugs, pottery, kachinas, historic photographs, and ancient artifacts.

Storyteller Indian Store, 970-387-5843, 1269 Greene St., Silverton. This high-altitude trading post has down-to-earth prices, especially for Navajo, Hopi, and Zuni jewelry.

Toh-Atin Gallery, www.toh-atin.com, 970-247-8277, 1-800-525-0384, 145 W. 9th St., Durango. The premier Native American art gallery in southwestern Colorado, dealing in contemporary Southwestern art and collectible Native American traditional crafts. This modern gallery space opened its doors over 50 years ago. Inside you'll find kachinas, fetishes, basketry, weavings, sandpaintings, and pottery by well-known indigenous artists. Western belts, buckles, bolos, horse tack, paintings, and prints are also sold.

Ute Mountain Pottery, www.utemountainute.com/pottery, 1-800-896-8548, 8 miles south of Cortez on US 160/491, Towaoc. Tribal-run pottery workshop primarily sells functional everyday pottery that is first poured into ceramic molds, then painted by hand with original, mostly black-and-white geometric designs before glazing.

7

Utah's Canyon Country

From Arches to Zion

The epic landscapes of southern Utah—forbidding deserts, waterfall oases, towering red-rock cliffs, and white-water river canyons and narrow gorges—draw adventurous travelers, vacationing shutterbugs, and wilderness seekers. The taxing stretches of interstate and other highway driving required elsewhere in the Four Corners region are absent in southern Utah, where small towns are instead connected by scenic byways. Two-lane roads roll through canyon country, all the way from the adventure base camp town of Moab, near Arches National Park, southwest to St. George outside Zion National Park. Slow down, relax, and enjoy the ride, whether it's a 4WD detour through deserted Grand Staircase–Escalante National Monument or a paved scenic loop inside busier Canyonlands or Bryce Canyon National Park.

By all means, get out of the car as much as you can, while spending time in southern Utah. This is a year-round adventure playground, especially for its colorful collection of national and state parks and in the variety of enviroscapes found around Moab, which extends from desert scrub and wetlands to sandstone cliffs overhanging the Colorado River to the high-elevation peaks of the Manti–La Sal Mountains. No matter which outdoor activity you're interested in, whether you're an absolute beginner or looking to polish expert skills, chances are southern Utah has the perfect place for you to get outdoors and just do it. Mountain bikers have challenging single-track trails to ride, especially around Moab, and canyoneers rappel down sheer cliffs in Zion National Park, while rock climbers top out in both places. Golfers tee off at championship courses outside St. George. Horse-back riders can explore the land of hoodoos outside Bryce Canyon, where Nordic skiers glide during winter. At the end of the day, desert spas await to tend to both peace of mind and body. And if you're going to camp anywhere in the Four Corners region, southern Utah has some unforgettably scenic spots for sleeping out under starry skies.

For insights into the history and prehistory of this frontier state, sleuth for dinosaur tracks, archaeological sites, pioneer settlements, mining ghost towns, and abandoned Hollywood movie sets scattered across southern Utah. The area was largely ignored by Spanish colonists, but when Brigham Young and his beleaguered followers of the Jesus Christ Church of Latter-Day Saints arrived near the Great Salt Lake in 1847, their leader

LEFT: *Hike, camp, or cycle among the eroded sandstone formations of Red Rock Canyon outside Bryce Canyon National Park.* Sara Benson

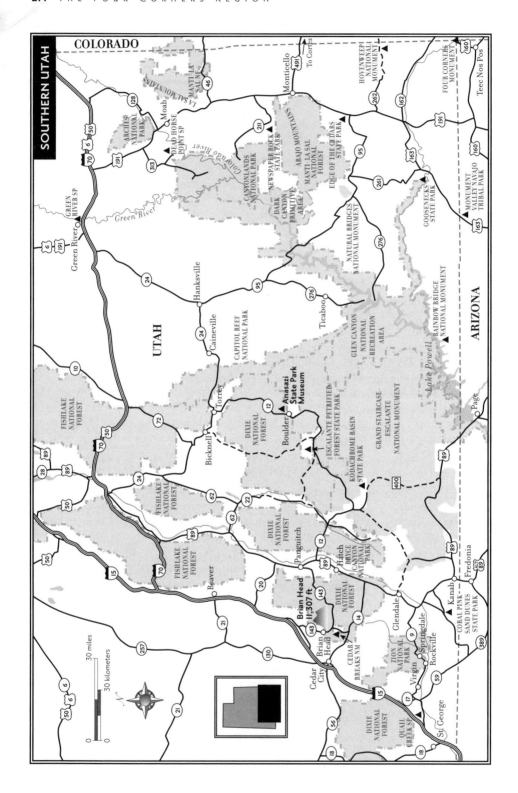

SOUTHERN UTAH

COLORADO

UTAH

ARIZONA

La Sal Mountains

Manti-La Sal NF

Moab

Green River SP

Green River

Colorado River

Arches National Park

Dead Horse Point SP

Canyonlands National Park

Newspaper Rock State Park

Dark Canyon Primitive Area

Abajo Mountains

Manti-La Sal National Forest

Edge of the Cedars State Park

Monticello

To Cortez

Hovenweep National Monument

Four Corners Monument

Teec Nos Pos

Natural Bridges National Monument

Goosenecks State Park

Monument Valley Navajo Tribal Park

Rainbow Bridge National Monument

Glen Canyon National Recreation Area

Lake Powell

Hanksville

Ticaboo

Green River

Caineville

Capitol Reef National Park

Anasazi State Park Museum

Escalante Petrified Forest State Park

Grand Staircase-Escalante National Monument

Page

Torrey

Boulder

Kodachrome Basin State Park

Fishlake National Forest

Dixie National Forest

Bicknell

Fishlake National Forest

Panguitch

Bryce Canyon National Park

Hatch

Dixie National Forest

Fredonia

Beaver

Brian Head 11,307 ft

Dixie National Forest

Glendale

Kanab

Coral Pink Sand Dunes State Park

Cedar City

Cedar Breaks NM

Brian Head

Zion National Park

Springdale

Rockville

Virgin

St George

Quail Creek SP

Dixie National Forest

30 miles

30 kilometers

N

declared "This is the place." And so Mormon pioneers chose to settle here in the Great Basin Desert after trekking halfway across the continent. They rapidly set up colonial outposts across the "State of Deseret," which extended into southern Utah. You'll see many well-preserved historic Mormon pioneer buildings, especially in downtown St. George, where Brigham Young built his winter home. Today Mormons still dominate the political and cultural landscape of southern Utah. However, visitors will also find a few more liberal-minded, artistic, and eclectic towns here, such as Springdale and Moab, which have all the earmarks of big-city life: independent bookstores and coffee shops, art galleries, fine dining, and boutique hotels.

The rural lifestyle that most locals follow, especially farmers, ranchers, and hard-core sports enthusiasts, keeps time with the rhythm of the seasons. Remember that many tourist-oriented businesses in southern Utah shut down completely between November and March, depending on how early winter arrives and how long it lasts. Be prepared for snowfall anytime between September and May. In contrast, the summer months can be extremely hot, so from June through August it's best to get an early start in the morning, especially if you are planning on playing outdoors in the desert sun.

LODGING

Bluff

CALF CANYON BED & BREAKFAST
Innkeepers: Duke and Sarah Hayduk
435-672-2470, 1-888-922-2470
www.calfcanyon.com
hosts@calfcanyon.com
7th St. E. (at Black Locust Ave.)
Bluff, UT 84512
Open: April through October
Price: Moderate
Credit Cards: None
Handicapped Access: No

Constructed in pioneer style, this modern bed-and-breakfast ensconced in gardens stands on the town's historic loop. The owners, who wandered the Southwest for some time before settling in Bluff, can inspire your vacation plans, including with regional books and maps in the common sitting area. Choose from the Chief's Room, where a Navajo rug overhangs a queen-size cedar bed; the Storm Room, which also has a handwoven Navajo rug, plus views over the San Juan River Valley; or the simpler Pioneer Room, a taste of East Coast style with a four-poster double bed. All rooms have private baths and ceiling fans. Rates include a full, hot homemade breakfast.

THE DECKER HOUSE INN
Innkeepers: Christa Monsen, Anthony Lott, and Sandra Patterson
435-672-2304, 1-888-637-2582
www.deckerhouseinn.com
deckerhouse@frontiernet.net
189 N. 3rd St. E. (at Mulberry Ave.)
Bluff, UT 84512
Price: Moderate
Credit Cards: AE, D, MC, V
Handicapped Access: No

In the same historic district as the town's other bed-and-breakfasts, this nationally registered site offers more creature comforts. The family who own the inn are truly welcoming. Each of the Victorian-style guest rooms has its own private entrance and bath, as well as heating and air-conditioning, mini-refrigerator, coffeemaker, and a VCR or DVD player with movies to borrow from the library. The Bluff, a spacious two-room suite, comes with a 1950s kitchenette. Rates include a self-serve continental breakfast, shared kitchen access in the evenings, and Wi-Fi Internet access.

DESERT ROSE INN

435-672-2303, 1-888-475-7673
www.desertroseinn.com
information@desertroseinn.com
701 W. Main St. (at 6th St. E.)
Bluff, UT 84512
Price: Moderate
Credit Cards: AE, D, MC, V
Handicapped Access: Yes

On a hilltop, this family-run, two-story timber lodge is the closest thing Bluff has to a hotel. Motel-style rooms in the main building cost only slightly less than private cabins with kitchenettes. All rooms have satellite TVs, Wi-Fi Internet access, and wraparound porches with redwood chairs for soaking up sunsets. The furnishings are simple with log-style beds and a South-western motif.

FAR OUT EXPEDITIONS GUESTHOUSE

Innkeepers: Vaughn and Marcia Hadenfeldt
435-672-2294
www.faroutexpeditions.com
tours@faroutexpeditions.com
7th St. E. (at Mulberry Ave.)
Bluff, UT 84512
Price: Moderate
Credit Cards: MC, V
Handicapped Access: Yes

Run by experienced outdoor outfitters, this laid-back inn is an amiable place. It's almost like a hostel, but with more ameni-ties and adult clientele. The historic home has two private bedrooms and two bunk-bed rooms, available nightly when groups haven't rented out the house. Hang out on the guesthouse's open-air porches, in the big living room, or in the shared guest kitchen.

RECAPTURE LODGE

Innkeepers: Jim and Luanne Hook
435-672-2281
www.recapturelodge.com
office@recapturelodge.com
P.O. Box 309, 220 E. Main St. (US 191)
Bluff, UT 84512
Price: Inexpensive
Credit Cards: AE, D, MC, V
Handicapped Access: Yes

A longtime favorite, this woodsy motel is a base camp for adventure, with miles of walking trails right on the grounds. Some of the tidy rooms are available with full kitchens. Breakfast is self-serve from a continental buffet. Amenities include a hot tub, playground, picnic areas, and seasonal swimming pool. The key attraction is a nightly slide show presented by naturalists and tour guides during peak season. A four-bedroom historic home, ideal for families and groups, rents on the Bluff River Ranch nearby.

Boulder

BOULDER MOUNTAIN LODGE

Manager: Susan Heaton
435-335-7460, 1-800-556-3446
www.boulder-utah.com
info@boulder-utah.com
P.O. Box 1397, UT 12, Boulder, UT 84716
Price: Moderate
Credit Cards: AE, D, MC, V
Handicapped Access: Yes

This Boulder landmark feels like more of a sanctuary than a lodge. The tin-roofed rose sandstone buildings may look rustic, but they're indulgent inside. Each hotel-style room has a down comforter, tapestry duvet, elegantly crafted furniture, and Aveda bath amenities. After a day of hiking, enjoy the outdoor hot tub and fire pit. Rates drop sig-nificantly outside of high season, and the lodge is open year-round. The gallery and gift shop showcase works by local artists and sell guidebooks and maps. The lodge also arranges activities, including guided tours, massage, and fireside chats. Dogs may be allowed for a surcharge.

BOULDER MOUNTAIN RANCH

Innkeepers: Gary and Sheri Catmull
435-335-7480
www.boulderutah.com/bmr
bmr@boulderutah.com
P.O. Box 1373, Boulder, UT 84716
Directions: Drive 3 miles south of Boulder
on UT 12. Turn left near mile marker 83
onto Hell's Backbone / Salt Gulch Rd., then
drive 3.5 miles.
Price: Moderate
Credit Cards: MC, V
Handicapped Access: No

People often stay at this working cattle
ranch, located outside town in pacific Salt
Gulch, before and after multiday pack trips.
A rustic overnight stop, it's a throwback in
time. Choose from a lodge room or a more
private cabin, all furnished in Western
style. There are no TVs, which leaves more
time for amazing stargazing. Daily horseback trail rides and winter snowshoeing,
cross-country skiing, and snowmobiling
are offered. No meals available.

POLE'S PLACE

Managers: Eugene Napoleon Griffin family
1-800-730-7422
www.boulderutah.com/polesplace
P.O. Box 1342, UT 12, Boulder, UT 84716
Price: Inexpensive
Credit Cards: AE, D, MC, V
Handicapped Access: Yes

Opposite Anasazi State Park, this well-kept,
family-run budget motel has been in business for 20 years. The owners are descendants of a homesteader who arrived in the
late 19th century, when Boulder was accessible only by mule trails. Looking as if it
was taken straight off a Western movie set,
this peaceful motel is a more comfortable
alternative to camping in Grand
Staircase–Escalante National Monument.
There are just a dozen nonsmoking rooms
with telephones, TVs, and air-condition-

ing. A small café serves old-fashioned
burgers, shakes, and salads.

Bryce

BEST WESTERN RUBY'S INN

435-834-5341, 1-866-1-866-6616
www.rubysinn.com
info@rubysinn.com
1000 S. US 63, Bryce, UT 84764
Price: Moderate
Credit Cards: AE, D, MC, V
Handicapped Access: Yes

This mammoth tourist complex is the closest lodging option outside Bryce Canyon
National Park. More than a motel, it's a village unto itself, complete with a general
store, restaurants, guided horseback riding, summer rodeo shows, a laundromat,
and indoor swimming pool. Almost 370
basic motel-style guest rooms have air-
conditioning, cable TV, and high-speed
Wi-Fi Internet access. Pets are welcome,
subject to a deposit and check-out room
inspection. The national park shuttle stops
outside the inn.

BRYCE CANYON LODGE

Regional General Manager: Jeff D'Arpa
435-834-8700, 1-888-297-2757
www.brycecanyonlodge.com
P.O. Box 640079
Bryce Canyon National Park, UT 84764
Price: Moderate
Credit Cards: AE, D, MC, V
Handicapped Access: Yes

This rustic-looking national park lodge
built in the 1920s is an officially registered
historic site with an unbeatable location
and peaceful atmosphere. All of the park's
outdoor activities are at your doorstep here.
Book a lodge suite, or a short walk away are
motel rooms and cabins, all decorated in
Western style. The modest cabins haven't
been remodeled recently but do have gas
fireplaces, bathrooms, phones, and

Creature comforts look inviting at Bryce Canyon Lodge inside Bryce Canyon National Park. Xanterra Parks & Resorts

porches near the canyon rim. The lodge has a general store and restaurant. Reservations are accepted 13 months in advance, starting on the first day of the month.

Cedar City

THE BIG YELLOW INN BED & BREAKFAST

Innkeepers: Scott and Barbara Hunt
435-586-0960
www.bigyellowinn.com
stay@bigyellowinn.com
234 S. 300 West (at W. 200 South)
Cedar City, UT 84720.
Price: Expensive
Credit Cards: AE, MC, V
Handicapped Access: No

As befits its imposing exterior, this butter-yellow-painted home is decorated in Georgian revival style. All the rooms are richly furnished but have a subtle theme, from the Mediterranean Room, which has a fireplace and mahogany bed, to the English room, with a fireplace and antique clawfoot tub. The romantic, oversize Gable Suite has a double whirlpool tub and a telescope for stargazing. At the moderately priced annex

across the street, simpler rooms have fish-pond views. Rates include Internet access and a full breakfast.

Escalante

CANYONS BED & BREAKFAST

Innkeepers: Cate Vining and Phil Heck
435-826-4747, 1-866-526-9667
www.canyonsbnb.com
info@canyonsbnb.com
120 E. Main St. (at N. 100 East)
Escalante, UT 84726
Open: March through November
Price: Moderate
Credit Cards: MC, V
Handicapped Access: No

Shaded by gardens and fruit trees, this bed-and-breakfast consists of a bunkhouse attached to an early 20th-century farmhouse painted the color of a folksy red barn. The hosts are amiable, the breakfasts outstanding, and the three guest rooms beckon with air-conditioning, modern furnishings, designer linens, down comforters, TVs, phones, Internet access, and private decks with French doors. The Garden Room has views and the Cabana Room has whimsical bamboo accents, while the Cowboy Room boasts authentic Western memorabilia.

KIVA KOTTAGE

Innkeepers: Barrie Ence
435-826-4550
www.kivakoffeehouse.com
kivakoffee@infowest.com
UT 12 mile marker 73.86
Escalante, UT 84726
Open: April through November
Price: Expensive
Credit Cards: MC, V
Handicapped Access: No

Although you might miss it driving past, this unique structure built into the hillside amidst canyon country is worth a stop. It took eight years to construct it out of logs, stone, and glass. Linger overnight inside the cottage nestled below the coffeehouse for peace and quiet. The furnishings are minimalist, but oversize guest rooms have bathrooms, whirlpool tubs, picture windows, ceiling fans, fireplaces, and private patios. While there are no TVs or telephones, Wi-Fi Internet access is available. Breakfast is served at the café upstairs.

LA LUZ DESERT RETREAT
Innkeeper: Ricki Brown
435-826-4708, 1-888-305-4705
www.laluz.net
stay@laluz.net
P.O. Box 537, Escalante, UT 84726
Price: Expensive
Credit Cards: MC, V
Handicapped Access: Yes

Surrounded by Utah's signature red rocks, this architect-designed vacation rental home is more private than most. Dramatic windows have big-sky views. In fact, the entire house is designed as an homage to Frank Lloyd Wright. It's also an eco-conscious retreat equipped with solar heating and evaporative cooling. The kitchen is fully equipped, featuring black marble countertops and antique Chinese cabinetry. An atrium shower is another feature not to be forgotten. Wi-Fi Internet access is available.

SLOT CANYONS INN
Innkeepers: Jeff and Joette Marie Rex
435-826-4901, 1-866-889-8375
www.slotcanyonsinn.com
3680 W. UT 12 (near mile marker 54)
Escalante, UT 84726
Price: Expensive
Credit Cards: AE, D, MC, V
Handicapped Access: Partial

A recently opened bed-and-breakfast, the Slot Canyons Inn stands in its own canyon where archaeological discoveries have been made. A contemporary multistory adobe house with a tranquil atmosphere, it has eight different guest rooms. Some have whirlpool tubs, fireplaces, river views, kitchenettes, and TVs with VCR/DVD players. The rooftop garden is a perfect place to unwind. Also available for rent is the Isaac Riddle Log Cabin, a two-bedroom house built from a century-old cowboy cabin perched on a hillside (two-night minimum stay).

SOUTHWESTERN RETREAT
435-826-4708
www.southwesternretreat.com
stay@southwesternretreat.com
P.O. Box 163, Escalante, UT 84726
Price: Moderate
Credit Cards: MC, V
Handicapped Access: No

Escalante is a jackpot for vacation rental homes. This spacious three-bedroom, two-bath house has a full kitchen, entertainment center, laundry facilities, and a front

Peaceful sleep awaits at the off-the-beaten-path Kiva Kottage in Escalante. Courtesy Kiva Kottage

porch with vistas that seemingly stretch on forever. The contemporary decor has a subtle Southwestern theme. The house, which is rented by the night or the week, is non-smoking. Pets are allowed.

WILD WEST RETREAT

Innkeepers: Shannon and Jennifer Steed
435-826-4849, 1-866-292-3043
www.wildwestretreat.com
yahoo@wildwestretreat.com
269 S. 200 East (at E. 200 South)
Escalante, UT 84726
Price: Moderate
Credit Cards: MC, V
Handicapped Access: Partial

Hosted by friendly cowgirl cooks, this remodeled pole barn has all sorts of rustic Wild West touches. Natural wood was used to make everything from gnarled door handles to the shady front porch. The private cabin is heated by a wood-burning stove and has a log-style king-size bed in a loft bedroom accessed via a spiral staircase, plus a hot tub, fully equipped kitchen, and air-conditioning. Rates include a breakfast basket delivered to your door. If you happen to show up while they're cooking a traditional Dutch-oven meal for a big group, dinner may also be free.

Glendale

HISTORIC SMITH HOTEL BED & BREAKFAST

Innkeepers: Rochelle, Bunny, and Mike
1-800-528-3558
www.historicsmithhotel.com
reachus@historicsmithhotel.com
295 N. Main St. (US 89)
Glendale, UT 84729
Price: Inexpensive
Credit Cards: MC, V
Handicapped Access: Partial

It's the legendary hospitality of the family of hosts that draws folks. Positioned between Zion and Bryce Canyon National Parks, this rambling 1920s boardinghouse is outfitted with antiques and cozy, country-kitsch rooms. The biggest has a king-size bed, private bath, and garden-view porch. Smaller rooms have bunk beds for kids. There's a pioneer wood-burning stove in the shared kitchen and a coin-op guest laundry. Kick back on one of the screened-in porches with orchard views, or play croquet. Hot breakfasts may include waffles or an apple crisp.

WINDWHISPER CABIN & BREAKFAST

Innkeepers: Terry and Audrey Behling
435-648-2162
www.windwhisperbb.com
P.O. Box 127, Glendale, UT 84729
Directions: US 89, south of mile marker 92
Price: Moderate
Credit Cards: AE, D, MC, V
Handicapped Access: No

A lovingly tended inn on the outskirts of town, Windwhisper is a more intimate experience. Pick the Shoshoni Room that opens onto a flagstone patio or the Mountain View Room in the main house. A detached cabin with a full kitchen affords privacy. All rooms have private baths. Rates include full breakfasts with homemade jams made from orchards and berry bushes on the property.

Green River

BEST WESTERN RIVER TERRACE

435-564-3401, 1-800-780-7234
www.bestwestern.com
880 E. Main St., Green River, UT 84525
Price: Moderate
Credit Cards: AE, D, MC, V
Handicapped Access: Yes

This riverfront Best Western is a good value, especially compared with motels in Moab. The shady grounds have garden patios and an outdoor swimming pool and hot tub that are open seasonally. Guest accommodations have standard-issue furnishings, with high-end mattresses, down pillows, and Wi-Fi Internet access. Some oversize rooms have balconies overlooking the Green River. At this oasis in the desert, rates include a considerable hot breakfast.

Kanab

AIKENS LODGE

Managers: Bill and Krista Erickson
435-644-2625, 1-800-790-0380
www.aikenslodge.com
info@aikenslodge.com
29 W. Center St. (at N. 100 West)
Kanab, UT 84741
Price: Moderate
Credit Cards: AE, D, MC, V
Handicapped Access: Yes

This friendly, family-owned motel is among the best budget lodgings along southern Utah's byways. You can walk anywhere downtown from here. All the rooms are nonsmoking and have air-conditioning and cable TV. Some also have mini-refrigerators. Amenities include high-speed Wi-Fi Internet access, coin-op laundry machines, and a seasonal heated pool. Two-and three-bedroom family units are available.

ANGEL CANYON GUEST COTTAGES

435-644-2001
www.bestfriends.org
cottages@bestfriends.org
Best Friends Animal Sanctuary, 5001 Angel Canyon Rd., Kanab, UT 84741
Directions: Off US 89 at mile marker 69, 5 miles north of town
Price: Moderate
Credit Cards: AE, D, MC, V
Handicapped Access: Yes

By staying here, not only do you get the peaceful atmosphere of Angel Canyon, but proceeds go toward running the nonprofit Best Friends Animal Sanctuary. Located

next to outdoor koi ponds, the contemporary, modular cottages are one-bedroom suites with kitchens and a full bath, while studio cabins have a kitchenette and shower. All the cabins and cottages have air-conditioning, TVs, and high-speed Wi-Fi Internet access.

CORAL CLIFFS TOWNHOMES

1-800-707-9706
www.cctownhomes.com
cctownhomes@kanab.net
Check-in: Holiday Inn Express, 815 E. US 89, Kanab, UT 84741
Price: Expensive
Credit Cards: AE, D, MC, V
Handicapped Access: Partial

Kanab's most luxurious accommodations are condo-style townhomes by the golf course. Each has a unique floor plan, but all have multiple bedrooms, full kitchens, washer/dryers, satellite TV, air-conditioning, and backyard barbecue grills and picnic tables. Guests get discounted greens fees and access to a hot tub, swimming pool, and high-speed Wi-Fi Internet access at the Holiday Inn Express in town. Pets are allowed in most units for a surcharge.

KANAB GARDEN COTTAGES

Manager: John Ehlert
435-644-2020
www.kanabcottages.com
kanabcottages@kanab.net
Various addresses in Kanab, UT 84741
Price: Expensive
Credit Cards: MC, V
Handicapped Access: Yes

In downtown Kanab, these quaint vacation cottages have enough space for even large families. The styles vary from Arts-and-Crafts to Victorian bungalow, with furnishings that are mostly contemporary. The Tudor Cottage has a full kitchen, TVs with VCR/DVD players, air-conditioning, and a washer/dryer. The largest Juniper Cottage also has a telephone and high-speed Internet access. Fireplaces and outdoor living areas encourage relaxation. A three-night minimum stay is required.

PARRY LODGE
435-644-2601, 1-888-289-1722
www.parrylodge.com
sales@parrylodge.com
80 E. Center St. (at S. Main St.)
Kanab, UT 84741
Price: Moderate
Credit Cards: AE, D, MC, V
Handicapped Access: Yes

With over 80 rooms, this centrally located motel with attractive two-story white buildings has a lot of history. Movie stars from Dale Evans to Sammy Davis Jr. stayed here while filming Hollywood Westerns in the desert nearby. It's nothing fancy, but it's among the friendliest places to stay in Kanab. The large old-fashioned rooms have character, full-size refrigerators, and sometimes kitchenettes. The leafy-green grounds have an outdoor swimming pool and hot tub. Guests enjoy free admission to classic films shown in the old barn between mid-April and mid-October.

QUAIL PARK LODGE
Owners: Guinn family
1-866-702-8099
www.quailparklodge.com
125 N. US 89 (at N. 300 West)
Kanab, UT 84741
Price: Inexpensive
Credit Cards: AE, D, MC, V
Handicapped Access: Yes

Another decent budget choice in Kanab, this family-owned motel north of downtown offers basic, no-frills lodging for a fair price. Rooms have air-conditioning, cable TV, mini-fridges, microwaves, and full baths. Families might want to pay more for a multi-bed suite. There's a heated out-door pool and a park conveniently next door. High-speed Internet access is free; pets are accepted.

Mexican Hat
THE HAT ROCK INN
435-683-2221
www.hatrockinn.com
UT 163, Mexican Hat, UT 84531
Price: Moderate
Credit Cards: AE, MC, V
Handicapped Access: Yes

Although the rates are slightly higher than the competition's and the exterior is not the most appealing, the simple motel-style rooms are pleasantly outfitted with comfortable beds, contemporary furnishings, antique photographs on the walls, bathtubs, and extra tables and chairs for a little more comfort. In the common area you'll find a gas fireplace, cable TV, and Internet-connected computer.

MEXICAN HAT LODGE
Owners: Bobbie and Vonnie Mueller
435-683-2222
www.mexicanhat.net
bob@mexicanhat.net
P.O. Box 310175, UT 163
Mexican Hat, UT 84531
Price: Inexpensive
Credit Cards: MC, V
Handicapped Access: Yes

Run by a family of traveling musicians who passed through Mexican Hat once and decided to stay, this motel is a social hot-spot, thanks to a steakhouse that attracts bikers, hippies, and rock climbers after sunset. Inside a former pioneer bar and dance hall there are just 10 rooms, each uniquely decorated with oddball antiques, country crafts, and more. It's got rustic Western appeal, and the staff will make you feel at home.

SAN JUAN INN

1-800-447-2022
www.sanjuaninn.net
sanjuaninn@citlink.net
P.O. Box 310276, UT 163,
Mexican Hat, UT 84531
Price: Moderate
Credit Cards: MC, V
Hanicapped Access: Yes

You can't miss this landmark two-story
motel built right against the cliffside beside
the San Juan River. It has the most picturesque setting in town. Rooms are basic but
do have TVs and phones—it's the views
you're paying to enjoy, though. A trading
post, diner, and laundry facilities are on
site, along with an air-conditioned workout
room and riverside walking trails.

VALLEY OF THE GODS
BED & BREAKFAST

Innkeepers: Gary and Claire Dorgan
970-749-1164
www.zippitydodah.com/vog
P.O. Box 310307, Mexican Hat, UT 84531
Directions: Take UT 163 east of town, then
UT 261 north for 6.5 miles. Turn right on
Valley of the Gods Rd.
Price: Moderate
Credit Cards: None
Handicapped Access: No

Boasting what must be one of the most
majestic and lonely settings in the
Southwest, this private ranch home made of
stone and wood is an idyllic escape from the
dusty town of Mexican Hat. Million-dollar
views from the wooden chairs set on the
front porch are alone worth the detour. The
owners take care of four guest rooms in the
main building and a split-level lodge next
door, which has private decks. The entire
property is solar- and wind-powered.
Breakfast is included in the rates, but for
dinner you'll have to drive into town or bring
your own food. Enjoy stargazing and chatting with other travelers in the evenings.

Moab

ADOBE ABODE
BED & BREAKFAST

Innkeeper: Keith R. Herrmann
435-259-7716
www.adobeabodemoab.com
info@adobeabodemoab.com
778 Kane Creek Blvd. (at S. 500 West)
Moab, UT 84532
Price: Moderate
Credit Cards: AE, D, MC, V
Handicapped Access: Yes

There's a touch of Southwestern style at this
modern adobe home on the outskirts of
downtown. A creek runs through the property, which has a natural setting. Each of
the four contemporary rooms and two
suites has a private patio, cable TV, ceiling
fans, and en-suite bath with terrycloth
robes for trips to the hot tub. Guests also
enjoy free high-speed Wi-Fi Internet
access, a library with satellite TV and books
and videos, plus a billiards table. A two-
night minimum stay is required; rates
include breakfast.

ADVENTURE INN

435-259-6122, 1-866-662-2466
www.adventureinnmoab.com
info@adventureinnmoab.com
512 N. Main St. (at W. 400 North)
Moab, UT 84532
Price: Moderate
Credit Cards: AE, D, MC, V
Handicapped Access: Yes

On the highway west of downtown, this single-story motel is run by a family who love
outdoor activities as much as the repeat
guests do. Basic rooms have bathtubs and
showers inside private attached baths,
individual air-conditioning and heating
units, cable TV, and telephones; some also
have mini-fridges. There's secure bike
storage for guests.

BEST WESTERN CANYONLANDS INN

435-259-2300, 1-800-649-5191
www.canyonlandsinn.com
canyonlandsinn@frontiernet.net
16 S. Main St. (at E. Center St.)
Moab, UT 84532
Price: Moderate
Credit Cards: AE, D, MC, V
Handicapped Access: Yes

This chain motel is ideally located down-town. It's an especially good deal in the off-season, when prices drop up to 50 percent. Spacious rooms are equipped with air-conditioning, cable TV, and mini-refrigerators. Guest amenities include an outdoor swimming pool, hot tub, fitness room, laundry facilities, secure mountain-bike storage, and a small children's playground. Rates include complimentary hot breakfast.

CALI COCHITTA BED & BREAKFAST

Innkeepers: David and Kim Boger
435-259-4961, 1-888-429-8112
www.moabdreaminn.com
calicochitta@moabdreaminn.com
110 S. 200 East (at E. 100 South)
Moab, UT 84532
Price: Moderate
Credit Cards: AE, D, MC, V
Handicapped Access: No

Secluded but within walking distance of downtown, this peaceful bed-and-breakfast inhabits a late-19th-century Victorian cottage. The furnishings harmonize with the era but have a contemporary appeal that

Take breakfast outside when the sun shines at Cali Cochitta Bed & Breakfast in Moab. Courtesy Cali Cochitta Bed & Breakfast

never feels stuffy. Private cottages have air-conditioning, refrigerators, and off-road parking. Rooms in the main house are almost as tranquil. Each is uniquely deco-rated, such as with a sleigh bed or French doors, but not all have private bathrooms. Amenities include a hot tub, high-speed Wi-Fi Internet access, and in-room TVs and VCRs. After enjoying a full hot breakfast, take time to swing in a hammock or relax on the backyard patio. The inn is gay-friendly.

CASTLE VALLEY INN

Innkeepers: Jim and Mary Germain
435-259-6012
www.castlevalleyinn.com
info@castlevalleyinn.com
HC-64 Box 2602, Moab, UT 84532
Directions: Follow UT 128 east along the Colorado River for 15.5 miles. Turn right onto La Sal Mountain Loop Rd., then right again after 1.7 miles.
Price: Expensive
Credit Cards: D, MC, V
Handicapped Access: Yes

Seeking a romantic getaway with plenty of solitude? This unique inn surrounded by private orchards outside Moab is run by friendly hosts who are full of hiking and birding tips. All rooms and suites have pri-vate baths, coffeemakers, telephones, mini-refrigerators, and TVs with VCRs and movies to borrow. Rooms in the main house are cozy, but private bungalows and cabins are more appealing, with orchard-view patios and full kitchens. The decor is contemporary Southwestern, with large picture windows. Rates include a full breakfast. The inn is gay-friendly.

DESERT HILLS BED AND BREAKFAST

Innkeepers: Winni and John Souvereyns
435-259-3568
www.deserthillsbnb.com
info@deserthillsbnb.com
1989 S. Desert Hills Lane, Moab, UT 84532

Directions: Drive 4 miles south of Moab on US 191. Turn left onto Spanish Trail Rd., left again onto Murphy Lane at the round-about, and take the first right.
Price: Moderate
Credit Cards: AE, D, MC, V
Handicapped Access: No

Located in the upscale Spanish Valley near a golf course, this residential bed-and-breakfast has a welcoming atmosphere. Some rooms have picture windows with sunset views of the La Sal Mountains. Simply furnished, contemporary rooms have cable TV, air-conditioning, pillow-top mattresses on log-style beds, and bathrobes for trips to the backyard hot tub; not all have attached private baths. Hot breakfasts may include treats like waffles. Dutch, German, and French are spoken. The inn is gay-friendly.

DREAM KEEPER INN
Innkeepers: Dave and Kim Pettit
435-259-5998, 1-888-230-3247
www.dreamkeeperinn.com
dreamkeeperinn@citilink.net
191 S. 200 East (at E. 200 South)
Moab, UT 84532
Price: Moderate
Credit Cards: D, MC, V
Handicapped Access: No

More formal than most of Moab's other bed-and-breakfasts, this well-kept guesthouse pays painstaking attention to detail in the guest rooms, a few of which have a detached private bath. Even the smallest, the Kava Room, has a fetching queen-size iron bed, a fireplace, and a small TV/VCR combo with movies to borrow from the library. Amenities include an outdoor hot tub and swimming pool, mini-refrigerator, guest telephone, and high-speed Wi-Fi Internet access. The garden cottages enjoy more privacy.

INCA INN
435-259-7261, 1-866-462-2466
www.incainn.com

reservations@incainn.com
570 N. Main St. (at N. 600 West)
Moab, UT 84532
Open: March through November
Price: Moderate
Credit Cards: AE, D, MC, V
Handicapped Access: Yes

Price gouging is not uncommon in Moab, especially on weekends. For a fair shake, try this tidy motel at the west edge of town. Rooms have ultra-comfortable beds, big-screen TVs, private baths, and individual heating and air-conditioning units, ready for any kind of weather. There's a small seasonal swimming pool in the parking lot by the highway. Secure mountain-bike storage and high-speed Wi-Fi Internet access are provided.

KOKOPELLI LODGE
Manager: Katy
435-259-7615, 1-888-530-3134
www.kokopellilodge.com
info@kokopellilodge.com
72 S. 100 East (at E. 100 South)
Moab, UT 84532
Price: Inexpensive
Credit Cards: AE, D, MC, V
Handicapped Access: Yes

A good budget motel in Moab is hard to find, but this remodeled downtown property caters well to mountain bikers. The enthusiastic owner fosters community spirit and has loaner bikes for guests to tool around town on. The eight standard motel rooms share a common patio, barbecue grills, and a gazebo hot tub. The rooms themselves are nothing fancy, but all have queen-size beds, cable TV, a microwave, mini-fridge, and coffeemaker stocked with organic grounds. High-speed Wi-Fi Internet access is complimentary; pets welcome for a surcharge.

LOS VADOS CANYON HOUSE
Innkeepers: Dave and Susan Valenti
801-532-2651
www.losvados.com

reservations@losvados.com
contact address: 777 E. Temple, Suite 5J
Salt Lake City, UT 84102
Mill Creek Canyon, Moab, UT 84101
Price: Very Expensive
Credit Cards: AE, MC, V
Handicapped Access: No

On a high-clearance 4WD dirt road in a red-rock canyon, this vacation rental affords true privacy. The relaxed contemporary furnishings are rustic but elegant. The house features outdoor living spaces, fireplaces, two bedrooms, a bathroom with a deep soaking tub, and an airy tent cabin pitched across the stream. Take advantage of a small seasonal swimming pool, full kitchen, and washer/dryer for guests. A three-night minimum stay is required.

MAYOR'S HOUSE BED AND BREAKFAST

Innkeepers: Cary Cox and David Ingalls
435-259-6015, 1-888-791-2345
www.mayorshouse.com
info@mayorshouse.com
505 Rose Tree Lane (at S. 4th St. East)
Moab, UT 84532
Price: Moderate
Credit Cards: AE, D, MC, V
Handicapped Access: No

Built by a former mayor of Moab, this contemporary brick house downtown has all the amenities you could desire after a day spent in the great outdoors, such as a heated swimming pool, two hot tubs, barbecue grills, secure bike storage, and in-room TVs and VCRs with a library of movies to borrow. Each of the six simple southwestern-style rooms has handcrafted furniture and air-conditioning; some have jetted soaking tubs, too. Rates include a full breakfast served at a communal table. The inn is gay-friendly.

MOUNT PEALE RESORT

Innkeepers: Teague, Lisa, and J. R.
435-686-2284, 1-888-687-3253
www.mtpeale.com
relax@mtpeale.com
1415 E. UT 46, mile post 14.1
Old La Sal, UT 84530.
Directions: From Moab drive 20 miles south on US 191, then 14.1 miles east on UT 46.
Price: Moderate
Credit Cards: MC, V
Handicapped Access: Partial

The owners of this forest lodge and cabins hidden in the Manti–La Sal Mountains put flannel sheets on the bed even in summer, as it's a cool retreat from the sweltering desert below. Loft rooms in the lodge have deck access to a hot tub, while cabins are more like mountain houses, with full kitchens, fireplaces, barbecue grills, satellite TV with VCR and DVD players, and washer/dryers. All are outfitted in rustic country style. High-speed Wi-Fi Internet access is available in the common areas. Meals and spa treatments are offered. The inn is gay-friendly.

RED CLIFFS LODGE

Managers: Colin Fryer and Sandy Bastian
435-259-2002, 1-866-812-2002
www.redcliffslodge.com
info@redcliffslodge.com
UT 128, mile marker 14, Moab, UT 84532
Price: Expensive
Credit Cards: AE, D, MC, V
Handicapped Access: Yes

Beside the Colorado River, this cowboy-style ranch lodge is outside town but close to hiking trails and river rafting. All rooms and cabins have private patios with views, kitchenettes, air-conditioning, and Spanish-tiled floors. Detached cabins, which are more like vacation homes, are equipped with satellite TV, high-speed Internet access, and telephones. Other amenities include a swimming pool and hot tub, horse corrals, restaurant, and winery. For nonfussy travelers who want a more rustic setting, it's a good choice. The lodge is gay-friendly. Pets may be accepted.

SORREL RIVER RANCH
RESORT AND SPA

Owner: Robbie Levin

435-259-4642, 1-877-359-2715

www.sorrelriver.com

stay@sorrelriver.com

Mile marker 17, UT 128, Moab, UT 84532

Directions: From Moab take UT 128 east for 17 miles.

Price: Very Expensive

Credit Cards: AE, D, MC, V

Handicapped Access: Yes

This century-old homestead and cattle ranch was rescued by a rock star. Today, Sorrel River Ranch Resort and Spa is Moab's most luxurious boutique hotel, designed for families and couples seeking an active outdoor vacation without sacrificing many creature comforts. Service here is attentive. Enormous guest rooms have private decks, kitchenettes, custom-made furnishings, and log-beam ceilings; suites up the ante with jetted soaking tubs and overstuffed sofas. Perks include high-speed Internet access, a fitness room, swimming pool and hot tub, and tennis courts. Spa appointments and reservations for horseback rides and restaurant tables should be made in advance.

SUNFLOWER HILL

Innkeepers: Stucki family

435-259-2974, 1-800-662-2786

www.sunflowerhill.com

innkeeper@sunflowerhill.com

185 N. 300 East (at E. 200 North)

Moab, UT 84532

Price: Expensive

Credit Cards: AE, D, MC, V

Handicapped Access: No

This award-winning upscale inn has a dozen quaint rooms spread between the ranch house and the garden cottage. Deluxe rooms and suites have jetted tubs, while classic suites enjoy a balcony or patio. Although the antique furnishings are a bit fussy and the staff can be stiffly formal, most guests find it charming.

There's a seasonal swimming pool, barbecue grills, secure mountain-bike storage, laundry facilities, and guests' kitchenette. Breakfast in the farmhouse dining room includes fresh smoothies, homemade honey granola, and a hot entree. Rates also include complimentary snacks and evening refreshments. A two-night minimum stay is required.

Mount Carmel

ARROWHEAD COUNTRY INN & CABINS

Innkeepers: Jane and Jim Jennings

435-648-2569, 1-888-821-1670

www.arrowheadbb.com

duelj1@color-country.net

P.O. Box 5561, US 89, near mile marker 84

Mount Carmel, UT 84755

Directions: Drive 2 miles north of Mount Carmel Junction.

Price: Moderate

Credit Cards: AE, MC, V

Handicapped Access: No

This country inn with hospitable owners and farmyard animals on the property has front porches made for lazing the afternoon away. Rooms in the main house are less expensive, but it's worth paying more for a bigger cabin with a full kitchen or a cottage with a kitchenette. Families will find plenty to occupy kids, from a movie library and billiards table to an outdoor seasonal swimming pool and walks around the gardens, orchard, and horse corrals. Rates include home-cooked breakfasts.

BEST WESTERN EAST ZION
THUNDERBIRD LODGE

435-648-2203, 1-800-780-7234

www.bestwestern.com

UT 9 and US 89, Mount Carmel, UT 84755

Price: Moderate

Credit Cards: AE, D, MC, V

Handicapped Access: Yes

The highway junction of the roads to Zion National Park, the North Rim of the Grand Canyon, and Bryce Canyon is a major crossroads for travelers. You're better off staying closer to the parks themselves, but this motel is the town's best choice. Spacious rooms each have a private balcony or patio, satellite TV, Wi-Fi Internet access, and rustic wood furnishings. An outdoor hot tub and swimming pool are open seasonally.

ZION MOUNTAIN RESORT
Innkeeper: Mark Wade
435-648-2555, 1-866-648-2555
www.zionmountainresort.com
9065 E. UT 9, Mount Carmel, UT 85755
Directions: 11 miles west of Mount Carmel Junction
Price: Expensive
Credit Cards: AE, D, MC, V
Handicapped Access: Yes

Outside the east entrance of Zion National Park, these remote lodgings offer peaceful surroundings and are a good bet for big families who want proximity to the parks and plenty of room to move around. Private cabins have wood furnishings, satellite TV, individual heating and air-conditioning units, and kitchenettes; suites also have jetted tubs. The vacation lodges are more than generously sized, with gas fireplaces and VCR/ DVD players, too.

ZION PONDEROSA RANCH RESORT
Manager: Michael Caane
435-648-2700, 1-800-293-5444
www.zionponderosa.com
resort@zionponderosa.com
P.O. Box 5547, Mount Carmel, UT 84755
Directions: Drive 2 miles east of Zion National Park's east entrance on UT 9, then 5 miles north on North Fork Rd.
Price: Moderate
Credit Cards: AE, D, MC, V
Handicapped Access: Partial

To get away from it all, try this rustic resort elevated at cooler mountain climes outside Zion National Park. Most guests come here for activities from ATV riding to mountain biking. Cowboy cabins are arranged around a dirt road that encloses a grassy camping area, with bathrooms in a shared modern shower house. Cabin suites and vacation homes enjoy more amenities, such as private bathrooms, air-conditioning, and front porches, but no telephones or TVs. There's an extra-large swimming pool and hot tub with a scenic view for guests, plus basketball and tennis courts and free high-speed Wi-Fi Internet access.

ZION WATERSIDE INN
Innkeepers: Kriss Gates and Dixie McCorvey
435-648-2300
www.zionwatersideinn.com
information@zionwatersideinn.com
Clear Creek Ranch, 1 North Fork Rd., East Zion, UT 84767
Directions: Drive 2 miles east of Zion National Park's east entrance on UT 9, then turn left onto North Fork Rd.
Price: Moderate
Credit Cards: D, MC, V
Handicapped Access: No

Beautifully set on a thousand-acre mountain ranch, this rural bed-and-breakfast is an escape from the crowds. Rooms are decorated in rustic Western style, with wooden furnishings, ceiling fans, private bathrooms, and even window seats. For guests there's a book and video library, fishing ponds, and laundry facilities. At night, kick back on the porch for stargazing or gather around the fireplace in the common area, which has satellite TV.

Panguitch
COLOR COUNTRY MOTEL
Managers: Lance and Cindy
435-676-2386, 1-800-225-6518
www.colorcountrymotel.com
bobbie@color-country.net
526 N. Main St. (US 89, at W. 500 North)

Panguitch, UT 84759
Price: Inexpensive
Credit Cards: AE, D, MC, V
Handicapped Access: Yes

Open year-round, this budget motel near downtown consistently gets good reviews. It offers just over two dozen recently refurbished rooms that are quiet. While the furnishings are just average, rooms have cable TV, phones, and heating and air-conditioning. There's a seasonal heated swimming pool and outdoor hot tub. German is spoken. Pets are allowed.

HIETT LAMP LIGHTER INN

435-676-8362, 1-800-322-6996
www.colorcountry.net/
~gsexpeditions/index
gsexpeditions@color-country.net
581 N. Main St. (US 89, at W. 500 North)
Panguitch, UT 84759
Price: Inexpensive
Credit Cards: AE, D, MC, V
Handicapped Access: Yes

Another well-kept budget motel near downtown, this AAA-approved property offers smoke-free, pet-free rooms with mini-fridges, cable TV, heating and air-conditioning, and coffeemakers (but no phones). The rooms' interior brick walls are cheerfully painted, and barbecue grills are available outside.

PURPLE SAGE MOTEL

435-676-2659, 1-800-241-6889
www.purplesagemotel.biz
info@purplesagemotel.biz
132 E. Center St. (at N. 100 East)
Panguitch, UT 84759
Open: March through October
Price: Inexpensive
Credit Cards: AE, D, MC, V
Handicapped Access: Partial

This tidy, nonsmoking, and pet-free motel is in downtown Panguitch. High-speed Wi-Fi Internet access is available in remodeled guest rooms. The furnishings are standard but with more than a modicum of taste; beds have pillow-top mattresses. Guests at this two-story motel also have access to a seasonal outdoor hot tub.

RED BRICK INN

Innkeepers: Peggy and Brett Egan
435-676-2141, 1-866-733-2745
www.redbrickinnutah.com
redbrick@color-country.net
161 N. 100 West (at W. 200 North)
Panguitch, UT 84759
Price: Moderate
Credit Cards: MC, V
Handicapped Access: No

A 1920s Dutch colonial bungalow, this quaint inn stands on the outskirts of downtown. Guests gather in the common room with a fireplace, big-screen TV, and board games, or in the shady yard. Small rooms decorated with Western and neo-Victorian themes have TVs and VCRs. Try the Northwoods Lodge Room, with a queen-size sleigh bed, private attached bath, and hardwood floors covered in plush rugs. Rates include a hot breakfast and, if you're lucky, afternoon chocolate chip cookies. The inn is gay-friendly.

Rockville

BUNK HOUSE AT ZION BED & BREAKFAST

Innkeepers: Meg and Bo Orton
435-772-3393
www.zionbunkhousebedandbreakfast.com
reducereuserecycle@bunkhouseatzion.com
149 E. Main St. (UT 9), Rockville, UT 84763
Price: Inexpensive
Credit Cards: None
Handicapped Access: No

Formerly Serenity House, this rustic guesthouse is committed to providing environmentally conscious lodging. The hosts live off the land, even doing their own organic farming. There are just two simple but tidy rooms with shared or private baths, a comfortably lived-in common area, and a porch shaded by the fruit orchard. If you're looking for a low-key overnight close to Zion National Park, the rates are reasonable, though it's nothing fancy.

DESERT THISTLE BED & BREAKFAST

Innkeeper: Maureen Edgel
435-772-0251
www.thedesertthistle.com
maureenedgel@hotmail.com
37 W. Main St. (UT 9), Rockville, UT 84763
Price: Moderate
Credit Cards: AE, D, MC, V
Handicapped Access: Yes

Near Zion National Park, this low-slung Rockville ranch house is more peaceful than the touristy town of Springdale. There's ample space to unwind in guest rooms that feature firm mattresses, flat-screen satellite TVs, and spacious bathrooms. The decor suggests a bit of luxury in the desert, but it's actually a down-to-earth experience. The outdoor swimming pool is perfect for hot days. The friendly owners are animal lovers, so some guests' pets may be accepted.

DREAM CATCHER INN
BED & BREAKFAST

Innkeepers: Dawna and Norm
435-772-3600, 1-800-953-7326
www.dreamcatcherinnzion.com
dcinn@redrock.net
225 E. Main St. (UT 9), Rockville, UT 84763
Price: Inexpensive
Credit Cards: None
Handicapped Access: No

Another bed-and-breakfast ensconced in the small town of Rockville, just west of Zion National Park, it's set apart by its affordable rates and the affable owners. Each room has country-style decor and harmonizes with a

different season, and most rooms have private baths. The Summer Suite boasts a California king-size bed with plenty of pillows, a wicker love seat, and the most privacy. There's a gas fireplace in the common area where guests read, watch TV, and make cups of hot chocolate. The walls of the inn are hung with original paintings.

Springdale

BEST WESTERN ZION PARK INN

435-772-3200, 1-800-934-7275
www.zionparkinn.com
info@zionparkinn.com
1215 Zion Park Blvd. (UT 9)
Springdale, UT 84767
Price: Moderate
Credit Cards: AE, D, MC, V
Handicapped Access: Yes

Spacious hotel rooms are in low-lying timber lodge–style buildings set beneath red canyon cliffs. In-room conveniences include coffeemakers, mini-refrigerators, and high-speed Internet access. Ask for a second-story room for better views and a patio. A seasonal swimming pool and hot tub are available for guests. Also popular with families are basketball, volleyball, and badminton courts. Pets are accepted.

CANYON RANCH MOTEL

435-772-3357, 1-866-946-6276
www.canyonranchmotel.com
info@canyonranchmotel.com
668 Zion Park Blvd. (UT 9)
Springdale, UT 84767
Price: Moderate
Credit Cards: D, MC, V
Handicapped Access: Yes

One of the town's tidiest little motels, this property looks straight out of the 1950s, with small brick cottages arranged around shady green lawns. Basic rooms have standard furnishings, telephones, and private patios; kitchenettes are available for a surcharge. An outdoor swimming pool and hot tub are located away from the highway, and there's free high-speed Internet access.

CANYON VISTA BED AND BREAKFAST
Innkeepers: Matt and Trista Rayner
435-772-3801
www.canyonvistabandb.com
email@canyonvistabandb.com
2175 Zion Park Blvd. (UT 9, at mile marker 30), Springdale, UT 84767
Price: Moderate
Credit Cards: MC, V
Handicapped Access: No

Located in a residential neighborhood, this inn beside the Virgin River is run by outdoor enthusiasts. They offer a continental breakfast for early risers who can't wait for full breakfast to be served. There's a library with books about the Southwest and movies to borrow, as well as a front porch and garden hot tub for unwinding. All four guest rooms have private entrances and baths; heating, air-conditioning, and ceiling fans; TVs with VCRs and DVD players; and a kitchenette with a microwave and mini-refrigerator. The Sinewava Room is enormous, while the Mukuntuweap Room has a cherry-wood four-poster bed. The resident dog can be borrowed for walks. The inn is gay-friendly.

CLIFFROSE LODGE & GARDENS
Manager: Colin Docksteader
435-772-3234, 1-800-243-8824
www.cliffroselodge.com
cliffrose@zionnationalpark.com
281 Zion Park Blvd. (UT 9)
Springdale, UT 84767
Price: Expensive
Credit Cards: AE, D, MC, V
Handicapped Access: Yes

More expensive than other Springdale hotels, this lodge surrounded by flower gardens is nonetheless recommendable. The two-story motel buildings back up against cliffs outside the west entrance of Zion National Park. Spacious rooms are outfitted with tasteful furnishings, pillow-top mattresses, mini-refrigerators, big-screen satellite TVs, and high-speed Wi-Fi Internet access. The heated outdoor pool is open seasonally, while the waterfall Jacuzzi stays open year-round. Out back is a beach with fire pits for riverside barbecues.

DESERT PEARL INN
Manager: Carl Palmer
435-772-8888, 1-888-828-0898
www.desertpearl.com
info@desertpearl.com
707 Zion Park Blvd. (UT 9)
Springdale, UT 84767
Price: Expensive
Credit Cards: AE, D, MC, V
Handicapped Access: Yes

A boutique hotel, the Desert Pearl lives up to its name. Built from old-growth Douglas fir and redwood trees abandoned on a Salt Lake City railway, these immaculately kept rooms come with luxurious bedding, hardwood floors, private balconies or patios, kitchenettes, cable TV and VCRs, telephones, and high-speed Wi-Fi Internet access. An outdoor swimming pool is open seasonally. You're in the middle of town, but the atmosphere is laid back.

EL RIO LODGE
Innkeepers: Gregoric family
435-772-3205, 1-888-772-3205
www.elriolodge.com
elrio@infowest.com
995 Zion Park Blvd. (UT 9)
Springdale, UT 84767
Price: Inexpensive
Credit Cards: AE, D, MC, V
Handicapped Access: Yes

This small, family-owned motel is the place to connect with independent travelers starting out or finishing their Southwest journeys. The no-frills, two-story lodge has spartan but tidy, old-fashioned rooms with air-conditioning; some also have private baths, microwaves, and TVs. The exterior entrances are sliding glass doors, but the amiable atmosphere allays most security concerns. Dogs are accepted for a surcharge.

FLANIGAN'S INN

Manager: Roger Reese
435-772-3244, 1-800-765-7787
www.flanigans.com
info@flanigans.com
428 Zion Park Blvd. (UT 9)
Springdale, UT 84767
Price: Expensive
Credit Cards: AE, D, MC, V
Handicapped Access: Yes

From the outside Flanigan's looks like just another faux-Western lodge. But inside the rooms have been artfully redone with modern color schemes and ultra-comfy furnishings. Rooms and suites with decks or patios are more spacious and have more amenities, such as mini-fridges, VCRs, and jetted tubs. Extended-stay villas are also available. All guests enjoy a swimming pool with views of the canyon's cliffs and high-speed Wi-Fi Internet access. There's a spa offering massage treatments and more.

HARVEST HOUSE BED AND BREAKFAST

Innkeepers: Tom and Mary Ann
435-772-3880, 1-800-719-7501
www.harvesthouse.net
29 Canyon View Dr. (off Zion Park Blvd.)
Springdale, UT 84767
Price: Moderate
Credit Cards: MC, V
Handicapped Access: No

Among Springdale's most highly regarded inns, the Harvest House is set on a quiet residential street at the east edge of town. The multistory building meshes well with the stunning sandstone cliff backdrop. Each room is tastefully decorated, for example, with Mission furniture or an airy deck for sunset views. The grounds include a Southwestern cactus garden and pond. The common living room has a big-screen TV and gas fireplace. High-speed Wi-Fi Internet access is available.

NOVEL HOUSE INN

Innkeepers: Ross and Norma Clay
435-772-3650, 1-800-711-8400
www.novelhouse.com
novelhouse@novelhouse.com
73 Paradise Rd. (off Zion Park Blvd.)
Springdale, UT 84767
Price: Moderate
Credit Cards: D, MC, V
Handicapped Access: Yes

On a residential side street, this contemporary home provides some of Springdale's most luxurious bed-and-breakfast rooms, with a waterfall koi pond bordered by a rose garden. Each room has a different literary theme and is beautifully outfitted with a writing desk, antique wardrobe, small sitting area, private bathroom, and air-conditioning. The Louis L'Amour Room shows off Western flair, while the Rudyard Kipling Room has a canopied bed. A common living room has a TV and a library of DVDs, which can also be viewed in your room. Rates include high-speed Internet access and a full breakfast. A two-night minimum stay may apply.

PIONEER LODGE

Manager: Heidi Gledhill
435-772-3233, 1-888-772-3233
www.pioneerlodge.com
frontdesk@pioneerlodge.com
838 Zion Park Blvd. (UT 9)
Springdale, UT 84767
Price: Expensive
Credit Cards: AE, D, MC, V
Handicapped Access: Yes

Not only are the staff wonderful, but the renovated hotel rooms feature deluxe beds, microwaves, refrigerators, and quiet air-conditioning and heating units. The lodge goes above and beyond expectations, with its quirky cowboy theme and log cabin furnishings. There are guest laundry facilities, an outdoor hot tub, swimming pool, and on-site Internet café.

RED ROCK INN
Innkeeper: Eileen
435-772-3139
www.redrockinn.com
rrinn@infowest.com
998 Zion Park Blvd. (UT 9)
Springdale, UT 84767
Price: Moderate
Credit Cards: AE, D, MC, V
Handicapped Access: Partial

These semidetached bed-and-breakfast cottages are a serene option in central Springdale. With country-style Southwestern decor, the studio units have private attached baths, cable TV, whirlpool tubs, and picture windows. Enjoy your privacy by sleeping in while a breakfast basket filled with organic breads, seasonal fruits, and a home-cooked egg dish is delivered to your door. Limited shared Internet access is available. The inn is gay-friendly.

UNDER THE EAVES B&B
Innkeepers: Steve and Deb Masefield
435-772-3457, 1-866-261-2655
www.under-the-eaves.com
eavesinfo@infowest.com
980 Zion Park Blvd. (UT 9)
Springdale, UT 84767
Price: Moderate
Credit Cards: AE, D, MC, V
Handicapped Access: No

A landmark 1930s pioneer home in the center of town, this English-run bed-and-breakfast has flower gardens and a cozy fireplace with a library of good books and

high-speed Wi-Fi Internet access. Each of six rooms has its own character, ranging from a basic backpacker's room with two single beds and gear storage space to a deluxe honeymoon suite that truly sits "under the eaves," with a kitchenette and an antique stained-glass window. The front porch is a great place to perch while you wait for breakfast. The hosts are knowledgeable about the local area. The inn is gay-friendly.

St. George

AMERICA'S BEST INNS & SUITES
435-652-3030, 1-800-718-0297
www.stgeorgeinnsuites.com
245 N. Red Cliffs Dr. (off I-15 exit 8),
St. George, UT 84790
Price: Inexpensive
Credit Cards: AE, D, MC, V
Handicapped Access: Yes

The gateway to Zion National Park, St. George is full of roadside motels. This two-story property near an outlet mall is the most reliable budget choice in town. All the spacious, sound-insulated rooms have microwaves, mini-refrigerators, cable TV, and high-speed wired/wireless Internet access. Families love to splash around the outdoor swimming pool. Staff are friendly, and rates include continental breakfast.

AVA HOUSE INN AND SPA
Innkeeper: Jill Burnett
435-673-7755
www.avahousespa.com
avahouse@qwest.net
278 N. 100 West (at Diagonal St.)
St. George, UT 84770
Price: Moderate
Credit Cards: AE, MC, V
Handicapped Access: No

This artful, modern bed-and-breakfast could not be closer to the historic district. Its flower-bedecked front porch faces a pedestrian-friendly street lined with other stately homes. Though not large, the rooms are eminently tasteful and outfitted with down comforters, comfy mattresses, satellite TV, and high-speed Wi-Fi Internet access. Romantics should book the suite with a whirlpool tub or the shabby-chic room with an antique clawfoot tub. Spa treatments, in-room massage, and yoga classes are available. Rates include an excellent breakfast.

GREEN GATE VILLAGE HISTORIC INN
Manager: Ed Sanstrom
435-628-6999, 1-800-350-6999
www.greengatevillageinn.com
stay@greengatevillageinn.com
76 W. Tabernacle (at N. 100 West)
St. George, UT 84770
Price: Expensive
Credit Cards: AE, D, MC, V
Handicapped Access: Partial

A short walk from the historic district, this bed-and-breakfast hotel is an oasis of calm, with a collection of Mormon pioneer houses set among gardens and walking paths. While some may call the decor outdated, others find it charmingly mismatched. Choose from over a dozen rooms and suites, mostly found in quaint 19th-century cottages, houses, and cabins, ranging from simple rooms to suites with kitchenettes, jetted tubs, and fireplaces. Rates include a hearty communal breakfast with gourmet coffee.

GREEN VALLEY SPA AND RESORT
Manager: Michael Rice
435-628-8060, 1-800-237-1068
www.greenvalleyspa.com
spasales@greenvalley.com
1871 W. Canyon View Dr.,
St. George, UT 84770
Directions: Take I-15 exit 6. Turn left onto Hilton Dr., right onto Dixie Dr., and left at Canyon View Dr.

Price: Very Expensive
Credit Cards: AE, D, MC, V
Handicapped Access: Yes

This health-oriented spa resort has been around for a while. Run with the help of energy-efficient improvements such as solar panels, each renovated residence has two master bedroom suites, a personal fitness studio, fully equipped kitchen, and private garden with a whirlpool tub and barbecue grill. Older yet still spacious suites that have fireplaces, whirlpool tubs, and flower-laden private patios are much less expensive. Guests have access to all spa facilities, including six swimming pools, tennis courts, and a fitness center. Spa packages are available; pets welcome.

THE INN AT ENTRADA
Manager: Rheanne Laubscher
435-634-7100
www.innatentrada.com
relaubscher@troongolf.com
2588 W. Sinagua Trail,
St. George, UT 84770
Directions: Take I-15 exit 6. Follow Bluff St. north, turn left on Snow Canyon Pkwy., and drive 2 miles west to the Kachina Cliffs entrance.
Price: Very Expensive
Credit Cards: AE, D, MC, V
Handicapped Access: Yes

Reserve one of the luxury vacation villas, which vary from studio duplexes to three-bedroom suites, and get access to the golf course and premier resort amenities, such as a fitness center with an indoor lap pool and spa, outdoor tennis courts, and concierge services. With a country-club atmosphere, each of the units is done up with adobe Southwestern style and boasts a fireplace, private patio, high-speed Wi-Fi Internet access, and kitchen facilities. Evening turndown service charmingly includes milk and cookies.

SEVEN WIVES INN

Innkeepers: Vanessa and Brent Calder
435-628-3737, 1-800-600-3737
www.sevenwivesinn.com
seven@infowest.com
217 N. 100 West (at W. 200 North),
St. George, UT 84770
Price: Moderate
Credit Cards: AE, D, MC, V
Handicapped Access: Yes

This well-regarded bed-and-breakfast,
where polygamist outlaws once hid in the
attic, is handy to the historic district. Fans
of traditional bed-and-breakfast experiences, complete with candelabra and frilly
decor, will be in heaven here.
Accommodations range from the Ada
Cottage, with reproduction pioneer furniture, a kitchenette, gas fireplace, whirlpool
tub, and stained-glass church windows, to
more modest rooms with TVs and VCRs,
queen-size beds, and private baths and balconies. There's a small seasonal swimming
pool, in-room massage appointments, and
high-speed Wi-Fi Internet access for
guests. Rates include a hot breakfast.

Teasdale

MULEY TWIST INN
BED AND BREAKFAST

Innkeepers: Eric and Penny Kinsman
435-425-3640, 1-800-530-1038
www.muleytwistinn.com
muley@rof.net
195 W. 125 South, Teasdale, UT 84773
Open: April through October
Price: Moderate
Credit Cards: AE, MC, V
Handicapped Access: No

Set in a cool, high-elevation grove of piñon
trees, this wooden ranch house has just five
guest rooms. All have private baths and
hardwood floors and are outfitted with
country-style furnishings and Southwestern patterned rugs. Take a break in one of
the rocking chairs on the front porch to
chat with the hosts, who offer expert advice
about outdoor activities around Capitol
Reef. Rates include a full hot breakfast.

THE LODGE AT RED RIVER RANCH

Managers: Dave and Charlene Van Dyke
435-425-3322, 1-800-205-6343
www.redriverranch.com
thelodge@redriverranch.com
2900 W. UT 24, Teasdale, UT 84773
Price: Expensive
Credit Cards: AE, D, MC, V
Handicapped Access: Yes

Claiming more than 2,000 acres of ranch
land, this luxurious hideaway is a natural
choice for those who crave creature comforts after a day spent hiking, four-wheel
driving, or rock climbing. The sprawling
main house with its three-story fireplace
feels like a hunting lodge. Guest rooms are
uniquely decorated with antiques and artifacts, from airy alcoves with views of the
river to the Anasazi Room, where hardwood
floors are covered in Native American wool
rugs. All have gas fireplaces and step-out
balconies. Rates include breakfast, boxed
lunches are available for purchase, and
dinner is available some nights.

Torrey

AUSTIN'S CHUCKWAGON MOTEL

435-425-3335, 1-800-863-3288
www.austinschuckwagonmotel.com
info@austinschuckwagonmotel.com
12 W. Main St. (UT 24, at N. Center St.)
Torrey, UT 84775
Price: Moderate
Credit Cards: AE, D, MC, V
Handicapped Access: Yes

A long-running motel with a Western
theme, Austin's is a reliable value in downtown Torrey. All rooms, suites, and cabins
have high-speed Wi-Fi Internet access,
cable TV, and heating and air-conditioning,

while the family suite also has a full kitchen. The two-bedroom, nonsmoking cabins have a private bath and kitchenette. Beware that budget rooms above the store are thin-walled and hot in summer. There's an outdoor swimming pool and hot tub for guests, plus free coffee from the general store by the coin-op laundry room out front.

BEST WESTERN CAPITOL REEF RESORT

435-425-3761, 1-800-780-7234
www.bestwestern.com
2600 E. UT 24, Torrey, UT 84775
Price: Moderate
Credit Cards: AE, D, MC, V
Handicapped Access: Yes

Spread across a hilltop off the highway at the edge of town, these low-lying buildings are closer than many other lodgings in town to the entrance to Capitol Reef National Park. Typical motel rooms here have better-than-average views of the red rock cliffs, especially rooms with balconies. All rooms and suites have satellite TV, high-speed Wi-Fi Internet access, and coffeemakers. Active guests can enjoy an outdoor swimming pool, hot tub, and lighted tennis and basketball courts.

CAPITOL REEF INN

435-425-3271
www.capitolreefinn.com
cri@capitolreefinn.com
360 W. Main St. (UT 24), Torrey, UT 84775
Open: April through October
Price: Inexpensive
Credit Cards: AE, D, MC, V
Handicapped Access: Partial

This funky, independent property is an alternative to chain motels. There's a desert garden and a stone kiva to explore, as well as a children's playground. Some of the large rooms have handcrafted furniture and Southwestern accents, in addition to satellite TV, telephones, mini-fridges, and an outdoor tub. It's an older property, so expect cramped bathrooms, but it's in reasonable repair.

TORREY PINES
BED AND BREAKFAST INN

Innkeepers: Erika and Eldon Reed
435-425-3401, 1-866-425-3401
www.torreypinesinn.com
torreypinesinn@color-country.net
250 S. 800 East (off UT 12)
Torrey, UT 84775
Price: Moderate
Credit Cards: None
Handicapped Access: No

Outside town, this country bed-and-breakfast offers three suites with private entrances and baths and a veranda for sitting out and enjoying fresh mountain air. A timber log–style cottage with a fully equipped kitchen and a condo, both equipped with telephones, satellite TVs, and VCRs, are also available. Breakfast is included for the suites, but not cabin or condo guests. One of the owners is a retired park ranger who has helpful tips for hiking and exploring around Capitol Reef. German is spoken.

TORREY SCHOOLHOUSE B&B INN

Innkeeper: Ty Markham
435-425-2116, 1-877-425-2116
www.torreyschoolhouse.com
bednbreakfastinfo@earthlink.net
150 N. Center St. (off UT 24)
Torrey, UT 84775
Open: April through October
Price: Moderate
Credit Cards: D, MC, V
Handicapped Access: Partial

A unique choice in downtown Torrey, this wonderfully renovated 1914 schoolhouse offers suites full of amenities, including private baths, deluxe mattresses, air-conditioning, high-speed Internet access, and vibrating massage recliner chairs; cable TV may be available. All the rooms are decorated with classical elegance, inspired by French impressionist, English tea garden, Italian opera, and Native American designs. Rates include a healthy full breakfast. Shared kitchenettes are available for guests.

Tropic

BRYCE COUNTRY CABINS
435-679-8643, 1-888-679-8643
www.brycecountrycabins.com
brycecc@color-country.net
320 N. UT 12, Tropic, UT 84776
Price: Moderate
Credit Cards: AE, MC, V
Handicapped Access: Yes

These newly built log cabins are better kept and more hospitable than many identical-looking roadside pit stops in southern Utah. Step off the front porch and inside each cabin you'll find patchwork bed quilts, cable TV, and private showers or full bathrooms. Outdoor barbecue grills and Wi-Fi Internet access are bonuses.

You can stay at Zion Lodge in the heart of beautiful Zion Canyon National Park. Sara Benson

BRYCE TRAILS BED AND BREAKFAST
Innkeepers: Frank and Shauna
435-679-8700, 1-866-215-5043
www.brycetrails.com
brycetrail@yahoo.com
1001 W. Bryce Way (off UT 12)
Tropic, UT 84776
Price: Moderate
Credit Cards: AE, D, MC, V
Handicapped Access: No

Warm and informative hosts await you in this modest contemporary home close to Bryce Canyon. Each guest room has a queen- or king-size bed, private bathroom, TV, telephone, central air-conditioning and heating, and high-speed Internet access. A favorite is the Navajo Loop Room for its Southwestern-style decor and extra futon bed perfect for families or friends traveling together. Rates include a country-style breakfast.

Zion National Park

ZION LODGE
Regional General Manager: Jeff D'Arpa
435-772-7700, 1-888-297-2757
www.zionlodge.com
P.O. Box 925, Springdale, UT 84767
Directions: Off UT 9 inside Zion National Park
Price: Expensive
Credit Cards: AE, D, MC, V
Handicapped Access: Yes

Backed by Zion's towering cliffs, this heritage lodge today ranks among the USA's most classic national-park lodgings. Motel-style rooms and suites come with air-conditioning and private patios or balconies. There are also 40 cabins, each with its own porch, full bath, and gas fireplace. All lodgings surround a large grassy area, a gathering place for park visitors. Yet the atmosphere remains tranquil, and there's a swimming pool and hot tub exclusively for guests. The free park shuttle stops outside.

Culture

Art Galleries

Anne Weiler-Brown, www.anneweilerbrown.com, 435-772-0770, 17 W. Main St., Rockville. With a home-studio west of Springdale, this abstract expressionist works with mixed media on canvas to create evocative images of the Southwest, including Zion.

Authentique Gallery of Art and Design, 435-688-7278, 199 N. Main St., St. George. Landscape paintings, mixed-media works, and sculptures await inside this tranquil house in the historic district. A fountain garden has benches for reflection.

Coyote Gulch Art Village, www.coyotegulchartvillage.com, 435-688-8535, 875 Coyote Gulch Court, Ivins. If you visit only one art complex in southern Utah, make it Coyote Gulch. It's a scenic drive from downtown St. George to the Kayenta desert community, where you'll find over a half dozen Southwestern galleries. Coyote Hungry coffee shop vends salads, baked goods, and espresso drinks on site. There's also a small arboretum and free public events, such as music concerts and movies under the stars.

David Pettit Photography, www.davidpettitphotography.com, 435-772-3206, 868 Zion Park Blvd., Springdale. Scenic landscape and environmental photography focuses on southern Utah's national and state parks, wilderness areas, and other remote locations.

Gallery Escalante, www.galleryescalante.com, 435-826-4080, 425 W. Main St., Escalante. Small-town art space displays mixed-media works, photography, wood carvings, jewelry, and fiber arts, including heritage rugs woven by Lillian Lyman.

The Museum of Photography, www.fatali.com, 435-772-2422, 145 Zion Park Blvd., Springdale. In the same complex as Zion's giant-screen theater, this gallery mounts exhibits by local photographers, ranging from natural landscapes and portraits to abstracts.

The Rafters Gallery, www.rockingvcafe.com, 435-644-8001, 97 W. Center St., Kanab. Upstairs from The Rocking V Cafe, this art gallery has an intriguing mix of photography, pastel drawings, oil paintings, wood sculpture, metalwork, and ceramics by Southwestern artists.

Red Rock Jewelry & Artworks, www.redrockjewelry.com, 435-772-3836, 998 Zion Park Blvd., Springdale. At her gem shop, this artist creates memorable gold and silver wearable art and displays sculpture, metalwork, and watercolors by other creative minds.

Tom Till Gallery, www.tomtill.com, 435-259-5327, 1-888-479-9808, 61 N. Main St., Moab. Drop by a timber-walled gallery to browse limited-edition prints, including southern Utah landscape photography.

Torrey Gallery, www.torreygallery.com, 435-425-3909, 80 E. Main St., Torrey. At this quiet gallery near Capitol Reef, Navajo rugs cover hardwood floors, impressionist Southwestern landscapes hang on the wall, and abstract sculptures stand tall.

Worthington Gallery, www.worthingtongallery.com, 435-772-3446, 1-800-626-9973, 789 Zion Park Blvd., Springdale. With its shady gardens and house full of treasures, this is a fine place to see works by southern Utah artists. The owner, who is a potter himself, displays Lyman Whitaker's wind sculptures in the front yard.

In Kanab, the upstairs Rafters Gallery shows paintings and more works by local artists. Victor Cooper/Courtesy
Rafters Gallery

Cinema
Crescent Moon Theater, www.crescentmoontheater.com, 435-644-2350, 150 S. 100 East,
Kanab. Multipurpose venue screens classic Western movies and hosts events.

Slickrock Cinemas 3, 435-259-4441, 580 Kane Creek Blvd., Moab. First-run Hollywood
releases projected with Dolby THX sound.

Sunset Corner Stadium 8, www.westatestheatres.com, 435-673-1994, 1091 N. Bluff St.,
St. George. Watch big-screen Hollywood flicks in stadium seating.

The Wayne Theatre, 435-425-3123, www.waynetheatre.com, 11 E. Main St., Bicknell. A
classic small-town cinema screens first-run Hollywood movies and hosts the quirky
Bicknell International Film Festival in mid-July.

Zion Canyon Giant Screen Theatre, www.zioncanyontheatre.com, 435-772-2400, 1-888-
256-3456, 145 Zion Park Blvd., Springdale. Utah's largest movie screen shows the documentary *Zion Canyon: Treasures of the Gods*, other outdoor-oriented movies, and new
Hollywood releases.

Historic Places
Many towns along southern Utah's byways have historic districts for strolling. Self-guided
walking-tour pamphlets are often available at tourist information centers, including in St.
George, Moab, and Kanab.

BLUFF

On the west side of the highway in **downtown Bluff** (www.bluffutah.org) is the original 1880s town site. The residential streets are filled with historic homes built in the late 19th and early 20th centuries. The library was originally a settlers' schoolhouse and later the county jail. On the bluffs overlooking town, the pioneer cemetery has panoramic views that make it worth the winding drive.

GREEN RIVER AND MOAB

A high-clearance 4WD vehicle may be required to reach **Sego Ghost Town** (www.ghost towns.com/states/ut/sego). This lonely, early 20th-century coal mining boomtown has the added bonus of being located near the ancient rock-art petroglyphs of Sego Canyon. Dinosaur footprints were also once found here. Today all you'll find in this once-bustling town are the impressive ruins of a wooden boardinghouse and the stone foundations and sunset-colored plaster walls of the old company store. Look hard for explosives bunkers, the historic cemetery, and rotting railroad trestles. To get here, take I-70 to exit 187. Drive 3.5 miles north of the town of Thompson to the first rock art panels, then another .5 mile up the canyon. Take a right at the fork to reach Sego Canyon, then drive another mile to reach the ghost town.

MOUNT CARMEL

Open from May to September, the quaint **Mount Carmel Rock Church** (www.eastzion tourismcouncil.org/history, 1-800-733-5263, 2610 S. State St. / US 89, Mount Carmel) was built of logs in 1890. After burning down in 1919, it was rebuilt using locally quarried sandstone. Today it's a small tourist information center.

PARIA

The adventure is just getting to **Pahreah Ghost Town and Paria Movie Set** (www.blm.gov/az/asfo/paria/driving.htm, 435-644-4600). Between Kanab, Utah, and Page, Arizona, turn north off US 89 at mile marker 30.5 and follow Paria River Road north for 6 miles to the movie set, then another 2 miles to reach the ghost town. The gold-mining town of Pahreah had faded by the 1900s, but replicas of the original pioneers' buildings were constructed later for a Rat Pack–era movie set and episodes of *Gunsmoke*. The authentic wooden buildings of the ghost town and the pioneer cemetery are found beyond the movie set along a sometimes muddy, impassable dirt road. For updates on road conditions, contact the Paria Ranger Station or the BLM Kanab Field Office at the phone number listed above before setting out.

Mining ghost towns dot the landscape across Utah, including in Sego Canyon. Sara Benson

A pioneer schoolhouse in the ghost town of Grafton stands against Zion's red rock cliffs. Sara Benson

ROCKVILLE

From UT 9 in Rockville turn south on Bridge Lane to find **Grafton Ghost Town** (www.graftonheritage.org, 435-635-2133). As seen in the movie *Butch Cassidy and the Sundance Kid*, this mid-19th-century ghost town set on the banks of the Virgin River has stunning mesa and cliff views all around. The adobe schoolhouse with its lava-rock foundation is the most photogenic, but there's a pioneer cemetery and several early settlers' homes still standing, too. It's a short detour en route to Zion National Park.

ST. GEORGE

The Mormon pioneer town of St. George was founded at the behest of Brigham Young in the 1850s. Pick up a walking-tour map of the downtown historic district at the **Visitor Center** inside the stately old courthouse (www.stgeorgechamber.com, 435-628-1658, 97 E. St. George Blvd.). Then drop by **Brigham Young's winter home** (435-673-5181, 67 N. 200 West), open daily for free tours. The **St. George Tabernacle** (435-673-5181, 18 S. Main St.) is also open daily for free tours. Admire the red sandstone walls, stained-glass windows, and twin spiral staircases with hand-carved balustrades leading to the balcony. The costumed period actors of **Historic St. George Live!** (435-634-5942 ext. 112, 125 E. 200 North) lead walking tours of the historical district during summer, usually leaving from the Pioneer Center for the Arts on Tuesday through Saturday mornings; tickets are inexpensive.

SILVER REEF GHOST TOWN

Originally named "The Rockpile," **Silver Reef** (www.leedsutah.org/silverreef.html, 435-879-2254, 2002 Wells Fargo Rd., Leeds, UT) was a rich silver-mining settlement that went bust at the end of the 19th century when water flooded the mines and the market crashed.

The St. George Tabernacle is one of the finest examples of Mormon pioneer architecture still standing. Sara Benson

Mormon pioneer leader Brigham Young's winter home in downtown St. George's historic district. Sara Benson

At its peak, Silver Reef pumped out over a million dollars of ore annually. Today you can wander around the remains of mining operations and the cemetery. Inside the brick Wells Fargo Bank, which has been restored, are a small museum and gift shop. To get here take I-15 exit 22, about 20 miles north of St. George. Drive a few miles north of Leeds, then turn left onto Silver Reef Road.

Museums

ANASAZI STATE PARK MUSEUM

435-335-7308
www.stateparks.utah.gov/parks/anasazi/
460 N. UT 12, Boulder, UT 84716
Open: Daily 9–5; extended summer hours 8–6. Closed Thanksgiving, Christmas, and New Year's Day.
Admission: Individuals $3

Built at the Coombs Site archaeological excavations, which have revealed over 100 structures so far, this museum displays interesting artifacts from an Ancestral Puebloan community. What makes this site west of the Colorado River unique is that it once bordered another prehistoric community, the Fremont Culture. Since extensive trading networks have been found, the museum's collections contain many unique pieces.

DAN O'LAURIE MUSEUM

435-259-7985
www.moab-utah.com/danolaurie/museum.html
118 E. Center St. (at S. 100 East), Moab, UT 84532
Open: Monday through Friday 10–3, Saturday through Sunday 12–5; extended summer
hours until 6 PM daily
Admission: Adults $2, children under 12 free

This diminutive downtown Moab museum has displays on history, geology, archaeology, and
just about everything else related to southeastern Utah. Exhibits are outdated but informative:
Learn about rock art and the pottery of the Ute people, see how railroads changed Western life
forever, and find out about the town's
uranium boom in the 1950s.

THE DINOSAUR MUSEUM

435-678-3454
www.dinosaur-museum.org
754 S. 200 West (at W. 800 South,
west of US 191), Blanding, UT 84511
Open: Mid-April to mid-October,
Monday through Saturday 9–5
Admission: Adults $2, seniors and
children $1

For school-age children and the
young at heart, this warehouse-size
museum is devoted to dinosaurs.
Inside you'll find life-size dinosaur
sculptures, real dinosaur skeletons,
fossilized skin, eggs, and casts of
footprints taken from around the
globe. Thought-provoking touring
exhibits are always topical.

*Replicas of prehistoric dinosaurs delight kids at the
Dinosaur Museum in Blanding.* Stephen Czerkas / Courtesy the
Dinosaur Museum

EDGE OF THE CEDARS
STATE PARK MUSEUM

435-678-2238
www.stateparks.utah.gov/parks/edge-of-the-cedars/
660 W. 400 North (at W. 600 North), Blanding, UT 84511
Directions: From US 191 drive .5 mile west on 200 North. Turn right on N. 300 West, then
left on W. 400 North.
Open: Daily 9–5; extended summer hours 9–6
Admission: Individuals $3, or $6 per vehicle

This state-sponsored complex is southern Utah's finest museum of ancient cultures, boasting
the largest collection of Ancestral Puebloan pottery and artifacts in the entire Four Corners
region. Don't miss the rare turkey-feather blankets or the glass-encased storage room where
pots are stacked from floor to ceiling. Native American crafts, fine art, and photography are
also on display here. Behind the museum are the excavated ruins of an authentic Pueblo village.

FRONTIER MOVIE TOWN

435-644-5337
www.frontiermovietown.com
297 W. Center St. (off US
89), Kanab, UT 84741
Open: Daily (seasonal hours
vary)
Admission: Free

In downtown Kanab, which is
nicknamed Utah's "Little
Hollywood," this sprawling
place lets visitors poke
around old Western movie
sets, including from director
Clint Eastwood's 1976 classic
The Outlaw Josey Wales. Who
can resist taking a picture of
themselves in front of an old
saloon door by the wooden
silhouette of an Old West

Experience the Wild West, Hollywood-style, at Frontier Movie Town in Kanab. Sara Benson

gunslinger while tumbleweeds blow by? If the heat of high noon gets to you, grab a beer from the Hole in the Wall Saloon.

HURRICANE VALLEY HERITAGE PARK AND THE BRADSHAW HOUSE MUSEUM

435-635-3245
35 W. State St. (at S. Main St.), Hurricane, UT 84737
Open: Monday through Saturday 9–5
Admission: Donations accepted

At the main crossroads in town, this hodgepodge collection of pioneer artifacts, from settlers' journals to antique kitchen implements, is worth a quick browse for history buffs
who are passing through on the way to Zion National Park. Nearby the Bradshaw House has
displays of blacksmithing, farm equipment, and medical kits from the old days.

IRON MISSION STATE PARK MUSEUM

435-586-9290
www.stateparks.utah.gov/parks/iron-mission/
635 N. Main St. (UT 130), Cedar City, UT 84720
Directions: .5 mile north of UT 56, off I-15 exit 59
Open: Monday through Saturday 9–5; extended summer hours daily 9–6. Closed
Thanksgiving, Christmas, and New Year's Day.
Admission: Individuals $3, or $6 per vehicle

Preserving a pioneer home and cabins, along with vintage horse-drawn farm equipment,
this small museum narrates the story of Mormon pioneers starting in 1850, when Brigham
Young dispatched followers here to mine iron. All that remains of those efforts is the
town's original bell, but there are plenty of other artifacts and also artwork on display.

JOHN WESLEY POWELL RIVER HISTORY MUSEUM

435-564-3427
www.jwprhm.com
1765 E. Main St., Green River, UT 84525
Open: Daily 8–5, extended summer hours daily 8–8
Admission: Adults $2, children 3–12 $1, children under 3 free

Beside the Green River, this modest museum documents the early expeditions of John Wesley Powell, who famously explored the Colorado River and made passage through the Grand Canyon after the Civil War. Highlights include full-size replicas of the original expedition boats. Other exhibits portray the indigenous prehistory of the region and modern-day river running in the Four Corners region.

KANAB HERITAGE HOUSE

435-644-3966
www.kanabheritage.com
115 S. Main St. (at S. 100 East), Kanab, UT 84741
Open: Monday through Friday 1–5 during summer; other seasonal hours vary
Admission: Free

A nationally registered historic site, this late-19th-century Mormon pioneer home houses a small historical museum. Docents give guided tours of the structure itself and hand out self-guided historical walking tour pamphlets of Kanab. The lower-level Juniper Fine Arts Gallery exhibits works by local artists.

MAYNARD DIXON HOME AND STUDIO

435-648-2653, 801-533-5330
www.maynarddixon.com
Mile marker 84, US 89
Mount Carmel, UT 84755
Open: Self-guided tours available daily, May through October
Admission: Individuals $20

Celebrated Western painter Maynard Dixon, whose landscapes evoke the variegated beauty of the Southwest, built a log home in southern Utah as his summer retreat. The natural setting is still inspirational, surrounded by cottonwood trees and backed up against iconic sandstone cliffs. A thunderbird-shaped memorial marks the spot where Dixon's ashes were interred in 1946. Although the home and studio are now on private property, tours of the grounds may be available. Inquire at the art gallery next door.

Edge of the Cedars State Park Museum in Blanding is a trove of Ancestral Puebloan pottery. Sara Benson & Mike Connolly

MOAB MUSEUM OF FILM & WESTERN HERITAGE

435-259-2002, 1-866-812-2002
www.redcliffslodge.com/museum
Mile marker 14, UT 128, Moab, UT 84532
Open: Daily 8–8
Admission: Free

Tucked away in the basement of the main lodge at Red Cliffs Ranch, this hodgepodge of Western movie memorabilia and cowboy history is for enthusiasts only. Most of the material derives from films by director John Ford, who discovered the cinematic scenery of Moab's canyonlands during the 1940s. John Wayne, Maureen O'Hara, and Jimmy Stewart are among the stars who stayed and worked here once upon a time.

ST. GEORGE ART MUSEUM

435-627-4525
www.sgcity.org/arts/sgartmuseum.php
47 E. 200 North (at N. Main St.), St. George, UT 84770
Open: Tuesday through Saturday 10–5; extended hours third Tuesday of the month 10–9
Admission: Adults $2, children 3–11 $1, children under 3 free. Free on third Tuesday of every month.

Located in the Pioneer Center for the Arts Complex, this art museum was once a humble storehouse for beet seeds. Today it has a small permanent collection of paintings, sculptures, ceramics, prints, drawings, and photographs, including artworks by key regional artists such as Maynard Dixon and historical photographs of Mormon pioneers.

ST. GEORGE DINOSAUR DISCOVERY SITE AT JOHNSON FARM

435-574-3466
www.dinotrax.com
2180 E. Riverside Dr. (at S. 2700 East), St. George, UT 84770
Directions: From I-15 exit 10 turn right onto Green Springs Dr. (UT 212). Pass through the intersection of Red Cliffs Dr. / Telegraph St., which becomes S. 3050 East, then Riverside Dr.
Open: Monday through Saturday 10–6
Admission: Adults $3, children 4–11 $2, children under 4 free

This site's claim to fame is what some experts have called the best-preserved dinosaur tracks in western North America. But that's not all you'll find here on the western edge of Early Jurassic–era Lake Dixie. You can view replicas of fossilized fish and plants uncovered by paleontologists nearby. Check the Web site for schedules of family-day activities, scientific lectures, and all-day guided paleontology tours that include hands-on excavation of a real fossil bed.

ZION HUMAN HISTORY MUSEUM

435-772-3256
www.nps.gov/archive/zion/HHMuseum.htm
UT 9, Zion National Park, UT 84767

Open: Daily 9–5; extended hours during fall 10–5, spring 10–6, and summer 9–7. Closed Christmas Day.
Admission: Included with park entrance fee (seven-day vehicle pass $25)

Inside Zion National Park, this busy interpretive center briefly covers the history of the region from the perspectives of Native Americans, pioneers, railway employees, Civilian Conservation Corps workers, and park engineers. It also tells the story of how the canyon was shaped largely through the forces of water found in this surprising desert oasis. A free 10-minute orientation film is shown continuously.

Music, Theater, and Dance

Bumbleberry Theatre, www.bumbleberrytheatre.com, 435-772-3611, 897 Zion Park Blvd., Springdale. This tiny venue puts on Broadway-style shows that are fun for family.

Cox Performing Arts Center, www.dixie.edu/concerts, 435-652-7994, Dixie State College, 325 S. 700 East, St. George. The Celebrity Concert Series features performances by big-name operatic singers, classical orchestras, ballet companies, and country-and-western singer-songwriters.

Crescent Moon Theater, www.crescentmoontheater.com, 435-644-2350, 150 S. 100 East, Kanab. Multipurpose venue stages concerts by traveling musicians, cowboy poetry nights, and local theater and dance productions.

Festival Hall and Heritage Theater, www.heritagectr.org, 435-865-2896, 1-866-882-3327, 105 N. 100 East, Cedar City. Multipurpose venue for the Orchestra of Southern Utah and classical concerts by chamber groups and opera singers.

Moab Arts and Recreation Center, www.moabcity.state.ut.us/marc, 435-259-6272, 111 E. 100 North, Moab. Community space with a performance schedule as diverse as the residents of Moab, offering everything from Afro-Cuban dance to Tibetan music.

Neil Simon Festival, www.simonfest.org, 435-327-8673, 1-866-357-4666, Heritage Theater, 105 N. 100 East, Cedar City. Small theater festival stages three Neil Simon plays every summer.

O. C. Tanner Amphitheater, www.dixie.edu/tanner, 435-652-7994, 300 Lion Blvd., Springdale. Backed by Zion's red-rock cliffs, the summer twilight concert series hosts symphony orchestras and a variety of bluegrass, folk, and rock bands.

St. George Musical Theater, www.sgmt.org, 435-628-8755, St. George Opera House: 212 N. Main St., box office: 200 N. 100 East, St. George. Amateur troupe puts on Broadway shows, melodramas, and dramatic classics in the downtown historic district.

St. George Tabernacle, 435-673-5181, 18 S. Main St., St. George. This landmark Mormon church hosts daily music recitals and the weekly Dixie History and Music Series.

Southern Utah Heritage Choir, www.heritagechoir.org, 435-673-5507, St. George Tabernacle, 18 S. Main St., St. George. Mormon choir performs religious music in the historic tabernacle and elsewhere around town when not touring nationally.

Southwest Symphony Orchestra, www.southwestsymphony.org, St. George, UT. Performs classical music and pops in St. George between October and May.

Tuacahn Amphitheatre and Center for the Arts, www.tuacahn.org, 435-652-3300, 1-800-746-9882, 1100 Tuacahn Dr., Ivins. Spectacular 2,000-seat outdoor amphitheater outside St. George puts on Broadway-style shows and recitals by ballroom superstars to modern troupes. Preshow backstage tours are offered.

Utah Shakespearean Festival, www.bard.org, 1-800-752-9849, 351 W. Center St., Cedar City. Downtown venues are enlivened by this dramatic festival staged from June through October, with works by the Bard and emerging American playwrights.

Nightlife

You won't find an abundance of nightspots in the Mormon-run state of Utah. The state's liquor control laws may strike visitors as odd. By law most bars and dance clubs are private clubs, although they are open to the public; visitors must purchase a temporary membership before entering (similar to a cover charge). At restaurants you may not drink at the bar without also ordering food, and there's a one-drink-at-a-time limit per person.

Bar-M Chuckwagon, www.barmchuckwagon.com, 435-259-2276, 1-800-214-2085, US 191, Moab. Four miles north of the Arches National Park turnoff, live Western music dinner shows with mock gunfights happen from April through October; make reservations.

Eddie McStiff's, www.eddiemcstiffs.com, 435-259-2337, 57 S. Main St., Moab. A rowdy, casual microbrewery and restaurant, McStiff's has a dozen handcrafted brews on tap and a giant menu of pizzas, pastas, seafood, burritos, barbecue, and burgers. Fun-loving young crowds take over the joint nightly.

Frankie D's Bar and Grill, www.frankieds.explorefourcorners.com, 435-259-2654, 44 W. 200 North, Moab. A private club, this is one of Moab's local hangouts with live bands on weekends. They've got pool tables, horseshoes, and video games.

Moab Brewery, www.themoabbrewery.com, 435-259-6333, 686 S. Main St., Moab. This place is famed for its Lizard Light Ale and spicy Scorpion Pale Ale, though the Black Raven

Utah's peculiar liquor laws mean that most bars are actually private clubs for members only. But don't worry—new faces are welcome. Sara Benson

Oatmeal Stout and lemony Elephant Hill Hefeweizen are nothing to scoff at. Moab's best brewpub also has a streetside patio for sunny days and starry nights.

The Rio Sports Bar & Grill, 435-259-6666, 100 W. Center St., Moab. Another of Moab's private clubs, this sports bar and "no-frills grill" just west of Main Street is the place for karaoke and live music on weekends.

Zax Watering Hole, www.zaxmoab.com, 435-259-6555, 96 S. Main St., Moab. Though Zax is technically a private club, everyone is welcome at this boisterous sports bar with pool tables, big-screen TVs, a jukebox, arcade games, free popcorn, and a hardwood dance floor. It opens before the crack of noon.

Zion Canyon Brewery, www.majesticviewlodge.com, 435-772-0665, Majestic View Lodge, 2400 Zion Park Blvd., Springdale. Hidden inside a steakhouse and saloon, just a drunken stumble away from a bizarre museum of stuffed wildlife, this young microbrewery is one to watch, especially for extra-special bitter (ESB), Jamaican-style lagers, and Virgin Stout.

Seasonal Events

JANUARY
Bluff Balloon Festival, www.bluffutah.org, 435-672-2341, Bluff

FEBRUARY
Bryce Canyon Winter Festival, www.rubysinn.com/winter, 1-866-866-6616, Bryce

Dino Days, www.sgcity.org/dinotrax, 435-574-3466, St. George

MARCH
Easter Jeep Safari, www.rr4w.com, 435-259-2263, Moab

APRIL
Annual St. George Art Festival, www.sgcity.org/artfestival, 435-634-5850, St. George

April Action Car Show, www.moab-utah.com/aprilaction, 435-259-5858, Moab

MAY
Blue Mountain Festival of the Old West, www.bullhollow.com, 435-587-2332, 1-866-587-1005, Monticello

Cowboys Ain't Dead Yet Festival and National Senior Pro Rodeo, www.seniorrodeo.com, 435-676-8949, Panguitch

Escalante Heritage Festival and Craft Fair, www.escalante-cc.com, 435-826-4810, Escalante

Four Corners Indian Art Market, http://stateparks.utah.gov, 435-678-2238, Blanding

Moab Arts Festival, www.moabartsfestival, 435-259-2742, Moab

San Juan County Heritage Festival, www.sjcheritagefestival.com, 435-459-3539, Monticello

JUNE
Bryce Canyon Astronomy Festival, www.nps.gov/brca, 435-834-5322, Bryce Canyon National Park

Canyonlands Rodeo, www.prorodeo.org, 1-800-635-6622, Moab

Ebenezer Bryce Festival and HooDoo Chili Cook-off, www.brycecanyoncountry.com, 1-800-444-6689, Bryce

Panguitch Valley Balloon Rally, www.panguitchballoons.com, 435-676-2514, 1-866-590-4134, Panguitch

Quilt Walk, www.quiltwalk.com, 1-800-444-6689, Panguitch

Torrey Apple Days, www.capitolreef.org, 435-425-3721, Torrey

Zion Canyon Art and Flute Festival, www.zioncanyonartandflutefestival.com, 480-984-5820, Springdale

JULY
Boulder Heritage Festival, www.boulderutah.com/heritage, 435-335-7422, Boulder

Escalante Pioneer Days Celebration, www.escalante-cc.com, 435-826-4810, Escalante

Pioneer Day Parade and Celebration, www.monticelloutah.org, 435-587-2271, Monticello

AUGUST
Torrey Music Festival, www.torreymusicfestival.com, 435-425-3265, Torrey

Washington County Fair, www.washcofair.net, 435-652-5899, Hurricane

Western Legends Roundup, www.westernlegendsroundup.com, 435-644-3444, Kanab

SEPTEMBER
Ancient Trails Motorcycle Tour, www.bullhollow.com, 435-587-2332, 1-866-587-1005, Monticello

Green River Melon Days, www.emerycounty.com, 435-564-3427, Green River

Moab Music Festival, www.moabmusicfest.org, 435-359-7003, Moab

Lions Dixie Roundup Rodeo, www.prorodeo.org, 435-628-1658, St. George

Moab Artists Studio Tour, www.moabstudiotour.com, 1-800-635-6622, Moab

Utah Navajo Fair, www.bluffutah.org, 435-651-3755, Bluff

OCTOBER
Escalante Canyon Arts Festival and Everett Ruess Days, www.everettruessdays.org, 435-826-4199, 435-826-4810, Escalante

Annual Gem & Mineral Show, www.moabrockclub.com, 435-259-3393, Moab

NOVEMBER
Bluff Arts Festival, www.bluffutah.org, 435-672-2296, Bluff

Moab Folk Festival, www.moabfolkfestival.com, 435-259-3198, Moab

Zion Canyon Open Studio and Gallery Tour, www.zarts.org, 435-669-1491, Springdale

Restaurants

Bluff

COW CANYON TRADING POST
435-672-2208
163 Mission Rd. (at US 191)
Bluff, UT 84716
Open: Daily April through October
Price: Expensive
Cuisine: New American
Serving: D
Credit Cards: None
Handicapped Access: No
Special Features: Reservations recommended

It's all about atmosphere at this vintage stone-walled trading post, where diners are seated at tables set on cool flagstone floors or on a glassed-in patio with views over the San Juan River valley. The experimental menu changes almost daily, depending on what's freshly available from local farms, but it always includes a vegetarian option. While the dishes are hit or miss, and service is leisurely, Cow Canyon remains an amiable favorite.

LAS DOS HERMANAS
435-672-9955
P.O. Box 87, Main St. (US 191)
Bluff, UT 84716
Price: Inexpensive
Cuisine: Mexican
Serving: B, L
Credit Cards: None
Handicapped Access: Yes

This funky little roadside taqueria is set up inside a defunct gas station. Not only is all the fare super-fresh (try the Baja grilled fish tacos and today's flavors of *aguas frescas*), but the cook is sincerely eco-conscious: Just take a look at the recycled grocery-store produce bins and Department of Defense Survival Supplies canisters used for building materials. Discounts are given for bringing along your own plates, cups, and silverware.

TWIN ROCKS CAFE
435-672-2341
www.twinrockscafe.com
913 E. Navajo Twins Dr. (off US 191)
Bluff, UT 84716
Price: Moderate
Cuisine: American
Serving: B, L, D
Credit Cards: AE, D, MC, V
Handicapped Access: Yes

Next to Twin Rocks Trading Post, this casual country diner is great for stuffing yourself silly at breakfast. Then it's the slow-smoked apple and mesquite-wood barbecue lunch and dinner plates that bring in crowds later in the day. Pizzas made with Navajo fry bread are for carbo-loading, especially when they're washed down with a microbrewed beer. There's a small selection for vegetarians.

Boulder

BOULDER MESA RESTAURANT
435-335-7447
www.bouldermesa.com
155 E. Burr Trail Rd. (off UT 12)
Boulder, UT 84716
Open: Daily
Price: Moderate
Cuisine: International
Serving: B, L, D
Credit Cards: AE, D, V
Handicapped Access: Yes

The slogan at this log-cabin, family-style restaurant is "Good Homecookin'." But the surprisingly contemporary menu of comfort food is done in a fresh, healthy way that makes the place a standout. It's a good place to fuel up for a day of exploring 4WD roads inside Grand Staircase–Escalante National Monument. Desserts and seasonal salads are made fresh daily.

HELL'S BACKBONE GRILL
435-335-7464
www.hellsbackbonegrill.com

20 N. UT 12, Boulder, UT 84716
Open: Daily mid-March to mid-November
Price: Expensive
Cuisine: Eclectic/Southwestern
Serving: B, D
Credit Cards: D, MC, V
Handicapped Access: Yes
Special Features: Reservations strongly rec-
ommended; dress business-casual

A unique destination for foodies, Hell's
Backbone Grill has a lot to love about it. It's
run on Tibetan Buddhist principles, with
sustainability, regional organic produce,
and cruelty-free animal products all made
priorities. The award-winning menu
changes with the seasons, but classics
include avocado-jalapeño soup, house-
made quesadillas and tamales with tempting fillings, and pots of chili-spiced
chocolate for dessert. Ask for the lengthy
list of microbrewed beers and imported
wines. It's always busy indoors, so you may
find more breathing room out on the patio,
which boasts sweeping canyon views.

Bryce

BRYCE CANYON DINING ROOM

435-834-8760
www.brycecanyonlodge.com
P.O. Box 640079, Bryce Canyon Lodge,
Bryce Canyon National Park, UT 84764
Open: Daily April through October
Price: Expensive
Cuisine: American
Serving: B, L, D
Credit Cards: AE, D, MC, V
Handicapped Access: Yes
Special Features: Reservations accepted two
months in advance starting April 1; casual
dress

Although tourists in Bryce Canyon National
Park are a captive audience, the Bryce
Canyon Lodge does serve decent food with
excellent ambience. Dinner entrees include
pastas, steaks, and seafood, with average

burgers and sandwiches at lunch. A select
list of Utah microbrewed beers are served.
Hikers can show up early in the A.M. for the
all-you-can-eat breakfast buffet and order
a boxed lunch the night before.

BRYCE CANYON PINES

435-834-5441, 1-800-892-7923
www.brycecanyonmotel.com
P.O. Box 64000-43, UT 12, mile marker 10
Bryce, UT 84764
Open: Daily
Price: Moderate
Cuisine: American
Serving: B, L, D
Credit Cards: AE, D, MC, V
Handicapped Access: Yes

This small motel's restaurant outside Bryce
Canyon National Park gets rave reviews for
its award-winning pies; the house specialties are banana-blueberry and banana-
strawberry. The full menu of steaks, freshly
cooked rainbow trout, real mashed potatoes, and more comfort food is worth stop-
ping in for. On chilly nights there's a
fireplace to warm your hands by, in addition to the kitchen's antique wood-burning
stove.

Cedar City

MILT'S STAGE STOP

435-586-9344
3560 E. UT 14, Cedar City, UT 84720
Directions: 5 miles east of Cedar City
Open: Daily
Price: Expensive
Cuisine: Steakhouse/seafood
Serving: D
Credit Cards: AE, D, MC, V
Handicapped Access: Yes

A rustic roadside steakhouse is where locals
go for rib eye and prime rib done right, as
well as seafood dishes. The old-fashioned
place has Western appeal, with hunting tro-
phies on the walls and splendid views of the

mountains and Cedar Canyon. A fireplace is lit inside during winter, while during summer the higher elevations are a much-needed cool relief.

PASTRY PUB

435-867-1400
86 W. Center St. (at S. 100 West)
Cedar City, UT 84720
Open: Monday through Saturday
Price: Inexpensive
Cuisine: American
Serving: B, L, D
Credit Cards: AE, D, MC, V
Handicapped Access: Yes

The best coffeehouse in Cedar City, it's also the first place to head to for fresh salads and sandwiches, healthy wraps, and decadent pastries and desserts. Pub favorites include the roast beef sandwich and delicious strawberry shakes. Beware that the place can get packed during the Utah Shakespearean Festival season.

Escalante

COWBOY BLUES

435-826-4577
530 W. Main St. (UT 12)
Escalante, UT 84726
Open: Daily February through December
Price: Moderate
Cuisine: American
Serving: D
Credit Cards: AE, D, MC, V
Handicapped Access: Yes

A popular gathering place for locals and tourists alike, this Escalante institution serves up full plates of hot wings, smoked trout, burgers with fries, and other tried-and-true crowd-pleasers. After a long day of hiking, who can resist wolfing down a hot fudge brownie sundae either? The boisterous full bar pours wine and micro-brewed beers, too.

ESCA-LATTE INTERNET CAFE & PIZZA PARLOR

435-826-4266
www.escalanteoutfitters.com
Escalante Outfitters, 310 W. Main St. (UT 12), Escalante, UT 84726
Open: Daily
Price: Moderate
Cuisine: American
Serving: B, L, D
Credit Cards: AE, D, MC, V
Handicapped Access: No

Stop by at any time of day, whether it's just for a quick breakfast of homemade baked goods and fruit yogurt parfaits or to settle in on the porch for a full meal, such as a seasonal salad, overstuffed sandwich, or fresh-baked signature pizza. It's an amazing place to connect with other independent travelers, perhaps over a pint of home-brewed beer.

Escalante Outfitters, including the Esca-Latte Internet Café & Pizza Parlor, is a one-stop shop for outdoor gear, fresh meals, espresso, and more.
Courtesy Escalante Outfitters

TRAILHEAD CAFE & GRILL

1-800-839-7567
www.excursionsofescalante.com
125 E. Main St. (UT 12)
Escalante, UT 84726
Open: Daily mid-April to October
Price: Inexpensive
Cuisine: Deli
Serving: B, L

Credit Cards: MC, V
Handicapped Access: Yes

Inside one of Escalante's oldest log cabins, which was built in 1880, this outdoor out-fitter has a yummy kitchen serving up fresh-fruit smoothies, home-baked bread and croissants, grilled burgers, herb-marinated chicken sandwiches, and espresso drinks. Since it's a tiny place, it's best not to be in a hurry. Take time to browse the books for sale or relax on the stone patio until your food arrives.

Green River

RAY'S TAVERN
435-564-3511
25 S. Broadway (at Main St.)
Green River, UT 84525
Open: Daily
Price: Moderate
Cuisine: Steakhouse
Serving: L, D
Credit Cards: D, MC, V
Handicapped Access: Yes

Don't be deterred by the rough-and-tumble crowd that hunkers down at old-school Ray's. Venture inside and get yourself all settled with a draft microbrew in hand, then order up a charbroiled burger or a locally raised steak that's fresh-cut daily. It's serious red meat for an audience that's notoriously hard to please, made up of longtime locals, bikers and river rafters.

Kanab

HOUSTON'S TRAIL'S END RESTAURANT
435-644-2488
32 E. Center St. (US 89 at S. Main St.)
Kanab, UT 84741
Open: Daily March through December
Price: Expensive
Cuisine: American
Serving: B, L, D

Credit Cards: AE, D, MC, V
Handicapped Access: Yes

A quirky Kanab institution, Houston's Trail's End is an Old West theme restaurant where the waitstaff dress up to match, sporting six-shooter gun holsters and all. Load up on carbs at breakfast, where you'll definitely get your money's worth of grub, or turn up later in the day just for the home-style chicken-fried steak with rich gravy. Beware of long waits and subpar steaks, however.

NEDRA'S TOO
435-644-2030
www.nedrascafe.com
310 S. 100 East (US 89 at E. 300 South)
Kanab, UT 84741
Open: Daily
Price: Moderate
Cuisine: Mexican/Southwestern
Serving: B, L, D
Credit Cards: AE, D, MC, V
Handicapped Access: Yes

Serving excellent home-cooked Mexican food for over 50 years, the second incarnation of Nedra's Cafe is the handiwork of three generations of pioneering women. Fresh guacamole, pork chili verde, stewed *machaca* (shredded beef), seafood enchiladas, chicken chimichangas in the house white sauce, Navajo tacos, and fried ice cream are among the filling specialties here. Vegetarians will be happy to find dishes made without lard or any other animal byproducts.

THE ROCKING V CAFE
435-644-8001
www.rockingvcafe.com
97 W. Center St. (US 89 at N. 100 West)
Kanab, UT 84741
Open: Daily mid-March to December
Price: Expensive
Cuisine: Southwestern
Serving: L, D

The Rocking V Café is an artful place to dine in rural Kanab. Victor Cooper / Courtesy Rocking V Cafe

Credit Cards: MC, V
Handicapped Access: Yes
Special Features: Reservations recommended; full bar

Inside a late-19th-century mercantile building and downstairs from the Rafters Gallery, this eclectic bistro devises outstanding, creative fusion fare made from fresh ingredients sourced locally (occasionally borrowed from neighbors' gardens!). Come for overstuffed muffaletta sandwiches at lunch, or leafy greens and perhaps blue cornmeal-encrusted trout at dinner. They cater to "vegetabulous" and "veganacious" palates, as well as kids (but heed the warning that "wild children of poorly behaved parents will receive a triple espresso, 6 scoops of ice cream, a drum set and a bullhorn upon ejection"). Outside are sidewalk tables where pet owners are welcome to perch.

THE THREE BEARS CREAMERY COTTAGE

435-644-3300
www.threebearscreamerycottage.com
210 S. 100 East (US 89 at W. 200 South)

Kanab, UT 84741
Open: Monday through Saturday
Price: Inexpensive
Cuisine: Deli
Serving: L, D
Credit Cards: MC, V
Handicapped Access: Yes

Feel a rush of childhood nostalgia when you enter this fairy-tale cottage. Known for its 20 flavors of homemade ice cream, thick milkshakes, and sundae creations, this family-owned café and deli also sells hearty soups and sandwiches made with fresh-baked bread. Vegetarians and even kids who are as finicky as Goldilocks will find plenty to eat here.

Mexican Hat

THE OLDE BRIDGE GRILL

435-683-2322
www.sanjuaninn.net
San Juan Inn, UT 163
Mexican Hat, UT 84531
Open: Daily
Price: Moderate

Cuisine: Southwestern
Serving: B, L, D
Credit Cards: MC, V
Handicapped Access: Yes

Sure, there's a full Southwestern family-style menu here, including ubiquitous Navajo tacos, but the real reason to come on down to the San Juan Inn is to unwind next to the river. Boasting panoramic windows, the casual restaurant is full of Western antiques and memorabilia, with a billiards table and a coffee and smoothie bar serving takeout.

THE SWINGIN' STEAK

435-683-2222
www.mexicanhat.net
Mexican Hat Lodge, UT 163
Mexican Hat, UT 84531
Open: Daily March through October
Price: Expensive
Cuisine: Steakhouse
Serving: D
Credit Cards: MC, V
Handicapped Access: Yes

After the sun sinks below the horizon, this is a social spot for cold beers and sizzling-hot steaks grilled over an open fire made of sweet-smelling cedar wood. Sidle up to the wooden bar and order a fresh, juicy cut with a side of pinto beans, toast, and a salad. While the home-style food is pricey, the place is memorable enough to have been featured on the Food Network. An alt-country band even named themselves after it, too.

Moab

BUCK'S GRILL HOUSE

435-259-5201
www.bucksgrillhouse.com
1393 N. US 191, Moab, UT 84532
Open: Daily
Price: Expensive
Cuisine: Southwestern

Serving: D
Credit Cards: AE, D, MC, V
Handicapped Access: Yes

Run by a Utah-born chef, this Western-style steakhouse serves up fresh cuts of beef, country favorites such as grilled pork chops with barbecue butter, and game specialties like elk stew, duck tamales, and buffalo meat loaf. The laid-back eatery is north of town, near where Moab's original pioneer fort once stood.

THE CENTER CAFE

435-259-4295
www.centercafemoab.com
60 N. 100 West (at W. 100 North)
Moab, UT 84532
Open: Daily March through November
Price: Very Expensive
Cuisine: New American
Serving: D
Credit Cards: D, MC, V
Handicapped Access: Yes
Special Features: Reservations recommended; dress business-casual

The chef-owners of this intimate restaurant just off Main Street have dreamt up a globally inspired menu that has devoted followers. Show up early in the evening to taste the Eurasian tapas menu, or later to experience the ever-evolving dinner menu, which might feature a winter vegetable timbale or grilled rack of lamb with mustard-currant sauce. The soothing environment with warmly colored walls, gentle lighting, a garden patio, and top-notch service enhances any special occasion.

DESERT BISTRO

435-259-0756
www.desertbistro.com
1266 N. US 191, Moab, UT 84532
Open: Tuesday through Sunday, early March to mid-December
Price: Expensive
Cuisine: Southwestern

Serving: D
Credit Cards: AE, D, MC, V
Handicapped Access: Yes
Special Features: Reservations recommended; dress business-casual; full bar

In a historic ranch house draped by cottonwood trees, this elegant dining room is brightened with works by local artists, from landscape paintings on the walls to metalwork flower vases on linen-clothed tables. A menu of Southwestern classics and creative dishes, which changes seasonally, may include homemade bread and rabbit sausage, tequila-cured salmon, or seared caribou medallions in whiskey sauce.

JAILHOUSE CAFE

435-259-3900
101 N. Main St. (at E. 100 North)
Moab, UT 84532
Open: Daily
Price: Moderate
Cuisine: American
Serving: B, L
Credit Cards: AE, D, MC, V
Handicapped Access: Yes

There's always a long line waiting outside the door at this Moab favorite, but it's worth the wait for their ginger pancakes drizzled with apple butter, Southwestern-spiced omelettes, and spicy new twists on classics like eggs Benedict. Tables inside this former courthouse and private residence are crushed together, but outdoor seating on an airy covered patio is available.

MIGUEL'S BAJA GRILL

435-259-6546
51 N. Main St. (at E. 100 North)
Moab, UT 84532
Open: Daily March–November
Price: Moderate
Cuisine: Mexican
Serving: L, D
Credit Cards: AE, D, MC, V
Handicapped Access: Yes

You can almost imagine palm trees waving at this authentic Baja-style eatery, where a glass-ceilinged walkway overhangs a pretty patio. Run by a chef (who used to sail boats in Mexico) using recipes passed down by his parents, the joint dishes up homemade guacamole, fish tacos, seafood ceviche, fresh-fruit margaritas, and other refreshing favorites.

MILT'S STOP & EAT

435-259-7424
365 S. 400 East (at Millcreek Dr.)
Moab, UT 84532
Open: Daily
Price: Inexpensive
Cuisine: American
Serving: L, D
Credit Cards: D, MC, V
Handicapped Access: Yes

Sating ravenous appetites since 1954, retro Milt's has a drive-up window for takeout orders. There are shady picnic tables and fewer than a dozen counter stools inside for devouring the all-American diner fare, from remarkable bowls of homemade chili and burgers made from locally dry-aged beef to the famous banana ice-cream shakes.

MOAB BREWERY

435-259-6333
www.themoabbrewery.com
686 S. Main St. (at Cedar Ave.)
Moab, UT 84532
Open: Daily
Price: Moderate
Cuisine: American/Southwestern
Serving: L, D
Credit Cards: AE, D, MC, V
Handicapped Access: Yes

More than just a big ol' brewpub pouring excellent libations like the Scorpion Pale Ale, here the kitchen dishes up overstuffed plates of truly excellent fare. Sweet-potato fries, beer cheese soup, whiskey chicken sandwiches, and Texas-style barbecue are just a sampling of the super-satisfying menu. Vegetarians have loads of choices, from garden burgers and hummus wraps to rainbow tortellini.

MOAB DINER
435-259-4006
www.moab-utah.com/diner/
189 S. Main St. (at W. 200 South)
Moab, UT 84532
Open: Daily
Price: Moderate
Cuisine: American
Serving: B, L, D
Credit Cards: AE, D, MC, V
Handicapped Access: Yes

If you need an escape from reality, this nostalgic 1950s-style American diner with checkered tablecloths will transport you back in time to another place. Service from the flouncy skirted-waitresses is lightning fast. Menu classics include green chili cheeseburgers, spicy chicken sandwiches, and Southwestern breakfast skillets (a mash-up of potatoes, veggies, bacon, cheese, and other heart-stopping goodies).

THE RIVER GRILL
435-259-4642, 1-877-359-2715
www.sorrelriver.com
Sorrel River Ranch, UT 128, mile marker 17
Moab, UT 84532
Open: Daily
Price: Very Expensive
Cuisine: Fusion
Serving: B, L, D (except no lunch during winter)
Credit Cards: AE, D, MC, V
Handicapped Access: Yes
Special Features: Reservations recommended; dress business-casual; full bar

On the serene grounds of an upscale boutique hotel outside Moab, this foodie destination offers so much more than its elemental name suggests. A seasonal menu of American ranch classics has a few French fusion twists, so come with an adventurous palate and be ready for anything from elk carpaccio with minced jalapeños and asiago-cheese chips to whole trout stuffed with crab and topped with a red-pepper coulis. The ambience feels as richly composed as the wine list.

ZAX PIZZA
435-259-6555
www.zaxmoab.com
96 S. Main St. (at W. 100 South)
Moab, UT 84532
Open: Daily
Price: Moderate
Cuisine: American
Serving: L, D
Credit Cards: AE, D, MC, V
Handicapped Access: Yes

Yes, it's a sports bar that also has pool tables and a jukebox. But the boisterous restaurant is better known for its wood-fired pizzas and calzones. The all-you-can-eat pizza, soup, and salad bar deal helps replenish all those calories worked off during mountain-bike rides, especially when you finish it off with an ooey-gooey slice of Mississippi mud pie.

Mount Carmel
BUFFALO BISTRO
435-648-2778
www.visiteastzion.info/buffalobistro
305 N. Main St. (US 89)
Glendale, UT 84720
Open: Thursday through Monday, April through October
Price: Expensive
Cuisine: Southwestern
Serving: D
Credit Cards: AE, D, MC, V
Handicapped Access: No
Special Features: Reservations recommended

Just about in the middle of nowhere, this Western cookhouse has an old pioneer wagon propped out front. Tables are covered in plastic flowered cloths, and the chairs are straight out of a vintage diner. There's cold beer and buffalo burgers hot off the grill, or try a full dinner of rattlesnake-rabbit sausage, wild boar, or barbecue ribs. Show up at the Testicle Festival in June for beer, live bands, and some Rocky Mountain oysters.

Panguitch

COWBOY'S SMOKEHOUSE CAFE
435-676-8030
www.cowboyssmokehousecafe.com
95 N. Main St. (US 89 at W. 100 North)
Panguitch, UT 84759
Open: Daily mid-March to mid-October
Price: Moderate
Cuisine: Barbecue
Serving: L, D
Credit Cards: MC, V
Handicapped Access: Yes

At this downtown grill they've always got mesquite-fired barbecue and steaks with baked beans on the menu. Although it's not always fantastic food, it's one of the best options in town. There's live entertainment some nights, especially on weekends.

Springdale

BIT & SPUR
435-772-3498
www.bitandspur.com
1212 Zion Park Blvd. (UT 9)
Springdale, UT 84767
Open: Daily
Price: Expensive
Cuisine: Southwestern
Serving: D
Credit Cards: AE, D, MC, V
Handicapped Access: Yes
Special Features: Reservations recommended; full bar

On the outskirts of town, this rustic-looking kitchen serves up spicy Mexican-Southwestern fare, such as chicken taquitos with spicy ketchup, brie quesadillas with jalapeño jelly, and rib eye steak with port wine sauce. The leafy grounds and patio make this a tried-and-true dinner choice. Live bands occasionally play here.

BLONDIE'S DINER
435-772-0595
736 Zion Park Blvd. (UT 9)
Springdale, UT 84767
Open: Daily
Price: Inexpensive
Cuisine: American
Serving: L, D
Credit Cards: AE, D, MC, V
Handicapped Access: No

If you want solid comfort food without any of the fuss or sky-high prices found elsewhere, walk onto the front porch and inside for a freshly made burger or chicken sandwich with a chocolate milkshake and a slice of homemade pie.

CAFE SOLEIL
435-772-0505
205 Zion Park Blvd. (UT 9)
Springdale, UT 84767
Open: Daily
Price: Moderate
Cuisine: Southwestern/deli
Serving: B, L
Credit Cards: MC, V
Handicapped Access: Yes

Almost the last stop for food before Zion National Park, this colorful café has funky artwork on the walls and free Wi-Fi Internet access. Just about everything on the menu is healthy-minded and handmade, including fresh-fruit smoothies, panini sandwiches, spicy Southwestern wraps, and espresso drinks, too.

OSCAR'S CAFE

435-772-3232
www.cafeoscars.com
948 Zion Park Blvd. (UT 9)
Springdale, UT 84767
Open: Daily
Price: Moderate
Cuisine: Mexican/American
Serving: B, L, D
Credit Cards: AE, D, MC, V
Handicapped Access: Yes

At this laid-back beatnik grill, the menu is
split between Mexican fare with a Southwestern twist, such as pesto quesadillas and
marinated rib eye burritos, and traditional
burgers, cheesesteaks, and chicken sandwiches topped with jack cheese. Grab a
chair out on the patio, which is ideal on
cool summer nights. Vegetarians are welcome.

SPOTTED DOG CAFÉ & PUB

435-772-0700
www.flanigans.com
Flanigan's Inn, 428 Zion Park Blvd. (UT 9)
Springdale, UT 84767
Open: Daily
Price: Expensive
Cuisine: Southwestern
Serving: B, D
Credit Cards: AE, D, MC, V
Handicapped Access: Yes
Special Features: Reservations recom-
mended; full bar

At Flanigan's Inn, this friendly restaurant
with a flower-bedecked sidewalk patio may
look casual, but the invigorating seasonal
menu of seafood and game dishes, homemade soups and salads, pastas, and wood
oven–fired pizzas ranks as gourmet. Look
for seared sushi-grade tuna served with
mango salsa and organic apple pie. There's
a 2,000-bottle wine cellar and Utah microbrews on tap.

ZION PIZZA & NOODLE CO.

435-772-3815
www.zionpizzanoodle.com
868 Zion Park Blvd. (UT 9)
Springdale, UT 84767
Open: Daily
Price: Moderate
Cuisine: Italian-American
Serving: L, D
Credit Cards: None
Handicapped Access: No

The social atmosphere inside this former
pioneer Mormon church spills over into the
beer garden, where pints and pitchers of
microbrews are shared. True to their name,
they offer a huge selection of pizzas, from
the vegan Tree Hugger Pizza with carrots
and sesame seeds to the Cholesterol Hiker
Pizza loaded with Canadian bacon and
Italian sausage, as well as pastas, calzones,
and salads.

St. George

BEAR PAW COFFEE COMPANY

435-634-0126
www.bearpawcafe.com
75 N. Main St. (at St. George Blvd.),
St. George, UT 84770
Open: Daily
Price: Inexpensive
Cuisine: American
Serving: B, L
Credit Cards: AE, D, MC, V
Handicapped Access: Yes

Unquestionably, this homespun café is the
place to go for breakfast. There's always a
line out the door, but it's all worth it to fork
into peanut-butter or apple-pecan pancakes, a plate of berry crepes dusted with
powdered sugar, a slice of salmon quiche,
or Idaho baked potatoes loaded with top-
pings. Breakfast is served all day, along
with espresso drinks, fruit smoothies, and
nonalcoholic juice cocktails. Panini and
deli sandwiches are available after 11 AM.

COSMOPOLITAN RESTAURANT

435-879-6862
www.cosmodining.com
1915 Wells Fargo Rd., Silver Reef, UT 84746
Directions: Take I-15 approximately 20
miles north of St. George to exit 22. Drive a
few miles north of Leeds, then turn left
onto Silver Reef Rd.
Open: Monday through Saturday
Price: Very Expensive
Cuisine: European
Serving: D
Credit Cards: MC, V
Handicapped Access: Yes
Special Features: Reservations recom-
mended; dress business-casual

An unlikely location for a fine-dining destination, Silver Reef ghost town is worth
the drive for dinner. Hungarian chef Imi
Kun offers a menu of classics that shows
German, French, and Italian influences,
including lamb osso bucco and
chateaubriand. The neo-Victorian decor
has Western flair, especially as you watch
the sun sink over the hills.

THE PAINTED PONY

435-634-1700
www.painted-pony.com
Ancestor Square, 2 W. St. George Blvd.,
St. George, UT 84770
Open: Daily
Price: Very Expensive
Cuisine: New American
Serving: L (Monday through Saturday), D
Credit Cards: AE, D, MC, V
Handicapped Access: Yes
Special Features: Reservations recom-
mended; dress business-casual; full bar

Known as one of southern Utah's top
restaurants, the Painted Pony is found
upstairs at the Ancestor Square courtyard
near the downtown historic district. The
chefs emphasize seasonal organic produce,
some of which their own gardeners grow,
with unusual offerings like beet salad,

pheasant or butternut squash ravioli, and
coconut key lime pie. Lunch is much simpler. The wine list covers Europe and the
West Coast.

Torrey

BRINK'S BURGERS DRIVE-IN

435-425-3710
165 E. Main St. (UT 24), Torrey, UT 84775
Open: Daily April through October
Price: Inexpensive
Cuisine: American
Serving: L, D
Credit Cards: None
Handicapped Access: Yes

This family drive-in right in downtown
Torrey is a reliable pit-stop for burgers,
chicken sandwiches, thick-cut potato fries,
and even thicker milkshakes. Although it's
fast food, everything here is cooked to
order, so don't show up in a hurry.

CAFE DIABLO

435-425-3070
www.cafediablo.net
599 W. Main St. (UT 24), Torrey, UT 84775
Open: Daily mid-April to mid-October
Price: Expensive
Cuisine: Eclectic/Southwestern
Serving: D
Credit Cards: MC, V
Handicapped Access: Yes
Special Features: Reservations recom-
mended

Trained in NYC, award-winning chef Gary
Pankow makes it his mission to create
innovative Southwestern cuisine inside this
charming house. Kitchen herbs and seasonal produce grow in the garden, while
eclectic specialties such as rattlesnake
cakes and pumpkin seed trout are featured
on the menu, along with house-made ice
cream and breads, and desserts whipped up
by the pastry chef. Beware of large tourist
groups descending, when you should give
this busy restaurant a miss.

CAPITOL REEF CAFE

435-425-3271
www.capitolreefinn.com
360 W. Main St. (UT 24), Torrey, UT 84775
Open: Daily April through October
Price: Moderate
Cuisine: International
Serving: B, L, D
Credit Cards: AE, D, MC, V
Handicapped Access: Yes

While it can't be recommended for snappy service or for its substantial lunches or dinners, this restaurant dishes up decent hot breakfasts. The specialty is smoked local trout, but classic diner-style plates, such as buttermilk pancakes and omelettes, are best. The honeyed pies and carrot cake are also sweet bites.

RIM ROCK RESTAURANT & PATIO

435-425-3388
www.therimrock.net
2523 E. UT 24, Torrey, UT 84775
Open: March through November
Price: Moderate
Cuisine: American
Serving: D
Credit Cards: AE, MC, V
Handicapped Access: Yes

Heading toward Capitol Reef National Park, you'll find this Western-style ranch restaurant at the edge of town, with inspiring views of the red-rock cliffs. The hearty menu is stuffed with down-home favorites like meat loaf, pot roast, stews, and fresh trout. Dine at a table in the main room with its timber-beamed ceilings or grab a seat out on the patio, where travelers and locals both gather after sunset for cold beer, hot pizza, and spicy fries.

Zion National Park

RED ROCK GRILL

435-772-7760
www.zionlodge.com
Zion Lodge, P.O. Box 925
Springdale, UT 84767
Directions: Off UT 9 inside Zion National Park
Open: Daily
Price: Expensive
Cuisine: Southwestern
Serving: B, L, D
Credit Cards: AE, D, MC, V
Handicapped Access: Yes
Special Features: Dinner reservations required; full bar

Atmospherically set deep inside Zion National Park, this classic timber lodge has a rustic Western grill with panoramic windows allowing views of the canyon's cliffs. Admittedly, the scenery is more spectacular than the menu, which offers flatiron steaks, prime rib, roasted pork loin, roasted eggplant, and more. Try a prickly-pear margarita or a mojito.

Bakeries, Coffeehouses, and Juice Bars

Comb Ridge Coffee, www.combridgecoffee.com, 435-672-9931, Main St. (US 191) at 7th St. East, Bluff. Lose yourself in the overstuffed couches and check your e-mail while sipping a cappuccino. Fruit muffins, quiche, and organic oatmeal get the day started right.

Dave's Corner Market, 435-259-6999, 401 Mill Creek Dr., Moab. Locals and mountain bikers congregate at this corner shop run by the mayor of Moab, who keeps it stocked with excellent shade-grown coffees and loose-leaf teas.

Eklecticafe, 435-259-6896, 352 N. Main St., Moab. This convivial cottage on the north side of town has a short menu of vegetarian-friendly dishes made with fresh, seasonal, and organic produce. Wi-Fi Internet access available.

Esca-Latte Internet Café, wwww.escalanteoutfitters.com, 435-826-4266, 310 W. Main St., Escalante. This outdoor outfitter makes a rich latte and has an airy front porch, plus free Wi-Fi or wired Internet access on shared computers.

Green River Coffee Company, 435-564-3411, 17 E. Main St., Green River. You'll find alternative types, artists, and sleepy tourists lined up here for their morning dose of java and hot breakfast sandwiches.

Jazzy Java, 435-674-1678, 285 N. Bluff St., St. George. This full-fledged coffee shop, where they roast their own beans and sell baskets full of baked goodies and deli sandwiches, attracts tattooed clientele in indie-rock T-shirts.

Kiva Koffeehouse, www.kivakoffeehouse.com, 435-826-4550, UT 12, mile marker 73.86, Escalante, UT 84726. Open: Wednesday through Monday, April through October. Both the canyon views and the espresso drinks will make your head spin. Homemade soups and breads are the specialty of the day.

The Mean Bean Coffee House, www.meanbeancoffee.com, 435-772-0654, 932 Zion Park Blvd., Springdale. This is where real people come for strong liquid stimulation and home-made scones and muffins. All the coffees and teas are organic, and the former are shade-grown and fair-trade.

Mondo Café, www.mondocafe.com, 435-259-5551, McStiff's Plaza, 59 S. Main St., Moab. For caffeinated rocket fuel and so much more, including Belgian waffles, pesto eggs on focaccia bread, grilled panini sandwiches, and microbrewed beer.

Peace Tree Juice Café, 435-259-8503, www.peacetreecafe.com, 20 S. Main St., Moab. This fruit and vegetable smoothie shop doubles as a healthy deli serving salads and quick wraps. There's another branch in Monticello.

Red Rock Bakery, 435-259-5941, 74 S. Main St., Moab. Baking goodies from scratch, from cinnamon rolls to soups, deli sandwiches, and desserts, this place always has a queue at the espresso bar. Wi-Fi Internet access available.

Robbers Roost Books, www.robbersroostbooks.com, 435-425-3265, 185 W. Main St., Torrey. Beautifully set beside a creek, this coffeehouse is warmed by a fireplace. It serves the finest brews for a hundred miles and hosts the local farmer's market on most Saturday afternoons.

Willow Canyon Outdoor Company, www.willowcanyon.com, 435-644-8884, 263 S. 100 East, Kanab. You may find it hard to tear yourself away from this outdoor gear store, book-store, and coffee bar. The baristas just couldn't be nicer.

Delis and Grills

Adobe Deli, 435-735-4014, 16 N. Main St. (US 89), Hatch, UT. The longest lines and biggest crowds of hungry patrons are found here, chowing down on signature, fresh-made sandwiches and salads. Espresso drinks are also served. Open March to mid-November.

Austin's Chuckwagon Deli, www.austinschuckwagonmotel.com, 435-425-3290, 12 W. Main St. (UT 24), Torrey. A grocery store with a deli that makes hot and cold sandwiches and a bakery for daily fresh bread and pastries.

Burr Trail Grill & Deli, www.burrtrailgrill.com, 435-335-7503, Burr Trail and UT 12, Boulder. This trading post serves up no-fuss meals on its patio, perfect for hungry families. Burgers, sandwiches, soups, salads, espresso drinks, and beer available.

Georgie's Corner Cafe & Deli, 435-826-4784, 190 W. Main St. (UT 12), Escalante. Pick up a salad, sandwich, piping-hot plate of fully loaded nachos, or a milkshake at this friendly local shop.

Hills and Hollows General Store and Mama Cyta's Wood Fired Bakery, www.original tradegoods.com, 435-335-7349, 840 W. UT 12, Boulder. Stop off for wood-fired European breads and pizzas, deli sandwiches, and monster-size cookies.

Pole's Place Eatery, 1-800-730-7422, www.boulderutah.com/polesplace, opposite Anasazi State Park, Boulder. This rustic motel café dishes up filling beef and garden burgers, salads, and super-thick milkshakes.

Village Market, 435-259-3111, 702 S. Main St., Moab. Big breakfasts, boxed lunches, and full chicken dinners are available for takeout. Every morning there's a 99-cent special for coffee and a doughnut.

Desserts and Ice Cream

Bulloch Drug, 435-586-9651, 91 N. Main St., Cedar City. An old-fashioned, atmospheric drugstore soda fountain in downtown Cedar City.

Bumbleberry Restaurant, www.bumbleberry.com, 435-772-3224, 897 Zion Park Blvd., Springdale, UT 84767. Swing by this casual diner for a slice of their famous bumbleberry pie or pancakes with bumbleberry syrup.

Grandee's Old-Fashioned Ice Cream & Bake Shoppe, 435-867-1179, 1166 Sage Dr., west of I-15 via W. 600 South, Cedar City. Come for 30 flavors of homemade ice cream, stay for a cup of soup or salad as the 1950s jukebox plays.

The Reel Scoop, 435-676-2820, 37 N. Main St., Panguitch. At this old-fashioned malt shop, order up a classic banana split or a towering ice cream sundae.

Restoration Creamery, www.livingrivers.org/creamery.cfm, 435-259-1063, 21 N. Main St., Moab. This unique ice cream shop scoops up temptingly named flavors and engages visitors with interpretive displays about its nonprofit environmental campaigns.

Grocery Stores and Markets

Griffin Grocery, 435-826-4226, 30 W. Main St., Escalante. The mom-and-pop operation stocks fresh produce and has a takeout deli.

Melon Vine Food Store, 435-564-3228, 72 S. Broadway, Green River. Basic grocery store vends fresh produce and camp-ready foodstuffs.

Mesa Market, www.mesafarmmarket.com, 435-456-9146, UT 24, mile marker 102, Caineville. Have a chat on the front porch at this organic farm, which offers the season's best produce, plus boxed salads and sandwiches to go.

Moonflower Market, 435-259-5712, 39 E. 100 North, Moab. This local health food store with a small local art gallery is the place for vegans, vegetarians, and other health-minded folks to get picnic supplies, hiking snacks, and more.

Ruby's Inn General Store, www.rubysinn.com, 435-834-5484, 1000 S. US 63, Bryce. Pick up picnic supplies here before heading into Bryce Canyon National Park for the day.

Sol Foods Market & Deli, www.solfoods.com, 435-772-0277, 95 Zion Park Blvd., Springdale. This well-stocked supermarket just outside Zion National Park has everything campers and hikers need, including rockin' deli lunches for takeout.

Springdale Fruit Company, www.springdalefruit.com, 435-772-3822, 2491 Zion Park Blvd. (UT 9), Springdale. Set beautifully among apple orchards, this high-priced juice bar, deli, and organic produce shop is closed during winter.

RECREATION

Bicycling

Cycling is a popular sport in Utah. Paved roads for cycling and some bike paths are found in national parks, from Arches to Zion. West of Bryce Canyon in Dixie National Forest (www.fs.fed.us/r4/dixie/recreation, 435-865-3700), the **Red Canyon bike trail** is gorgeous. Long-distance cyclists are seen on **UT 12**, southern Utah's scenic byway. For bike rentals and repair shops, see the "Mountain Biking" section, below.

Events include Moab's **Skinny Tire Festival** (www.skinnytirefestival.com, 435-259-2698) in March, the **Escalante to Boulder—There and Back Again Bike Ride** (www.escalanteoutfitters.com, 435-826-4266) in April, Monticello's **Blue Mountain Bike Chase** (www.monticelloutah.org/activities, 435-587-2029) and **Moon Shadows in Moab** (www.moonshadowsinmoab.com, 435-259-2698) during July; and the **Moab Century Tour** (www.skinnytirefestival.com, 435-259-2698) in October.

Birding

A premier spot for birding in southern Utah, the **Scott M. Matheson Wetlands Preserve** (www.nature.org, 435-259-4629, 934 W. Kane Creek Blvd., Moab) is a desert oasis surrounded by red-rock cliffs. Birding checklists and self-guided tour maps showing walking trails, boardwalks, and wildlife blinds are available at the information kiosk. Visit during spring or fall to see migratory species. Bring binoculars and bug repellant. To get there from Moab, drive south on US 191, then west on Kane Creek Blvd.; bear left at the Y-intersection after .75 mile, then drive another .50 mile to the entrance. The preserve is open daily from dawn until dusk; admission is free.

Most national parks in southern Utah also offer excellent birding opportunities and ranger-guided walks, with species checklists available from visitor centers and bookstores. **Utah Birds** (www.utahbirds.org) offers free downloadable birding checklists, a photo gallery, calendar of events, reports of rare-bird sightings, and driving directions to bird-watching hot spots. Hosted by the **Red Cliffs Chapter of the National Audubon Society** (www.redcliffsaudubon.org, 435-673-0996), the annual **St. George Winter Bird Festival** (www.sgcity.org/birdfestival) takes place in January.

Camping

Many national and state parks (see "Parks and Natural Attractions," below) and other federal recreation lands offer developed campgrounds with tent and RV sites and basic facilities (flush toilets, water, fire pits). Some campsites are first-come, first-served; others can be reserved in advance. Contact **ReserveAmerica** (www.reserveamerica.com) for campsite reservations at national parks and other federal recreation lands (1-877-444-6777, 518-885-3639), as well as at **Utah state parks** (1-800-322-3770); a surcharge applies per reservation. Private roadside campgrounds, which cater more to RVs than tent campers, usually offer better amenities, such as Wi-Fi Internet access, swimming pools, and laundry facilities. Expect to pay up to $20 for campsites at private campgrounds, and at least $30 for RV sites with hookups.

Recommended campgrounds around southern Utah include:

Boulder Mountain Campgrounds, www.ut.blm.gov/monument/visitor-centers.php, 435-826-5499, Escalante Interagency Visitor Center, 755 W. Main St., Escalante. Stop by the visitor center for information about these primitive campgrounds, off UT 12 between Escalante and Torrey. Open June– September.

Cedar Canyon Campground, www.fs.fed.us/r4/dixie/, 435-865-3200, off UT 14, approximately 13 miles southeast of Cedar City. West of Bryce Canyon, this Dixie National Forest campground has tent and RV sites with picnic tables, vault toilets, and nonpotable water.

Escalante Outfitters, www.escalanteoutfitters.com, 435-826-4266, 310 W. Main St., Escalante. Outdoors store offers grassy tent sites, an RV site with hookups, and bunkhouse cabins with fans (no air-conditioning), along with shared showers and free Wi-Fi Internet access. Dogs are welcome.

Grand Staircase–Escalante National Monument, www.ut.blm.gov/monument/, 435-826-5499, 755 W. Main St., Escalante. The vast monument has only two developed campgrounds. Between Escalante and Boulder on UT 12, Calf Creek Recreation Area has tent and RV sites in a beautiful canyon. Six miles from Boulder along the Burr Trail, Deer Creek Campground has a few shady tent and RV sites with vault toilets (no water).

Paria Canyon Adventure Ranch, www.pariacampground.com, 928-660-2674, US 89, between mile markers 21 and 22. Between Page, Arizona and Kanab, Utah, outdoor outfitter offers tent and RV sites, tipis, and shared shower and laundry facilities.

Red Canyon, www.fs.fed.us/r4/dixie/recreation/campgrounds/campindex, 435-676-9300, off UT 12 west of Bryce Canyon. This Dixie National Forest campground has tent and RV sites, flush toilets, and showers. Open mid-May– September.

Red Cliffs Recreation Area, www.ut.blm.gov, 435-688-3200, off I-15 exit 22, about 15 miles northeast of St. George. This hosted BLM campground has tent and RV sites with drinking water, vault toilets, and picnic tables.

River Road Campgrounds, www.blm.gov/utah/moab, 435-259-2100, along UT 128 east of US 191, Moab. Moab's most scenic campsites are at this first-come, first served campground set beneath the cliffs of the Colorado River.

Ruby's Inn RV Park & Campground, www.rubysinn.com, 435-834-5301, 1-866-1-866-6616, 1000 S. US 63, Bryce. Just outside Bryce Canyon National Park, this tourist complex rents cabins and Native American–style tipis with hot showers, an outdoor heated swimming pool, and hot tub.

Sand Island Campground, www.blm.gov/utah/monticello/camping.htm, 435-587-1500, off US 191, 3 miles west of Bluff. Set beside the San Juan River, this BLM campground has shady tent and RV sites, picnic areas, drinking water, and vault toilets.

Sunglow Campground, www.fs.fed.us/r4/fishlake, 435-836-2811, off UT 24 west of Torrey. In the Fishlake National Forest, this hidden, remote campground has basic sites backed by gorgeous red-rock cliffs. Open May through October.

Up the Creek Campground, www.moabupthecreek.com, 435-260-1888, 210 E. 300 South, Moab. This small private campground in downtown Moab offers shady walk-in tent sites with picnic tables and a shared bathhouse with hot showers and flush toilets. Open March through October.

Zion Ponderosa Ranch Resort, www.zionponderosa.com, 435-648-2700, 1-800-293-5444, North Fork Rd., off UT 9 east of Zion National Park. Offers a small grassy tent-camping area surrounded by cabins, plus RV sites, canvas-tent rentals, laundry facilities, hot showers, an outdoor swimming pool and hot tub, mountain-biking trails, and free Wi-Fi Internet access.

Canoeing and Kayaking

For more canoeing and kayaking adventures in southern Utah, visit Glen Canyon National Recreation Area (see the "Recreation" section of the "Native America" chapter).

Canyon Voyages Adventure Co., www.canyonvoyages.com, 435-259-6007, 1-800-733-6007, 211 N. Main St., Moab. Offers half-day and multiday kayak trips on the Green River in tandem and sea kayaks. Also runs a kayak school on the Colorado River.

Escalante Petrified Forest State Park, stateparks.utah.gov/parks/escalante, 435-826-4466, 710 N. Reservoir Rd., Escalante. From March through November, rental canoes allow visitors to paddle lazily around the reservoir.

Red River Adventures, www.redriveradventures.com, 435-259-4046, 1-877-259-4046, 1140 S. Main St., Moab. Rents canoes and inflatable kayaks and offers lessons.

Red River Canoe Company, www.redrivercanoe.com, 1-800-753-8216, 1371 N. US 191, Moab. Offers canoe rentals, shuttle services, and guided tours of Green River, the Colorado River, and the San Juan River from Bluff to Mexican Hat and beyond. One- and two-day canoe workshops and private lessons available.

Tex's Riverways, www.texsriverways.com, 435-259-5101, 691 N. 500 West, Moab. Tex's provides rental canoes, touring tandem and sea kayaks, and overnight camping gear, as well as shuttle services to/from put-in / take-out points on the Green and Colorado Rivers, including Meander, Labyrinth, and Stillwater Canyons.

Canyoneering

You can rope up and rappel your way into slot canyons across southern Utah. No experience is required for easy trips, although lessons are available.

Moab Cliffs and Canyons, www.cliffsandcanyons.com, 435-259-3317, 1-877-641-5271, 63 E. Center St., Moab. Offers easy half-day trips in Zion National Park, as well as more difficult half- and full-day trips farther afield in the desert.

Moab Desert Adventures, www.moabdesertadventures.com, 435-260-2404, 1-877-765-6622, 415 N. Main St., Moab. Premier rock-climbing outfitters offer canyoneering trips to

*Guided canyoneering trips with Zion Adventure
Company are an all-ages thrill.* |onathan D. Zambella /
Courtesy Zion Adventure Company

more remote slot canyons, plus rappelling off Corona Arch.

North Wash Outfitters, www.north washoutfitters.com, 435-672-9942, 255 N. 700 East, Bluff. Offers introductory, advanced, technical canyoneering, and canyon rescue courses, as well as day trips around the San Juan River Valley and women-only technical canyoneering workshops.

Zion Adventure Company, www.zion adventures.com, 435-772-0990, Zion Outdoor Center, 868 Zion Park Blvd., Springdale. Experienced rock-climbing outfitter offers guided canyoneering trips and prep courses for DIY canyon descents.

Zion Rock & Mountain Guides, www.zionrockguides.com, 435-772-3303, 1458 Zion Park Blvd., Springdale. Owned by an ex–national park ranger, this multi-sport outfitter offers guided tours and courses from introductory to advanced.

Fishing

For fishing regulations and to buy licenses online, contact the **Utah Division of Wildlife Resources** (wildlife.utah.gov, 801-538-4700). Popular fishing spots include the **Green River** near Moab; **Duck Creek** and **Navajo Lake** off UT 14, east of Cedar City and west of Bryce Canyon; **Pine Lake** northwest of Bryce Canyon; **Panguitch Lake,** west of Panguitch; **Barker Lake** and the **Escalante River** outside Escalante; in the **Manti–La Sal Mountains** and along the **Colorado River** outside Moab; along the **San Juan River** outside Bluff; **Kolob Reservoir** at the edge of Zion National Park outside Virgin; **Quail Creek State Park** outside Hurricane; and **Baker Dam Reservoir** off UT 18 and **Gunlock State Park** off UT 91, northwest of St. George. Near major lakes and reservoirs you'll find rustic cabin resorts and tackle shops that sell fishing gear and bait and rent watercraft.

For fly-fishing, head to the lakes around Boulder Mountain, west of Torrey. **Boulder Mountain Fly Fishing** (www.bouldermountainflyfishing.com, 435-335-7306, Boulder) rents fly-fishing gear and provides guide services. **Alpine Angler's Shop & Boulder Mountain Adventures** (www.fly-fishing-utah.net, 435-425-3660, 310 W. Main St., Torrey) and **Red River Outfitters** (www.redriveroutfitter.com, 435-425-3669, 135 E. Main St., Torrey) are full-service fly shops that arrange personalized guided trips; the latter shop has a private catch-and-release ranch on the Fremont River.

Fitness Facilities

Better business hotels may also have workout facilities for guests.

Adobe Fitness, www.adobefitness.com, 435-644-5474, 163 S. 100 East (US 89), Kanab. Although small, this rural gym offers low-priced day passes and a variety of equipment and exercise classes.

St. George Recreation Center, www.sgcity.org/recreation/sgreccenter.php, 435-627-4560, 285 S. 400 East, St. George. This inexpensive public gym has a fully equipped exercise room, racquetball and basketball courts, and aerobic fitness classes.

Golf

Some courses are open year-round, while others close in winter. For more golf courses open to the public, contact the **Utah Golf Association,** www.uga.org, 801-563-0400.

Coral Canyon Golf Course, www.coralcanyongolf.com, 435-688-1700, 1925 N. Canyon Greens Dr., off I-15 exit 16, Washington. This course outside St. George has views of Utah's canyon country. Public, 18 holes, 7,029 yards, par 72; club and cart rentals, driving range, lessons, pro shop, putting green, restaurant.

Coral Cliffs Golf Course, www.coralcliffsgolfcourse.com, 435-644-5005, 755 E. Fairway Dr., Kanab. A scenic course backed by the Vermillion Cliffs. Public, 9 holes, 3,400 yards, par 36; cart and club rentals, driving range, putting green.

Dixie Red Hills Golf Course, www.sgcity.org/golf/sgredhills.php, 435-627-4444, www.sgcity.org\golf\redhills.asp, 645 W. 1250 North, St. George. Tee off next to cottonwood and mesquite trees overshadowed by sandstone cliffs. Public, 9 holes, 2,733 yards, par 34; cart and club rentals, driving range, lessons, putting greens, snack bar.

Entrada at Snow Canyon Country Club, www.golfentrada.com, 435-986-2200, 2537 W. Entrada Trail, St. George. Golfing privileges at this challenging, award-winning course are extended only to those staying at The Inn at Entrada (see "Lodging," above). Private, 18 holes, 7,059 yards, par 71; cart and club rentals, driving range, lessons, pro shop, putting green, snack bar.

Green Spring Golf Course, www.greenspringgolfcourse.com, 435-673-7888, 588 N. Greenspring Dr., Washington. Near St. George, this course with a mountain backdrop has two signature holes crossing a red-rock ravine. Public, 18 holes, 6,830 yards, par 72; cart and club rentals, driving range, lessons, pro shop, putting green, snack bar.

Green River State Park, http://stateparks.utah.gov/parks/green-river/, 435-564-8882, Green River Blvd. south of Main St., Green River. Casual, laid-back course on the banks of the Green River shaded by cottonwood trees. Public, 9 holes, 3,548 yards, par 36; cart and club rentals, driving range, lessons, pro shop, putting green, snack bar.

The Hideout Golf Course, www.monticelloutah.org/golf.html, 435-587-2200, 549 S. Main St., Monticello. In the Abajo Mountains, southern Utah's favorite public golf course is also its highest (over 7,000 feet above sea level). Public, 18 holes, 6,768 yards, par 72; cart and club rental, driving range, lessons, pro shop, putting green, snack bar.

Moab Golf Course, 435-259-6488, 2705 S. East Bench Rd., Moab. Built into the Spanish Valley, this short but scenic course beneath sandstone bluffs is nevertheless demanding.

Public, 18 holes, 6,819 yards, par 72; carts and club rentals, driving range, lessons, pro shop, putting green, snack bar.

St. George Golf Club, www.sgcity.org/golf/sggolfclub.asp, 435-627-4404, 2190 S. 1400 East, St. George. A natural setting cut into desert terrain is the reason for this course's popularity. Public, 18 holes, 7,217 yards, par 73; cart and club rentals, pro shop, putting green, snack bar.

Sunbrook Golf Course, www.sgcity.org/golf/sunbrook.asp, 435-634-5866, 2240 Sunbrook Dr., St. George. This municipal course has an unmatched variety of holes and scenery, including black lava rock. Public, 27 holes, 10,202 yards, par 108; cart and club rental, driving range, pro shop, putting green, café, snack bar.

Hiking and Backpacking

For first-time visitors to southern Utah, the best hikes are inside national and state parks and recreation areas (see "Parks and Natural Attractions," below). Information about trails, ranging from easy nature walks to moderate day hikes and rugged overnight trips, is available at any park visitor center and online at the parks' official Web sites. Regional highlights include the head-spinning trip to Angels Landing and the splashy trek through The Narrows inside **Zion National Park**; walking past the hoodoos of **Bryce Canyon National Park**; the riverside trail to lower Calf Creek Falls inside **Grand Staircase– Escalante National Monument**; epic descents into **Canyonlands National Park**; and sandy day hikes across slick-rock to awesome sandstone formations inside **Arches National Park**.

Horseback Riding

Southern Utah is idyllic country for horseback riding, particularly at many national parks and around Moab.

Boulder Mountain Ranch, www.boulder utah.com/bmr/, 435-335-7581, Hell's Backbone Rd., Boulder, UT 84716. This working cattle ranch in Grand Staircase– Escalante National Monument organizes daily trail rides, beginners' overnight trips, and multiday pack trips for experi-enced riders.

Canyon Trail Rides, www.canyonrides.com, 435-679-8665, P.O. Box 128, Tropic, UT 84776. It's the only outfitter for cowboy-led horse and mule rides inside Bryce Canyon and Zion National Parks.

Easy walking trails overlook the wild backcountry of Canyonlands National Park. Sara Benson

Capitol Reef Backcountry Outfitters, www.ridethereef.com, 1-866-747-2972, 677 E. UT 24, Torrey. Arranges trail rides and overnight pack trips in Capitol Reef country.

Hondoo Rivers & Trails, www.hondoo.com, 435-425-3519, 1-800-332-2696, P.O. Box 98, Torrey. Tour operator specializes in horseback holidays: multiday trail rides with overnights inn stays or camping out in Capitol Reef country and Escalante canyons.

Red Canyon Horseback Rides, www.brycecanyonmotel.com, 1-800-892-7923, Bryce Canyon Pines Resort, UT 12, mile marker 10, Bryce. Tamer outfit offers short rides in the ponderosa forests of Red Canyon outside Bryce Canyon National Park.

Red Cliffs Lodge, www.redcliffslodge.com, 435-259-2002, 1-866-812-2002, UT 128, mile marker 14, Moab. Arranges half-day rides and customized overnight pack trips starting from the Colorado River.

Ruby's Inn, www.rubysinn.com, 435-834-5341, 1-866-782-0002, 1000 S. UT 63, Bryce. Accepts last-minute reservations for trail rides around Red Rock Canyon outside Bryce Canyon from April through October. Longer rides near the Paria River in Grand Staircase–Escalante National Monument in spring and autumn require advance bookings.

Trailhead Station, www.trailheadstation.com, 435-679-8536, Kodachrome Basin State Park, UT. Offers day rides through sandstone formations led by real cowboys.

Zion Mountain Resort, www.zionmountainresort.com, 435-648-2555, 1-866-648-25555, 9065 E. UT 9, Mount Carmel. Offers short trail rides in meadowlands outside Zion National Park's east entrance.

Mountain Biking

Moab is the center of southern Utah's mountain-biking universe. Whether you're seeking a scenic desert ride or the ultimate technical single-track challenge, this is the place. Famous rides include the **Slickrock Trail** atop an eroded sandstone plateau, the technical downhill **Porcupine Rim**, and the **White Rim Trail**, a 100-mile marathon on 4WD roads in Canyonlands. Dozens of more trails will get you beautifully doused in red dirt. Local bike shops can point you in the right direction, or stop by the **Moab Information Center** (www.discovermoab.com, 1-800-635-6622, corner of Main and Center Sts., Moab).

Moab is not the only place to ride, however. **Red Canyon** in the Dixie National Forest (www.fs.fed.us/r4/dixie/recreation/, 435-865-3700) near Bryce Canyon has more than 30 miles of single track through spectacular red-rock scenery. Northwest of Bryce, **Brian Head Resort** (www.brianhead.com, 435-677-3101, 329 S. UT 143, Brian Head) has a mountain bike park with chairlifts and over 200 miles of trails. Over 100 miles of dirt roads beckon in enormous **Grand Staircase–Escalante National Monument** and on nearby **Boulder Mountain**, as well as in **Capitol Reef country** (see "Parks and Natural Attractions," below). Outside Zion National Park near St. George there are phenomenal desert rides, including single track atop **Gooseberry Mesa** and along the **Bear Claw Poppy Trail**.

SingleTrackTreks (www.singletracktreks.com) and **Utah Mountain Biking** (www.utahmountainbiking.com) have helpful online trail directories, discussion forums, and announcements of group rides and special events. The **24 Hours of Moab Mountain Bike Race** (www.grannygear.com, 304-259-5533) takes place every October. Local bike shops and tour outfitters providing equipment rentals, repairs, and trail information and shuttles include:

Bicycles Unlimited, www.bicyclesunlimited.com, 1-888-673-4492, 900 S. 100 East, St. George.

Capitol Reef Backcountry Outfitters, www.capitolreefoutfitters.com, 1-866-747-3972, 677 E. UT 24, Torrey.

Chile Pepper Bike Shop, www.chilebikes.com, 435-259-4688, 1-888-677-4688, 702 S. Main St., Moab.

Moab Cyclery, www.moabcyclery.com, 435-259-7423, 1-800-559-1978, 391 S. Main St., Moab. Also functions as the office for **Escape Adventures** (www.escapeadventures.com, 1-800-596-2953).

Poison Spider Bicycles, www.poisonspiderbicycles.com, 435-259-7882, 1-800-635-1792, 497 N. Main St., Moab. Also the headquarters for **Nichols Expeditions** (www.nichols expeditions.com, 1-800-648-8488).

Red Rock Bicycle Company, www.redrockbicycle.com, 435-674-3185, 446 W. 100 South, St. George.

Rim Cyclery, www.rimcyclery.com, 435-259-5333, 1-888-304-8219, 94 W. 100 North, Moab.

Rim Tours, www.rimtours.com, 1-800-626-7335, 1233 S. US 191, Moab.

Ruby's Inn, www.rubysinn.com, 1-866-1-866-6616, 1000 S. US 63, Bryce.

Springdale Cycle Tours, www.springdalecycles.com, 435-772-0575, 1-800-776-2099, 1458 Zion Park Blvd., Springdale.

Zion Cycles, www.zioncycles.com, 435-772-0400, 868 Zion Park Blvd., Springdale.

Parks and Natural Attractions
To find more out-of-the-way recreation areas, dinosaur-track trails, and 4WD routes, check out the free online brochure rack sponsored by the Moab Information Center (www.discovermoab.com, 1-800-635-6622, Main and Center Sts., Moab, UT 84532).

National Parks and Monuments
ARCHES NATIONAL PARK
435-719-2299
www.nps.gov/arch
P.O. Box 927, Moab, UT 84532
Directions: Off US 191, about 5 miles north of Moab
Open: 24/7/365; visitor center daily 7:30–6:30, April through October; 8–4:30, November through March
Admission: seven-day entry pass per vehicle $10

Outside the adventure town of Moab, this park protects millennia-old sandstone arches, fins, and other beautifully eroded formations. Rent an audio tour CD from the visitor center, then drive uphill on the paved scenic loop road past famous Balanced Rock, detour to Delicate Arch Viewpoint, and arrive at Devils Garden, the starting point for rugged hikes out to Dark Angel and Double O Arch. Ask about ranger-led programs in the Fiery Furnace.

BRYCE CANYON NATIONAL PARK

435-834-5322
www.nps.gov/brca
P.O. Box 640201, Bryce Canyon, UT 84764
Directions: On UT 63, south of UT 12
Open: 24/7/365; visitor center daily 8–4:30, spring and fall daily 8–6, summer daily 8–8
Admission: seven-day entry pass per vehicle $25

Not as big as the Grand Canyon, Bryce Canyon is an outdoor playground for budding geologists and anyone else who can appreciate the naturally carved amphitheaters and strangely shaped "hoodoo" spires. In summer, hop aboard the park shuttle, which connects over a dozen viewpoints and trailheads atop the canyon rim. Ask about ranger-led geology talks and walks.

CANYONLANDS NATIONAL PARK

435-719-2313
www.nps.gov/cany
Mailing Address: 2282 SW Resource Blvd., Moab, UT 84532
Open: 24/7/365. Needles visitor center daily 9–4:30, with extended hours March through October; Island in the Sky visitor center daily 9–4:30; both closed Christmas and New Year's Days.
Admission: seven-day entry pass per vehicle $10

Less crowded than nearby Arches National Park, this massive collection of kaleidoscopic canyons is divided into three main districts. The Needles is easiest to get to from Moab, while Island in the Sky is worth the detour from I-40. The Maze is the wildest and least accessible place, bordering Glen Canyon National Recreation Area. Most people come to hike or take backpacking trips along the canyon's river bottoms. 4WD trips are popular with experienced drivers.

CAPITOL REEF NATIONAL PARK

435-425-3791
www.nps.gov/care
HC-70 Box 15, Torrey, UT 84775
Directions: Off UT 24, east of Torrey
Open: 24/7/365; visitor center daily 8–4:30, with extended summer hours
Admission: seven-day entry pass per vehicle $5

Stretched along a wrinkle in the earth's crust, this geologically fascinating park also treats the natural and cultural history of the area. Visitors can pick in-season fruit from the orchards of the Fruita pioneer district. The paved park loop road also passes more historic buildings and trailheads for hikes along canyon washes and to scenic viewpoints. Four-wheel-drive adventurers explore the Cathedral Valley and Waterpocket Fold formations.

CEDAR BREAKS NATIONAL MONUMENT

435-586-9451
www.nps.gov/cebr
Mailing Address: 2390 W. UT 56, Suite 11, Cedar City, UT 84720
Directions: From Cedar City take UT 14 east 18 miles, then UT 148 north 4 miles.

Open: Daily 8–6, June to mid-October (weather permitting)
Admission: seven-day entry pass per individual $4

Climb high onto the Colorado Plateau for views of a natural horseshoe-shaped amphitheater painted with many colors. Short hiking trails lead atop the rim past gnarled ancient bristlecone pines, which are among the oldest living things on earth, and alpine ponds. Always call ahead to see if the main park access road is open at the time of your visit.

GRAND STAIRCASE–ESCALANTE NATIONAL MONUMENT
435-826-5499
www.ut.blm.gov/monument
Escalante Visitor Center, 755 W. Main St., Escalante, UT 84726
Directions: South of UT 12 and north and east of US 89
Open: 24/7/365
Admission: Free (except Calf Creek Recreation Area day-use pass $2)

This Wild West wilderness area bridges the geological gap between the Grand Canyon and Bryce Canyon. Exploring the back roads should be done only during good weather, however, as flash floods and washouts are possible. With limited time, drive the paved section of the Burr Trail just outside Boulder and hike the trail to Lower Calf Creek Falls in Calf Creek Recreation Area, between Escalante and Boulder. For information, maps, and current road conditions, stop by the Escalante Visitor Center or BLM offices in Cannonville, Kanab, and Big Water (see "Tourist Information" in the "Information" chapter).

ZION NATIONAL PARK
435-772-3256
www.nps.gov/zion
Springdale, UT 84767
Directions: Off UT 9, east of Springdale
Open: 24/7/365
Admission: seven-day entry pass $25 per vehicle

An oasis in the desert of southern Utah, Zion's waterfall pools and river canyons are a respite for road-weary travelers. Photographers, birders, rock climbers, and hikers are all drawn to the massive sandstone cliffs that make this giant place feel intimate. Hop on the seasonal park shuttle that travels along the scenic loop road, then exit the park by driving east through the 1.1-mile-long Zion–Mount Carmel Tunnel, an engineering marvel. In the northwest corner of the park, the epic Kolob Canyons are accessed off I-15.

State Parks
Most state parks charge $5 or more per vehicle for day-use passes.

Coral Pink Sand Dunes State Park, http://stateparks.utah.gov/parks/coral-pink/, 435-648-2800. On Sand Dunes Rd., approximately 22 miles northwest of Kanab. Red sandstone cliffs and pine forests frame the Colorado Plateau's only sand dunes.

Dead Horse Point State Park, http://stateparks.utah.gov/parks/dead-horse/, 435-259-2614. Take US 191 about 9 miles northwest of Moab, then UT 313 southwest 23 miles. Where cowboys once corralled wild mustangs, visitors now soak in panoramic vistas of the buttes and pinnacles of Canyonlands National Park.

Remote overlooks of the winding San Juan River at Goosenecks State Park. Sara Benson & Mike Connolly

Escalante Petrified Forest State Park, http://stateparks.utah.gov/parks/escalante/, 435-826-4466, 710 N. Reservoir Rd. (UT 12), Escalante, UT 84726. A mile west of Escalante, this small piece of ancient petrified forest borders a recreational reservoir.

Goblin Valley State Park, http://stateparks.utah.gov/parks/goblin-valley/, 435-564-3633. Approximately 24 miles south of I-70 (exit 149) on UT 24. The alien-looking eroded formations at this remote park appear like scenes from a sci-fi movie.

Goosenecks State Park, http://stateparks.utah.gov/parks/goosenecks/, 435-678-2238. About 10 miles north of Mexican Hat on UT 316. Detour to this head-spinning overlook with canyon walls carved by a horseshoe bend in the muddy San Juan River.

Kodachrome State Park, http://stateparks.utah.gov/parks/kodachrome/, 435-679-8562. From UT 12 drive 8 miles south of Cannonville. Sky-scraping sandstone chimneys and sand pipes are colorful evidence of ancient hot springs and geysers. For cowboy trail rides, see "Horseback Riding," above.

Racquet Sports

Larger towns and cities usually have public tennis courts that are first-come, first-served. Upscale hotels, spa resorts, and golf clubs often have tennis or racquetball courts, too. **Vic Braden Tennis College** (www.vicbradentennis.com, 435-628-1068, 1-800-237-1068, Green Valley Spa and Resort, 1871 W. Canyon View Dr., St. George) offers multiday workshops, crash courses, and private lessons on indoor and outdoor courts.

River Rafting

Although not as epic as the Grand Canyon, the **Green River's Desolation Canyon** and the **Colorado River's Cataract Canyon** outside Moab are thrilling passages. For calmer waters, head for the **San Juan River** outside Bluff and Mexican Hat. The river-running season lasts from March or April through October.

Adrift Adventures, www.adrift.net, 435-259-3127, 1-800-874-4483, 53 W. 100 North, Moab. Offers guided white-water rafting (motorized or rowing) trips on the Green and Colorado Rivers, and jet-boat tours between Moab and Canyonlands.

Canyon Voyages Adventure Co., www.canyonvoyages.com, 435-259-6007, 1-800-733-6007, 211 N. Main St., Moab. Arranges calm-water and white-water rafting trips on the Colorado River and the Dolores River in Colorado.

Float trips on the San Juan River are excellent for first-time river runners. Sara Benson

Moki-Mac River Expeditions, www.mokimac.com, 1-800-284-7280, P.O. Box 71242, Salt Lake City, UT. With over 20 years' experience, Moki-Mac runs multiday white-water trips on the Green and Colorado Rivers and daylong introductory river-rafting trips, all starting from the town of Green River.

Navtec Expeditions, www.navtec.com, 435-259-7983, 1-800-833-1278, 321 N. Main St., Moab. Well-established tour company arranges white-water rafting trips and short calm-river floats on the Colorado, Green, and Dolores Rivers, plus rents rafts and equipment for DIY adventurers.

OARS, www.oars.com/utah, 209-736-4677, 1-800-346-6277, P.O. Box 67, Angels Camp, CA 95222. Renowned international tour company offers locally guided multiday trips on the Colorado, Green, and San Juan Rivers.

Red River Adventures, www.redriveradventures.com, 435-259-4046, 1-877-259-4046, 1140 S. Main St., Moab. Experienced outfitter offers a variety of trips on local rivers. Private trips available in wooden dories, the same kind used by 19th-century explorers.

Sheri Griffith Expeditions, www.griffithexp.com, 435-259-8229, 1-800-332-2439, P.O. Box 1324, Moab. Family-oriented tour operator offers a variety of white-water rafting trips (motorized or rowing) on the Green and Colorado Rivers, as well as Colorado's Yampa River. Ask about luxury, multisport, and women-only expeditions.

Wild River Expeditions, www.riversandruins.com, 1-800-422-7654, 101 Main St., Bluff. Experienced outfitter runs trips of a variety of lengths on the San Juan River with guides that emphasize natural history.

Rock Climbing

Most rock-climbing routes in southern Utah are outside Moab, with an enormous variety of climbs up slabs, cracks, and desert towers, and around Zion National Park, famed for its big-wall climbs and canyon bouldering. Spring and fall are the best seasons for rock-climbing in the desert. For DIY climbing gear and advice in Moab, visit **Pagan Mountaineering** (www.paganmountaineering.com, 435-259-1117, 59 S. Main St.) or **GearHeads**, (435-259-4327, 471 S. Main St.).

For details of climbing regulations and restrictions in national parks, contact **Arches, Capitol Reef, and Zion National Parks** (see "Parks and Natural Attractions," above); overnight bivouacs typically require wilderness permits, while daylong climbs usually don't. Outside St. George, **Snow Canyon State Park** (http://stateparks.utah.gov/parks/snow-canyon/, 435-628-2255, 1002 Snow Canyon Dr., Ivins) offers a few technical climbing routes.

Moab Desert Adventures, www.moabdesertadventures.com, 435-260-2404, 1-877-765-6622, 415 N. Main St., Moab. Long-running guide service offers basic to expert instruction, as well as guided climbs of towers and cracks. Female instructors host the popular three-day Chicks on Cracks climbing event in mid-November, and Splitter Camps attract both sexes during spring and fall.

Paragon Climbing, www.paragonclimbing.com, 435-673-1709, 1-888-412-5462, P.O. Box 2234, St. George. Professional guides operate rock-climbing and zipline trips and courses for all skill levels around southern Utah.

Red River Adventures, www.redriveradventures.com, 435-259-4046, 1-877-259-4046, 1140 S. Main St., Moab. River-running company offers half- and full-day rock climbing courses, including for women, and rafting-and-climbing combination trips.

Zion Adventure Company, www.zionadventures.com, 435-772-0990, Zion Outdoor Center, 868 Zion Park Blvd., Springdale. Organizes guided rock climbs and climbing camps and offers beginning to advanced climbing instruction.

Zion Rock & Mountain Guides, www.zionrockguides.com, 435-772-3303, 1458 Zion Park Blvd., Springdale. This multisport outfitter specializes in rock climbing, including guided tours, introductory to advanced courses, and technical skills clinics.

Running

The desert isn't hydration-friendly, but many joggers, marathoners, and triathletes use southern Utah's scenic byways and national park loop roads as training grounds. Trail runners will find plenty of wilderness routes to follow. Amateurs compete in regional races and events, including the **Canyonlands Half Marathon** (www.moabhalfmarathon.org, 435-259-4525) and the **Blue Mountain to Canyonlands Triathlon** (www.monticelloutah .org/activities, 435-587-2029) in March; the **Bryce Canyon Half Marathon and 5K Run/Walk** (brycecanyonhalfmarathon.com, 1-800-444-6689) in July; the **Bryce Canyon Rim Run** (www.rubysinn.com/run, 435-834-8023, 1-866-1-866-6616 ext. 7239) in August; **The Other Half Marathon** (www.moabhalfmarathon.org, 435-259-4525) and the **St. George Marathon** (www.stgeorgemarathon.com, 435-624-5850) in October; and **Springdale's Butch Cassidy 10K Run / 5K Walk** (www.zionpark.com/events, 1-888-518-7070) in November.

Skiing, Snowboarding, and Other Winter Sports

Most of the Olympic-worthy powder and downhill ski resorts are found farther north in Utah. However, there are limited opportunities for downhill and cross-country skiing, snowboarding, snowshoeing, snowmobiling, and sledding during winter here.

Brian Head, www.brianhead.com, 435-677-2035, 329 S. UT 23, Brian Head, UT. Near Cedar Breaks National Monument, Utah's highest-elevation ski resort has a variety of easy to expert runs on two mountains equipped with six lifts. Equipment rentals and lessons, snow tubing and terrain parks, and night skiing and snowboarding available.

Duck Creek Village, www.duckcreekvillage.com, 1-800-733-5263, off UT 14, Duck Creek Village, UT. Several rustic resorts west of Bryce Canyon like this one can arrange snowmobile rentals and tours, as well as point out cross-country ski trails.

Manti–La Sal National Forest, www.fs.fed.us/r4/mantilasal/, 435-259-7155, 435-259-7669, off US 191 south of Moab. The **La Sal Mountains** are a high-country escape for cross-country skiing, sledding, and some snowmobiling. Equipment rentals are available from Moab outfitters, including **GearHeads** (435-259-4327, 471 S. Main St.) and **Rim Cyclery** (435-259-5333, 1-888-304-8219, www.rimcyclery.com, 94 W. 100 North). **Tag-A-Long Expeditions** (www.tagalong.com, 435-259-8946, 1-800-453-3292, 452 N. Main St., Moab) handles overnight reservations at Nordic ski huts.

Ruby's Inn Nordic Center, www.rubysinn.com, 435-834-5341, 1-866-1-866-6616, 1000 S. US 63, Bryce. Cross-country skis and snowshoe rentals are available at the inn, from where groomed trails connect to others inside Bryce Canyon National Park. Guided snowshoe tours and cross-country ski races are held during the Bryce Canyon Winter Festival in February.

Spas

Advance reservations are essential at all spas.

Deep Canyon Adventure Spa, www.flanigans.com/spa, 435-772-3244, 1-800-765-7787, Flanigan's Inn, 428 Zion Park Blvd., Springdale. This modest hotel spa offers facials, body wraps, massage, and a meditative labyrinth looking onto red-rock cliffs.

Desert Mountain Spa, www.mtpeale.com/dmspa, 435-686-2284, 1-888-687-3253, Mount Peale Resort, 1415 E. UT 46, at mile post 14.1, Old La Sal. In the Manti–La Sal Mountains outside Moab, this rustic mountain lodge offers a small menu of relaxing services, including several styles of massage, facials, salt scrubs, and citrus body polishes.

Green Valley Resort, www.greenvalleyspa.com, 435-628-8060, 1-800-237-1068, 1871 W. Canyon View Dr., St. George. Holistic treatments include aromatherapy, herbal wraps, reflexology, and chakra analysis, as well as more traditional body work and facials. Access to the swimming pools, tennis courts, and fitness center entails a surcharge.

Sagestone at Red Mountain Spa, www.redmountainspa.com, 435-673-4905, 1-800-690-9215, 1275 E. Red Mountain Circle, Ivins. In a red-rock canyon outside St. George, this spa resort offers treatments for both sexes, including massage, body treatments, skin care, and salon services. There's an exercise room and swimming pool.

Swimming

Butch Cassidy's King World Waterpark, www.butchcassidyskingworldwaterpark.com, 435-259-2837, 1500 N. US 191, Moab. Open from Memorial Day through Labor Day, this humongous water park has multiple pools, waterslides, and paddleboats on a natural spring-fed pond.

Hurricane City Pool, 435-635-0256, 750 N. 100 West, Hurricane. This municipal lap pool is open May through Labor Day; call for open-swim hours.

Sand Hollow Aquatic Center, www.sgcity.org/swimming/sgshac.php, 435-634-5938, 1144 N. Lava Flow Dr., St. George. Indoor facilities include a family-friendly leisure pool and a competition-size pool with diving boards; call for open-swim hours.

St. George City Pool & Hydrotube, 435-627-4584, 250 E. 700 South, St. George. This outdoor municipal pool is open May through Labor Day; call for open-swim hours.

Zion National Park, www.nps.gov/zion, 435-772-3256, Springdale. Although swimming is not permitted in the park's Emerald Pools, it's allowed in the Virgin River, best accessed at Watchman Campground. Beware of swift cold currents and flash floods.

Zion Tubing, 435-772-8823, www.ziontubing.com, Tsunami Juice & Java, 180 Zion Park Blvd., Springdale. From mid-May to early September, you can drift downstream from Springdale to Zion National Park on the Virgin River in an inner tube. It's typically a two-hour trip, including a shuttle ride back to town.

Tours and Guided Adventures

In addition to guided trips offered by outdoor outfitters, there are many tour agencies offering overland 4WD trips, scenic flights, and more unusual tours.

Bryce Canyon Airlines & Helicopters, www.rubysinn.com/bryce-canyon-airlines, 435-834-8060, 1000 S. US 63, Bryce. Flies around the Bryce Canyon region and to Zion National Park, the Grand Canyon, and Monument Valley.

Canyonlands by Night and Day, www.canyonlandsbynight.com, 435-259-2767, 1-800-394-9978, 1861 N. US 191, Moab. Scenic daytime tours, sunset dinner cruises, and after-dark sound-and-light shows along the Colorado River on jet boats and slower craft.

Canyonlands Field Institute, www.canyonlandsfieldinst.org, 435-259-7750, 1-800-860-5262, 1320 S. US 191, Moab. Natural history association operates educational hiking and van tours around Arches and Canyonlands National Parks.

Conservation Adventures, www.plateaurestoration.org, 435-259-7733, 1-866-202-1847, P.O. Box 1363, Moab. Nonprofit organization dedicated to protecting and restoring native wildlife habitats on the Colorado Plateau runs land-based and river-running tours focused on natural history and geology, plus volunteer vacations.

Dreamland Safari Tours, www.dreamlandtours.net, 435-644-5506, 515 S. 475 East, Kanab. Family-owned 4WD tour company offers customized trips—for example, to visit rock-art petroglyphs, explore slot canyons, or do landscape photography.

Elite Motorcycle Tours, www.elitemotorcycletours.com, 435-259-7621, 1-888-778-0358, 1310 Murphy Lane, Moab. Offers guided motorcycle tours into Moab's canyon country, including off-road adventures for experienced riders.

Escape Goat Tours, www.utahpackgoats.com, 435-826-4652, P.O Box 532, Escalante, UT 84726. This unusual company arranges pack trips in Escalante's canyons from March to October and in the mountains during summer, all taken with goats as porters.

Excursions of Escalante, www.excursions-escalante.com, 1-800-839-7567, 125 E. Main St., Escalante. Locally based outfitter arranges guided hiking, backpacking, and canyoneering tours and photo safaris.

Far Out Expeditions, www.faroutexpeditions.com, 435-672-2294, 7th St. E. at Mulberry Ave., Bluff. Established outfitter guides hiking, trekking, and 4WD tours around Cedar Mesa and beyond.

Hondoo Rivers & Trails, www.hondoo.com, 435-425-3519, 1-800-332-2696, P.O. Box 98, Torrey. Professional outfitter runs 4WD tours and photography safaris around Capitol Reef country, Escalante canyons, and the San Rafael Swell outside Green River.

M&S Aero, www.msaero-bryce.com, 435-679-8440, 435-559-8440, UT 12, Tropic. Fly more affordably with a retired National Park Service employee as your pilot and tour guide to Bryce Canyon.

Navtec Expeditions, www.navtec.com, 435-259-7983, 1-800-833-1278, 321 N. Main St., Moab. Organizes multiday jeep tours in the backcountry of Canyonlands National Park from March through October.

Paria Outpost and Outfitters, www.paria.com, 928-691-1047, US 89, mile marker 21, Big Water. Guided tours and shuttle services for independent travelers exploring Paria Canyon, Vermillion Cliffs, and Grand Staircase–Escalante National Monument.

Red Rock 'n Llama Tours, 1-877-955-2627, www.redrocknllamas.com, 80 Roadrunner Rd., Sedona, AZ. Based in Boulder, this eco-conscious outfitter runs hiking trips into the outback around Escalante with llamas as trekking porters.

Skydive Moab, www.skydivemoab.com, 435-259-5867, Moab Airport / Canyonlands Field, US 191, Moab. Arizona outfitter organizes skydiving trips from March through mid-November.

Slickrock Air Guides, www.slickrockairguides.com, 435-259-6216, 1-866-259-1626, P.O. Box 901, Moab. Offers flight-seeing tours of Canyonlands and Monument Valley.

Tag-A-Long Expeditions, www.tagalong.com, 435-259-8946, 1-800-453-3292, 452 N. Main St., Moab. Experienced outfitter organizes half- and full-day 4WD trips around Canyonlands, with river-running and jet-boat tour combos offered. Ask about hot-air balloon rides.

Wild Hare Expeditions, www.color-country.net/~thehare, 435-425-3999, 1-888-304-4273, 116 W. Main St., Torrey. Local guides lead hiking, backpacking, and 4WD tours of the Capitol Reef backcountry.

Zion Canyon Field Institute, www.zionpark.org, 1-800-635-3959, Zion National Park, Springdale. Zion Natural History Association schedules family-friendly tours, geology and wildlife walks, photo safaris, and geology trips around the park.

SHOPPING

Art, Antiques, and Collectibles

For more art galleries, turn to the "Culture" section, above.

Ancestor Square, 435-628-1658, Main St. and St. George Blvd., St. George. This shady downtown courtyard on the edge of the historic district has a few shops specializing in art and crafts, design, home decor, and unique made-in-Utah items.

Canyon Offerings, www.canyonofferings.com, 435-772-3456, 1-800-788-2443, 933 Zion Park Blvd., Springdale. Small shop carries over 10,000 handcrafted works, including jewelry, sculptures, and paintings by Southwestern artists.

Cowboy Collectibles, www.cowboycollectiblesutah.com, 435-676-8060, 57 N. Main St., Panguitch. An enormous showcase for Western memorabilia, this shop houses a collection of saddles, spurs and bits, cowboy boots, and vintage furniture and clothes, including from movie stars like Roy Rogers.

Desert Wolf Gallery, 435-826-4210, Moqui Motel, 480 W. Main St., Escalante. This motel gift shop showcases local artisans and cowboys, as well as Native American potters and jewelry makers; the selection is small but stimulating.

Manzanita Trading Co., http://manzanitatrading.home.att.net, 435-772-0123, 205 Zion Park Blvd., Springdale. In the middle of Moab, this local art gallery and gift shop sells paintings, sculpted metalwork, pottery, jewelry, blown glass, and photography.

Nature Sounds, www.tribalsounds.com, 435-826-4700, 450 W. Main St., Escalante. These Native American-style drums are handcrafted from elk, buffalo, and deer. It's worth a browse just to see the fine workmanship.

Old Bryce Town Shops, www.rubysinn.com, 435-834-5341, Ruby's Inn, 1000 S. US 63, Bryce. Especially if you've got kids, these faux Old West storefronts are worth a stroll. Don't miss the rock shop.

Virgin Goods, 435-635-7730, 3 E. UT 9, Virgin. Near the Kolob Road turnoff, this quirky store sells antique and vintage pieces collected from around the Southwest and the world, including Navajo jewelry, Pueblo pottery, and retro clothing.

Western Hills, www.westernhills.com, 435-644-2390, 288 W. Center St., Kanab. Sells bookends and sculptures made from locally quarried, rainbow-colored sandstone.

Books, Clothing, Maps, Gifts, and Outdoor Gear

At national park visitor centers in Utah, including at Zion, Bryce Canyon, Capitol Reef, and Arches National Parks, cooperative natural history associations stock excellent books on natural history, outdoor activities, and photography, as well as high-quality maps, posters, CDs and DVDs, and other souvenirs.

Arches Book Company, http://arches.booksense.com, 435-259-0782, 78 N. Main St., Moab. With a full espresso bar, this alternative-minded bookstore sells thought-provoking new titles in all genres.

Back of Beyond Books, www.backofbeyondbooks.com, 435-259-5154, 1-800-700-2859, 83 N. Main St., Moab. Stop by this small independent bookstore for regional interest and natural history titles, rare and signed first editions, guidebooks, and maps.

Escalante Outfitters, www.escalanteoutfitters.com, 435-826-4266, 310 W. Main St., Escalante. This crowded shop run by an outdoor adventure company is full of performance clothing, active footwear, and gear and supplies for active pursuits.

Escalante Rock Shop, www.escalanterockshop.com, 435-826-4796, 475 N. Wide Hollow Rd., Escalante. More of a roadside attraction, this rock shop, about a mile west of town near Escalante Petrified Forest State Park, carries a kaleidoscopic assortment of minerals, petrified food, and dinosaur bones.

The Moab Rock Shop is stuffed full of geological gems and antiques. Sara Benson

Escalantees, www.escalantees.com, 435-826-4796, 23 W. Main St., Escalante. Unique, cool, and durable souvenir T-shirts in a rainbow of colors and themed to fit the region, from Ancestral Puebloan rock-art designs to UT 12 highway logos.

GearHeads, 435-259-4327, 471 S. Main St., Moab. One of the premier, long-running outdoors stores in Moab, it's built for climbers, with walls of rope, racks of shoes, and an insane collection of water bottles. Rely on the expert staff's advice.

Hollow Mountain Gas & Grocery, 435-542-3298, 2 UT 95 N., Hanksville. Get your bait, local maps, T-shirts, and kitschy souvenirs at a gas station and market blasted out of the side of a humongous rock. At least take a photo, folks.

Moab Rock Shop, 435-259-7312, 600 N. Main St., Moab. You can't miss the antique prospecting equipment tossed out front. Browse tables full of nature's geological gems, including fossils, crystals, rare minerals, and dinosaur bones, at this enormous rock shop.

Pagan Mountaineering, www.paganmountaineering.com, 435-295-1117, 59 S. Main St., Moab. Pagan sells everything to outfit rock climbers from head to toe, as well as river sandals, logo hoodies, gloves, and backpacks. Name-brand gear includes Mountain Hardwear, Patagonia, and Prana.

Utah Canyons Desert Store, www.utahcanyons.com, 435-826-4967, 325 W. Main St., Escalante. This outdoor outfitter carries activity guidebooks and customizes topographic maps printed on waterproof paper with handy annotations for trailheads, routes, and mileages.

Willow Canyon Outdoor Company, www.willowcanyon.com, 435-644-8884, 263 S. 100 East, Kanab. Carries a high-quality, hand-picked selection of outdoor clothing and gear for both sexes, including name-brand backpacking and camping gear. The attached espresso bar and bookstore sells travel books, regional interest titles, and maps.

Native American Trading Posts and Galleries

Cow Canyon Trading Post, 435-672-2208, 163 Mission Rd., Bluff. In a picturesque historic adobe building, this small but select trading post has a cool, stone-floored showroom filled with Navajo and Zuni rugs, pottery, baskets, and jewelry.

Hogan Trading Company, 435-259-8118, 100 S. Main St., Moab. Unlike shops that deal strictly in traditional wares, this place carries contemporary sculptures, innovative Pueblo pottery, and one-of-a-kind handmade jewelry.

San Juan Inn Trading Post, www.sanjuaninn.net, 1-800-447-2022, San Juan Inn, UT 163, Mexican Hat. Just outside the Navajo Nation boundary, this riverside motel has an authentic trading post that deals in Navajo rugs, jewelry, pottery, and baskets.

Tribal Arts Gallery, www.tribalartszion.com, 435-772-3353, 291 Zion Park Blvd., Springdale. Outside Zion National Park, this culturally sensitive shop carries an extensive selection of beaded and metalwork jewelry, baskets, kachinas, fetishes, sandpaintings, Navajo rugs, and Pueblo pottery.

Twin Rocks Trading Post, www.twinrocks.com, 435-672-2341, 1-800-526-3448, 913 E. Navajo Twins Dr., Bluff. Curated as if it were a museum, this top-notch trading post deals in all kinds of artisan crafts, from turquoise jewelry to Navajo rugs and pottery, and from folk art to fetishes. Drop by to admire the Native American handiwork and chat with the knowledgeable staff.

The beautiful Twin Rocks Trading Post is a veritable museum of Native American art and artisan crafts.
Courtesy Twin Rocks Trading Post

8

Information

Practical Matters

What follows is essential information for making a visit to the Four Corners region more enjoyable, for both planning your trip and while on your vacation. This chapter briefly covers the following topics:

AMBULANCE, FIRE, AND POLICE

Dial 911 in the event of an emergency (ambulance, fire, or police) in major towns and cities. Most rural counties and Native American reservations have basic emergency services. The following are some helpful telephone numbers for emergency and nonemergency situations. If you have trouble reaching the right agency, dial "0" for operator assistance.

LEFT: *Follow the cowboy to find the helpful visitor center by the railroad tracks in Mancos, Colorado.* Sara Benson

Poison Control

Arizona	1-800-362-0101
Colorado	1-800-332-3073
New Mexico	1-800-432-6866
Utah	1-800-222-1222

Police (nonemergency)

Albuquerque, NM	505-242-2677
Aztec, NM	505-334-6622
Blanding, UT	435-678-2916
Cedar City, UT	435-586-2956
Cortez, CO	970-565-8441
Durango, CO	970-375-4700
Farmington, NM	505-599-1070
Flagstaff, AZ	928-774-1414
Gallup, NM	505-863-9365
Grants, NM	505-287-4404
Green River, UT	435-564-8111
Holbrook, NM	928-524-3991
Kanab, UT	435-644-5854
Kayenta, AZ	928-697-5600
Kingman, AZ	928-753-2191
Moab, UT	435-259-8938
Navajo Nation (Window Rock, AZ)	928-871-6581
Page, AZ	928-645-4355
Pagosa Springs, CO	970-264-4151
Panguitch, UT	435-676-2678
Silverton, CO	970-387-5531
Springdale, UT	435-634-5730
St. George, UT	435-634-5001
Williams, AZ	928-635-4461
Winslow, AZ	928-289-2431

Rape Crisis Centers

Albuquerque Rape Crisis Center, www.rape-crisis.org, 505-266-7711, 1025 Hermosa St. SE, Albuquerque, NM 87108

Northern Arizona Center Against Sexual Assault (NACASA), www.victimwitness flagstaff.org/nacasa.htm, 928-779-6163, 5200 E. Cortland Blvd., Flagstaff, AZ 86004

Seekhaven, 435-259-2229, P.O. Box 729, Moab, UT 84532

Sexual Assault Services Organization (SASO), www.durangosaso.org, 970-352-7273, P.O. Box 2723, Durango, CO 81302

State Police and Highway Patrol
Arizona Highway Patrol
Flagstaff, Grand Canyon, and Page areas	928-773-3608
Holbrook area	928-524-6177
Kingman area	928-753-5552

Colorado State Patrol
Cortez and Mancos areas	970-564-9556
Durango area	970-385-1675
Pagosa Springs area	970-731-0039

New Mexico State Police
Anywhere in the state	1-888-442-6677

Utah Highway Patrol
Cedar City, Panguitch, and Escalante areas	435-865-1970
Moab area	435-259-5441
St. George, Hurricane, and Kanab areas	435-628-1966
Torrey area	435-896-2780

AREA CODES, ZIP CODES, AND LOCAL GOVERNMENT

In addition to major towns and cities, there are many Native American reservations in the Four Corners region. Politically and legally, each reservation is a sovereign nation led by a tribal government and has its own police force. For information on specific destinations in the Four Corners region, call the following numbers or contact the relevant tourist information organization instead (see "Tourist Information," below).

CITY, TOWN, OR RESERVATION	TELEPHONE	ZIP CODE
Albuquerque, NM	505-768-3555	87103
Aztec, NM	505-334-7600	87410
Blanding, UT	435-678-2791	84511
Cedar City, UT	435-586-2950	84720
Cortez, CO	970-565-3402	81321
Durango, CO	970-375-5000	81301
Farmington, NM	505-599-1100	87401
Flagstaff, AZ	928-774-5281	86001
Gallup, NM	505-863-1254	87305
Grants, NM	505-287-7927	87020
Green River, UT	435-564-3448	84525
Holbrook, AZ	928-524-6225	86025
Hopi Nation (Kykotsmovi, AZ)	928-734-3000	86039
Kanab, UT	435-644-2534	84741
Kingman, AZ	928-753-5561	86401
Mancos, CO	970-533-7725	81328
Moab, UT	435-259-5121	84532
Navajo Nation (Window Rock, AZ)	928-871-6000	86515
Page, AZ	928-645-8861	86040

Pagosa Springs, UT	970-264-4151	86040
Silverton, CO	970-387-5522	81433
Springdale, UT	435-772-3434	84767
St. George, UT	435-634-5800	84770
Williams, AZ	928-635-4451	86046
Winslow, AZ	928-289-2422	86047
Zuni Nation (Zuni Pueblo, NM)	505-782-7000	87327

BANKS

The Four Corners region is remote. You'll find national and state banks with 24-hour ATMs only in the biggest cities, towns, and tourist centers. Smaller places, especially along Route 66 and on Native American reservations, often do not have banks with 24-hour ATMs, although you may find an ATM inside a gas station or convenience store. All tribal casinos have ATMs, but the surcharges for withdrawing money using your bank card or credit card are typically much higher than at banks. Instead, try to withdraw cash in major cities to carry you through at least a few days.

BIBLIOGRAPHY

What follows is not an exhaustive list of worthy books written about the Four Corners area. It is a short list of suggested readings that will introduce you to Native American nations, natural history, diverse cultures, and artistic and religious traditions, as well as practical guides for outdoor recreation, interesting travel narratives, and inspirational photographic studies of the area. You'll find more titles to browse at independent bookstores around the region (see the "Shopping" sections of earlier chapters in this book).

Art and Cooking

Colton, Harold S., *Hopi Kachina Dolls.* Albuquerque: University of New Mexico Press, 1970. 160 pp., illus., photos, $18.95.

Dalrymple, Larry. *Indian Basketmakers of the Southwest.* Santa Fe: Museum of New Mexico Press, 2000. 156 pp., photos, $29.95.

Frank, Lois Ellen. *Foods of the Southwest Indian Nations.* Berkeley, CA: Ten Speed Press, 2002. 208 pp., $35.

Hayes, Allen, and John Blom. *Southwest Pottery: Anasazi to Zuni.* Flagstaff, AZ: Northland Publishing, 1996. 189 pp., photos, $21.95.

Indian Arts and Crafts Association. *Collecting Authentic Indian Arts and Crafts: Traditional Works of the Southwest.* Zuni, NM: Council for Indigenous Arts and Culture, 1999. 127 pp., photos, $16.95.

Kaufman, Alice, and Christopher Selser. *Navajo Weaving Tradition: 1650 to the Present.* Tulsa, OK: Council Oak Books, 1999. 834 pp., photos, $29.95.

Kavena, Juanita Tiger. *Hopi Cookery.* Tucson: University of Arizona Press. 109 pp., $15.95.

McManis, Kent. *Zuni Fetishes and Carvings: The Complete Guide.* Tucson, AZ: Rio Nuevo Publishers, 2004. 144 pp., photos, $14.95.

Rodee, Marian E. *One Hundred Years of Navajo Rugs.* Albuquerque: University of New Mexico Press, 1995. 199 pp., illus., photos, out of print.

Simpson, Georgia Kennedy. *A Guide to Indian Jewelry of the Southwest*. Tucson, AZ: Western National Parks Association, 1999. 46 pp., photos, $4.95.

Trimble, Stephen. *Talking with the Clay: The Art of Pueblo Pottery*. Santa Fe, NM: School of American Research Press. 128 pp., photos, $17.95.

Wright, Barton. *Hopi Kachinas: The Complete Guide to Collecting Kachina Dolls*. Flagstaff, AZ: Northland Publishing, 1977. 139 pp., photos, $14.95.

Autobiographies, Biographies, and Memoirs

Benedek, Emily. *Beyond the Four Corners of the World: A Navajo Woman's Journey*. Norman: University of Oklahoma Press, 1998. 343 pp.

Berke, Arnold, and A. Vertikoff. *Mary Colter: Architect of the Southwest*. New York: Princeton Architectural Press, 2003. 320 pp., illus., photos, $24.95.

Cahalan, James M. *Edward Abbey: A Life*. Tucson: University of Arizona Press, 2003. 357 pp., photos, $19.95.

Cumming, Dorothy. *Before the Roads Were Paved: Living with the Navajos at Canyon de Chelly, 1950–1952*. Victoria, BC, Canada: Trafford Publishing, 2006. 125 pp., $17.

Hirst, Stephen. *I Am the Grand Canyon: The Story of the Havusupai People*. Grand Canyon, AZ: Grand Canyon Association, 2007. 276 pp., photos, $18.95.

Iliff, Flora Gregg. *People of the Blue Water: A Record of Life Among the Walapai and Havasupai Indians*. Tucson: University of Arizona Press, 1985. 288 pp., $17.95.

Leavengood, Betty. *Grand Canyon Women: Lives Shaped by Landscape*. Grand Canyon, AZ: Grand Canyon Association, 2004. 297 pp., photos, $18.95.

Poling-Kempes, Lesley. *The Harvey Girls: Women Who Opened the West*. New York: Marlowe & Co., 1994. 252 pp., photos, $14.95.

Polingaysi, Qoyawayma, as told to Vada F. Carlson. *No Turning Back: A Hopi Woman's Struggle to Live in Two Worlds*. Albuquerque: University of New Mexico Press, 1977. 188 pp., $17.95.

Powell, John Wesley. *Exploration of the Colorado River and Its Environs*. Grand Canyon, AZ: Grand Canyon Association. 400 pp., $13.

Richardson, Gladwell. *Navajo Trader*. Tucson: University of Arizona Press, 1986. 244 pp., $22.95.

Stegner, Wallace. *Beyond the Hundredth Meridian: John Wesley Powell and the Second Opening of the West*. New York: Penguin, 1992. 496 pp., $16.

Wallis, Michael. *Route 66: The Mother Road*. New York: St Martin's/Griffin, 2001. 288 pp., photos, $19.95.

Cultural Studies and History

Brown, Dee. *Bury My Heart at Wounded Knee: An Indian History of the American West*. New York: Henry Holt, 2007. 512 pp., photos, $16.

Brown, Kenneth A. *Four Corners: History, Land, and People of the Desert Southwest*. New York: Harper Perennial, 1996. 400 pp., photos, $14.

Childs, Craig. *House of Rain: Tracking a Vanished Civilization Across the American Southwest*. New York: Little, Brown, 2007. 512 pp., $24.99.

Childs, Craig. *Soul of Nowhere*. New York: Back Bay Books, 2003. 240 pp., $18.99.

Farmer, Jared. *Glen Canyon Dammed: Inventing Lake Powell and the Canyon Country*. Tucson: University of Arizona Press, 1999. 312 pp., photos, $17.95.

Fontana, Bernard L. *A Guide to Contemporary Southwest Indians*. Tucson, AZ: Western National Parks Association, 1999. 96 pp., $10.95.

Keller, Robert H., and Michael F. Turek. *American Indians and National Parks*. Tucson: University of Arizona Press. 319 pp., $22.95.

Krakauer, Jon. *Under the Banner of Heaven: A Story of Violent Faith*. New York: Anchor Books, 2004. 400 pp., photos, $14.95.

McClain, Sally. *Navajo Weapon: The Navajo Code Talkers*. Tucson, AZ: Rio Nuevo Publishers, 2002. 300 pp., photos, $16.95.

McPherson, Robert S. *Sacred Land, Sacred View: Navajo Perceptions of the Four Corners*. Salt Lake City: Signature Books, 1992. 152 pp., photos, $8.95.

Moore, MariJo. *Genocide of the Mind: New Native American Writing*. New York: Nation Books, 2003. 352 pp., $16.95.

Pyne, Stephen J. *How the Canyon Became Grand: A Short History*. New York: Penguin, 1999. 240 pp., photos, $15.

Reisner, Marc. *Cadillac Desert: The American West and Its Disappearing Water*. New York: Penguin, 1993. 608 pp., $18.

Waters, Frank. *The Book of the Hopi*. New York: Penguin, 1977. 384 pp., illus., $16.

Fiction, Poetry, and Literary Anthologies

Bitsui, Sherwin. *Shapeshift*. Tucson: University of Arizona Press, 2003. 65 pp., $15.95.

Courlander, Harold. *The Fourth World of the Hopis: The Epic Story of the Hopi Indians as Preserved in Their Legends and Traditions*. Albuquerque: University of New Mexico Press, 1987. 239 pp., illus., $17.95.

Ellis, Rueben, ed. *Stories and Stone: Writing the Ancestral Homeland*. Tucson: University of Arizona Press, 2004. 244 pp., $19.95.

Erdoes, Richard, and Alfonso Ortiz, eds. *American Indian Myths and Legends*. New York: Pantheon, 1985. 544 pp., $18.

Gross, Matthew Barrett. *The Glen Canyon Reader*. Tucson: University of Arizona Press, 2003. 201 pp., $17.95.

Hershman, John. *I Swallow Turquoise for Courage*. Tucson: University of Arizona Press, 2007. 96 pp., $15.95.

Hillerman, Tony. *Dance Hall of the Dead*. New York: HarperTorch, 2004. 272 pp., $7.99.

Meléndez, A. Gabriel, M. Jane Young, Patricia Moore, and Patrick Pynes, eds. *The Multicultural Southwest: A Reader*. Tucson: University of Arizona Press, 2001. 294 pp., $24.95.

Ruess, Edward. *A Vagabond for Beauty / Wilderness Journals*. Layton, UT: Gibbs Smith, 2002. 448 pp., $29.95.

Various eds. *Blue Mesa Review*. Albuquerque: University of New Mexico, Creative Writing Program. $12 per issue.

Zolbrod, Paul G. *Diné Bahane': The Navajo Creation Story*. Albuquerque: University of New Mexico Press, 1987. 443 pp., $21.95.

Natural History and Field Guides

Baldridge, W. Scott. *Geology of the American Southwest: A Journey through Two Billion Years of Plate-Tectonic History*. Cambridge, MA: Cambridge University Press, 2004. 296 pp., illus. $34.99.

Cook, Terri, and Lon Abbott. *Hiking the Grand Canyon's Geology*. Seattle, WA: Mountaineers Books, 2004. 304 pp., photos, $16.95.

Fagan, Damian. *Canyon Country Wildflowers*. Guilford, CT: Falcon, 1998. 192 pp., photos, $19.95.

Grant, Campbell. *Canyon de Chelly: Its People and Rock Art*. Tucson: University of Arizona Press, 1977. 290 pp., photos, $19.95.

Hopkins, Ralph Lee. *Hiking the Southwest's Geology: Four Corners Region*. Seattle, WA: Mountaineers Books, 2003. 272 pp., illus., $16.95.

National Audubon Society. *National Audubon Society Field Guide to the Southwestern States*. New York: Knopf, 1999. 448 pp., illus., photos, $19.95.

Noble, David Grant. *Ancient Ruins of the Southwest: An Archaeological Field Guide*. Flagstaff, AZ: Northland Publishing, 2000. 160 pp., $15.95.

Patterson, Alex. *A Field Guide to Rock Art Symbols of the Greater Southwest*. Boulder, CO: Johnson Books, 1992. 256 pp., illus., $17.50.

Sprinkel, Douglas. *Geology of Utah's Parks and Monuments*. Page, AZ: Glen Canyon Natural History Association, 562 pp., illus., $34.95.

Whitney, Stephen. *A Field Guide to the Grand Canyon*. Seattle, WA: Mountaineers Books, 1996. 269 pp., illus., photos, $19.95.

Williams, David B. *A Naturalist's Guide to Canyon Country*. Guilford, CT: Falcon, 2000. 192 pp., illus., photos, $22.95.

Photographic Studies

Bryant, Kathleen. *The Four Corners: Timeless Lands of the Southwest*. Flagstaff, AZ: Northland Publishing, 2003. 64 pp., photos, $9.95.

Strutin, Michael, and George H. H. Huey. *Chaco: A Cultural Legacy*. Tucson, AZ: Western National Parks Association, 1994. 64 pp., photos, $9.95.

Chesher, Greer, and Michael Plyler. *Zion Canyon: A Storied Land*. Tucson: University of Arizona Press, 2007. 96 pp., photos, $14.95.

Decourten, Frank, and John Telford. *Shadows of Time: The Geology of Bryce Canyon National Park*. Bryce, UT: Bryce Canyon Natural History Association, 1994. 155 pp., $12.95.

Dutton, Bertha P. *American Indians of the Southwest*. Albuquerque: University of New Mexico Press, 1983. 317 pp., $21.95.

Eves, Robert L. *Water, Rock, and Time: The Geologic Story of Zion National Park*. Springdale, UT: Zion Natural History Association, 2005. 132 pp., photos, $19.95.

Murray, John A. *Cinema Southwest: An Illustrated Guide to the Movies and Their Locations*. Flagstaff, AZ: Northland Publishing, 2000. 161 pp., photos, $21.95.

Nichols, Tad, and Gary Ladd. *Glen Canyon: Images of a Lost World*. Page, AZ: Glen Canyon Natural History Association. 176 pp., photos, $29.95.

Simonelli, Jeanne M. *Crossing Between Worlds: The Navajos of Canyon de Chelly*. Santa Fe, NM: SAR Press, 1997. 118 pp., photos, $19.95.

Strom, Stephen E., and Laura Tohe. *Tséyi' / Deep in the Rock: Reflections on Canyon de Chelly*. Tucson: University of Arizona Press, 2005. 72 pp., photos, $15.

Suran, William C. *The Kolb Brothers of the Grand Canyon*. Grand Canyon, AZ: Grand Canyon Association, 1991. 60 pp., photos, $7.95.

Williams, Brooke, and Chris Noble. *Escalante: The Best Kind of Nothing*. Tucson: University of Arizona. 96 pp., photos, $14.95.

Travel Guides and Literature

Abbey, Edward. *Desert Solitaire: A Season in the Wilderness*. New York: Ballantine Books, 1985. 352 pp., $7.99.

Benson, Sara. *Road Trip: Route 66*. Oakland, CA: Lonely Planet Publications, 2003. 64 pp., $10.

Hillerman, Tony, and Laurence Linford. *Tony Hillerman's Navajoland: Hideouts, Haunts and Havens in the Joe Leaphorn and Jim Chee Mysteries*. Salt Lake City: University of Utah Press, 2005. 312 pp., maps, photos, $19.95.

Meloy, Ellen. *Raven's Exile: A Season on the Green River*. Tucson: University of Arizona Press, 2003. 256 pp., $17.95.

Myers, Thomas M. *Over the Edge: Death in the Grand Canyon*. Flagstaff, AZ: Puma Press, 2001. 408 pp., $22.95.

Padget, Martin. *Indian Country: Travels in the American Southwest 1840–1935*. Albuquerque: University of New Mexico Press, 2006. 266 pp. $37.95.

Preston, Douglas. *Talking to the Ground: One Family's Journey on Horseback across the Sacred Land of the Navajo*. Albuquerque: University of New Mexico Press, 1996. 284 pp., $19.95.

Rittenhouse, Jack D. *A Guide Book to Route 66*. Albuquerque: University of New Mexico Press, 1989. 128 pp, illus., $7.95.

Roberts, David. *In Search of the Old Ones*. New York: Simon & Schuster, 1997. 272 pp., $14.

DISABILITY SERVICES

Services for travelers with disabilities are unreliable in the Four Corners region. If you're renting a car, don't forget to bring along your disabled parking placard from home. Rental cars with hand controls are available from national car-rental agencies, but reserve them well in advance. The same advice applies for the limited number of ADA-accessible rooms available at motels and hotels. For wheelchair-accessible van rentals, **Wheelchair Getaways** (1-800-642-2042, www.wheelchair-getaways.com) has locations in Arizona, Utah, New Mexico, Colorado, and Nevada (if you're flying into Las Vegas).

In major towns and cities, you can expect dropped curbs and wheelchair ramps on public streets and buildings, including at most motels and hotels, some restaurants, and many museums and popular attractions. Some public buses have wheelchair-accessible lifts. Taxicab companies sometimes can provide a wheelchair-accessible vehicle if you call ahead. More specific information about accessible travel and disability services can be obtained from local tourist information offices (see "Tourist Information," below).

Typically, the farther you get away from the urban centers, the less infrastructure there will be to aid those with disabilities, especially those who are mobility-impaired. Notable exceptions are sites administered by federal agencies, such as the National Park Service (NPS). Developed areas of national parks have many of the same amenities and services for travelers with disabilities as cities do, including dropped curbs, paved sidewalks, wheelchair-accessible public transport, and assisted-listening devices and braille signage. For accessibility details about specific parks, consult the NPS Web site (www.nps.gov).

Governmental, nonprofit, and private organizations may be great resources for figuring out the practicalities of accessible travel and finding adaptive outdoor adventures. **Access Anything** (www.accessanything.net, 970-846-9859, P.O. Box 880763, Steamboat Springs,

CO 80488) publishes the *Access Anything: Colorado* guidebook ($15.95). The **Access Utah Network** (www.accessut.state.ut.us, 1-800-333-8824, relay line 711, 155 S. 300 West, Suite 100, Salt Lake City, UT 84101) is that state's official information agency for those with disabilities. It provides handy links to adaptive outdoor adventure outfitters, paratransit services, and wheelchair-accessible van rentals on its Web site. The **Society for Accessible Travel and Hospitality** (www.sath.org, 212-447-7284, 347 Fifth Ave., Suite 605, New York, NY 10016), a worldwide advocacy group for travelers with disabilities, provides consumer-oriented information, travel tips, and destination advice.

GUIDED TOURS

Wherever you go in the Four Corners region, there are tour guides and outfitters waiting to show you everything the area has to offer. Their tours range from two-hour trail rides to multiday, multisport adventures. For longer and/or more expensive tours, make reservations well in advance. But you can often make same-day bookings for shorter, more popular tours, especially ranger-led activities in national parks. The best guided tours are listed under the relevant activity subheadings in the regional destination chapters.

HOSPITALS

The quality of medical services in the Four Corners area varies erratically. In smaller towns and on Native American reservations, 24-hour emergency services may be extremely limited or nonexistent. Albuquerque, New Mexico, Flagstaff, Arizona, and St. George, Utah, have the best medical facilities in the region.

Before leaving home, check with your health-insurance provider to see if you're covered for medical emergencies that may occur on the road, and to ask about any necessary procedures for preauthorizing treatment. If you are uninsured (or underinsured) for health-care services away from home, consider purchasing additional travel medical insurance before your trip. Auto clubs and credit cards may offer discount travel insurance plans for members.

Arizona

Flagstaff Medical Center, 928-779-3366, 1200 N. Beaver St., Flagstaff, AZ 86001

Fort Defiance Indian Hospital, 928-729-8000, P.O. Box 649, Fort Defiance, AZ 86504

Grand Canyon Walk-In Medical & Dental Clinic, 928-638-2551, Clinic Rd., Grand Canyon Village, AZ 86023

Kingman Regional Medical Center, 928-757-2101, 3269 Stockton Hill Rd., Kingman, AZ 86409

Page Hospital, 928-645-2424, 501 N. Navajo Dr., Page, AZ 86040

Colorado

Mercy Regional Medical Center, 970-247-4311, 1-800-345-2516, 1010 Three Springs Blvd., Durango, CO 81301

New Mexico

Rehoboth McKinley Christian Health Care Services Hospital, 505-863-7000, 1901 Red Rock Dr., Gallup, NM 87301

San Juan Regional Medical Center, 505-325-5011, 801 W. Maple St., Farmington, NM 87401

University of New Mexico Hospital, 505-272-2411, 2211 Lomas Blvd. NE, Albuquerque, NM 87106

Utah

Allen Memorial Hospital, 435-259-7191, 719 W. 400 North, Moab, UT 84532

Dixie Regional Medical Center, 435-251-1000, 1380 E. Medical Center Dr., St. George, UT 84790

Garfield Memorial Hospital, 435-676-8811, 200 N. 400 East, Panguitch, UT 84759

Kane County Hospital, 435-644-5811, 355 N. Main St., Kanab, UT 84741

Valley View Medical Center, 435-586-6587, 1303 N. Main St., Cedar City, UT 84720

LATE-NIGHT FOOD AND FUEL

Smaller towns in the Four Corners region roll up their sidewalks early in the evening, so finding a place to eat dinner after 8 PM or a motel with the lights on after 10 PM can be difficult. Except in major cities and tourist centers, be sure not to arrive at your night's destination too late to grab a bite to eat or to find a place to lay your head. Booking rooms at least a day ahead of time will help you avoid becoming stranded with no place to stay—or alternatively, with overpriced accommodations as your only option.

Gas stations with 24-hour pumps are available in the biggest cities, such as Flagstaff and Albuquerque, and along major highways, such as I-40 in Arizona and New Mexico and I-70 in Utah. Given the great distances you'll often have to drive between towns, you should fill up your gas tank whenever you have a chance.

MEDIA

Magazines and Newspapers

Every major town and city publishes its own newspaper or two. The biggest metropolitan areas have free alternative weekly newspapers for offbeat, up-to-date local guides to the arts, culture, and entertainment. Glossy lifestyle magazines slanted toward upscale residents sometimes have valuable information for discerning travelers, especially foodies and art lovers.

Among the best regional publications currently available:

Albuquerque Journal, www.abqjournal.com, 505-823-3800, 7777 Jefferson St. NE, Albuquerque, NM 87109. New Mexico's largest daily newspaper.

Albuquerque: The Magazine, 505-842-1110, 20 First Plaza NW, Suite 213, Albuquerque, NM 87102. The city's lifestyle magazine includes restaurant reviews.

Alibi, www.alibi.com, 505-346-0660, 2118 Central Ave. SE, Suite 151, Albuquerque, NM 87106. Albuquerque's alternative weekly guide to arts, culture, politics, and entertainment.

Arizona Daily Sun, www.azdailysun.com, 928-774-4545, 1751 S. Thompson St., Flagstaff, AZ 86001. Northern Arizona's largest daily newspaper.

Durango Herald, www.durangoherald.com, 970-247-3504, 1275 Main Ave., Durango, CO 81301. A daily newspaper for southwestern Colorado.

Durango Magazine, www.durangomagazine.com, 970-385-4030, 124 W. 21st St., Durango, CO 81302. General-interest magazine covering outdoor recreation, arts and culture, events, and dining.

Durango Telegraph, www.durangotelegraph.com, 970-259-0133, 556 Main Ave., Durango, CO 81301. Southwestern Colorado's alternative weekly newspaper.

Flagstaff Live! www.flaglive.com, 928-779-1877, 1751 S. Thompson St., Flagstaff, AZ 86001. Flagstaff's alternative weekly guide to arts, culture, and events.

Gallup Independent, www.gallupindependent.com, 505-863-6811, 500 N. 9th St., Gallup, NM 87305. Daily newspaper for the city and nearby Native American tribal lands.

Kingman Daily Miner, www.kingmandailyminer.com, 928-753-6397, 3015 Stockton Hill Rd., Kingman, AZ 86401. Small local newspaper in western Arizona.

Lake Powell Chronicle, www.lakepowellchronicle.com, 928-645-8888, P.O. Box 1716, Page, AZ 86040. Small local newspaper covering Page and surrounding areas.

Moab Happenings, www.moabhappenings.com, 435-259-8431, P.O. Box 698, Moab, UT 84532. Free monthly magazine covering arts, events, lifestyle, and travel in southeastern Utah.

Moab Times-Independent, www.moabtimes.com, 435-259-7525, 35 E. Center St., Moab, UT 84532. Moab's daily newspaper.

Spectrum, www.thespectrum.com, 435-674-6200, 275 E. St. George Blvd., St. George, UT 84770. Southern Utah's daily newspaper.

Local chambers of commerce and tourist agencies (see "Tourist Information," below) distribute free booklets, magazines, and newspapers designed specifically with travelers' interests in mind.

Radio and Television Stations

Throughout the Four Corners region, you'll find all the major domestic TV networks, including cable and satellite TV channels and the Public Broadcasting Service (PBS). Radio reception is excellent, even in some of the most remote areas. Tune in to a variety of news, music, and talk stations, including National Public Radio (NPR).

REAL ESTATE

Much of the land in the Four Corners area has been set aside by the federal government for public use. Thousands of acres have been designated as national parks, while other tracts have been reserved for Native Americans. Vast parcels already belong to private ranching and farming businesses, too.

There is good news for prospective homeowners. The city of St. George, Utah, is among the fastest-growing metropolitan areas in the country, with a six-year growth rate of 40 percent and median home price of $186,000. Flagstaff, Arizona, and Albuquerque, New Mexico, are also expanding (albeit less rapidly), with median home prices of $206,000 and $163,000, respectively. Small towns like Springdale, Utah, outside Zion National Park, offer heartening prospects for small-business owners and new residents alike.

If you decide to settle here for a while, real-estate agencies can provide information about local housing markets and leads on available properties for sale or rent, everything from suburban homes to vacation condos. Most real estate agencies advertise in the yellow pages of local telephone directories. The **Utah Association of Realtors** (www.utahrealtors .com, 801-676-5200, 1-800-594-8933), **Northern Arizona Association of Realtors** (www.nazrealtor.com, 928-779-4303), **Realtor Association of New Mexico** (www.nmrealtor .com, 505-982-2442, 1-800-224-2282), and the **Colorado Association of Realtors** (www.coloradorealtors.com, 303-790-7099, 1-800-944-6550) provide referrals.

RELIGIOUS ORGANIZATIONS

Around the Four Corners region, a variety of ancient, modern, and new-age philosophies are religiously followed by some local residents. Many Native Americans carry on their tribal traditions, from powwows to shamanic rituals. The historical influence of early Christian missions to the New World is still evidenced in many Pueblo communities, where centuries-old syncretism has preserved Native American traditions by combining them with European rituals of the Catholic Church. The Church of Jesus Christ of Latter-Day Saints (the Mormon church) is the foundation of the present-day state of Utah. The Southwest has also attracted many followers of New Age philosophies, especially to communities in northern New Mexico, southern Utah, and in Sedona, Arizona, south of Flagstaff.

ROAD SERVICES

The following is a short list of towing and emergency roadside assistance services in the Four Corners region; some offer 24-hour services. Members of auto clubs should be sure to call their organization's toll-free roadside assistance number instead.

Arizona

ATR Towing & Recovery, 928-753-2626, 111 N. 2nd St., Kingman, AZ 86401

B&B Auto Repair, 928-645-2223, 809 Aqua St., Page, AZ 86040

Northern Arizona Towing, 928-774-6644, 310 W. Birch Ave., Flagstaff, AZ 86001

Scotty & Son Towing & Auto, 928-524-2500, 405 Navajo Blvd., Holbrook, AZ 86025

Value Tire Union 76, 928-289-5611, 2800 W. Route 66, Winslow, AZ 86047

Colorado

Basin Towing & Repair, 970-247-2444, 25823 E. US 160, Durango, CO 81301

Buckskin Towing & Repair, 970-264-2500, 1435 E. US 160, Pagosa Springs, CO 81147

Doug's Quality Towing, 970-565-1500, 1113 Edith St., Cortez, CO 81321

Silverton Towing, 970-799-1621, 1129 Greene St., Silverton, CO 81433

New Mexico

Discount Towing, 505-341-0800, 109 Headingly Ave. NW, Albuquerque, NM 87107

Four Corners Towing, 505-327-9513, 1120 Madison Lane, Farmington, NM 87401

Interstate Towing, 505-290-7510, 1210 E. Santa Fe Ave., Grants, NM 87020

Speedway Towing Services, 505-863-3755, 601 W. Highway 66, Gallup, NM 87301

Utah

AA Service & Towing, 435-564-3291, 50 N. Walnut St., Green River, UT 84525

Bryce Towing, 435-834-5222, 1000 S. UT 63, Bryce, UT 84764

Bracken's Auto Tech & Tires, 435-673-8828, 86 N. 1000 East, St. George, UT 84770

Moss Towing, 435-635-2722, 191 N. 1380 West, Hurricane, UT 84737

Nations Towing, 435-259-6900, 2870 S. UT 191, Moab, UT 84532

Ramsay Towing, 435-644-2468, 43 E. Center St., Kanab, UT 84741

Superior Service, 435-586-0118, 1221 S. Main St., Cedar City, UT 84720

TOURIST INFORMATION

Almost every city and small town in the Four Corners region has its own tourism office or chamber of commerce to promote that area's attractions. How helpful they are depends on the staff working that day, but all of these offices stock free, glossy brochures and maps. If you're lucky, they'll also have up-to-date information about what's going on in the region and make specific recommendations about things to see and do that day. Associated online resources vary from not-so-helpful to comprehensive, but the Web sites listed below will give you some places to start researching and planning your trip.

Arizona

Arizona Office of Tourism, www.arizonaguide.com, 1-866-275-5816, 1110 W. Washington St., Suite 155, Phoenix, AZ 85007

Flagstaff Visitor Center, www.flagstaffarizona.org, 928-774-9541, 1-800-842-7293, 1 E. Route 66, Flagstaff, AZ 86001

Grand Canyon Chamber of Commerce, www.grandcanyonchamber.com, 928-638-2901, 1-888-472-2696, P.O. Box 3007, Grand Canyon, AZ 86023

Historic Route 66 Association of Arizona, www.azrt66.com, 928-753-5001, 120 W. Route 66, Kingman, AZ 86401

Holbrook Visitors Center, www.ci.holbrook.az.us, 928-524-6558, 1-800-524-2459, 100 E. Arizona St., Holbrook, AZ 86025

Kingman Visitors Bureau, www.kingmantourism.org, 928-753-6106, 1-866-427-7866, Powerhouse Tourist Information & Visitor Center, 120 W. Route 66, Kingman, AZ 86401

Navajo Tourism Department, www.discovernavajo.com, 928-810-8501, P.O. Box 663, Window Rock, AZ 86515

Oatman–Gold Road Chamber of Commerce, www.oatmangoldroad.com, 928-768-6222, P.O. Box 423, Oatman, AZ 86433

Page Tourism Bureau, www.pagelakepowelltourism.com, 928-645-9496, 1-888-261-7243, 6 N. Lake Powell Blvd., Page, AZ 86040

Page–Lake Powell Chamber of Commerce, www.pagelakepowellchamber.org, 928-645-2741, 1-888-261-7243, Safeway Plaza, 608 Elm St., Suite C, Page, AZ 86040

Williams Chamber of Commerce, www.williamschamber.com, 928-635-4061, 200 W. Railroad Ave., Williams, AZ 86046

Winslow Chamber of Commerce, www.winslowarizona.org, 928-289-2434, 101 E. Second St., Winslow, AZ 86047

Colorado

Cortez Area Chamber of Commerce & Colorado Welcome Center, www.mesaverde country.org, www.colorado.com, 970-565-3414, 1-800-265-6723, 928 E. Main St., Cortez, CO 81321

Durango Area Tourism Office, www.durango.org, 1-800-525-8855, 111 S. Camino del Rio, Durango, CO 81302

Mancos Valley Chamber of Commerce Visitor Center, www.mancosvalley.com, 970-533-7434, Main St. at Railroad Ave., Mancos, CO 81328

Pagosa Springs Area Chamber of Commerce, www.pagosaspringschamber.com, 970-264-2360, 1-800-252-2204, P.O. Box 787, Pagosa Springs, CO 81147

Silverton Chamber of Commerce, www.silvertoncolorado.com, 970-387-5654, 1-800-752-4494, The Wye, Hwys. 550 and 110, Silverton, CO 81433

New Mexico

Albuquerque Convention & Visitors Bureau, www.itsatrip.org, 505-842-2282, 1-800-284-2282, Plaza Don Luis, off Romero Ave. NW, Albuquerque, NM 87125

Aztec Welcome Center, www.aztecchamber.com, 505-334-9551, 1-888-838-9551, 110 N. Ash St., Aztec, NM 87410

Farmington Convention & Visitors Bureau, www.farmingtonnm.org, 505-326-7602, 1-800-448-1240, 3041 E. Main St., Farmington, NM 87402

Gallup Chamber of Commerce, www.gallupnm.org, 505-722-2228, 103 W. Route 66, Gallup, NM 87301

Grants / Cibola County Chamber of Commerce, www.grants.org, 505-287-4802, 1-800-748-2142, 100 N. Iron Ave., Grants, NM 87020

New Mexico Route 66 Association, www.rt66nm.org, 505-852-2995, 1415 Central Ave. NE, Albuquerque, NM 87106

Northwest New Mexico Visitor Center, 505-876-2783, off I-40 exit 85, Grants, NM 87020

Utah

Big Water Visitor Center, www.ut.blm.gov/monument/visitor-centers.php, 435-675-3200, 100 Upper Revolution Way, Big Water, UT 84741

Cannonville Visitor Center, www.ut.blm.gov/monument/visitor-centers.php, 435-826-5640, 10 Center St., Cannonville, UT 84718

Capitol Reef Visitor Information Center, www.capitolreef.org, 435-425-3365, 1-800-858-7951, Hwys. 12 and 24, Torrey, UT 84773

Escalante Interagency Visitor Center, www.ut.blm.gov/monument/visitor-centers.php, 435-826-5499, 755 W. Main St., Escalante, UT 84726

Garfield County Travel Council, www.brycecanyoncountry.com, 435-676-1160, 1-800-444-6689, 55 S. Main St., Panguitch, UT 84759

Green River Chamber of Commerce Information Center, www.emerycounty.com/travelbureau, 435-564-3427, 1765 E. Main St., Green River, UT 84525

Iron City Visitor Center, www.chambercedarcity.org, 435-586-4484, 581 N. Main St., Cedar City, UT 84720

Kanab Visitor Center, www.ut.blm.gov/monument/visitor-centers.php, 435-644-4680, 745 E. US 89, Kanab, UT 84741

Kane County Office of Tourism, www.kaneutah.com, 435-644-5033, 78 S. 100 East (US 89), Kanab, UT 84741

Moab Information Center, www.discovermoab.com, 1-800-635-6622, corner of Main and Center Sts., Moab, UT 84532

St. George Area Chamber of Commerce, www.stgeorgechamber.com, 435-628-1658, 197 E. St. George Blvd., St. George, UT 84770

Utah Office of Tourism & Utah Travel Council, www.utah.com, travel.utah.gov, 1-800-200-1160, 300 N. State St., Salt Lake City, UT 84114

Zion Canyon Visitors Bureau, www.zionpark.com, 1-888-518-7070, P.O. Box 331, Springdale, UT 84767

Weather and When to Go

The climate of the Four Corners region varies depending on elevation and topography. In spring-time a balmy afternoon in the deserts of Utah feels nothing like the gusty, dusty winds sweeping across New Mexico or freezing snowstorms on the high plateaus and mountains of Colorado. Whichever season you visit in, you may drive through several climatic zones in one day.

Nature is a dominating force. Flash floods can completely wash out lowland roads, especially during winter and spring. Snowstorms may cut off mountain passes in Colorado and access to the high plateaus of Arizona any time of year, though not usually during peak summer season. Summer temperatures in the deserts of Utah, New Mexico, and Arizona easily reach over 100 degrees Fahrenheit, while overnight lows during winter in south-western Colorado average just 15 degrees F. The weather during spring and fall may be more moderate, but these seasons are highly unpredictable times to visit the Four Corners, due to the extreme variance in temperature and precipitation that can occur. If you travel in April or October, it could be hot and dry as a bone on the Navajo Nation, or a sudden downpour might wash out bridges and leave a dusting of snow on high buttes and mesas. So be prepared for anything, weather-wise—it's part of the adventure.

Schedule your trip based on your own itinerary of must-see destinations and activities. Peak summer season (from Memorial Day through Labor Day) is when most people visit the Grand Canyon region of Arizona and Mesa Verde country in southwestern Colorado. For the deserts and canyons of Utah, late spring and early fall trips reward visitors with cooler weather and fewer crowds, although the weather doesn't always cooperate. In fact, many tourist centers in Utah open in April and shut down again in October. Much of cen-tral New Mexico can be visited year-round, although the most popular time to go is in summer. Book hotel rooms far in advance for major events, such as the Navajo Nation Fair in early September or the Albuquerque International Balloon Festival in early October (see the "Seasonal Events" sections of the regional destination chapters earlier in this book).

For recorded weather forecasts, call:

Arizona

Northern Arizona (including Flagstaff)	928-774-3301

Colorado

Alamosa area (including Pagosa Springs)	719-589-3232
Grand Junction area (including Durango and Mesa Verde)	970-243-0914

New Mexico

Albuquerque area	505-821-1111

What to Wear

No matter what time of year you're traveling through the Four Corners region, pack for all four seasons, just in case. Bring comfortable walking shoes and a pair of sturdy sandals, preferably ones that have soles with textured tread. Wraparound sunglasses and a wide-brimmed hat will shade you from the sun, and swimwear will come in handy. Also pack a waterproof layer—at least a jacket and possibly pants made of Gore-Tex or another material that will keep the rain from drenching your skin. A lightweight, wind-resistant fleece jacket, a ski hat, and warm, water-resistant gloves will help insulate you from colder weather. Most restaurants and entertainment venues don't have dress codes, so one smart, dressy outfit in your luggage is all you'll need.

9

IF TIME IS SHORT

Suggested Itineraries

You don't always have as much time as you'd like to travel. Or because the Four Corners region is enormous, you don't know exactly where to start exploring. The following are personal suggestions of where to visit first and what to do in the Four Corners region, if your time is limited. These are truly special places along the road, whether they exhibit historical character, quirky charm, or exceptional natural beauty; provide insights into Native American cultures; or are simply legendary landmarks that shouldn't be missed. They're always worth a detour and are exceptionally good value for the money. You can rely upon them to offer experiences that you'll remember for years to come, and maybe to inspire return visits to this fascinating, flavorful corner of the country.

Flagstaff and Grand Canyon

Spend a day on the South Rim of the Grand Canyon, taking a short nature walk along the rim trail, joining a ranger-led program, or hiking partway down into the canyon. Back in Grand Canyon Village, browse Native American arts at the historic Hopi House, then dine next to panoramic windows in the Arizona Room at Bright Angel Lodge. In Flagstaff, make time for the Museum of Northern Arizona and a loop detour to Wupatki and Sunset Crater Volcano National Monuments. If you want a less touristy experience of the Grand Canyon, head for the North Rim—just remember to make reservations first.

Route 66

West of Flagstaff, Williams is an alternative gateway to the Grand Canyon. It was also the last Route 66 town to be bypassed by the interstate, so you'll find lots of Mother Road relics there. From Williams take a day trip west via Seligman to Kingman, Arizona, with its Route 66 museum, then wind over Gold Hill Grade up to the Old West mining town of Oatman, where wild burros roam the streets.

Heading east from Flagstaff, Route 66 wanders all the way to Albuquerque, New Mexico, with stop-offs at kitschy Meteor Crater or the Jack Rabbit Trading Post, and the beautifully restored La Posada Hotel with its Turquoise Room, an homage to the great days of rail travel. Stay overnight at the Wigwam Motel in Holbrook before cruising through the Painted Desert of Petrified Forest National Park, past Gallup's trading posts and the uranium mining boom-and-bust town of Grants, and by the historic Rio Puerco Bridge into Albuquerque.

Native America

It is not easy to explore Native American nations or pueblos if you're in a hurry. The driving distances are long, roads are often in rough condition, and the pace of life is slow. For many guided tours and other worthwhile cultural experiences, you'll need to make reservations in advance, or at least arrive the day before to make arrangements for activities. The main tourists hubs are Gallup, New Mexico; the Navajo tribal capital of Window Rock, Arizona; and the Second Mesa of the Hopis. More accessible to visitors are Acoma Pueblo ("Sky City") and various national and tribal parklands scattered around the reservations, including Hubbell Trading Post National Historic Site, Monument Valley Navajo Tribal Park, Navajo National Monument, Canyon de Chelly National Monument, and Chaco Culture National Historic Park. Check if your trip schedule coincides with any of the sacred ceremonial dances open to the public at pueblos around Albuquerque.

Colorado's Plateau

Southwestern Colorado is one of the easiest places to explore in the Four Corners region. You can almost see and do it all in just two or three days. Devote a full day to Mesa Verde National Park, then kick back overnight in Durango, with its top-notch restaurants and microbreweries. After resting up overnight at one of Durango's historic hotels, wake up early to catch the vintage narrow-gauge railroad to Silverton, a high-altitude mining town in the San Juan Mountains. Drive west to Cortez and stop at the Anasazi Cultural Center in Dolores before visiting Ancestral Puebloan sites in Canyon of the Ancients National Monument or at Hovenweep National Monument, next to the Utah border.

Informative rangers lead interpretive tours of Ancestral Puebloan cliff dwellings inside Mesa Verde National Park Sara Benson & Mike Connolly

Utah's Canyon Country

Even if you're in a hurry, there's only one main driving route through southern Utah. You can travel in either direction. Either start from the arty town of Springdale outside Zion National Park, or in adventurous Moab, the gateway to Arches and Canyonlands National Parks. In between these anchor points, it takes two or three days to drive scenic byways past natural wonders, such as Bryce Canyon National Park, Grand Staircase–Escalante National Monument, Calf Creek Recreation Area, Glen Canyon National Recreation Area, and Natural Bridges National Monument. Along the way are memorable places to stay, notably national park lodges and bed-and-breakfast inns. Food lovers shouldn't miss Hell's Backbone Grill in Boulder, Desert Bistro in Moab, Cow Canyon Trading Post in Bluff, Rocking V Cafe in Kanab, or the Kiva Koffeehouse outside Escalante.

General Index

Lodging by Price

Dining by Price

Dining by Cuisine